PRIVATE RIGHTS AND PUBLIC ILLUSIONS

PRIVATE RIGHTS AND PUBLIC ILLUSIONS

Tibor Machan

Transaction Publishers
New Brunswick (U.S.A.) and London (U.K.)

This book is printed on acid-free paper that meets the American National Standard for Permanence of Paper for Printed Library Materials.

Library of Congress Catalog Number: 93-45616
ISBN: 1-56000-176-3 (cloth); 1-56000-749-4 (paper)
Printed in the United States of America

Library of Congress Cataloging-in-Publication Data

Machan, Tibor R.
  Private rights and public illusions / Tibor R. Machan.
    p. cm.
  Includes bibliographical references and index.
    ISBN 1-56000-176-3 : $34.95. — ISBN 1-56000-749-4 (pbk.) : $19.95
    1. Civil rights—United States.   2. Human rights—United States.
3. Trade regulation—United States.   4. Labor policy—United States.
5. Individualism. 6. Libertarianism. 7. Welfare state. I. Title.
JC599.U5M265 1994
323'.0973—dc20   93-45616
                                                                     CIP

The INDEPENDENT INSTITUTE

THE INDEPENDENT INSTITUTE is a non-profit, scholarly research and educational organization which sponsors comprehensive studies on the political economy of critical social and economic problems.

The politicization of decision-making in society has largely confined debate to the narrow reconsideration of existing policies, the prevailing influence of partisan interests, and a stagnation of social innovation. In order to understand both the nature of and possible solutions to major public issues, the Independent Institute's studies adhere to the highest standards of independent inquiry and are pursued regardless of prevailing political or social biases and conventions. The resulting studies are widely distributed as books and other publications, and are publicly debated through numerous conference and media programs.

Through this uncommon independence, depth, and clarity, the Independent Institute pushes at the frontiers of our knowledge, redefines the debate over public issues, and fosters new and effective directions for government reform.

For further information and a catalog of publications, please contact:
THE INDEPENDENT INSTITUTE
134 Ninety-Eighth Avenue, Oakland, CA 94603
(510) 632-1366   FAX: (510) 568-6040

For further information and a catalog of publications, please contact:

THE INDEPENDENT INSTITUTE
(510) 632-1366 FAX: (510) 568-6040

Contents

Foreword

Tibor Machan's *Private Rights and Public Illusions* is a work at once passionate and brimming with critical intelligence. Often as not, a book is best characterized in terms of what it opposes, and Machan's target is the all-pervasive present-day tendency to address social problems by way of collective governmental regulation rather than through the distributive efforts of individuals and volunteer organizations. In pursuing this project, Machan has given us a comprehensive and systematic critique of the modern welfare state with its bloated public sector and its pervasive meddling in people's lives. The readers of this book will find themselves not only informed but challenged by Machan's rich and complex critique of a fashionable liberalism that sounds well-intentioned in theory but engenders dire consequences in practice.

Traditionally, political philosophers have regarded rights as correlative with obligations. They insisted that to enjoy a right is also to take on the burden of an associated duty. Even inalienable rights—life, liberty, and the pursuit of happiness—come joined with correlative obligations to preserve, protect, and defend the comparable right of others. But apparently *nous avons changé tout celà*. In recent years rights theorists have grown myopic and been reluctant, perhaps unable, to see beyond rights to those correlative obligations. And in mandating the contemporary omni-state with the guardianship of an ever proliferating cornucopia of rights, our contemporaries have seldom been eager to require a fair price from the beneficiaries involved. And so the doctrine of rights adopted by contemporary liberalism—welfarism as Machan calls it—offers to provide an ever more ample free lunch for some at the expense of others sufficiently powerless to keep their tax authorities at bay: generally a virtually open-ended "middle class."

As a philosopher, Machan puts the issue of rights squarely in the setting of philosophical and constitutional first principles. The traditional public philosophy of the United States is predicated on an individualistic concept of liberty, a commitment to a free-market economy, and a

vii

democratic concept of property rights—all of which are steadily being eroded away by welfarism.

The prime social objective in the sphere of public welfare is surely the creation of a set of arrangements in all relevant areas—economic, biomedical, and educational—to assure that the welfare interests of people-in-general are duly secured. The critical task here is that of forging a social and economic order to achieve these basic objectives, be it by the unfettered workings of a free market or through some sort of planning. But one must not be misled in this connection by this emphasis upon planning. For there is a wide difference between centralized public *planning* for realization of the social welfare on the one hand, and centralized public *control* for the realization of these objectives on the other.

The implementation of planning does indeed require coordination and mutual adjustment, but this need not call for any comprehensive centralized control in the sense of actual direction, let alone dictation. It may well—nay, usually does—turn out to be quite sufficient to operate in this area with a partial control and a large measure of incentives (both positive and negative). The health aspects of welfare afford a good example of this: only a very modest list of health measures are legally available and the incentives of individual concern are allowed free play over a very wide area. And much the same picture can prevail on the economic side of public welfare in the U.S., with a modicum of control to assure, for example, national uniformity in the provision of certain minimum essentials but a wide scope for incentives to encourage innovation and creativity.

This line of thought points to the concept of what might be called "second-order centralism": a system of planning and its implementation without actual operational control of the activities at issue and consequently with first-order decentralization. The regulation of vehicular traffic in cities affords a good example of the workings of this concept. No driver is constrained to use a certain route. But some are made easier than others (by supplementing the natural differences with such artificial instrumentalities as traffic lights, stop signs, and the like), with the result that the traffic in a given direction can be channeled in a predictable way along selected routings in a manner that, as far as concerns the motorist, is entirely free of the factor of control. Control in the domain of social and economic arrangements is often simply indicated by less drastic means. Sometimes, of course, actual control is unavoidable (considering the traffic analogy, think now not of automobiles but of aircraft near heavily used airways and airfields). The optimal arrangement is doubtless a mixture into which control enters at some points, producing a balance of directive elements with elements of incentive. The key fact is that the requirement for the implementation of plans as such need not result in any pervasive *control* over the planned-for activities. Planning without operational control is more than a possibility, it is an ongoing reality in many spheres of human life.

Everyone is by now familiar with the depressing catalogue of the problems of urban, present-day America: dirt, noise, snarled traffic, physical ugliness, crowding, crime, friction in interpersonal contracts. The corresponding results have often been discussed and lamented: personal demoralization, group tensions, and the social alienation that comes about when people interact with others not as people but as parts of a system. These conditions have conspired to produce an anomalous result: "Uniquely in human history, Americans have been evacuating their cities not because there is an invader at the gates but because they are less and less viable as communities in which to work and raise families."[1] A prime task of the post-welfare society is to devise means for securing pleasantness in urban life—to restore convenience to city living, to make the city physically attractive, to decompose the city (insofar as possible) into units of human scale, to facilitate civility in interpersonal dealings under the crowded conditions of mass interactions, etc.

Here then we have one typical example of the reorientation of the focus of society's attention that will characterize the situation of the post-welfare state. In the era of the welfare state, society's attention was directed to the basics needed to make life viable on a mass basis in the context of a developed industrial economy. With the post-welfare state, the prime task will be making the circumstances of life richer and fuller for a mass population in the context of a "postindustrial" economy oriented heavily toward the production of services rather than goods. The welfare state has seen its problem in terms of making life in a mass society physically and economically secure; the post-welfare state faces the enormously more difficult and challenging problem of making life socially more civilized, personally fuller, and environmentally more pleasant. Accomplishing this monumental task will tax to the utmost the resources of effort and initiative that even a clever and resourceful people can muster. But order and system in human affairs do not emerge magically by themselves from the independent, uncoordinated activities of people pursuing their diverse purposes in separate ways. Only the confluent initiative and effort of individuals can forge that coordination and cooperation without which social goals—those of the postwelfare era included—can never come to concrete realization.

Machan's many-faceted assault on the political mainstream's blind dedication to the welfare state could be seen as a commentary on the doctrine he quotes from Herbert Spencer: "The ultimate result of shielding men from the effect of folly is to fill the world with fools." Machan's target is a deserving one—state paternalism run amuck. He clearly sees that the state that protects is a state that controls, and that an all-controlling state is for all intents and purposes a prison.

Deeply rooted in a widely informed background in political philosophy and U.S. constitutional thought, Machan's book issues a clarion call against such an assault on citizen sovereignty and individual liberties. And not content with deliberations at the level of general principles, Machan proceeds to examine a great host of issues in the domain of contemporary public policy disputes: governmental regulation, prior restraint, occupational health and safety, the right to know, pollution control, product liability, freedom of expression, and various others. His discussion does not simply ride some ideological hobby horse—as so many in this area do—but is deeply concerned, its deliberations grounded in a combined care for philosophical principles, empirical realities, and contemporary texts. (The range of literature he takes into account is truly impressive.)

Henry Simpson had a favored dictum: "The only way to make someone trustworthy is to trust them." He was thinking of individuals, but exactly the same holds for a nation's citizenry at large. In its protective care for people, the welfare state neither trusts its citizens to be intelligent guardians of their own good nor to be responsible guardians of the good of others. And in taking this line, the welfare state has produced a citizenry that is neither good nor responsible. Machan's book is an open invitation to say "Halt!" to this catastrophe.

—Nicholas Rescher
University Professor of Philosophy
University of Pittsburgh

1. Harry K. Girvetz in *Encyclopedia of the Social Sciences*, s.v. "Welfare State."
   This phenomenon is the source of the financial dilemma of the modern U.S. city—
   a vast expenditure for costly municipal and social services in the face of drastic
   balance-of-payments problems as more and more well-paid workers become com-
   muters who depend on the city for their jobs but pay most of their taxes in the
   suburbs.

Preface

A serious confusion has infested much prominent thinking about government's role in our lives, a confusion well-illustrated in the way members of the various media think about government. They assume, in the way they address politicians or report on social problems, that whatever is important in society must be a matter of *public* or state concern. An example may be found in the way some reporters bemoaned the absence of federal regulations concerning the recreational use of dolphins at various Florida and Hawaii hotels. It was not the fate of the dolphins but the absence of government regulation that these reporters found objectionable—which clearly assumes that with such regulation the danger to the dolphins would seriously diminish.

The first point to be noted when we reflect on this proliferation of a faith in rendering everything a public concern is that the state or government is but a small feature of any society suitable for human community life. The exact nature of government is a complicated issue. But there is little doubt that only a totalitarian government aims to take on every possible concern of the citizenry. Yet, the concept *public* is used in our culture in such a way that it has come to encompass any problem area that some vocal members of the population want government to address. Only habit and custom—and occasional judicial review—make it improbable that our society will become totalitarian; legislation and dominant ideology are no longer resistant to that eventuality (consider how unself-consciously and unflinchingly Dr. C. Everett Koop, President Ronald Reagan's surgeon general, could declare, "I want to see a smoke-free America by 1990!").

This book developed from my policy-oriented work—in the form of numerous papers in professional journals and collections of essays—on the proper scope of public authority, of government. I have integrated all of my relevant discussions, many of them previously published in different form, so that they now make up a complete and continuous book. I wanted to deal in one work with the various aspects of the topic, arguing against addressing various social problems by way of government and arguing for addressing them by way of the efforts of individuals and their various voluntary organizations in a free society. The different chapters are self-contained discussions of each main theme and some points are occasionally repeated, albeit briefly, so that the reader may be reminded of the basic principles that guide my thinking throughout the work.

Some of what will be discussed in this work presupposes certain views I have tried to defend elsewhere. In particular, my book, *Individuals and Their Rights* (1989), is a full-scale attempt to develop the case for the basic natural rights theory on which much of what I say in the following pages ultimately rests. Other works of mine, such as *The Pseudo-Science of B. F. Skinner* (1974), *Human Rights and Human Liberties: A Radical Reconsideration of the American Political Tradition* (1975), and *Marxism: A Bourgeois Critique* (1988), touch on several of the foundational aspects of my political thought. Some readers might wish to consult these works so as to gain an appreciation for how the following more-applied areas gain their philosophic support. Here and there in the ensuing pages I do, of course, provide a sketch of that support, but by no means fully. This work may then be understood as, in part, the development of some policy implications of my more abstract political theory of natural rights libertarianism; and in part, as a series of test cases— sometimes even "hard" cases—by which to check the soundness of my basic political outlook.

One cannot do everything all at once, so I can only hope that such a division of my labors will be seen as useful if not always immediately satisfactory.

Concerning the title of this book, let me stress that I do not for a moment believe that one's life can be divided simply into a private and a public sphere. Human life is multidimensional; it involves public or political concerns, as well as concerns that are purely personal or private, as well as those in-between these two poles: familial, social, communal, professional, commercial, scientific, athletic, artistic, etc. The private versus public division is useful only so as to appreciate where political—that is, necessarily forcible—organization and action have a decisive role in our lives. The rest, though by no means purely private, needs to be kept distinct from and free of governmental authority and is not to involve any use of force to accomplish objectives. The public realm is one wherein we must act collectively and subject individual wills to a common purpose. In the rest of our spheres of concern no such subjugation is necessary or even desirable. In this book I have combined what comes the closest to "empirical" work with philosophical analysis and argument (I eschew the term empirical because it embodies assumptions from a philosophical perspective I find flawed, one in which the world is divisible into its empirical and conceptual aspects). It is, I maintain, impossible to understand the facts without the analysis, or engage in the analysis without attention to the facts. Understanding is indeed a matter of constant interplay between two aspects, namely, the universal and the particular. They are distinct but inseparable.

Furthermore, I have focused mostly on moral and normative concerns, even when I draw on the fortunate legal recognition of some of the principles and ideals involved. I wish to contribute to the rejuvenation of normative political thought and public policy analysis.

The main theme of this book is the proper scope of government conduct, especially in regard to people's economic or commercial affairs. I argue that the concept *public policy* means something specific, not what it is now used to mean, which is anything some politically powerful portion of the citizenry is concerned about.

In our time, even in a relatively free society such as the United States, people tend to think that the public realm includes virtually anything people think about aloud or communicate "in public." Of course, there are different uses of the concept of *public*, but not all are well suited for the context of politics. A public conversation, for example, is simply a conversation held in a place that allows others to be privy to what is being said. A public debate is one widespread throughout a community. And a public phone is available to anyone with the requisite change or calling-card code. But when we use the concept *public* with political overtones, we have in mind something that ought to come under government supervision, regulation, or enforcement.

In the United States, not to mention most other countries, many hold that the public realm includes such concerns as childcare for working mothers, AIDS, rampant crime, drug abuse, teenage pregnancy, nuclear military defense, pollution, traffic congestion, oil spills, medical care and insurance, unemployment, inflation, bank failures, forest fires, farm failures, plant closings, in vitro fertilization, surrogate motherhood, genetic engineering, hate speech, bilingual education, college tuition, affirmative action toward minorities and women, etc., etc.—the list could go on indefinitely.

But are all these problems public when rightly understood? I will explore that issue, and indicate where proper public policy must be focused. I will argue mostly a negative position, namely, that the public or political realm is smaller and more restricted than is generally believed, and that the contrary position tends toward totalitarianism and is unbecoming to a free society when it regards individual liberty as an obstacle to the more important progress of society. (The few apparent extant exceptions, such as Sweden, need not concern us here; their peculiar historical situation accounts for their burgeoning *public* realm and seems tolerable—albeit by no means uniformly welcome—there and being dismantled in parts as of late.)

Despite the negative beginning of my position, the thesis behind it is decidedly positive: It is a thesis in support of human liberty, of individual and all varieties of community initiative—familial, fraternal, professional, religious, and more. It is a thesis that deems coercive human interactions destructive, even where the coercion is urged from honorable motives, and advocates confining the use of physical force in human relationships to instances of the administration of justice understood as the protection and maintenance of individual (negative) human rights.

When slaves are asked what they want, the answer is respect for the right to liberty. But, one might reply, liberty is merely negative, the absence of bad, humanly imposed conditions, not the presence of a good. What good flows from it? The right answer, in this case, is for the slave to say: That's my business and trust me to take care of it. As a matter of public policy, however, my first concern is with the right to individual liberty, with not having my or other persons' initiative thwarted, preempted, or depleted by regimentation and dictatorship.

All this may sound hyperbolic. Indeed, some economists who are generally friendly to the free society and the free marketplace, with their correspondingly small public sphere, have said to me that this kind of (normative) talk is more like music than science—that is, more an expression of taste and preference than the proposition of a defensible thesis.

I make note of this because views similar to those developed in this work often hail from the pens of economists; at least some of the policy recommendations they advance would be congruent with those implicit in the present work. However, my book does not approach the matter from the familiar *homo economicus* viewpoint.

Such thinking stems from a troublesome bias. It is advanced because too many people, even among freedom's friends, have accepted the false notion that the only intellectually respectable way to think and talk about human affairs is without reference to values, especially to moral values. This false notion, stemming from the scientistic—not scientific—tradition of several hundred years in Western intellectual history, should not be accepted uncritically. After all, even in the prescription to practice the value-free approach there is a clear value judgment—a prescription that by that very theory should be withheld by anyone who wants to make clear, defensible good sense. I have dealt with that issue elsewhere, namely, in my *Capitalism and Individualism* (1990), which is subtitled *Reframing the Argument for the Free Society.*

Acknowledgements

I thank *The Journal of Social and Political Studies, Philosophia, Harvard Journal of Law and Public Policy, Notre Dame Journal of Law, Ethics and Public Policy, Theory and Decision, DePaul Law Review, Public Affairs Quarterly*, and *Reason* magazine, as well as Random House Inc., for permission to draw on my materials previously published by them.

I wish also to thank The Independent Institute and its president David J. Theroux and research director M. Bruce Johnson for sponsoring this book. Many persons have helped me with the development of my ideas: Douglas B. Rasmussen, Douglas J. Den Uyl, Howard Dickman, Randall R. Dipert, Clifton Perry, J. Roger Lee, Eric Mack, Fred D. Miller, Jr., Robert Hessen, the late Sidney Hook, Bill Puka, Thomas Morawetz, Morton L. Schagrin, William Davis, Robert W. Poole, Jr., James Sterba, and David L. Norton were among the most influential recently. Of course, I am deeply indebted to the central contemporary figures of the classical liberal tradition, especially its philosophical champions such as Ayn Rand, Ludwig Von Mises, Murray Newton Rothbard, Friedrich A. von Hayek, Milton Friedman, and many others. John Ahrens and Jim Chesher gave very helpful editorial suggestions. And I thank the John M. Olin Foundation for its support of my research on this and other projects.

1

The U.S. Polity and the Welfare State

The culminating point of administration is to know
well how much power, great or small, we ought to
use in all circumstances.
                                        —Montesquieu

Does the conception of a public realm limited in scope by the basic human individual rights of every citizen—the conception that I explore and develop in the following chapters—accord with America's unique political tradition? I argue that it does, certainly more so than the alternative of a broad, unlimited conception.

Whether we ought to maintain and promote this limited idea of the public realm or broaden it as most political theorists appear to want to do, is a question I shall touch upon in the body of this work. For now, let me briefly indicate why the idea of a restricted, limited public scope is more consonant with the unique U.S. political tradition than is the idea of the welfare state, with its bloated public sector. This historical point is not vital to a philosophical inquiry, of course, yet in view of the fact that some socialists, such as the late Michael Harrington, as well as some conservatives, such as George F. Will, insist that the framers of the U.S. Constitution established a welfare state—a society with a largely unrestricted, democratically administered public realm—the question bears some attention.

Welfarism on the Rise

Conservatives and neoconservative's often seem to suppose that the U.S. government was meant to be a crafter of souls as well as a provider of (at least) an economic safety net. Democratic socialists, in turn, would

1

aver that the framers put the first touches to an economic welfare state, a government that ought to coordinate the production of our diverse prosperity. Out of these "bipartisan" efforts to graft onto the U.S. political tradition a welfare statist doctrine, the conviction is allowed to emerge that public policy in the United States ought to address practically anyone's or any group's vested interests, concerns, wishes, desires, and complaints.[1]

As the late Harry Girvetz notes, what amounts to the welfare state was already on Nassau Senior's mind around 1834, when he designed the English Poor Laws (i.e., the Poor Law Amendment Act). "It is the duty of a government", he said, "to do whatever is conducive to the welfare of the governed." In the United States the same idea surfaced only in the late nineteenth century, when Richard T. Ely, an institutional economist, denounced laissez-faire as "unsafe in politics and unsound in morals." The idea had its origins, partly, in the belief that because in modern societies the family, church, and other nonpolitical institutions would be unable to provide the basic needs of people, the state should come to the rescue.[2]

The claim that the welfare state expresses America's political design gains some plausible support when we read the Preamble to the U.S. Constitution and indeed from certain portions of the document itself. The Preamble states that the framers "do ordain and establish this Constitution for the United States of America" partly so as to "promote the general Welfare."

But does the welfare clause in the Preamble support the view that the U.S. political system was meant to be a welfare state? And thus do we really live in a country whose political traditions treat the concept *public* (or *state*) as if it were synonymous with *social* (or *community*)?

From the constitutional tradition of the U.S. federal government, there is no reason to construe "general Welfare" as referring to the economic and economically related well-being of the citizenry. In short, the *general* welfare means no more than those legal foundations that facilitate the achievement of the well-being, economic and otherwise, of the people on their own, not government's, initiative.

The framers appear to have wanted the Constitution and its implicit legal development to enable us all to prosper. By *promoting* the general welfare they meant to secure the conditions that are of political or legal, as distinct from particular and specialized, necessity for people's well-being.

Also, the promotion of the general welfare should not be given a utilitarian rendition meaning, "establishing the greatest happiness (or good or satisfaction) of the greatest number." Instead it makes far better sense to read it as meaning "securing the general prerequisites for everyone so that each person may seek prosperity or welfare." The most sensible way to read the founders' and framers' words—remembering that they were not utilitarians but largely influenced by the Lockean doctrine of natural individual rights—is that they wanted to secure the conditions for prosperity by means of establishing a government that would secure each individual's basic rights.[3]

It is unlikely, then, that the basic underpinnings of the U.S. polity imply a bloated public domain such as we find in the welfare state. The framers specifically guarded against that interpretation. In drafting Article I, Section 8 of the Constitution, they rejected putting the point in a way that would include the innumerable special-interest objectives served by the welfare state.[4] Given the full context of the Preamble, it is clear enough that the framers believed that protecting individual rights—to life, liberty and the pursuit of happiness, as expressed in somewhat more complex fashion through the U.S. Constitution—is exactly how to promote the general welfare politically (that is, by way of government). Individual rights to life, liberty, and the pursuit of happiness—when spelled out in the Bill of Rights to meet contemporary and long-range legal needs—are the standard of political and legal justice. It is this that the framers wanted first and foremost, since their complaints focused mostly on the great scope and powers of European and English governments. Thus they could not, consistently, also have wanted the same kind of interventionist government on the federal level.

Private Property in the Constitution

There is good reason to think that the U.S. Constitution supports a stringent adherence to the principle of private property rights. True, Justice Oliver Wendell Holmes, Jr. claimed (in *Lochner v. New York*) that "the Fourteenth Amendment does not enact Mr. Herbert Spencer's Social Statics."[5] By this he meant that capitalism is not constitutionally mandated by the Fourteenth Amendment, which does protect certain features of a free-market system. Holmes did not consider, however, that what the various principles expressed in the Constitution did very likely accomplish was, among other things, to imply a laissez-faire economy, not a mercantilist, socialist, or even a welfare economy. If one goes through the first ten amendments, one finds that each either endorses or presupposes the right to private property. Thus, there cannot be freedom of speech without the freedom to own places where speeches may be given. No freedom of the press is possible without ownership of equipment, buildings, transportation facilities, and so on. One cannot have the right to bear arms if one cannot own them. And prohibitions against unreasonable search and seizure have little force unless one has the right to own one's place of residence.

Among the nations of the West, the United States is often taken to have long enjoyed a virtual laissez-faire economic system. Yet the United States never had the benefit of pure laissez-faire; it did not even have the principles of economic liberalism fully and explicitly embodied in its main legal document, the U.S. Constitution. Article I, Section 3, for example, gave the federal government the power to regulate at least interstate commerce. Article I, Section 10 was for long ineffective in the effort to bar legislatures' impairment of contractual obligations. The same is true of the "privileges and immunities" clause of the Fourteenth Amendment as possible legal protection against state intrusion in the economic and commercial lives of citizens. It has not been invoked in this vein since Justice Holmes declared it inapplicable to economic matters in his *Lochner* dissent. It is also worth mentioning that much of our states' common law, which originated in England, does not favor the separation of state and economics but harks back, in large measure, to the feudal conception of "police power." This is the doctrine that the state is responsible for economic well-being within its realm of jurisdiction. Some of this influence has been blocked by various court decisions such as that of Judge Lemuel Shaw in *Commonwealth v. Hunt*.[6] Nevertheless, police power continues to be an instrument of state interference in citizens' commercial affairs.

Judge Shaw's argument, however, does help to support the view that the United States has rested more on the idea of freedom of commerce— including the free movement of labor—than on some kind of centrally governed system of economic behavior. Shaw argued that when groups of workers withhold their labor they are not engaging in a conspiracy because,

"Associations may be entered into, the object of which is to adopt measures that may impoverish another, that is diminish gains and profits, and yet so far from

being criminal or unlawful, the object may be highly meritorious and public spirited. The legality of such an association will therefore depend upon the means to be
used for its accomplishment. If it is to be carried into effect by fair or honorable
and lawful means, it is, to say the least, innocent; if by falsehood or force, it may be
stamped with the character of conspiracy."[7]

This clearly is not a utilitarian argument; it concerns what Robert
Nozick has called the issue of side-constraints, that is, of whether the
means employed for some purpose violate rights. According to Shaw's
position, the consequences themselves are irrelevant as far as the law is
concerned. But Shaw's ruling had been influenced by the natural rights
tradition of constitutional jurisprudence, not so much by legislative edict
or common (or case) law. The latter are the sources for the bulk of the
utilitarian influence, no doubt considerable in Western legal systems.

But surely one major difference between other political systems and
Western liberal democracy is the latter's provision of far greater economic opportunity than is found in other nations, opportunity afforded
through the institution of relatively free markets. The United States is a
relatively free society and marketplace, compared to other past and
present societies. Is this mere habit and custom, or is there evidence that
the U.S. Constitution was framed with the objective of making the country
economically free?

The Constitution and the Free Market

There are indeed reasons why we should view the U.S. Constitution
as a protector of a free-market system of economics, that is, of the economic liberty of persons, rather than a welfare state. But ever since the
time of Justice Holmes's famous but entirely gratuitous quip about the
Fourteenth Amendment and Herbert Spencer, the dominant view of utilitarian welfare statism has opposed this idea.[8] First, there is the general
point that the American Revolution was preceded by a Declaration of
Independence, wherein our founders boldly asserted that they would
hold it to be self-evident that we all have "unalienable rights [to] life,
liberty, and the pursuit of happiness."[9] Having these rights logically
implies the more concrete liberty to engage in commercial transactions
with others.[10] Indeed, it seems clear, from both supporters and radical
critics, that this was one of the founders' and framers' major concerns.
They did not wish to be regimented in their concrete living, including
their religious, journalistic, or commercial endeavors. As James Madi-

son said, "if industry and labor are left to their own course, they will generally be directed to those objects which are the most productive . . . in a more certain and direct manner than the wisdom of the most enlightened legislature could point out."[11] So, at least, the founders believed—pace Justice Holmes.

The U.S. Constitution itself seems to contain an acknowledgment of this, although not as explicitly as some might welcome now that the idea is not so widely embraced among our intelligentsia. But as Robert Hessen has suggested,[12] the founders did not see the point of giving explicit protection to the right to private property. Rather, they took it to be politically self-evident that it should be protected, as our rights to life and liberty ought to be.[13]

Indeed, the right to property was to the founders almost as vital an aspect of human life and liberty as the right to physical sovereignty is to women in our time. Furthermore, the right to the pursuit of happiness surely must include the more particular right to seek economic prosperity by means of the free ownership and disposition of property. How could one pursue happiness in this life if one were regimented in one's economic affairs? Certainly the happiness connected with economic matters that might come one's way would not be the result of any rightful pursuit of one's own but at best a matter of public policy.

It seems, then, that the founders and even the framers meant for us to have the right to private property clearly protected, along with other rights. Of course they might have believed that some other rights—to worship, to speak and publish, and to associate freely—were under more immediate threat and needed more clear-cut protection. Ergo, the near absolutism of the First Amendment. But this by no means need be interpreted as a disparagement of the right to private property. Some recent court decisions seem to reaffirm this. We are told, for example, that

> the right to enjoy property without unlawful deprivation, no less than the right to speak or the right to travel, is in truth a "personal" right, whether the "property" in question be a welfare check, a home, or a savings account. In fact, a fundamental interdependence exists between the personal right to liberty and the personal right to property. Neither could have any meaning without the other. That rights in property are basic civil rights has long been recognized.[14]

Furthermore, Article I, Section 3 of the Constitution contains the famous interstate commerce clause and this might also be read as a rejection of the idea of a fully free market. But once again, there is good reason to think that, as the framers saw things, the opposite conclusion should be drawn from the presence of this element of the Constitution. The framers did not approve of interstate duties, restraints on trade, or anything similar, so they refused to grant this authority to states but kept it for Congress, presumably to meet some emergency contingencies but not to make it federal policy. As Walter Fairleigh Dodd has said,

> the primary purpose of the framers of the Constitution was to prevent state restrictions upon interstate and foreign commerce. Our modern economy places an emphasis upon affirmative regulation by the national government.[15]

At first glance it would appear that the Fifth Amendment sanctions the government's taking private property. But once it is understood that such taking may occur only when there is a "public purpose" for it, and provided that the owners are justly compensated, it becomes clear that this Amendment provides strong evidence for the present thesis. Of course, by reference to the wording of the takings clause, innumerable incursions on the right to private property and freedom of trade appear to be warranted. When we read that "nor shall private property be taken for public use without just compensation," this seems to open the door to all kinds of takings. But that is partly the result of the bloated contemporary sense of the concept *public*. In our increasingly more majoritarian system—espoused by Benjamin R. Barber as "strong democracy"—the public realm includes virtually anything for which there is a sufficiently large constituency to make it politically feasible to place on the government's agenda.[16] In fact, however, the Fifth Amendment acknowledges the vital importance of private property when it allows government to abridge it only when a bona fide public purpose demands. If we consider the point argued in more detail in chapter 2, namely, that *public* does not in fact mean (nor did it mean for the founders and the framers) anything that is wanted by some members of the polity, but rather what concerns every member of the public as such, then this is indeed a powerful affirmation of private property rights.[17]

Little Room for Doubt

We have considered some of the salient elements of our political documents and found that what appear to be compromises on the right to private property really are nothing of the kind. But are there certain unambiguous pieces of evidence in the Constitution in support of that right?

Article I, Section 10 also affirms the sanctity of contract. Granted, the Supreme Court later made numerous exceptions to this and other protections. But that is not the issue here; we are talking about the Constitution, not the judges who have interpreted it. No doubt, in the last 150 years of U.S. intellectual history, there have emerged many trends hostile to private property. Justice Holmes, for example, advanced a populist sentiment about this idea and was himself under the influence of the U.S. philosophical movement known as pragmatism, which is skeptical about the idea of fundamental determinate principles, including moral and political ones. He held that unless "a rational and fair man necessarily would admit that the statute proposed would infringe fundamental principles as they have been understood by the tradition of our people and our law," a statute should be left intact by the Supreme Court.[18] No one can satisfy such an impossibly strict standard in the case of any legislation that has been ruled unconstitutional by the Supreme Court; just imagine such a standard vis-à-vis the rights to free speech, fair trial, or unreasonable search and seizure. Justice Holmes was perfectly willing to compromise on principles because he believed in the final authority of convention or majority rule. His support for the First Amendment, just like Robert H. Bork's, stemmed from his belief in the doctrine of majoritarianism: the people, he held, wanted that idea to be enshrined into law. That, and nothing more, is what gives the amendment its high standing.

With Justice Holmes's philosophy of the meaning of the rights spelled out in the Constitution (not just of those to property and economic liberty) the executive branch, the legislatures, and the law-enforcement agencies could abandon probable cause requirements, prohibitions of unreasonable search and seizure or prior restraint, and various exclusionary rules in the effort to stem crime—or, indeed, so as to reach any other valued objectives—provided the majority approved. Consistently applied, his very influential doctrine of when courts may oppose legislatures namely, only if they can show that the majorities are necessarily wrong, is dangerous not just to the right to private property but to practically any constitutional principle.

The Natural Right to Private Property

Before we consider the reasons why the political framework of the founders and framers became discredited, it will be useful to attempt a brief defense of the principle designated as "the right to private property." The reason is that throughout this work we will have numerous occasions for evaluating doctrines and policies that stand in opposition to private property principles and such a defense will help us to see at the outset why, despite the bad press private property principles have gotten lately, they should nevertheless be respected and given full legal protection.

One instructive way to understand the nature of the right to private property is to consider how it was understood by its main critic, Karl Marx. Marx states that "the right of man to property is the right to enjoy his possessions and dispose of the same arbitrarily without regard for other men, independently from society, the right of selfishness."[19] This is a rather good definition. The right to private property, be it to a toothbrush or a steel factory, authorizes a person to use what one owns as he or she sees fit without regard for other persons. And this use can be reckless as well as prudent—or have any other quality—but may not be so reckless as to invade the rights of others.[20]

Now the largely practical usefulness of the institution of private property rights has been defended by many, starting perhaps with Aristotle.[21] More recently, Garrett James Hardin restated Aristotle's point in his essay "The Tragedy of the Commons."[22] Yet there is more to the merits of the right to private property than practical usefulness. The following may help to make this clear.

If one is on a desert island all by oneself, the issue of property rights is of no significance, because there is no one else who could threaten one's authority over what one is going to do and how one will set out to manage the natural world that surrounds one. But if there is somebody else—if, for example Robinson Crusoe is met by Friday—both now have the choice to do good, bad, or mediocre deeds, and either may have an impact on the other. They are moral agents who may get in each other's way with their morally wrong choices and actions. In his choice of actions, for instance, Friday might help himself in a morally significant fashion from which Crusoe ought not to benefit without Friday's permission. There should be some way to tell what Robinson Crusoe does and what Friday does and to let both of them have a say whether and when they want to cooperate. This, in brief, spells out one of the moral functions of private property rights: Such rights identify what Robert Nozick called "moral space" around persons—within which, if adequately protected, they can be sovereign agents.[23]

We can appreciate, then, that from the point of view of morality everyone needs to know his or her proper scope of personal authority and responsibility. One needs to know that some valued item, skill, or liquid asset is in one's own jurisdiction to use before one can be prudent, creative, courageous, charitable, or generous. If one does not know that some particular area of human concern is under one's own or other people's proper authority, then one cannot know if it would be courageous, foolhardy, or silly to protect it, whether it would be generous or reckless to share it, and so on.[24]

It follows that private property rights are, in the first place, a social precondition to the possibility of an extensive, personally guided, and morally significant life. If one is to be generous to the starving human beings in Somalia but has nothing of one's own from which to be generous, generosity will not be possible.[25] So there is, in effect, a necessary connection between a practical moral code or set of guiding moral principles and the institution of private property rights.[26]

John Locke was only partially aware of the moral significance of private property rights. He made a connection, roughly along lines sketched above, between acting freely and responsibly as a moral agent and having the right to private property. He defended the institution of the right to private property as well as the way that property might be assigned. But his defense of the latter is in need of some repair. The fact that private property rights are a necessary condition for the personal moral life of human beings—without a sphere of personal authority they will not know what to do with what there is in the world for them to relate to—does not yet solve the problem of how property rights ought to be assigned over various candidates, including one's skills and time.

Why is such assignment important? One reason is that property rights have to be "compossible"—each person's right to private property must be compatible with all other persons' similar right. Any system of "incompossible" rights is a flawed system. It is inconsistent and leads to internal conflict. Of course, conflicting claims to having rights (rights to something, that is) can still arise because if people have free will they are able to either exercise their property rights or violate those of others, unless they are stopped or somehow they are prevented. So just because private property rights may be in principle compossible—just because they can coexist next to each other—it does not follow that people will not violate each other's rights. If, however, these rights are not compossible, and no harmonious assignment of them can be brought about, at least in principle, then there is no way to avoid violating other people's rights and the system is not possible to implement.

Can Property Rights Be Assigned?

But is there some method whereby a correct or justified assignment of property rights is possible? What might be a justified assignment of property rights to various items that can be owned by people?

Locke advanced the theory that when one mixes one's labor with nature, one gains ownership of the part of nature with which the labor was mixed. While initially nature is a gift from God to us all, once we individually mix our labor with some portion of it, it becomes ours alone.

Yet this idea causes problems partly because the idea of "mixing labor with nature" seems ambiguous. Does discovering an island count? Does exploring it? Does fencing it in? Does identifying (or discovering) a scientific truth count as mixing labor with nature? What about inventing something? And how about trade: Should the act of coming to mutually agreed-upon terms count as mixing one's labor with something of value?

A revised notion uses the theory of entrepreneurship. It was advanced at about the same time by the Fordham University philosopher James Sadowsky, S.J., and the New York University economist Israel M. Kirzner.[27] Ayn Rand also advanced a sketch of a moral case for the system that emphasizes the central role of individual mental initiative, of which entrepreneurship is a species.[28]

The notion is that it is the judgment that fixes something as of potential value to oneself or others that earns oneself the status of a property holder. Judgment, after all, is not automatic, nor need it involve actual overt physical labor. It is a freely made choice involving the quintessential human capacity to think, to reason things out, in this case applied to some aspect of reality and its relationship to one's goals and purposes in life.[29] One makes the choice to identify something as having potential or actual value of a personal and/or social nature. This choice gives such reasoning or judgment a practical dimension, something to guide one's actions in life. One may be right or wrong, but in either case choosing to make the judgment brings the item under one's jurisdiction on a kind of first-come, first-served basis. George, let us call him, identifies and claims for himself some hole in the ground as of potential value, and then George has rightful jurisdiction over it and may explore it for oil, minerals, a museum or a private home. George may have been right or wrong to embark upon this venture; indeed, the hole may not come to anything at all—it may be dry, so to speak. But by his selecting it he has appropriated it. And the appropriation has moral significance because it exhibits an effort of prudence, of taking proper care of himself and those he is responsible for. George's attempt to act prudently, to exercise the virtue of prudence, by his judgment and subsequent exploitation of what he has chosen to appropriate, may turn out to be potentially morally meritorious. And to live as a moral agent, George must be free to make such attempts without intrusions by others.

This is the beginning. In complex social contexts such as industrial society, such acquisition occurs via thousands of small and large acts of discovery, investment, saving, buying, and selling, with willing participants who embark upon the same, more or less focused, entrepreneurial approach to life. Yet no one is coerced into one particular approach, either, a circumstance that accounts for capitalism's hospitality to diversely conceived utopias, to experiments with great varieties of human conceptions of the good social life.[30] This hospitality is evident in all the experimental communities, churches, and artistic colonies, and in the economic, educational, and scientific organizations that abound in what has come to be perhaps the most closely capitalist, private-property-respecting large society in human history.

Moreover, theoretical defenses of the system of private property rights do not begin to answer all the questions that arise concerning the best application of that system vis-à-vis the multitude of complex problems involving property acquisition and use. While the 1980s have ushered in the movement toward privatization, including Eastern Europe's abandonment of the planned economic system, throughout the globe we are still far from having full confidence in the power of such a system of individual property rights.

Defenders argue, however, that compared to all other alternatives, the system has proven itself. And if it is consistently upheld, then, when problems arise, the courts will arrive at the required answers concerning it on everything from radio signals to frozen embryos, from the air mass to segments of water. Without elaborate legal and technical discussion, which will be prevented by the application of alternative models, the great potential of the system will remain unexploited—for example, regarding environmental and ecological concerns.

Summarizing, then, we have two related grounds for giving the system its moral justification: First, the right to private property is a necessary component of "moral space" and, second, it makes the realization of rational or prudential conduct possible vis-à-vis both our nonhuman and our social world. Unless these are sound grounds, that system is probably going to be defeated sooner or later as a political alternative for the modern world—defeated for lack of moral support.

Why is Freedom in Decline?

It seems clear that the case for the principle of private property rights is a reasonably strong one. Why then did the (classical) liberal or libertarian reading of the U.S. Constitution and its antecedents fall into disrepute? Two main reasons may well explain this. One is the denial of a certain conception of human life, the other the relativization of political theory. Both of these can be rejected now, although for some time it may have appeared that these reasons amounted to insurmountable obstacles.

The earlier view of human life holds that human beings, if left free, dealt with justly, and not faced with constant conflicts and wars, will proceed most effectively to promote their own individual or special welfare. That is how they will flourish best in their various circumstances. That is what will lead to mutual prosperity. Here we have the insight of Adam Smith and all those political economists who, from either the natural law or the utilitarian traditions, see an intimate tie between liberty and flourishing, including prosperity. Smith argued that when individuals have the right to pursue their own best interest as they understand it, the result will be the maximization of overall wealth in the community. (This view derives, in part, from the earlier Hobbesian idea that individuals are single-minded pursuers of their own advantage as they understand it. Smith argued that making room for them to do this will be to the overall advantage of the community.)

What only a few saw—among them the poet John Milton, at least in connection with his campaign to free the presses of government control—is that the same connection exists between liberty and prosperity. And prudence, the trait that secures well-being and prosperity for us, is of course, the first of the cardinal virtues.[31]

But why is there so little confidence in this idea now? A large part of the explanation lies in an element of modern science and philosophy.[32] When religion still had a hold on intellectuals or, before that, when the ancient Greek vision of human nature could still command some respect, the idea that free men and women should live decent, honorable lives made intellectual sense. The Greeks held that human beings could act purposefully. Aristotle, for example, explained that the morally virtuous life had to be chosen by the person; prudence, for example, is a virtue only if the person elected it, not if he or she was forced to conform to it by nature or by others. The Greeks and Christians were not radical individualists. Yet they did consider it most important that a human community make the morally virtuous life possible. For Aristotle, government existed to promote moral virtue. Augustine held a similar political position. They also laid one important foundation for liberalism by acknowledging that moral virtue requires choice.[33] It remained for later thinkers, such as John Locke, to suggest that the crucial requirement for the promotion of moral virtue so understood was to limit the power of government, indeed to restrict it to a few essential functions.

The Greek view was improved upon, accordingly, with the development of the idea of the liberal polity. If people are to live properly, then they need a substantial sphere of individual responsibility. Already William of Ockham, in the fourteenth century, characterized natural rights as "the power to conform to right reason."[34] Locke in the seventeenth century went much further with his doctrine of natural individual rights, one that the founding fathers drew upon in the Declaration of Independence.[35]

The crux of the thesis that emerged was that if people were not subjugated to the intrusive, meddling powers of others, including the government or state—in other words, if "laissez-faire, laissez-passer" were honored—they could make the most of their lives. They could pursue happiness. They could do it on their own, by their own initiative. It made sense that lack of this kind of right to freedom—lack of "negative liberty"—was the major obstacle to making progress on virtually all fronts in human life, even in helping the poor and the sick. Individual initiative, not state regimentation, would make life good. Thus, with government confined to resisting aggressors, settling disputes by respecting standards of justice (that is, individual rights), defending the community, and securing liberty—the general welfare would be promoted, that is, the welfare of all as members of the public. There would be no need under these conditions for government to become paternalistic. Individuals themselves would have ample opportunity to promote their own diverse welfare, by doing well at living their lives.

Once, however, the idea of the basic capacity for individual initiative of every person had been abandoned, this view embraced by the founders and framers could not be intellectually sustained. Most philosophers, enamored by scientism or the mechanistic view of nature, had by then applied reductive (and/or dialectical) materialism to reconceive human nature along more passive lines, even while political thought was still being shaped by elements of the earlier view. The new idea took root that, to put it succinctly, the forces of nature made us as we are. Some of us then ended up lacking in basic needs or talents, while others were more fortunate. The most efficient way to remedy this seemed to be a forceful welfare state that evened up these discrepancies.

From Ideas to Consequences

This is, of course, a much simplified view of the development of ideas. The development of any human creation is influenced by numerous subtle and not so subtle factors, some benign or unavoidable, others insidious and even demeaning. Nevertheless, the central idea that human beings merely reacted to their environment and did not initiate their conduct, and so could not flourish when all they could obtain from politics and law was the absence of coercion—others oppressing them—became a decisive influence in political thinking. Intellectuals began to lose confidence in the view that securing our right to liberty via the law would gain us the greatest opportunity for a good life in society. John Stuart Mill is a good example of a classical liberal who seriously wavered in his commitment to the idea of limited government. Something else would have to be secured besides the forbearance of everyone to set upon the person and property of another, i.e., to violate negative rights.

Many intellectuals also lost confidence in firm moral and political principles. In our time a version of pragmatism, one that sees all basic principles as ultimately unfounded and a matter of convention, holds sway among many thinkers concerned with politics. It now extends into even the hardest of the natural sciences, physics. From the mid-twentieth century onward, this view came to undermine not only the specific ideas that animated the U.S. system of law and politics but the very idea of finding lasting, stable principles of moral and political life. The frequently heard notion that the principles of the Declaration of Independence are eighteenth-century myths, needed for the time but no longer relevant and true, gives clear evidence of this development.

In earlier times, the possibility of personal initiative on everyone's part except those entirely incapacitated had been assumed as a universal fact. It made the idea of private, voluntary progress sensible. That accounted for the initial libertarian features of liberalism. But once personal initiative became incongruous, because it appeared to conflict with the reigning mechanistic science, the kind of liberalism that was meant to accommodate it fell into disrepute. Instead, the reconceived liberalism began to require setting people free of their hardship by the force of the state. It is just this that is meant by Marxist "liberation."[36]

In addition to these developments, another idea began to exert influence, one that was not so much novel as handy. The idea gained respect that society is a kind of team. The various social contract theories encouraged this view. In terms of these views, human communities found their principles by way of a kind of bargain, sometimes merely imagined but always useful for determining how the society ought to be structured. Members of the "team" possessed very different talents, circumstances, assets, and so on, with each equally helpless in the face of his or her lot. This suggested a certain idea of justice, namely, fairness: "It's not fair—that some are uglier than others, richer than others, more talented than others." In this way the idea of personal achievement meriting a different station in community life lost its philosophical standing.

One of the leading political philosophers of our time, John Rawls, has given extensive expression to this notion, a notion in the making for several centuries.[37] We are all on the same team, the argument runs, yet some of us are better off than others. This is unfair! No one can do anything to deserve his or her lot, so why should anyone be better off than anyone else? Success is just a matter of bad luck or good luck, nothing more. Only if some general benefit could be derived from unequal positions in the community would such positions be justified; otherwise they are unjust. From this the welfare statist egalitarian impulse is but a few steps away: Let's try to do something about the unfairness. We must, as a society, do everything we can about it—it's a matter of social justice—even if the chances of rectifying matters are minimal and seeking such rectification could produce greater and greater poverty. It is our duty as a society to at least try.

Collective Welfare Statism Is a Mistake

The whole story is more complex. But even this sketch of it clearly traces the abandonment of the great idea that particular welfare ought to be promoted by free individuals in cooperation and competition among themselves. It begins to explain, in part, why many influential people today expect far more of their governments than the mere provision of a suitable setting in which everyone is free to promote his or her welfare without coercive interference by others.

However, this abandonment is a tragic mistake. Sometimes, it is even an excuse for grabbing the power to achieve goals that arguments could not support. First, society is no team. Pace Karl Marx, who wrote that "the Human essence is the true collectivity of man," we are all essentially individual human beings.[38] We do have roughly the same capacity to start out on our journeys, never mind our starting point. But how well we will do on these journeys is ultimately up to us—provided we are left to our own resources even in the company of others. Individual initiative is, contrary to the dictates of scientism, the driving force of human life. We think by our own initiative and live by our own initiative, often—even largely—in the company and with the assistance of others. But without that initiative which makes us all human, we would not even have ideas about ethics, politics, science, law, and the arts.[39]

The belief that we are moved by forces that work on us is itself the result of hasty generalization if not extrapolation. The fact that some events in nature occur by virtue of efficient causation does not demonstrate that all events do so. I have explained this elsewhere but will repeat some of the needed points in later chapters.[40] The essential point is that human initiative and nothing else is the central cultural force. If it were not, nothing we think and do would be wrong or right, true or false. We could not even know which of our "knowledge" would simply be programmed belief.

Accordingly, what counts most for us together, in each other's company, is not fairness but the right to liberty. A team is a wrong and destructive analogy for political life. A friendly marathon race, perhaps, or carnival, would do much better.

While John Rawls calls his a theory of "justice as fairness," the better conception is that of "justice as liberty." The central feature of political justice for human individuals is to acknowledge everyone's sovereignty, whether he or she be humble or great, rich or poor, beautiful or ugly, healthy or ill. All we need from politics—from the power of legalized force—is to do everything possible to secure justice. Once this is achieved, prosperity will usually be taken care of by free people, in roughly the right proportion. They will clearly do so better than will administrators of justice who get in the fray to "help out" some at the expense of others.

To those who still hang on to the scientistic idea of classical mechanics, we must say that nothing discovered by science precludes us from causing much of our own behavior and that it is we who are responsible for how well or ill we do in life. In the complex universe we now know, self-determination is indeed possible. There is very good reason to conceive of human beings thus.[41] Normally, people are their own agents and thus responsible for facing up to the challenges of their lives.

Moreover, not only is this idea closer to what the framers had in mind than welfare statism, but it also makes better common sense. The power of initiation, as noted earlier, is well entrenched as a quintessential human characteristic; awareness of a new idea forged by anyone should make this evident and everyone with a critical or creative idea—the base of all innovation—testifies to this. Given the logic and context of the founding of the U.S. republic, the welfare clause in the Preamble suggests that we are all to enjoy the protection of our rights so that we may then strive to promote our well-being. Government is to preserve justice, tranquillity, the common defense, and liberty for all. Each of these objectives is to be secured—with none compromised.

The unique and radical conception forged by the founders and framers did not tell the whole story. Their vision was eclipsed by contrary ones based on a plausible scientism as well as on many leftover notions about the need for the supposedly superior wisdom of either the elite or, somewhat later, of the majority. This loss of vision may account in part for why we now have on our hands a massive, ineffective, bureaucratically regimented welfare state instead of a government administering the laws of a free and vibrant country.

It is perplexing that so many will not acknowledge that we ought to and can flourish in life, provided our rights are respected and protected. Surely, acknowledging that we are mostly capable, potent creatures rather than wards of the elect could have that result. At least the chances for a decrease in statism would improve.

Probably one of the most potent ideas confronting us in this undertaking is the belief in a growing, expanding, nearly unlimited public realm. What does the concept *public* properly mean? Can we find a meaning in the first place, one that is rationally defensible and not merely dogmatically asserted, the result of some kind of ideological predilection? It is to these questions we turn in our next chapter.

Notes

1. I am here focusing mostly on the impact of ideas, not on the numerous other forces that influence the direction of government. The claim that ideas do not matter, proposed by the late George J. Stigler, is self-defeating. See Tibor R. Machan, "Politics and Ideology: Do Ideas Matter?" *Mid-Atlantic Journal of Business* 28 (June 1992): 159–167. I would argue, also, that only if the dominant ideas make allowance for it can these other forces exert their full impact on political-legal developments. For example, only if there are accepted legal avenues for influencing Congress will special-interest groups be able to carry their considerable weight in directing the nation's affairs.
2. "Welfare State," in *Dictionary of the History of Ideas: Studies of Selected Pivotal Ideas*, ed. Philip P. Wiener, (New York: Scribner, 1973), pp. 509, 512. It needs to be noted, though, that the welfare state is not a great departure from the patriarchal state in which the monarch is the "keeper of the realm." Indeed, one avenue through which many of the welfare state's policies have gained entrance into the U.S. system is the common-law concept of police power, which has its origins in feudal orders. The welfare state is also similar to mercantilism, with the main difference being that in the patriarchal state other objectives besides achieving economic power take either an equal or more prominent place on the nation's agenda.
3. Of course there is dispute about what this phrase means. It seems to me, however, that the case for their essentially Lockean view is much stronger than the alternatives. For a balanced discussion, see Gilman Marston Ostrander, *The Rights of Man in America, 1606–1861* (Columbia, MO: University of Missouri Press, 1960).

4. Section 8 spells out the powers of Congress and though, for example, the support of science and the arts is mentioned, that support amounts to issuing copyrights and patents, not providing subsidies. This is fully consistent with how I understand the founders' and framers' concerns with "promoting" facets of U.S. culture. For a more detailed explanation of these features of the Constitution and its history, see Forrest McDonald, *Novus Ordo Seclorum: The Intellectual Origins of the Constitution* (Lawrence, KA: University Press of Kansas, 1985).

5. *Lochner v. New York* 198 U.S. 45(1905), p. 75. The reference is to Herbert Spencer's 1850 treatise of that name.

6. *Commonwealth v. Hunt* 45 Mass. 111.

7. *Commonwealth v. Hunt* 45 Mass. 111, p. 41.

8. A very insightful discussion of the Lochner decision and dissent may be found in William Letwin, "Economic Due Process in the Constitution and the Rule of Law," in *Liberty and the Rule of Law*, ed. Robert L. Cunningham, (College Station, TX: Texas A and M University Press, 1979), pp. 22–73.

9. The founders did not say that it is self-evident that we have these rights by nature, only that for purposes of their declaration they would take that to be self-evident. In every field of inquiry some propositions will be basic and unquestioned, excepting, of course, in philosophy.

10. Abraham Lincoln appears to have agreed:

    > All this is not the result of accident. It has a philosophical cause. Without the Constitution and the Union, we could not have attained the result; but even these are not the primary cause of our great prosperity. There is something back of these, entwining itself more closely about the human heart. That something, is the principle of "Liberty to all"—the principle that clears the path to all—gives hope to all—and, by consequence, enterprise, and industry to all.

    Quoted in Harry V. Jaffa, *How to Think about the American Revolution: A Bicentennial Cerebration* (Durham, NC: Carolina Academic Press, 1978), p. i.

11. James Madison, "Speech in First Congress, 9 April 1789," in *The Complete Madison: His Basic Writings*, ed. Saul K. Padover, (New York: Harper, 1953), pp. 269–270.

12. Personal discussion, September 1988.

13. Would we have to spell out today that a woman has a right not to be raped? Hardly. Simply because no right not to be raped is mentioned in our Constitution, one would not deny legal protection to such a right. Consider John Marshall's reference to "the right which every man retains to acquire property" in *Ogden v. Saunders*, 25 U.S. (12 Wheat.) 213, 346–347.

14. *Lynch v. Household Finance Corp.*, 31 L. Ed. 2d 424 (1972).

15. Walter Fairleigh Dodd, *Cases and Materials on Constitutional Law: Selected from Decisions of State and Federal Courts*, 5th ed., (St. Paul, MN: West Publishing, 1954), p. 390.

16. Benjamin R. Barber, *Strong Democracy: Participatory Politics for a New Age* (Berkeley, CA: University of California Press, 1984).

17. Just that thesis is argued by Richard Allen Epstein in *Takings: Private Property and the Power of Eminent Domain* (Cambridge, MA: Harvard University Press, 1985); and, earlier, by Bernard M. Siegan in *Economic Liberties and the Constitution* (Chicago: University of Chicago Press, 1981). This and related topics are discussed in Ellen Frankel Paul, *Property Rights and Eminent Domain* (New Brunswick, NJ: Transaction, 1987).

18. *Lochner v. New York*, p. 76.

19. Karl Marx, *Selected Writings*, ed. David McLellan, (Oxford: Oxford University Press, 1977), p. 54.

20. The exact characterization of such rights is not simple. See my *Human Rights and Human Liberties: A Radical Reconsideration of the American Political Tradition* (Chicago: Nelson-Hall, 1975) and *Individuals and Their Rights*; (LaSalle, IL: Open Court, 1989) for the details as I have been able to assemble them.

21. According to Aristotle,

> that all persons call the same thing mine in the sense in which each does so may be a fine thing, but it is impracticable; or if the words are taken in the other sense, such a unity in no way conduces to harmony. And there is another objection to the proposal. For that which is common to the greatest number has the least care bestowed upon it. Every one thinks chiefly of his own, hardly at all of the common interest; and only when he is himself concerned as an individual. For besides other considerations, everybody is more inclined to neglect the duty which he expects another to fulfill; as in families many attendants are often less useful than a few. *Politics*, trans. Benjamin Jowett, 1262a30–37).

While put mostly in pragmatic terms, the analysis of both Aristotle and Garrett James Hardin (see note 22) of the function of private property rights contains a vital normative component, namely, that such rights are a necessary condition for some kinds of moral conduct in societies. For more, see my "Pollution, Capitalism, and Socialism," *Journal des Économiste et Étude de Humanités* 2 (March 1991): 83–102.

22. Garrett James Hardin, "The Tragedy of the Commons," *Science* 162 (December 13, 1968): 1243–1248.

23. Property rights are necessary for such protection since human beings are not disembodied souls who can carry out morally significant conduct away from nature. Property law in a society based on the individual's rights would keep track of the extent and nature of much of that moral space—in copyright, trespass, and nuisance law, for example.

24. In my *Human Rights and Human Liberties*, pp. 125–126, I recount a story told by Norman Malcolm about Ludwig Wittgenstein's impromptu conceptual analysis of "owning" something. It serves as a *reductio ad absurdum* of the idea that one may own something but others set standards for its use—just the sort of understanding of property rights prominent in the welfare statist, fascist and market socialist political economies.

25. When one critic, Jeffrey Friedman, remarks that "every 'man' in history has managed to survive without such a right [to unfettered individual ownership]," we might consider that de facto private property ownership has been far more pervasive in history than de jure private property ownership. It is arguable, however, that most human beings have had a significantly limited range of personal authority respected and protected throughout history, a situation that has most likely contributed to what I call "the moral tragedy of the commons." See Jeffrey Friedman, "The New Consensus: II The Democratic Welfare State," *Critical Review* 4 (Fall 1990): 664.

26. By "necessary" I do not mean "purely formal." See my "Epistemology and Moral Knowledge," *Review of Metaphysics* (September 1982): 23–49 for more on this point. I also discuss the issue in my *Individuals and Their Rights*.

27. James Sadowsky, "Private Property and Collective Ownership," in *The Libertarian Alternative: Essays in Social and Political Philosophy*, ed. Tibor R. Machan, (Chicago: Nelson-Hall, 1974), pp. 119-133; and Israel Kirzner, "Producer, Entrepreneur, and the Right to Property," *Reason Papers* 1 (Fall 1974): 1-17. Kirzner identifies Frank Hyneman Knight as having also identified "the ethical implications of producing" via entrepreneurship.

28. Ayn Rand, "The Objectivist Ethics", chap. 1 in *The Virtue of Selfishness: A New Concept of Egoism* (New York: New American Library, 1964). This line of defense of private property has been implicit in any ethics that stresses right reason and prudence as virtues. See also William of Ockham's characterization of "natural right [as] nothing other than a power to conform to right reason, without agreement or pact" in *Opus Nonaginta Dierum*, quoted in Martin P. Golding, "The Concept of Rights: A Historical Sketch," in *Bioethics and Human Rights: A Reader for Health Professionals*, ed. Elsie L Bandman and Bertram Bandman, (Boston: Little, Brown, 1978), p. 48. Ockham also defended the institution of private property in a way similar to John Locke, based on the view that God gave human beings this institution, that is, "that the right to private property is a dictate of right reason" (as expressed by Heinrich Albert Rommen, "The Genealogy of Natural Rights," *Thought* 29 (1954):419.

29. I develop these points—based on a defense of the possibility of formulating a noncircular definition of the concept *human being* that does not fall prey to familiar arguments against the possibility of objective definitions—in *Individuals and Their Rights*.

30. See, for more on this point, Robert Nozick, "Utopias," part 3 in *Anarchy, State, and Utopia* (New York: Basic Books, 1974).

31. For a detailed discussion of prudence and its relationship to commerce, see Douglas J. Den Uyl, *The Virtue of Prudence* (New York: Lang, 1991).

32. Some of these issues are explored in more detail in Friedrich A. von Hayek, *The Counter-revolution of Science: Studies on the Abuse of Reason* (Glencoe, IL: Free Press, 1952).

33. For a very good examination of these and related issues, see Douglas B. Rasmussen and Douglas J. Den Uyl, *Liberty and Nature; An Aristotelian Defense of Liberal Order* (LaSalle, IL: Open Court, 1991).

34. William of Ockham, *Opus Nonaginta Dierum*.

35. John Locke, *Two Treatises of Government* (1690).

36. I discuss this in my *Marxism: A Bourgeois Critique* (Bradford, England: MCB University Press, 1988).

37. John Rawls, *A Theory of Justice* (Cambridge, MA: Harvard University Press, 1971).

38. Marx, *Selected Writings*, p. 126.

39. I defend these points in detail in *Capitalism and Individualism*, chap. 1, (New York: St. Martin's Press, 1990).

40. See my *The Pseudo-Science of B. F. Skinner* (New Rochelle, NY: Arlington House, 1974); and my *Individuals and Their Rights*.

41. For more on this, see Roger W. Sperry, *Science and Moral Priority: Merging Mind, Brain, and Human Values* (New York: Columbia University Press, 1983).

2

Rational Choice and Public Affairs

*No gauge has been found yet by which we can
measure the value of public services that are not
sold to consumers but given away.*

—Roger A. Freeman

My first task in this chapter will be to answer the most basic question in the present context, namely, What is the public realm? In chapter 1 I showed why, within the U.S. political tradition, our common, bloated understanding of the concept *public* rests on shaky foundations. But it is not enough to consider our particular political tradition when we inquire into some topic of politics; such a parochial approach begs the important question of whether our tradition itself is sound. What we need is a broader inquiry about the very nature of human public affairs.

The Alleged Impossibility of Rational Public Choice

In some contemporary studies of public choice, economists and decision theorists argue that democratic politics leads to inherent contradictions when it attempts to rank collective priorities. I will explore the topic of the nature of the public realm by examining this question of the nature of rational public choice.

First, however, I need to note that in this discussion I will not be focusing on the public choice school of neoclassical economic analysis, led by James Buchanan and Gordon Tullock. I have already discussed certain aspects of their work in my *Capitalism and Individualism*.[1]

What I will do here is discuss the ancient topic of rational public choice, one that pertains to how we might evaluate the actions taken by political representatives, leaders, officials, or others whose work is to secure the public interest. This issue goes back at least as far as Plato's *Republic*. A central task Socrates embarked upon in that work was to establish the standard by which to judge a community's public affairs.

I argue here, as the first stage of my attempt to develop a theory of public choice for the free society, for the possibility of a rational—that is, a realistic, consistent, and unambiguous—determination of public policy. I will, in short, defend the rationality of politics thoroughly enough to make it possible to appraise the merits of my case.

Let me alert the reader to a feature of my discussion that may be methodologically controversial. This discussion is not carried on in the form of a linear, syllogistic argument. Rather it attempts to construct a set of definitions based on familiar uses of terms and the circumstances in which the terms seem to function clearly. Syllogistic arguments depend on premises that themselves rest on definitions of terms. At some point one needs to arrive at a sensible understanding of the crucial terms, and in this discussion that is my main objective. What the concept *public* means most felicitously is what is ultimately at issue, and for purposes of determining this we need to explore various related concepts and what they, too, ought to be taken to mean.

Clearly, we can begin with taking note of the fact that there exists widespread dissatisfaction with the prominent approaches to solving the problem of rational public choice. Edward I. Friedland and Stephen J. Cimbala point this out effectively.[2] They show how arguments such as Kenneth Arrow's, which challenge the rationality of public affairs, embody a misconception of the nature of rationality.[3] Thus, they propose, the conclusion that rational choice in public affairs is impossible should be challenged.

Kenneth Arrow argued that when we have a polity of roughly universal citizen participation, whereby everyone may give his or her input as to what the ranking of the political agenda should be, we will get impossible results; mutually exclusive ranking orders will emerge from such a process. The practical result is that two claims, mutually exclusive, could both be true concerning what priorities governments should pursue. Since these claims are impossible to act on, rational *public choice* is not possible within such a (liberal) polity.

But Friedland and Cimbala are mostly critical and stop short of offering an alternative framework from which to approach the problems Arrow and others have tried to tackle. They end their discussion by noting that "basically the problem facing us is this: How to rationally choose among alternative theories of rational choice."[4] Their summary description of the present state of affairs in the field indicates the enormity of the problem. They show, for example, that Arrow's proof is actually a demonstration of the logical inconsistency among a set of value postulates, not of some inconsistency between the roles of logic and nondictatorial methods of reaching social decisions. The assertion that social orderings ought to be transitive or that they ought to be independent of irrelevant alternatives are hardly principles of logic. Although they coincide with notions of rationality often accepted, they are no less value judgments than the statement that a dictatorship is undesirable. Therefore, one could easily reach a quite different conclusion, not the usual one, from Arrow's proof, namely, that prevailing utilitarian standards of rationality are inapplicable as guides to action in a democratic society.[5]

Friedland and Cimbala think that if today's practitioners were to abandon the search from within their analytical framework, it "would confirm suspicions that the decision theoretical conceptions of rationality must inevitably remain little more than window dressing and an amusing pastime, some sort of intellectual puzzle for otherwise unemployed economists, mathematicians, political scientists, etc."[6] This is a very cynical hypothesis about why decision theories keep emerging; that is, only to be knocked down and reemerge in slightly altered garb—even though in some cases the picture they paint may be correct. But given the impoverishment of philosophy's idea of "being scientific," not to mention "rational," one can hardly blame social scientists for keeping up the effort. The little that philosophy has done to revise the conception of science and reason has led toward conventionalism. Nevertheless, the trend may be changing.[7]

It seems to me, however, that improvements can be made and that once we reexamine the nature of rationality, including how to compare theories of rationality, we will be able to come close to a satisfactory answer to the problem faced by Arrow and his critics. I will begin my argument for the rationality of public choice by indicating the meaning the concept *rational* must have in the phrase *rational choice*. I will also go on to discuss what choice comes to mean in this context. Then I will consider what *public* properly means in the context of political economy. And I will show that, given this meaning, it is highly likely that rational choice in public affairs is possible. Accordingly, this portion of the present work may be considered as its theoretical center. If these basic issues are to be conceived of very differently from how I see them, it seems to me that the later arguments and conclusions will not have adequate support.[8]

On Choosing Theories of Rational Choice

Even though we will not be digging at the deepest recesses of philosophical exploration, still, with a verdict such as "prevailing utilitarian standards of rationality are inapplicable as guides to action in a democratic society," it is necessary to begin at a relatively basic level of analysis. As a start, let us take up Friedland and Cimbala's own hint as to where part of the difficulty may lie. They suggest that the decision theorists' problem is "so vexing because it is irremediable by logical means."[9] In other words, the employment of a single line of inquiry among decision theorists, namely, formal logical analysis, is the reason why solutions are not reached—that is, why we cannot reach a satisfactory answer to the question of, for example, public-policy decision making.

Let us notice at the outset that some of the most prominent participants in the discussion appear to understand by *rational* nothing more than "logically consistent." For example, Amartya Sen tells us that "rationality, as a concept, would seem to belong to the relationship between choices and preferences, and a typical question will take the form: Given your preference, was it rational for you to choose the actions you have chosen?"[10] Sen himself notes that, from this conception of rationality, paradoxes will arise "in a situation where the outcome depends on other people's actions in addition to one's own."[11] Since Sen is one of the central figures among decision and social choice theorists, his view of rationality is illustrative. It is equally illustrative that he believes that "morality would seem to require a judgment among preferences whereas rationality would not.[12]

The model of rationality invoked by Sen and most social scientists, especially economists, is that of internal consistency or coherence. But this model will not yield an approach to the problem facing public choice (or political) theorists, namely, how to settle on goals, judge among preferences, and end with an answer to the question, What is the right thing for us to do? With respect to these matters, the field of decision theory appears, then, to be ill-conceived, just as Friedland and Cimbala suggest, because of its narrow conception of rationality, one that is purely formalist and is thought to imply no substantive assumptions. This is why Sen believes that morality, which is a substantive field, might find itself in conflict with rationality. (Two substantive domains, both having a firm tie to reality, could not be in conflict with each other unless reality itself exhibited internal inconsistencies.) It is also why the idea of rational choice is taken to mean no more than consistent ranking (in terms of existing preferences involving existing alternatives), a point I will discuss in more detail in the following section.

We thus need to examine whether there isn't a viable, richer notion of rationality. Without denying that the decision theorists' use of *rational* is valid in part (since logic is an aspect of rationality), we need to examine the idea of rationality before concluding that there are no rational guides to public action. As I will show, Friedland and Cimbala gave up too early; there is a way to conceive of rationality and, also, of rational public choice that can meet at least the more telling objections to the idea.

My procedure will involve, first, the definition of the concepts describing our field of inquiry so as to identify the standards by which to evaluate the steps taken within the field. I will identify the criterion of rational choice (or formulation) of theories concerning any field of inquiry. From there I will move on to the specific requirements for formulating or selecting a theory of public choice. Here I will focus on the nature of public affairs and will indicate why the present treatment is superior to those offered by the usual decision theories. I will end by indicating how this discussion, if taken seriously, can enhance the actual institution of rational decision making within the domain of politics.

For the moment, however, we are not concerned with rational public choice itself but with choosing a theory of such choice. For both aspects of the discussion we need to know what a theory is. Only then will we come to the issue of what, in theories of pubic choice is the rational choice.

On Rationality

For purposes of initial scrutiny, let us separate *rational* and *choice*. But, lest we fail at the outset, we need to defend, briefly, a way of going about answering such questions as what *rational* and *choice* mean. This may look like trying to begin without the prospect of getting off the ground, since all beginnings seem to pose the problem of needing support. But it is just a mistake to believe that no starting point is warranted as such, as Aristotle noted long ago. Some matters really cannot be questioned or doubted with any hope of being understood, despite what some current schools of philosophy—Richard Rorty's form of pragmatism, for instance—suggest.[13]

We pose questions when we face problems (unless we are jokers or madmen).[14] An inquiry into the meaning of some term is commonly prompted by the occurrence of incompatible usage. The results sought from the inquiry are firm grounds—preferably, the truth of the matter—for resolving the incompatibility.

Why do we think that such grounds or foundations might be found? Because we are here asking these questions and by so doing already rest on some foundations in many of our activities. In other words, our presence at the inquiry, our interest in the problem itself, our ability to focus on the issue at hand, and similar factors affirm that our search is grounded or rests on something stable and ongoing, otherwise we would not be able to embark upon it. Once these grounds are uncovered, confusion and conflict in usage are more likely to cease, though no one is justified in expecting final guarantees.[15] Accordingly, let us briefly contrast some uses of the terms at hand with others to see which will yield better results in terms of the standard implicit in our purpose, namely, to discover an unambiguous rendering of what a term means within the context of the rest of our discourse and experience.[16]

Rational is a term with diverse and sometimes incompatible uses in both common discourse and philosophical dialogue. The term is used to characterize what we say and do; but, given the different meanings people attach to it, most will disagree about whether the same course of conduct is or is not rational. Some tend to mean by *rational* that, for example, one is in possession of one's (uniquely human) conscious faculties. Actions that are rational are then supposed to involve competent, unimpeded, undiluted use of these faculties or what is sometimes referred to as articulable or intelligible accounts. That, in turn, requires a large array of virtues guided by competent, alert awareness of the world around us. In this rendition of *rational*, both means and ends of action can be subject to evaluation as either rational or irrational. (Some matters, namely, anything not capable of being placed under one's conscious control, would of course not be subject to such evaluation).

Others tend to mean by *rational* that, for example, some action led efficiently or effectively to satisfactory results, to just what was desired. This is often designated as the "instrumental" conception of rationality: what counts as rendering some behavior rational is that the most effective (or even technically up-to-date) means are employed to get from some starting point to some desired objective. The meaning here is the one we have already found associated with Sen. Acting consistently, being (formally) logical and internally consistent in one's course of conduct, as well as employing the most advanced technical resources in one's carrying out of one's policies, is rational.

Some, in turn, hold that *rational* means whatever is widely accepted—conventionally agreed to in the relevant community—as the way to proceed.[17] Or it is argued that that is the most one can expect the term to mean, given the difficulties with attempts to defend the sense of it indicated above. *Rational* or, less strictly, *reasonable*, is whatever conforms to the commonly adhered-to standards. (In the law the "reasonable man" standard is sometimes taken to mean this.)

It is clear that in certain contexts some of the conceptions described above will conflict. To take *rational* as meaning both "self-consistent" and "widely accepted in the relevant community" is realistic, yet that is supposed to be a firm, universal conclusion about what *rational* must mean.[18] And this last sense of *rational* also conflicts with "action flowing from competent use of one's conscious faculties," since the bulk of the relevant group might not use its faculties competently.

What we are after in inquiring whether institutions, policies, goals, and so on are *rational* is a common standard. That is why the decision theorists' or economists' rendition of *rational* is of little use here. But can we use the other sense, just discussed, which introduces a rather conventionalist standard?

A common standard implies a framework for evaluating judgments, actions, and other behavior involving such matters as distance, time, size, speed, quality, and kind, in all sorts of areas such as the sciences, arts, humanities, and personal life. It presupposes some shared capacity on people's part to identify (even if they do not do so) the standard as indispensable, binding, and universal within the context of the inquiry or endeavor at hand.[19] In judgments as such, independently of the specific subject matter (but not of any subject matter), the context would be seeking knowledge or learning what exists or ought to be done, or why.[20] Given the purpose of gaining knowledge, therefore, there would be a common standard by which judgments or conclusions could be evaluated (at least concerning a minimum degree of success so that, for example, explicit contradictions would be ruled out from the start). *Rational* would thus mean abiding by such a standard.

Clearly, inquiry into the meaning of *rational* produces at least two mutually exclusive answers. Why should we select one answer over the other? (Although we perhaps should, some may still refuse.)[21] Can we give an answer to this question without encountering vicious circularity?

If adopting one of the answers to the question "What does *rational* mean?" implies that it is impossible to make ourselves clear about what exactly the answer is, then the answer should be rejected.[22] At this fundamental level of inquiry, accepting the criterion of internal consistency is necessary, for inquiries as such make no sense without it. Indeed, seeking solutions presupposes that that standard is fully applicable.[23] With other terms, such as *pleasure, love, happiness,* or *alienation,* it may not be so obvious that an internally consistent meaning is a must, but it is no surprise with the term *rational.* Some conceptions of rationality do allow contradictory procedures in the same context to be rational. But when "widespread acceptability in the relevant community" is used as a substitute for *rational,* too many matters are left ambiguous to yield the absence of avoidable conflict.

We cannot use the economic model or the conventionalist idea of rationality because these fail to provide us with any common ground, the main purpose that we appear to expect to be achieved when the term is employed. The economist and the conventionalist can take us closer to settling on common means or methods, but most often what concerns us are goals—especially, for example, in public policies that are being recommended to an entire nation, not just to those whose special goals are already accepted.[24]

We are left now with *rational* as "established by reference to common standards for judging choices or decisions in some specific context." When someone correctly asserts that "'*X* is right' is the rational evaluation," he or she must mean that "'*X* is right' is established by reference to common standards in a given context of inquiry such as chemistry, metaphysics, ethics, or public choice."[25] Does this result beg the question? If one believes that the method for establishing the proper meaning of *rational* is itself employed because it is considered rational, then one will think the result empty. But the approach rests on a com-

mon standard for evaluating a choice, in this case concerning the meaning of terms in usage. If so, it could be rational—that is, we could discover it is rational upon reflection—without rendering the approach
circular in any vicious sense, unless the common standard cannot be
shown to be in fact common.

But would not showing the standard to be common itself involve an
idea of what is the rational way of choosing standards? No, because
some very basic standard is identified, not by way of arguments, but by
recognition that it is indispensable for inquiry and must serve as the
ground of rationality. To object to this standard as arbitrary is to forget
that arbitrariness makes sense only in contrast to the possibility of being
well grounded. So the only reply that would make sense is one that
shows that some other standard is common, not that none is. Otherwise
the charge is unfounded, literally. We are dealing with very basic matters, although this tends to be disguised by the fact that we are dealing
with them in a situation in which they are extremely well hidden from
view. That is, we are using language, complicated concepts, and theories in relatively familiar ways, and this can mislead us into thinking
that we could go much further in our inquiries to reach the level of
fundamentality. Contrary to this impression, we are actually there.

We can now turn to an examination of the concept *choice*. First,
let me note that the same points concerning methodology apply here
as when we examined what *rational* meant. Second, the relationship
between rationality and a certain kind of (initial) choice has been
recognized as a very strong one by many philosophers, in particular
by Immanuel Kant. This relationship has been worked out in detail
by Joseph Boyle, Jr., and colleagues.[26] Third, we should take note of
the fact that decision theorists and economists often use the concept
choice in a way that tends to conflate the sense just described with
its sense of "selecting from among alternatives." For instance, when
economists speak of *choice*, they usually mean revealed preference,
that is, the action or behavior of someone who is exposed to an existing range of alternatives. The sense of the term in its strong relationship to rationality, however, concerns initiating one's actions—as
when we speak of freedom of choice or free will. With the decision
theorists' or economists' idea of rationality—so long as a given long-
or short-range goal is efficiently achieved—the selection that is made
from the available alternative would be rational. With the concep-

tion of rationality developed above, however, the choice of a goal or end, too, could be either rational or not.

Given that a choice can involve both selection from among alternatives and the initiation of some (possible) course of conduct, which sense of the term is appropriate for our purpose? Since we are speaking of rational choice, we are concerned with both possible uses, as well as with uses that indicate both aspects of choice within one particular phenomenon. Thus, if someone chose to learn to play an instrument, he or she would both initiate some available (but not existent) course of conduct and select from (existent) alternative kinds of conduct besides learning an instrument, such as learning to ski or taking a vacation.

Only where the possibility of initiating—of being the fundamental or first cause of—one's conduct exists can the possibility of rational choice arise. This explains in part why it does not make sense to speak of a dog making a rational choice, although dogs make many selections. (Again, the prevalent economic conception of rationality would not rule out considering a dog's selection of one dog food over another as a rational choice—nor yet the behavior of computers. That is one result of the view that many economists embrace, namely, that all internally consistent behavior patterns are rational.)

For our purposes, the kind of choice we wish to know about most is selection. But even this needs some qualification. If we try to select from among existing alternative theories of rational public choice, we may find that we end without a viable candidate. We may then have to initiate (the mental action of) formulating such a theory. Keeping this point in mind, we can propose as a definition of the concept *choice*: either the initiation of some course of conduct, or the selection from among alternatives, or both. *Rational choice*, in turn, would then mean: initiation of a course of conduct or selection from alternatives, or both in accordance with a common standard appropriate to the context.

On Theories

Our context in this discussion is a distinct area of reality and the range of phenomena, activities, and concerns of which it is comprised, namely, rational choice of public policies, programs, institution, and so on. We are trying to make a rational choice concerning what theory to adopt or formulate pertaining to this realm of reality. We need to consider what a theory is. Only by having a fairly clear idea of what one is can we determine what common standard should be invoked in choosing or selecting from among such theories.[27]

Theories are series of (allegedly) logically related and factually relevant claims concerning the phenomena (or a range of phenomena) regarding which understanding is desired.[28] A series of assertions or claims that disregard evidence and omit placing the claims in logical relationship to each other do not make up a bona fide theory. (By "logical" I mean related in accordance with the correct meanings of the terms employed and by application of laws of valid inference.) Thomas S. Kuhn, Paul Feyerabend, and Stephen Toulmin, among others, have argued that sorting out the initial phenomena for purposes of separate or distinct treatment, in view of their alleged "theory ladenness" and thus lack of objective status raises intractable problems. These problems may be solved, however, by referring to the arguments advanced by Carl Kordig, Roger Trigg, myself and others, who stress that being theory laden is only a problem if one already believes that formulating a theory is a kind of interference with the world—a form of distortion through problematic interpretation. But there is no justification for so viewing theory ladenness; the human mind does not mold reality but grasps it, does not reshape what is by placing it in a framework, but merely notes differences and similarities, and works with these to apprehend further nuances and complexities. Indeed, the central problem with indicting theory ladenness is that the indictment cannot have force if it is valid, for then it is no more than just one opinion about what is going on. Of course, theory ladenness does make it possible for one to go astray, but there is nothing inevitable about that.[29]

Sometimes a distinction is upheld between normative and descriptive theories, but this distinction is itself theory based and thus is not very useful here where we are seeking help at a fundamental level of inquiry. Normative theories pertain to how behavior ought to occur—what is best, the good, the valuable. Descriptive theories, as the term suggests, are not action guiding but merely describe and explain some range of phenomena. It is sometimes held that the standards of adequacy and success for these two different types of theories will themselves be different. But that itself depends on whether the theory alleging the difference is itself a successful one. Indeed, there is a common sense difference between normative and descriptive theories, namely, that the former are about guiding action, and the latter are about explaining behavior. (Of course, the two kinds of theories often meet practical applications; for example, what engineers ought to do often depends upon how something is explained within their field of expertise.)

For our purposes, however, we are concerned with theories in the broad sense of the term, apart from any attempt to subcategorize them. In this regard, let us observe that theories need not be closed systems and can admit of warranted revisions, modifications, and alterations. Thus, unlike certain conceptions of what definitions must be—namely, unalterable or final statements of what something must be to constitute an instance of a kind—the concept "theory," as defined above, can overcome perversely language-centered Wittgensteinian objections.[30] This is especially important to note in connection with ethical and political (normative) theories, so as not to expect of them the utopian goal of reaching timelessly final standards for guiding conduct.

To succeed in providing a plausible series of logically related and factually comprehensive claims concerning some (range of) experiences will serve as a criterion or standard for identifying bona fide theories. The theory with the strongest arguments in its favor, inclusive of logical and factual requirements (though not necessarily in a formalist or deductive mode) will be the best theory within some field of inquiry.[31]

Candidates for Rational Public Choice Theory

To determine whether a theory of public choice is bona fide requires an understanding of what public affairs are. Friedland and Cimbala are correct to note that the findings of Arrow et al. warrant moving our inquiry onto a different plane, namely, political theory. Much earlier, Leo Strauss—anticipating numerous contemporary disputers—provided an argument showing the need for such an inquiry in our time.

> If there is no standard higher than the ideal of our society, we are utterly unable to take a critical distance from that ideal. But the mere fact that we can raise the question of the worth of the ideal of our society shows that there is something in man that is not altogether in slavery to his society, and therefore that we are able, and hence obliged, to look for a standard with reference to which we can judge of the ideals of our own as well as of any other society. The standard cannot be found in the needs of the various societies, for the societies and their part have many needs that conflict with one another: the problem cannot be solved in a rational manner if we do not have a standard with reference to which we can distinguish between genuine needs and fancied needs and discern the hierarchy of the various types of genuine needs.[32]

Strauss might well have spoken of the public interest as conceived by political leaders instead of society's various ideals, and of preferences or desires instead of needs; the point would be the same. In contrast, the ideal of society—the highest or most fully developed idea of a just human community, the real public interest, as it were, is the guiding concept for distinguishing political from nonpolitical areas of human concern. Under this concept, we subsume the traditional concerns of political life—the national purpose, the public good, justice (as a community concern), the good of the community as such, and so on.

It bears noting first that *social* is not *public*. The distinction I am making involves three groupings of people: society, community, and state. The first requires only the presence of large numbers of people in no special relationship to one another at all; the second is the grouping suggested by the Greek term *polis* (city), where people are members of an association with no other special ties involved except to function well or successfully for their lives together (which, of course, calls forth an inquiry as to what such well or successful functioning would amount to); the state is the idea that a community of people is itself an independent or at least united entity or group with particular goals such as making everyone happy, achieving economic success, or striving for technological progress.[33]

In the context of politics and law, understood by means of common sense rather than some theory that has picked certain objectives as being of special significance for everyone, *public* means whatever pertains to the entire citizenry or membership of a given human community qua that citizenry or membership rather than as regards their varied and often conflicting totality.[34] Once it is appreciated that human beings are, contrary to Karl Marx, not first and foremost members of an "organic body" but have as their defining characteristic their individuality (as well as rationality, sociality, and so on), to include anything more in *public* must lead to an incoherent, internally inconsistent concept. For instance, the public purpose will involve, as it does so frustratingly in many democratic welfare states, both supporting some goal—smoking, economic growth, conservation, technological advances, historical preservation—and opposing it. It is just this that seems to me to be so powerfully underlined by Arrow's thesis about the paradox of public choice.

Of course, much familiar usage conflicts with this definition of *public* as in the case of public telephones or public accommodations, which are available to all citizens but not in their capacity as citizens. In many such cases the context explains the exception involved, although some apparent exception could be misuses of the concept. Such usage as public park, public building, or public debt supports the definition.[35]

Public interest involves the more troublesome concept *interest*, which can mean—and is used to mean—concern on the part of as well as benefit or value to the public. It is possible that utilitarian theories of what is good, or of benefit to someone, have led to the conflation of the two senses of *interest*.[36] *Concern* is suggested by "I have an interest in modern art." Yet it seems that when one speaks of the public interest, one is not including the actual, usually conscious, interests we all have in one thing or another. When we substitute for *interest* the concept employed by economists and decision theorists, namely, *preference*, it is most likely impossible to give a clear rendition of the public interest in terms they employ.[37] Whatever the correct thesis about the nature of goodness or benefit, it is what is good for the public or benefits the public that is consistently meant by the concept *public interest* not what the public has an interest in or conscious concern for. As such, the concept *public interest* is understandably employed as a possible guide in our effort to identify what the political sphere pertains to. And when the problematic and highly abstract elements of this concept are analyzed and provided with consistent meaning, we not only may obtain a standard for identifying bona fide public affairs, but can make use of this standard to evaluate different proposals concerning how best to accomplish what is required for the public interest.[38]

Decision theorists and political philosophers, as well as political scientists, are well aware of the problem of identifying the public interest. In his essay on this general topic, the economist Peter O. Steiner says that "with respect to the nature of the public interest, it is we theorists who are the primitives in the sophisticated world of public decision makers."[39] He defers to bureaucrats and politicians in the effort to become enlightened, but it is obvious to anyone who observes the usual controversies concerning what governments should do, that these individuals, or members of the public at large, have no clear idea of what the public interest is. This does not prove that no one knows or could know the nature of the public interest, but it does point to the need for further explorations in this area. This is hardly a mere academic exercise, then, as Friedland and Cimbala suggest.

Briefly, I would attribute the difficulties with the public interest to our ancestors' and our own attempts to impose on the study of community life a model of research appropriate to other fields of inquiry, such as physics, biology, even economics. Also, the lure of mysticism has been powerful enough that rational inquiry has often been put aside because of the belief that human affairs are fundamentally mysterious. Thus, many people have held that human affairs either are not really distinct from the rest of nature or must be left to secular or theistic mystics to "understand" and "explain."

Some fusionists—Marxists for instance—have tried to combine a scientific and humanistic approach, but the effort cannot be considered a success, and some of those most sympathetic to Marx's ideas have admitted as much.[40] Given our conceptual faculties and the resultant need we have for integrated, principled perspectives on reality and our place in it, the attractiveness of the Marxist approach can be appreciated in the light of its having received very little competition at that comprehensive level of philosophy.[41] Fortunately, trends have been improving in recent years on the philosophical level, and the Marxist approach has been vitiated by the colossal failure of those measures closest to the ones suggested by Marx.[42]

My aim at this point in the discussion is to develop a standard by which certain kinds of policies and programs loosely and inconsistently referred to as "public policies" may be evaluated and formulated. This too will be a fusionist approach, but nonhistoricist; that is, it will eschew the idea that all standards are relative to some period of human history. My approach is in line with a secular neo-Aristotelianism I began developing in other works on related topics.[43]

Why is it necessary to try such a grand-scale reconsideration? The prospect of identifying the standard Strauss refers to above has not been very good in recent decades because of the widespread rejection, in academic philosophical circles, of the possibility of defining concepts objectively.[44] Earlier I sketched an explanation of what is required to so define concepts, and I have relied on this approach in providing definitions of *rational, choice, theory, public,* and *interest.* The central feature of that approach is to disown the view that definitions must be "necessarily final" statements of the nature of something—or of what something must be for it to be correctly designated by a concept being defined.[45] Instead, definitions are contextual, so that it remains open whether in some realm of inquiry they could or could not be final. In metaphysics, certain axiomatic concepts are indeed very likely to be unchangeably, unalterably valid, while in other realms we could formulate correct definitions that are nevertheless open-ended, although change would only be warranted when good reasons were provided for it. This contextual approach avoids both extremes of the philosophical theses that have been addressed to the topic, namely, absolutism and relativism (or Platonism and conventionalism). Absolutism understands definitions to state the final truth about the nature of something, thus rendering the prospect of definition impossible, while relativism or conventionalism takes definitions to be stipulative, persuasive, ultimately arbitrary or unjustifiable (except within a framework that is itself incapable of being shown to be sound or correct).

The standard that Strauss asks for in his remarks could be identified with the aid of a clear definition of the concept *public*. In line with the earlier definition, we can specify the range of the applicability of the term *public* as whatever is, or is very probably, clearly related to the citizenry as such, that is, to each individual member of the community in his or her status as such a member. The sort of endeavor, program, policy, office, official, or service that may be rationally regarded as public is one that exists to function for ends that the citizens qua citizens of a community share. This implies a severe restriction, apparently quite unrealistic, on what is properly meant by *public*. But it may also be construed as one hypothesis advanced after consideration of alternatives that have produced havoc in the field, as indicated not only by theoreticians such as Arrow and Sen but by contemporary community affairs.[46] By way of the proposed definition, a clear standard for distinguishing bona fide from fancied public matters may be developed, and determining the excellence or lack of same of various bona fide public matters could thereby be facilitated (though not guaranteed, of course).[47]

Understanding the proper range of public affairs—that is, what is to be rationally considered part of this domain—will not provide what some people desire in theories of public choice; I have no deductive formula to answer whether something is or is not a public matter. Whether it is well administered as such can be deduced from axioms along the lines used in mathematical logic (and also involved with great optimism in much social science, as in economics). Unlike the structure of an abstract science such as mathematics, reasoning about public affairs must in many areas be inductive or contextual. And more than in other nondeductive fields of inquiry, in the humane sciences the context of application can vary from time to time and place to place, sometimes with enormous differences in judgments and evaluations.

We need to admit, in line with our contextual stance, that the substantive points made here are not a priori truths. Therefore, different developments in human knowledge could produce different valid interpretations of the general ideas involved.[48] Given our general context, and our present level of understanding, what criterion determines whether something is a public matter? The answer will enable us to judge the quality of various public affairs—to wit, various past, present, and proposed bona fide public programs, institutions, and policies and their administration.

Public Affairs, Citizen Concerns

Bona fide public affairs must relate to all citizens qua citizens. Although the concept "citizen" is not self-evidently clear, we are not far from right when we think of citizenship as membership in a community that is organized as a human community for the purposes for which such communities should exist.

Almost any political theory subscribes to some conception of the end(s) or purpose(s) of human communities as such, if only in the sense that some motive is identified as providing the impetus for community existence. Among such conceptions we may number Hobbes's motive for self-preservation; Locke's innate drive toward happiness or preserving our person and property; Hegel's dialectical drive toward the universal freedom that will relieve our inherent internal strife. More recently, there is Rawls's motive for ensuring the safest possible conditions of social compact; and Nozick's desire to allay the fear of arbitrary intrusion into our lives by others.

But we must be cautious here. The Greek's goal-oriented political discourse has changed (though mainly in form) by making the motives, passions, or instincts—or history's movement—the bearers of what in teleological discussion are taken to be ends or goals to be deliberated about and chosen. In the ancient philosophies the dominant—but by no means exclusive—outlook had been to regard, at least implicitly, such goals as imperative but subject to choice. For example, each person was supposed to have a natural or proper goal, which was possible to identify; but each person could also fail to attain it, through negligence, weakness of will, or some other flaw of character or, at times, misfortune or tragedy. In the modern philosophies, in contrast, the dominant view is that the goal of behavior is preset, or that drives or instincts "know" in which direction behavior will steer us, but that we can improve the efficiency of our progress in that direction by acquiring better information and instruments or techniques.

In the present discussion we are going to regard goals for human beings as derivable from the kind of being they are and the pursuit of those goals as something we are free to choose. What common goal, then, unites rational citizens? (We are considering only self-conscious citizenship as a possible model to work with, since it is impossible to discuss the principles of conduct of those careless or indifferent, not to mention destructive, of their proper goals in life.)[49] How, if at all, are citizens united in the pursuit of some goal(s) or end(s)?

There is no way to answer the question about what conduct is properly pursued by people in communities qua members of communities without learning what conduct is proper individually. Not that an answer to the basic ethical question has to be accepted by all who are members of a community. But for those who want to discover correct standards of community life as such, the questions of ethics must be answered, at least in their broadest outline. In other words, rational public choice theory logically presupposes rational private choice theory—unless we are to presuppose the radical statist treatment in terms of which the public is a separate individual with its own proper goals. Since, however, principles or standards of the sort we are interested in (namely, ones we can sensibly be said to be responsible for invoking to guide conduct) presuppose the existence of moral agency and whatever is conceptually and actually required for such agency to exist, the statist answer to questions of public choice theory faces severe difficulties. What faculty of choice does the public have? Do states have moral responsibilities apart from or over and above the general responsibilities of those who live in a community? The phrase "society's obligations" is often used, yet the society does not appear to have the capacity prerequisite to the exercise of choice (namely, conceptualization) that obligations, for instance, assume.

Because of these and related problems with the radical statist's theory, we need briefly to explore ethics and to focus on the moral responsibilities individual human beings are supposed to have.

Turning to Metaethics

We have reached the stage of our discussion that bears directly upon some of the points raised in the introduction to this work, namely, the ethical or moral foundations of a free political system and, thus, the distinctive political tradition of the United States. There is a hint about that foundation in the Declaration of Independence, where the right to "the pursuit of happiness" is mentioned. It seems clear that for the first time in history a major country paid attention in its founding document to the importance of the individual human being's happiness. It is not spelled out, of course, whether this happiness is one that a person might attain here on earth or in some supernatural realm.

Of course, the Declaration is not an ethical treatise but a political assertion. Naturally, then, it only makes mention of a "right to" the pursuit of happiness, not to any possible moral responsibility to exercise that right. Nevertheless, knowing something of the Declaration's philosophical background should enable one to take seriously the idea that the founders and framers did not look askance upon the idea that human beings ought to strive for their happiness. Hobbes and Spinoza, both prominent influences on liberal and democratic political thought, believed in a form of psychological egoism. Locke believed in the same, although he moderated it to allow for more choice and was closer to being an ethical egoist. And the ancient philosophers, whom the founders studied, also believed that—to quote Adam Smith from *The Wealth of Nations*—"the duties of human life [are] subservient to the happiness and perfection of human life."[50]

An investigation of the ethics underlying a sound public choice theory, with the result that a form of ethical egoism is found as the best candidate, will be eminently justifiable here. Let us start as close to the beginning as is workable by asking "What is the correct ethical position?" But before we can do that, we must first know what question ethics addresses or has as its purpose to answer.

Ethics is concerned with answering the question "How do human beings live well or properly?" This question arises quite naturally because, as I have noted earlier and argued elsewhere, human beings must initiate the bulk of their actions.[51] They face the responsibility of having to choose a course of conduct that will make it possible for them to live well. Because human beings are unable to rely solely on their sensory and physiological responses to guide them in living—they lack instincts, at least vis-à-vis the myriad complex objectives they could pursue—they need to initiate actions that will achieve for them the conceptual knowledge needed to live well, that is, live in accordance with the requirements of their nature.[52]

The fact that human beings are essentially free to choose their behavior—that they are beings of volitional consciousness, as Ayn Rand put it—explains our concern with morality in human affairs.[53] Because human beings are entities of a specific kind, the duration and the quality of their existence become tasks for them to achieve in their conduct. Life matters to other beings, but for people the quality and the duration of existence are (to some considerable extent) matters of choice. If the choices made are right, the quality and duration of existence are advanced in likelihood (for no guarantees can be offered, contrary to much ethical and political theory). And the most basic, universal standard for such advancement is what ethics or morality seeks to identify, with the correct ethical position presented being the most successful theory aimed at this end.[54] Let me simply outline the case for the position I think most successful as an ethical theory. It seems to me that, contextually, the most rational life of an individual is the goal which it is our moral responsibility to pursue. This necessarily very general basic ethical claim applies to all human beings for all times, by virtue of what human beings are, namely, rational animals. For any person, it is morally good to live by standards that render the achievement of this kind of life more rather than less likely. Or in Aristotelian language, the successful life of the individual as a human being is what we should pursue in our individual lives.[55] Both who and what we are become determinants of what these standards of conduct will be. Virtues vary from the general to the more and more specialized, but some of them are broadly enough defined to be demonstrably binding. The basic virtue by which the goal of successful human existence is secured (to the extent possible) is the choice to be rational, to be aware of reality, to employ principles of sound thinking, and to be guided by this thinking in all of one's activities. From this virtue others may be developed, and I would argue that the widely acknowledged virtues—integrity, honesty, justice, productivity, generosity, courage, prudence, and the rest—can be demonstrated to be proper guidelines for successful human existence in the various areas of human life where they are applicable.

But what interests me here is the central goal we all have, albeit with very different implications for us, depending on who we are and where and when we are in existence. If our central goal in our conduct is to live rationally, we have some clearly identifiable universally shared goals in community life. Our capacity for rational living and its value to us make community life a great value to us. Here we can learn, teach, produce, enjoy, create, and so forth with far greater success than in isolation from others. Yet, as so many political theorists have noted, community life poses unusual dangers to us as well, and the task is to make possible the enjoyment of its values with the fullest possible reduction of those dangers.

The danger we face that is unique to community life is the danger from others who either have made very bad choices or have simply failed to exercise reason in their conduct, thus exposing us to negligence and vice that can impair our existence. The value of community life is so crucial that it provides sound reasons for establishing institutional protection against its unique dangers. Not self-preservation or fear or some such negative factor (pace Hobbes and Nozick, for example), but the fact of the enormous potential value of community life gives rise to public affairs, to the establishment of the public sector, that is, to the institution of politics and law.

In summary, then, the ethics of classical egoism—that we should all pursue our success or happiness as human beings—gives us the central moral reason for community existence and, thereby, for existence of the public or political realm of life.[56] What we now need to find out is the specific value that public institutions or politics are supposed to secure for us so that we may pursue the values community existence makes possible. In short, what is the public interest? I will defend the view that, briefly, the value to be pursued by means of political or public activity is liberty, the necessary condition in society for the pursuit of the moral life.[57]

Delineating the Public Realm

Among the very few purposes we all share is to succeed as human beings in our individual lives; interference with our option to meet this challenge is a destruction of our moral dignity, of our opportunity to aspire to moral excellence within our context.

This assumption might be disputed on the ground that at least sometimes interference can restore us to a state where we can pick up our self-government and self-determination, while the absence of such interference (whether its motives are paternalistic or something else) would permanently cripple us. Yet it is more likely that such helpful interference alone would be impotent to save us unless we chose to use it wisely, and that would be improbable when we did not accept it in the first place (which is why it must be imposed on us). Furthermore, it is also likely that reaching an irreversible level of desperation entirely on our own—that is, not because we had been treated unjustly—would be the result of our own failings, of negligence, which would indicate that interference would be useless.

As members of human communities it is appropriate that we take measures to have the impediments to meeting this challenge stemming from community life—a challenge that faces us precisely because we aim to benefit so much from community life—competently resisted and restrained. Without community life being of benefit to us, the challenge could be met by opting for mere physical isolation. Even in contemporary society, one could carve out some space and remain utterly alone. But that would be a destructive course. Instead, it is more prudent to establish barriers against the uninvited intrusions of others. This objective is what gives rise to the distinctive sphere of public affairs as such—the concern with the establishment, maintenance, and administration of the basic unobtrusive constituents of a just community. The reason that benefiting citizens in such realms as health care, athletic aspiration, personal grooming, education, and the like are not part of this bona fide public concern is that in those matters the requirements of citizens vary and conflict, based on their distinctive individuality. Such benefits may be pursued by them without conflict, but the attempt to provide the benefits for them at the collective expense must irresolvably pit them against one another. This is the situation in democratic welfare states, where there is a Hobbesian war of all special or vested interest groups against all others for obtaining "public" support.

Evaluating rational choice theories in public affairs requires a clear identification of the domain of public affairs. Standards of proper decision and conduct concerning public affairs must enable us to aim successfully at protecting and preserving the liberty of the membership of a community qua such membership. This last qualifier is essential. For the actions of members of a community can be impeded by many forces, but the forces threatening individuals in relationship to community existence are other people and their many-faceted coercive behavior. The task of public policy is to cope with such distinctive community problems as are generated by the threat and reality of other people's coercive or liberty-impeding conduct. Human existence is always confronted with threats from nonhuman sources, in or outside the context of community life, so the public domain could not be singled out as requiring protection from nonhuman threats.[58]

If one maintains that equality of conditions and opportunities for achieving success in one's life is a moral and political imperative, then one will find this goal inadequate because, clearly, merely keeping the peace among the citizenry does not promote that objective. But there is no moral/political imperative of that sort that can be demonstrated.[59] Perhaps most importantly, the very attempt to secure such equality must involve undermining it by giving some the power to promote, maintain, and preserve it.

Of course, in a corrupted public realm, even if its official objective is merely keeping the peace—that is to say, protecting the basic negative rights of all citizens—some may temporarily be at a disadvantage, while others reap special (undeserved) benefits. If a judge or legislator or police officer is bribed, undeserved benefits can and will likely be the result, and the system must be prepared so that remedies may be sought in such cases. But a community structure that is focused on preserving peace will be least likely to precipitate corruption since not a great deal may be obtained from public officials who have no treasure beyond what is required for the administration of minimalist justice. The neo-Marxist claim that protecting individual negative rights "prevents" some from reaping benefits rests on the mistaken notion that there exists a natural obligation for human beings to promote the welfare of those in dire need. While the virtue of generosity is indeed defensible, such a natural and so enforceable obligation is not, unless one abandons the individualist conception of human nature and accepts the collectivist one Marx and some others adopt, whereby we all belong to one another.[60]

What standards need to be observed and upheld by law so as to achieve the task of public policy? The answer I would propose lies in natural rights or human rights theory.[61] Independent of any particular theory of human rights, the goal of governmental conduct is generally seen to be achieved when people's rights are protected and preserved. If we assume for a moment that government and public policy has as its proper goal the distribution of wealth equally among the citizens of a community, individual citizens will accordingly claim rights in the available wealth. Or suppose that public policy should aim at upholding the moral fiber of society. In that case individuals can claim rights in having immoral behavior prohibited and moral behavior supported. Or again, suppose that government and public policy should aim to bring about the communist society and the eventual withering away of the state; here, too, the rights (or entitlements) people may claim will be those rights which, protected and preserved, will enhance this future prospect.[62]

Since the goal of public policy is, contrary to the above examples, the protection and preservation of the right to liberty of the individual from others, the obligations people have are those that secure this right. It is inappropriate to elaborate here what I have discussed in considerable detail elsewhere, namely, that the value of negative liberty—which is required for moral choice and, thus, for human flourishing—is secured when the rights of individual members of a human community to life, to voluntary action (or to liberty of conduct), and to property are universally respected, observed, and defended. I want to explain merely that the central consideration is the right of everyone to life, that which each person must enhance and make excellent as a matter of his or her personal moral responsibility. From this basic right (itself grounded on the ethics of classical individualism and egoism), others are derived within the context of human social reality.

The right to liberty of conduct is necessary for purposes of upholding human dignity or the capacity of each individual to be a moral agent in life. One's right to life, based on the fact of one's moral agency and responsibility to live successfully, is hollow, indeed, if the right to liberty is not implied by it. The right to produce, hold, and acquire (by exchange or through gifts) valuables is again a derivative right, based on the recognition that to be free to act involves, in part, to be free to act so as to benefit oneself (whether in fact the consequence of such action yields benefit or loss). While derivative, concretely or practically the right to property is extremely important because it is the expression of the more abstract rights to life and liberty in the sphere of action. Everybody—from engineer and farmer to poet and composer—acts some place, however directly or indirectly, vis-à-vis some entities in nature.[63]

Other rights that may be derived from the right to life include the more specialized, contextually justified rights to enter into contracts; to have a role in the selection of political representatives; to speak one's piece and create one's science or art; and much more. The list here is familiar within the framework of U.S. political history because different groups of these rights have been held by various ideological and political factions, down to our own times, to be in need of defense. In few cases, however, and then usually based on different philosophical and other considerations, have theorists argued for a fully consistent policy of the defense of human rights.

As an example, modern liberals have tended to defend rights concerning political participation, such as the rights to free speech, assembly, voting, legal protection against violation of due process, and so forth, while conservatives have tended to give support to such rights as free trade, wealth acquisition, and private enterprise. Each faction has also tended to compromise on its list of preferred rights when defending them would have endangered the principal value for which it believes government should aim, namely, economic welfare in the case of modern liberals and spiritual welfare in that of conservatives.

The present thesis defends the view that public policy should be restricted to its natural, rationally warranted purpose, namely, to secure what is of benefit for citizens qua citizens, their liberty of conduct—however good, successful, attractive, or joyous that conduct, as well as however unappealing, immoral, unsuccessful, or distressing such conduct may be. (It is not necessary to add the caveat: provided the liberty of others is unabridged. The universal character of the normative or prescriptive nature of this thesis implies that only such liberty is to be secured as is possible for each person in the community to enjoy; "ought" implies "can.")

I must briefly acknowledge a major difficulty with the present thesis, one that it is hardly possible to dispel here. My position depends here on so many unfinished strands of argumentation, including comparative analyses of the theoretical merits of alternative answers to various philosophical questions—about free will versus determinism, as well as ethics, theories of definition, and other issues—that it may be imagined to be little more than a theoretical house of cards. In a sense I have been pleading my case, as that phrase is used in both the law and informal fallacy textbooks. But I have made every effort to shore up this case elsewhere, so I will not repeat the entire discussion here.

Applied Public Choice Theory

For the rest of this chapter I wish to indicate some of the advantages that the present position has in connection with the problem of making decisions and choices or guiding conduct and policy in the public domain.[64] To do this I want to sketch one of the standard hypothetical cases of policy conflict.

The Department of Human Services in the United States is directed by Congress to institute a program of day-care centers for "working parents"—parents who both work outside the home. Experts in finance, communication, community organization, and so on, are called in, and the specifications for the program are written up, based on information about the estimated needs. Eventually the program gets under way. Based on the satisfaction of working parents, incidence of mishaps, whether the system is administered fairly (do part-time workers receive some consideration, for instance) the system is up for evaluation and is assessed as successful, moderately successful, or poor.

In this sketch, crucial considerations are missing. When we introduce them, we will discover why public policy that aims to satisfy needs and desires of this type must end in being closed to evaluation qua public policy. Evaluating a public program or policy or institution requires us to rely on and invoke a standard, and standards that are unsuited to this purpose simply result in contradictory evaluations. That, in blunt terms, is the reason that utilitarian evaluation schemes have failed thus far. Within such a framework it is impossible to carry out what is referred to as interpersonal utility comparisons. This means that when we take as our starting point each person's unique (subjective) standard of value (or preference scale), then there exists no common standard of evaluation—the essential ingredient of rational public choice. On some people's preference scale, childcare centers rank very high, on others' they rank in the middle, and on the rest very low or not at all. With resources that are not infinite, public instituting childcare centers is impossible unless some people's preferences are negated in favor of others, yet there is no common standard (preference scale) to justify this. A strictly utilitarian analysis, not so much à la John Stuart Mill as Jeremy Bentham, yields no meaningful results in public decision-making situations. In principle, some notion of intensity of desire might be introduced and a kind of crude physical calculus proposed; but even if this were worked out, the result would be only an unmanageably volatile collation of overall preferences or desires.[65] The attempt to use this suspiciously fantastic idea as some kind of theoretical model has, I believe, yielded some of the preoccupations of decision theorists, political scientists, and others that Friedland and Cimbala refer to so cynically.[66]

Let us consider some other factors involved in our example. Instituting child-care centers is an objective that is important only for some people but if it is accepted as a valid public purpose, other objectives will arise rapidly enough and be proposed for representation. The concept of the public is well enough understood by most people for us to take it as given that if the desires of some people are valid public concerns, then those of others must be also. This cannot be avoided when the idea of *public* is left ambiguous, with only the vague idea that the more support something gets, the more public it is. Certainly some programs not naturally public may at any time receive virtually unanimous support, but even these would fail at being public in terms of the analysis here advanced. What is important to note is that this practical result of the ambiguous conception of public affairs, though not logically entailed, is reasonably predictable on the basis of what we know of human motivation and the function of conceptual understanding in how people plan their lives. Moreover, it is perfectly evident in the political affairs of mid-twentieth-century societies.[67]

Without a viable, rationally plausible alternative, in the face of the above-noted counts against feasibility, we might simply have to conclude that public program selection is inherently irrational. Let us then simply plow ahead with the combative, pressure-group politics evident in practice and apparently engendered as a last resort by utilitarian theory.[68] The existence of a sensible alternative brings forth a different situation.

In line with the value we have identified as properly sought via public action, namely, liberty, public programs must enhance individual liberty, not stifle it. Thus, requiring that all (or most) citizens pay for a program that will furnish only some with opportunities by which they might make personal advances in life violates the public interest. For it obstructs the liberty of those who would rather employ their own resources—spans of life time, skills, earnings, faculties, talents, and whatever else they can—in other ways. Furthermore, we need to consider the ethical issue that by providing some people with opportunities without generally regarding it as their responsibility to achieve them, the programs involved will cater to a demoralization of the citizens' lives and actions by preempting their personal moral involvement. (By "demoralization" I refer to the process of destroying the moral significance of something.) It is wrong to force others to obtain the goods and services needed to pursue any goals, even when they coincide with the goals of those who are being coerced. For example, even if someone ought to go to church or ought to insure herself against the likely illnesses that will befall her in old age, for another to coerce her to do these acts—in other words, to make her behave as she ought to—would be immoral. As such, the sorts of "public" programs we are here considering fly in the face of how persons ought to act toward each other—even when these persons occupy the role of government administrators. Such actions are normally immoral and such policies are categorically immoral.[69]

I am not here concerned with the motivations that may lie in back of instituting so called coercive public programs. It makes no difference whether child-care centers, for example, are instituted because many people feel compassion for and ought to act with proper generosity or charity toward working parents. Nor does it matter whether they are interested in child indoctrination or simply seek self-enrichment. These motives have inspired many worthy as well as unworthy policies. What is wrong is that the institution of these kinds of programs violates the central principle of the best political system available to us now, namely, the principle of the right to individual liberty. As such these programs should not be adopted. It is, furthermore, not surprising that when a system makes it structurally possible for such violation to occur, quirks, including inconsistent "public" policies, will be instituted.

The daycare center discussed in this case is an example. Irreconcilable conflicts accompany attempts to justify such programs and to determine which of the infinite number of them should be instituted, for whose benefit, and at whose expense. The reason conflicts arise is that no clear understanding exists, even among those who are conscientiously making the effort to get things right, of the nature of public affairs. Consider—as an illustration of this lack of understanding and as an indication of the comparative advantages of the present position—several recent attempts to define *public good*.

1. "There are certain goods that have the peculiarity that once they are available no one can be precluded from enjoying them whether he contributed to their provision or not. These are the public good." (Dorfman)[70]

2. "Any publicly induced or provided collective good is a public good. A 'collective good'...is not necessarily a collective consumption good. Collective goods arise whenever some segment of the public collectively wants and is prepared to pay for a different bundle of goods and services than the unhampered market will produce. When the coordinating mechanism of providing a collective good invokes the powers of the state I define the good as a public good." (Steiner)[71]

3. "A public good is any good or service which is de facto provided for or subsidized through Government budget finance." (Birdsall)[72]

In the first definition the concept of *public good* is defined in terms of some alleged peculiarities of community life, namely, that some goods and services produced at some cost by specifiable parties are enjoyable without payment by others. This fact entitles no one to institute measures to have these goods and services produced at the cost of everyone, even those who would not choose to contribute to the production but will, of course, readily enjoy the product if it is offered free of charge. Nor is there any argument available to show that the perhaps lamentable burdens some might have to shoulder from having chosen to engage in this kind of production should be distributed over all those who could enjoy the results. As a simple example, consider the attractiveness of those who frequent the same places where others enjoy this quality. Should the beneficiaries be forced to contribute to the cosmetic and clothing costs, even living expenses, of those who have unwittingly contributed this potential benefit? Why? Unless some relationship is demonstrated between promises made or obligations undertaken by the beneficiaries, no moral connection is evident between what they do and what they may freely enjoy on such occasions. In short, this definition of a public good trades on prevailing coincidences.

Turning to the second definition on our list, we find here what may be construed, I believe, as typical by positivists. This definition may be appreciated from its emphasis exclusively on what some segment of the public actually wants and is prepared to pay for, avoiding the issue of whether what is wanted is just, right, or good. No question of propriety is settled in such a definition, and, by its tenets, any sort of mad dash for the supply even of morally odious "goods" or services qualifies the supply as a public good. What if most people actually wanted addictive narcotics, prostitution, or sadomasochism and waged a political campaign to get it? Would it be a public good when any of these was delivered? Surely that stretches the concepts beyond any recognizable meaning. A public good would at once be a public bad. This is just the sort of difficulty that is raised by Strauss and by others conscious of the pitfalls of positivist—including the prominent *homo economicus* (or utility maximizing person)—analyses of law and politics. More particularly, there is no evidence of any restriction on the quality of the "coordinating mechanism" that might invoke the powers of the state; presumably then, anything from purely democratic to wholly totalitarian methods of coordination would be acceptable means for determining what would be a public good or service or policy. What is clear is that no rational social or public choice from among conflicting desires or needs or wishes can be identified if public goods or services or policies are identified in terms of the second definition.

The third definition is essentially the same definition as the second, but with even fewer precautions against dictatorial methods of implementing some wish or desire as if it were really public. Mere de facto state activity is sufficient here, so that the definition does not even tie the public good to some loosely specified range of goods and services governments might supply or subsidize. Again, no claim to rationality is possible in the selection of such public goods or policies.

In these and many other conceptions of what constitutes the public character or nature of some good, service, or policy, no possibility exists for distinguishing consistently between bona fide and fancied claims in behalf of something being a public matter. Thus, no standards could be available for determining the excellence of some public program, for these would depend on a coherent conception of what is to count as a public matter.

We need not, however, declare the field inherently irrational or even nonrational, as some have suggested. The nature of public affairs conceived along the lines presented earlier will secure the prospect of rational choice, decision, action, and evaluation of the bona fide public sector. By bona fide public programs I have in mind those such as police services, court reform and normal court business, prison upkeep and maintenance, administration of (the proper) political participation methods, and public (military) defense. These and related programs are public because they are the tasks the performance of which contributes to the achievement of the goals or ends of citizens qua citizens of a community. Evaluation of these types of programs and of the policies associated with them can ensue without the tangle of contradictions that has characterized so much policy assessment associated with activities now construed to be public.

The first conceptual task here is to discipline oneself about the distinction between genuine and fancied public affairs. However risky this may seem—and indeed be—as far as public sentiment is concerned, the task is to uphold the integrity of reaching the proper goals involved. No doubt this approach will engender criticism on grounds that the task is unlikely to be achieved. Some tasks are worth trying even without good odds, however. When one considers the alternative of ending up with frustration (because other methods yield no results that can be considered rationally justifiable), the risk no longer appears so great.

Given a proper conception of public programs, what standards are appropriate for purposes of designing, selecting, or evaluating such programs? Here the answer will be both quite simple and apparently vague. But that is to be expected from a philosophical investigation. Such a process can at best produce correct general standards, stated in terms that would have to be interpreted in the context of the actual public affairs being carried out. Just as in ethics we might be able to produce arguments to the effect that justice is a virtue that involves conducting oneself toward others in accordance with the moral qualities people achieve; and just as in physics we can produce sound arguments that yield the conclusion that certain principles apply in the case of the behavior of certain kinds of subatomic particles; so in political theory it is possible only to arrive at general principles concerning what is proper within this area of human concern.

What must be aimed for in public programs is the contextually warranted best method for achieving the proper ends involved. For example, we need to know the available means for carrying out the various proper public policies, and then we need to institute the organizational structure for so implementing them. Individually, those administering public programs need to be fully aware of their proper role as public officials, that is, that they must possess the personal moral quality of people who are entrusted with carrying out bona fide public tasks, in the sense discussion above.

The only point that can be added (without taking up a full consideration of specific bona fide public tasks) is that economics, psychology, anthropology, international relations, political science, and all the various technologies will bear on determining what can rationally be allotted to public affairs—which will be multitudinous even with the restriction required by a clear definition of the concept *public*. To a large extent these determinations are quite changeable. Thus, awareness of advances in the various sciences, with their expected potential for altering the specific standards of rationality (for instance, as to means for achieving what is itself a proper public purpose within the field of criminal justice), would be required. In general, philosophical analysis of the conditions of rationality within the public domain must remain on the high level of abstraction of philosophy proper, lest unwarranted limitations be imposed and the often-feared dogmatism concerning what counts as rational become a reality.

Put very briefly, then, evaluation of bona fide public matters would involve technical, scientific, market, legal, and moral considerations. In its essentials the process would not differ from what would count as rational regarding the guidance and evaluation of personal conduct. Guided by basic principles that are capable of gradual changes—though at times necessarily radical ones, because previously neglected—the system of public affairs could have the needed fixedness of rational judgment and the dynamism of a world where both our knowledge and reality itself are subject to change.[73]

In subsequent chapters of this book I will be exploring the question of just what kinds of tasks are fit to be regarded as "public," and how those that have appeared to some to belong in that class do not need to be approached in a polity properly suited to human community life. Throughout the ensuing discussions in this work, three main conclusions of this chapter need to be kept in mind. First, while there are rational answers to the questions we pose in the context of political life, they are not timelessly fixed, nor infinitely flexible or arbitrary; for example, while what we have seen clearly recommends a significant sphere of personal authority or sovereignty for every individual in society, the exact determination of the range of that sovereignty cannot be made a priori.[74] Second, what counts as public is by no means unproblematic, and only a conception that avoids Arrow's paradox of public choice can be counted on to do the job we broadly have in mind as we make use of the concept of *public* in the context of law and politics. Third, that concept involves an understanding of human beings as essentially individuals with certain specific and (limited) collective objectives that amount to public affairs.

Notes

1. Tibor R. Machan, *Capitalism and Individualism: Reframing the Argument for the Free Society* (New York: St. Martin's Press, 1990).
2. Edward I. Friedland and Stephen J. Cimbala, "Process and Paradox: The Significance of Arrow's Theorem," *Theory and Decision* 4 (1973): 51–64.
3. Kenneth Joseph Arrow, *Social Choice and Individual Values*, 2d ed., (New York: Wiley, 1963).
4. Friedland and Cimbala, "Process and Paradox," p. 60.
5. *Ibid.*, p. 61.
6. *Ibid.*, p. 62.
7. See Rom Harre and P. F. Secord, *The Explanation of Social Behaviour* (Totowa, NJ: Littlefield, Adams, 1973); Robert Hollinger, "A Defense of Essentialism," *The Personalist* (Autumn 1976): 327–343; Robert Nozick, *Anarchy, State, and Utopia* (New York: Basic Books, 1974); Hanna Fenichel Pitkin, *Wittgenstein and Justice: On the Significance of Ludwig Wittgenstein for Social and Political Thought* (Berkeley: University of California Press, 1972); Barry Stroud, "Wittgenstein and Logical Necessity," in *Wittgenstein*, ed. G. Pitcher, (Garden City, NY: Anchor Books, 1969); Roger Trigg, *Reason and Commitment* (Cambridge: Cambridge University Press, 1973).
8. Let me quickly mention that I will not enter fully the discussion of meaning, although clearly a philosophically comprehensive approach to our topic must deal with that problem to some extent. I do touch on it in my exploration of the nature of rationality. But I do not take up the currently fashionable but actually ancient idea satirized in Plato's *Cratylus*, that ultimately words have no right meaning, no correct interpretation, no best sense. That idea seems to me to be so hopelessly confused and confusing that it must lead to nihilism or utter nonsense.
9. Friedland and Cimbala, "Process and Paradox," p. 60.
10. Amartya K. Sen, "Choice, Orderings and Morality," in *Practical Reason*, ed. Stephan Koerner, (New Haven, CT: Yale University Press, 1974), p. 55.
11. *Ibid.*
12. *Ibid.*
13. Richard Rorty, *Objectivity, Relativism, and Truth* (Cambridge: Cambridge University Press, 1991). Other currently fashionable suggestions along these lines include deconstructionism and methodological anarchism. But see Tibor R. Machan, "Evidence of Necessary Existence," *Objectivity* 1 (Fall 1992): 31–62.
14. Gilbert Harman, *Thought* (Princeton, NJ: Princeton University Press, 1973). The dialogues of Plato are conceived along such lines—serious and goodwilled people trying to solve problems.
15. Guarantees are clearly impossible, since good arguments can be rejected.
16. Throughout the various stages of this work, some intermediary steps will not receive full treatment—inescapably since most of those could take up volumes apart from our objective here. But the notes and the brief outline of the argument will show clearly the merits the present approach has, if any.
17. Carl R. Kordig, *The Justification of Scientific Change* (Dordrecht, Holland: Reidel, 1972); and John Rawls, *A Theory of Justice* (Cambridge: Harvard University Press, 1971).

18. Compare with two articles by Morton L. Schagrin, "On Being Unreasonable," *Philosophy of Science* 40 (1973): 1-9; and "A Response to Machan and Zupan," *Philosophy of Science* 42 (1975): 311.

19. Rare exceptions do not damage the possibility of firm definitions. See Kenneth G. Lucey, "Counter-examples and Borderline Cases," *The Personalist* 51 (1976): 351-355.

20. We are concerned with what inquiry as such is for, namely, correct awareness of reality.

21. We assume free will here, of course.

22. To be understood, all parties must be able to fix the meaning of terms. Aristotle, in *Metaphysics*, Book 4, Chapter 4 still gives the best discussion of this issue. See also, Machan, "Evidence of Necessary Existence."

23. Even to understand a problem requires such standards.

24. Here we can consider the dismay with the influence of "special interests" on public policy, an influence that appears to render public policy impossible as any kind of integrated project.

25. For example flipping a coin can be the rational solution.

26. Joseph M. Boyle, Jr., Germain Grisez, and Olaf Tollefsen, *Free Choice: A Self-referential Argument* (Notre Dame, IN: University of Notre Dame Press, 1976). I discuss it, as well, in my *The Pseudo-Science of B. F. Skinner* (New Rochelle, NY: Arlington House, 1974); and *Individuals and Their Rights* (LaSalle, IL: Open Court, 1989).

27. See Stanley Malinovich, "Knowledge and Evaluation," *Canadian Journal of Philosophy* 4 (September 1974): 79-95.

28. This does not imply a reductionist approach. See Stephen Edelston Toulmin, *The Uses of Argument* (Cambridge: Cambridge University Press, 1958).

29. Kordig, *Justification of Scientific Change*; and Trigg, *Reason and Commitment*. For my own treatment of this issue, see Tibor R. Machan, "On the Possibility of Objectivity and Moral Determinants in Scientific Change," in *Determinants and Controls of Scientific Development*, ed. Karin D. Knorr, Hermann Strasser, and Hans Georg Zilian, (Dordrecht, Holland: Reidel, 1975), pp. 75-111. See, for a discussion of the basic epistemological issues, Tibor R. Machan, chap. 1 in *Individuals and Their Rights*.

30. Robert Hollinger, "Natural Kinds, Family Resemblance, and Conceptual Change," *The Personalist* 55 (Autumn 1974): 323-333; and Tibor R. Machan, "Law, Justice and Natural Rights," *Western Ontario Law Review* 14 (1975): 119-130.

31. Machan, "On the Possibility of Objectivity..."; and Toulmin, *The Uses of Argument*.

32. Leo Strauss, *Natural Right and History*, 2nd ed., (Chicago: University of Chicago Press, 1970), p. 39.

33. There is, of course, support for this view in Hegel, Marx, Skinner, and others. But most talk along these lines is simply of the generalizing and averaging sort. See Jerome Rothenberg, chap. 13 in *The Measurement of Social Welfare* (Englewood Cliffs, NJ: Prentice-Hall, 1961), pp. 309ff.

34. Common sense, as has been acknowledged by nearly all philosophers—notably Socrates, Aristotle, Hume, and Wittgenstein—is indispensable as the starting point of inquiry. Furthermore, concepts required for action by all persons cannot be specialized or technical.

35. Some of the discussions in Brian Barry, *Political Argument* (London: Routledge and Kegan Paul, 1965); and Bertrand de Jouvenel, *Sovereignty: An Inquiry into*

the Political Good, trans. J. F. Huntington, (Chicago: University of Chicago Press, 1957) can help us get clear on the definition of "public."

36. This may stem from a debt to Hobbes in neoclassical economics. See, for more on this, Machan, chap. 1 in *Capitalism and Individualism*.

37. Compare with Ronald Dworkin, *Taking Rights Seriously* (Cambridge: Harvard University Press, 1977). An attempt is made by Dworkin to distinguish between preferences involving oneself alone and those involving others. But Dworkin notes that "external preferences...present a great difficulty for utilitarians" (p. 30).

38. See Malinovich, "Knowledge and evaluation."

39. Peter O. Steiner, "The Public Sector and the Public Interest," in *The Analysis and Evaluation of Public Expenditures: The PPB System: A Compendium of Papers submitted to the Subcommittee on Economy in Government of the Joint Economic Committee,* Ninety-first Congress, First session, (Washington, DC: Government Printing Office, 1969) p. 14.

40. See Tibor R. Machan, *Marxism: A Bourgeois Critique* (Bradford, England: MCB University Press, 1988). See note 48 for more on this.

41. I think the post-Kantian hostility to metaphysics accounts for the absence of systems philosophy, combined with various liberal ethos fears of dogmas, closed systems, etc., à la Karl Popper.

42. Yet it is not at all clear that Marxism proper—as distinct from Leninism—has been decisively discredited by developments in Eastern Europe. See Tibor R. Machan, "How to Understand Eastern European Developments," *Public Affairs Quarterly* (Spring 1992): 24–34.

43. Tibor R. Machan, "Kuhn's Impossibility Proof and the Moral Element in Scientific Explanation," *Theory and Decision* 5 (1974):355–374 and Machan, "On the Possibility of Objectivity...."

44. See Thomas S. Kuhn, *The Structure of Scientific Revolutions*, 2d ed., (Chicago: University of Chicago Press, 1970); and Schagrin, "On Being Unreasonable." See especially, Rorty, *Objectivity*.

45. I elaborate and defend this point in chapter 1 of *Individuals and Their Rights*. My approach owes much to Ayn Rand, *Introduction to Objectivist Epistemology*, exp. ed., (New York: New American Library, 1990.)

46. Since work of the kind we are attempting here cannot be completed within the confines of this discussion alone, the thesis must for the present remain at best a strong conjecture or highly plausible theory.

47. Theories of human affairs cannot produce formulas that guarantee results. See Machan, "Kuhn's Impossibility Proof...."

48. Related views are worked out in and, most pertinently, by Richard J. Bernstein, *Praxis and Action: Contemporary Philosophies of Human Activity* (Philadelphia: University of Pennsylvania Press, 1971); Peter Winch, *The Idea of a Social Science and Its Relation to Philosophy* (London: Routledge and Kegan Paul, 1958); Mary Hesse, "In Defense of Objectivity," *Proceedings of the British Academy,* Vol. 48 (1962); and Hanna F. Pitkin, *Wittgenstein and Justice: On the Significance of Ludwig Wittgenstein for Social and Political Thought* (Berkeley: University of California Press, 1972).

49. Citizenship could imply some principles of conduct not explicitly made evident to the citizen, just as parenthood does to the parent. I discuss this in greater detail in chapter 7 of *Individuals and Their Rights*.

50. Adam Smith, *The Wealth of Nations* (New York; Modern Library, 1938). p. 726. It is very arguable that Aristotle advanced an ethical egoist position. See

W. F. R. Hardie, "The Final Good in Aristotle's Ethics," *Philosophy* 40 (1965): 277–295.

51. Machan, *The Pseudo-Science of B. F. Skinner*; see also Boyle, Grisez and Tollefsen, *Free Choice*.

52. Malinovich, "Knowledge and Evaluation"; and Machan, *Individuals and Their Rights*. See also, Ayn Rand, *The Virtue of Selfishness: A New Concept of Egoism* (New York: Signet Books, 1964); and Douglas B. Rasmussen and Douglas J. Den Uyl, *Liberty and Nature, An Aristotelian Defense of Liberal Order* (LaSalle, IL: Open Court, 1991).

53. Ayn Rand, *For the New Intellectual: The Philosophy of Ayn Rand* (New York: Signet Books, 1961), p. 120.

54. Ethics is the field of inquiry calling forth the various theories that amount to answers to the question, How should I, a human being, conduct my life? It is a field that could be every bit the science that biomedicine is, though with serious differences—in levels of precision, for instance—in view of the very different subject. (But this difference obtains between physics and biology, as well.) Methods of inquiry could also differ, given the nature of the subject matter.

55. "Successful life of the individual" might mean "happiness" if only the last term had not acquired its hedonist renditions. See W. F. R. Hardie, "The Final Good in Aristotle's *Ethics*," *Philosophy* 40 (1965): 277–295; and Douglas J. Den Uyl and Tibor R. Machan, "Recent Work on the Concept of Happiness," *American Philosophical Quarterly* 21 (1984): 1–31.

56. This egoism rejects the Hobbesian conception of the self and takes it as central that human beings have a specific nature. See Tibor R. Machan, "Recent Work in Ethical Egoism", *American Philosophical Quarterly* 16 (January 1979); 1–15. How such classical egoism gives support to the establishment of government is discussed in chapter 7 of my *Individuals and Their Rights*.

57. More precisely, politics has as its purpose to secure our basic rights, in particular, the rights to life, liberty, and property, by means of public administration.

58. The fact that human beings now are taken by many, mainly in the social sciences and in psychology, to be passive, moved by forces within or outside them and otherwise not self-responsible, has had a considerable impact on contemporary ideas of liberty. (This is evident both in highly abstract and academic discussions and from television and radio talk shows.) Thus, for Marx, liberty involves furnishing people with opportunities, abilities, goods, and so forth, since without these they are supposedly bound by necessity and cannot develop—hence the distinction between liberal and socialist efforts at liberating people, countries, etc. See Machan, *Marxism*.

59. I argue in *Individuals and Their Rights* against numerous efforts advanced by Rawls, Dworkin, Gewirth, Sterba, and others.

60. See Tibor R. Machan, *Marxism*. The idea of specie-being testifies to this quite directly, as developed by Marx.

61. Tibor R. Machan, *Human Rights and Human Liberties* (Chicago: Nelson-Hall, 1975). See also my *The Pseudo-Science of B.F. Skinner* and *Individuals and Their Rights*. A perhaps surprising source of support for this proposition comes from the Nobel Laureate Roger W. Sperry in his *Science and Moral Priority: Merging Mind, Brain, and Human Values* (New York: Columbia University Press, 1983).

62. See Sperry, *Science and Moral Priority*, for a discussion of collectivist ideas of (positive) rights.

63. See, for more on this, Tibor R. Machan, "Property Rights and the Decent Society," in *Ideology and American Experience*, ed. John K. Roth and Robert C. Whittemore, (Washington, DC: Washington Institute Press, 1986), pp. 121–144.

64. For dissatisfaction with much of social theory, due to the lack of comprehensiveness and a sound grasp of human nature, see Harre and Secord, *Explanation of Social Behavior*, and Eugene F. Miller, "Hume's Contribution to Behavioral Science," *Journal of the History of the Behavioral Sciences* 7 (April 1971): 154–168.

65. When decision theories and works about public choice forget the distinction between what is essentially public and what is merely public because of widespread desire, the confusions of current mainstream theories are to be expected. Nominalist approaches engender this since they deny the validity of the concept of "the nature of X" as having objective significance or the determinacy of conceptual knowledge. See, for the most cogent exposition of these views, Rorty, *Objectivity*. Note, incidentally, the direct attack on natural rights theory that springs from Rorty's framework—for example, on p. 31.

66. Friedland and Cimbala, "Process and Paradox" p. 62.

67. Fred R. Harris, ed., *Social Science and National Policy*, 2nd ed., (New Brunswick, NJ: Transaction, 1973); David Moller, "Ill Fares the Welfare State," *Encounter* (September 1976): 58–64; and William N. Nelson, "Special rights, General Rights, and Social Justice," *Philosophy and Public Affairs*, Vol. 3 (Summer 1974), 410–430.

68. In the United States there is, as in many other welfare states, a constant and relentless political war among interest groups with an eye to gaining a larger and larger share of the public treasury—presumably so as to advance the public interest by means of their own special interests. This phenomenon may be designated as the political tragedy of the commons, leading to deficit spending and, in the end, to a crisis in public finance.

69. Emergency cases can arise. See the treatment of these in my *Human Rights and Human Liberties*; and in Tibor R. Machan, "Prima Facie versus Natural (Human) Rights," *Journal of Value Inquiry*, 10 (Summer 1976): 119–131. I also discuss the argument, advanced by James Sterba in *How to Make People Just: A Practical Reconciliation of Alternative Conceptions of Justice* (Totowa, NJ: Rowman and Littlefield, 1988), that because of emergency cases, all political or legal systems must become welfare statists, in *Individuals and Their Rights*, postscript 2.

70. Robert Dorfman, "General Equilibrium with Public Goods," (Paper presented at International Economics Conference on Public Economics, September, 1966), p. 4.

71. Steiner, "Public sector and the public interest," p. 17.

72. William C. Birdsall, "A Study of the Demand of Public Goods," in *Essays in Fiscal Federalism*, ed. Richard A. Musgrave, (Washington, DC: Brookings Institution, 1965), p. 235.

73. See Kordig, *Justification of Scientific Change*; Machan, "Law, Justice and Natural Rights"; Ayn Rand, *Introduction to Objectivist Epistemology*, 2d ed., (New York: New American Library, 1990).

74. This is perhaps best brought to mind by the example of problems with the environment, as we will see in some detail in chapter 8.

3

Human Dignity and the Welfare State

It is better to go down on the great seas which
human hearts were made to sail than to rot at the
wharves of ignoble anchorage.

—Hamilton Wright Mabie

The purpose of my discussion here is to argue that the crucial ideal of human dignity is placed in serious jeopardy by the legal features of the welfare state. The ideal is the condition, which every adult person ought to enjoy, whereby his or her standing as a responsible individual (distinct, for example, from that of a slave or a ward) is legally recognized. Human dignity is better secured by a fully free society and free-market system.

The Legal and the Moral

Throughout this chapter—as well as in numerous other places in this book—I discuss normative politics. Mostly my aim is to give moral or ethical backing to certain kinds of legal principles and possible legal developments. What may be confusing is that I sometimes illustrate a moral point by reference to existing legal principles; for example, I show that government regulation is objectionable by reference to its violation of the principle of prior restraint. But that last is itself a legal principle, so how can it serve the purpose of offering a moral criticism?

Actually, in most cases when I make reference to such legal principles I do so for purposes of calling attention to the underlying moral notion that most people will accept—and that need not, therefore, be argued for in detail. It seems evident to most, for example, that before a person has done a wrong, he or she may not be punished for it. It would be plainly unjust; the point need not be argued for, at least not in every context. Suppose, in turn, it can be shown that some other practice, let us say of the government, fully satisfies the conditions of prior restraint, though in an area most people do not think about in such terms. One example might be government regulation, whereby people are constrained from acting and have to spend great sums of money and extensive periods of time even though it has not be shown that they have done anything wrong. In that case, a critical point will have been driven home sufficiently to move on, since we will have uncovered a rather significant malfeasance of that institution. If, for example, much of what the welfare state's government does involves such prior restraint because of its very nature as a welfare state, that state is seriously flawed.[1]

There should be no mistake about this, though: the point is always to invoke moral criteria, not only legal ones. Yet some legal principles are so evidently in accord with morality and by being legal principles also testify to their acceptance, that they become useful in making a moral point.

Looking at Some Basics

Human dignity is the capacity of individuals to be morally responsible. Moral responsibility, in turn, arises because human beings are capable of free choice and rational thought. Rational consciousness and the ability to make choices make an individual a moral agent, since his decisions can be made in accordance with a rational standard in which some actions are right while others are wrong.[2]

Of course, people can adopt improper standards of judgment—a putative moral position that has no rational foundation. Still, anyone who can identify, or accept and guide herself, by a rational ethics possesses human dignity because of her ability to execute significant choices in the performance of human tasks.[3] It is when one is blocked in this ability that one's human dignity has been denied.

I have already argued (here and in other works) that the basic institutions of the community should support human dignity. That is to say, the law that governs community life should recognize and uphold the individual's dignity. This end can be achieved through legal policies such as due process and equal protection under the law.

However, the concept of human dignity has come under serious attack from some segments of the social sciences, particularly behaviorist psychology. Perhaps the most drastic expression of this trend has been through the prominence of the school of psychology called behaviorism. While other schools of social science have perhaps been less forthright about their denial of the notion of human dignity, behaviorism has been quite explicit on this issue. And while many institutions and practices have not adopted this school of thought fully, underlying the methods of many we find the crux of the behaviorist thesis.

Behaviorists, for example, have openly and unabashedly expounded the view that human action is determined by influences beyond the control of the individual. Behaviorism denies a person's capacity to choose his conduct and thus it flatly rules out the meaningfulness of the idea of human dignity—of one's capacity to be morally responsible. B. F. Skinner's book *Beyond Freedom and Dignity* is perhaps the most popularly known work espousing the behaviorist view.[4]

Behaviorism has had a serious—although not always openly acknowledged—impact on our legal system, surfacing in the positive law of legislation, verdicts, and judicial policy. Encouraged by this view, legal institutions frequently treat people as if they were helpless and lacking free will and the capacity for purposeful action. This treatment is most obvious in policies such as involuntary mental hospitalization and psychosurgery.[5] It is accomplished far less obviously through preventive laws of various types, such as legislation forcing motorcyclists to wear helmets.[6] The requirement that drug manufacturers prove that their drug is harmless even if no evidence of harm is present is in the same category.[7]

Those who deny that freedom of choice plays any significant role in explaining the behavior of those whom they deem "victims" of society and whom they insist on protecting by means of government paternalism—the poor, the criminal, consumers, minorities, and so forth—are nonetheless usually anxious to condemn, in the strongest moral terms, capitalists and politicians and dissident (reactionary) intellectuals. The Exxon Corporation's defiling of the Alaskan coast line is not excused by them on grounds of how corporate executives are not free to make choices but are determined by their history to act as they do; Lt. Col. Oliver North or Speaker James Wright, to cite two notorious cases, are not excused on grounds that they could not help themselves and had to behave as they did; nor were the several Wall Street investment bankers who found themselves indicted for securities fraud declared mere victims of circumstances. Finally, intellectuals who find the government's efforts to paternalistically help people objectionable, even in the case of blacks or Hispanics, usually find themselves ridiculed by their mainstream adversaries. Thomas Sowell, the black economist at the Hoover Institution, Stanford University, comes to mind; he has been labeled an Uncle Tom by numerous civil rights leaders for not accepting the standard line on what leads to poverty and underdevelopment. In such cases moral reproach seems not to be abated on grounds of universal determinism.

Some argue that such preventive legislation is implemented for the good of the citizen and that many citizens would want to enjoy the protection, in any case. Nevertheless, such legislation is not voluntarily offered and accepted help, and thus undermines continued respect for human dignity. When the basic responsibility of an individual to make his own decisions is rejected in favor of governmental paternalism, the legal system stands in opposition to human nature itself. Such paternalism involves the subjection of citizens to edicts and rules enforced in their own interest and with the understanding that they are not quite adept at coping with the tasks in questions.

It is, in short, to treat citizens as if the government had the role of parent and citizens the role of children.

The impact of a denial of human dignity by paternalistic government may perhaps be resisted by private citizens in such areas as education, the arts, and personal relationships. Much of what ensues in these realms still manifests a substantial degree of independence from legal interference, although this is by no means uniformly true. Today the idea of what belongs within the "public" realm has grown immensely and tends to cover any concern accompanied by sufficiently loud demands for political solutions. In any case, the detrimental impact of the denial of dignity through positive law is inevitable.

As an example, when poetry is under government control (as it was largely in the Soviet Union) the essential human dignity of artists is often under fatal assault. In our own history, when members of different racial groups were legally forbidden to marry, the same kind of attack on human dignity was evident. Slavery was, of course, the most direct assault on human dignity in the case of those affected by it.

In order for the legal system to reaffirm the support of human dignity instead of state paternalism, the philosophical foundations for proper law must be uncovered. The legal community must be persuaded as to what values should be protected and what is wrong with the status quo. It should then develop a consistent legal system based on these values. (That this would be an arduous task and not rapidly achievable by no means vitiates the point, despite the often heard claim that broad social designs are mistaken and that it is arrogant, not to mention chauvinistic, to think we can construct them in any case.)

The legal system that promotes human dignity most successfully is the one that supports every individual's natural human rights. That is because such human rights, when fully respected, secure for everyone the full opportunity (within the bounds of nature) to act as a moral agent rather than as a subject of another moral agent. The most vital social condition for any person is the honoring of his or her dignity. If someone's dignity is destroyed, all other benefits that person reaps from others amount to very little and certainly serve as no compensation. Trading one's dignity is akin to selling one's soul; it takes away one's essential identity as the human being one is.

To be sure, numerous familiar public programs, such as entitlements (to services and goods secured at public expense) superficially appear to benefit recipients. In fact they are crucially flawed in large part because they erode respect for human dignity. So while certain features of a legal system may protect an individual's dignity, others familiar within the welfare state are harmful to it.

The Relationship Between Human Nature and the Legal System

A basic element of the present thesis, already defended to some extent, is Aristotle's observation that human beings are rational animals capable of choosing their actions with some end in mind. We are beings of volitional consciousness; each human individual's crucial and distinctive capacity for rationality consists of having the ability to think, and to distinguish between truth and falsehood and between right and wrong.

If the capacity to choose is essential to human beings, a proper or suitable legal order should function so as not to impair that choice.[8] Laws have as their best explanation that an orderly and well-governed political society is valuable to human beings.[9] Individuals actualize their full potential through the virtually unlimited enhancements that community life offers. And they need a system of principles, involving methods of adjudication, enforcement, and modification, by which the threats to such actualization may be averted.

Persons can develop most successfully by drawing on the talents and accomplishments of others.[10] Thus commerce, education, entertainment, science, sports, and law are all potential contributors to the enhancement of each person's life.[11] Whatever values social life enhances, people must still choose to better themselves, and they often refrain from doing so when in each other's company.

Aside from private failings, people can fail in ways that injure others. For example, when someone interjects physical violence or force into human relationships, there is a great potential for danger. A primary purpose of the legal system is to prevent all unjustified violence or coercion in human relationships. By acting as keeper of the peace, the legal system serves to prevent persons from interfering with another's independence of judgment. The law helps protect human liberty within the community and enables the individual to develop to his or her full capacity as a rational and creative being within a personally unique situation.

Because human beings are essentially animals with the capacity to live by the use of reason, they live properly, that is, by standards of moral goodness, when their actions are directed by the use of their minds.[12] A good legal system provides an individual with the opportunity to exercise his choice-making capacity and leaves the responsibility for achieving success to that person.[13] Each individual's moral responsibility is to excel as the human being that she is. This ethical system, namely, individualism or ethical egoism, is the basis of a good legal system.[14]

In a legal order laws must be developed to meet the challenges of change and thereby help to provide a detailed framework for continued freedom of action.[15] In order for our legal system to acknowledge this goal, the underlying interpersonal moral principles on which law should be based must be identified.[16] These principles provide a social condition in which the individual can benefit from living in a community while preserving moral independence and the freedom to choose between living as a good or an evil person.[17]

Dignity Versus Welfare

The major objection to the individualistic viewpoint comes from those who see guaranteeing economic or spiritual welfare as the primary goal of political life. The popular acceptance of either economic or spiritual welfarism, and the forceful intellectual support behind it, have produced statist trends. Current political debates have focused on how extensively should government guarantee a relatively high degree of economic welfare and quality of life. In our time they only rarely address the issue of the usurpation of human dignity through breach of the right to individual liberty. The case for dignity is admitted only in the abstract discussion of political theory, where the idea is that the rights to liberty and to welfare must be balanced.[18]

While individualism was once widely hailed in Britain and especially the United States, today it is deemed amoral and heartless. The individualist viewpoint is unable to promise honestly that everyone will eventually be completely well-off. Critics find this defeatist and insist that "we must do better" while calling upon the force of the state to see that we do.

These are utopian promises, expressing more a desire than a realistic, feasible idea. They rest on the view that human nature itself might be changed and social life thus radically altered. Yet such an idea is a mistake. Human nature is what is stable throughout human history, even though—because of the creative, active nature of human beings—change is equally stable. But change is not constant in human nature itself, so the utopian promises are unattainable.[19] The individualist ideal of a free society, in which each person can aspire to human excellence within the framework of respecting each other's similar possible aspiration, is therefore clearly a superior system, worthy of deeper study and support via the process of democratic political decision making.

Yet most intellectuals want to push society toward utopian perfection. Often this is because they develop their political principles by consulting common moral intuitions, which are based on certain entrenched, personal, nonpolitical, altruistic principles, such as equality, self-sacrifice, and sharing of one's wealth. They give support mainly to welfare-oriented public policy, so as to effectuate these ideals in the political sphere, disregarding that this makes objects of personal moral choices a matter of public coercion.

Thus, our culturally prominent ideas of morality and "public" policy often directly conflict with the political implications of the theory of ethical individualism or egoism. These ideas support the belief that economic or spiritual equality, not protection of the individual's basic right to liberty, should be the supreme political goal.[20] The prevailing view is that a good society must ensure equal economic or spiritual welfare. This is to be accomplished not only by providing equal opportunities to all citizens, but by eventually effectuating a nearly equal distribution of material goods and paternalistic care. It logically follows that if the law is to serve this conception of justice, it must sacrifice the individual's right to liberty when the exercise of that liberty leads to inequality.

If the proper political goal is the equal progress of all individuals, then obviously the proper function of laws is to achieve this goal. Clearly, bringing about full equality among citizens will require the widespread enforcement of economic and related changes required to eradicate the natural and inevitable differences among individuals. The totalitarian and dictatorial consequences are easy to infer. Voluntary cooperation and generosity are certainly encouraged by those who oppose governmental welfarism. Within the welfarist system, however, these benevolent qualities are not regarded as enough. Individuals are not trusted to live peacefully and to be responsible for reaching their full potential. The entire concern with equality of welfare, even in the framework of "upgrading the poor" and "upholding society's moral fiber," is inconsistent with the ideal that each person must make his or her own way in life.

This trend toward economic and spiritual equalization is so strong that when institutions do not meet the established norm, the government forces progress by utilizing its retaliatory powers for redistributive and paternalistic purposes. This can be seen in the use of, for example, forced busing to meet integration standards.[21] The government can also indirectly force institutions to meet various standards by making financial assistance conditional on certain requirements.[22] Such requirements treat members of society as tools for other people's programs. This personal responsibility for others' goals and well-being, which underlies political support for many desirable programs, also fuels—by making them conceptually and legally acceptable in the sphere of social engineering—the techniques of behavior modification and, at the extreme end, such measures as involuntary psychosurgery.

All governmental action that does not serve to repel or retaliate against coercion is antithetical to any respect for human dignity. While it is true that some people should give to others to assist them in reaching their goals, forcing those individuals to do so plainly robs them of their dignity. There is nothing morally worthwhile in forced giving. Generally, for a society to respect human dignity, the special moral relations between people should be left undisturbed. Government should confine itself to making sure that this voluntarism is not abridged, no matter how tempting it might be to use its coercive powers to attain some worthy goal. Obviously, this idea is neither accepted nor widely promulgated in our times. Most institutions are oriented in the opposite direction, where the state acts as the tool to foster a variety of special goals and produce desired ends for millions of disparate individuals and groups. It will help us to briefly sketch the background for the welfare statist position and then contrast it with the individual rights approach developed most fully (until recently) by the philosopher John Locke.

Freedom Versus Welfare: Some Historical Points

In the Middle Ages states were thought by most to possess supreme if not divine rights. This not only seemed to provide the states with the authority to lay down the rules for their subjects to follow but also conferred upon them a responsibility to do so. The doctrine of state sovereignty upholds both the authority and the responsibility of states to rule wisely.

John Locke, in the seventeenth century, argued effectively against the doctrine of the divine right of kings. He did this by refuting the biblical case Sir Robert Filmer advanced in his *Patriarcha* (1680). Locke went on to advance a radical position: It is individuals who possess natural rights, based on "a law of Nature...which obliges every one, and reason which is that law, teaches all mankind who will but consult it, that being all equal and independent, no one ought to harm another in his life, health, liberty, or possessions."[23]

Locke's argument was most influential. For many decades it supplied jurists and political thinkers with the intellectual and moral ammunition needed to oppose absolute monarchy and to defend the establishment of parliamentary checks on royal power and, eventually, of constitutional restrictions on the power of governments as such. The founders were influenced by Locke's thought. Jefferson read him and shaped the Declaration of Independence in part by reference to Locke's natural rights doctrine. He did not, however, manage to include as the third part of the crucial trio of rights the right to property. Instead it turned out to be the right to the pursuit of happiness. The change was a fateful one.

The beginnings of the U.S. legal system had been under the influence of conflicting political philosophies. The Constitution stressed individual rights—though not consistently enough, when we judge it by the Declaration of Independence and its doctrine of equal rights to all persons. But the common law kept within it much of the older, paternalistic legal idea of the supremacy of government. Many jurists and justices embraced elements of both of these viewpoints, which in part accounts for the conflicting tendencies within our legal institutions—and, indeed, for the ease with which a country of individualism could be turned, without revolution, into a country of substantial collectivism and statism.

But the natural rights individualism of Locke has certain features that many have found difficult to reconcile with conventional morality. Perhaps the most telling criticism against the natural rights thesis, which stresses private property rights and therefore free-market capitalism, is that it lacks compassion. For example, according to John Maynard Keynes, capitalism is a method of bringing the most successful profit-makers to the top by a ruthless struggle for survival, which selects the most efficient by the bankruptcy of the less efficient, ignoring the cost of the struggle, and looking only to the benefits of the final result.[24] It is to tame corporate capitalism that many features of the welfare state were introduced and embraced in the United States. What is this system?

The welfare state rests on the view that while individual liberty, including the freedom to earn and even amass wealth, needs to be respected in a legal system, so must be the needs of those, to use Keynes's phrase, "whose necks are shorter." The result of this expression of moral concern for those who could not flourish under capitalism—or who did not do so, for whatever reason—has been the modification of pure capitalist theory and the gradual emergence of the welfare state as a more humane alternative.

What is crucial here is that besides all the anticapitalist systems of thought there has emerged one that does not entirely dismiss capitalism and its moral-political foundations (a foundation that stresses negative liberty as the supreme political value). This system of welfarism, unlike socialism, fascism, communism, or some of the religiously inspired benevolent dictatorial regimes (such as Islamic theocracy), tries to combine some of the fundamental values of capitalism with certain other and even alien values, such as the notion of the right to welfare or well-being or happiness.[25]

One of the major consequences of this idea has been the rejection of the doctrine of caveat emptor or "let the buyer beware."[26] This notion is to the effect that wherever trade occurs, either party is legally obligated merely to act in a nonviolent and nonfraudulent manner, and that is all.[27] No special assistance or help is owed, in law, to those with whom one is doing trade. Of course, none may perpetrate fraud, for example, via the misrepresentation of one's wares or services. But in trade all parties are concerned primarily with what seems to benefit them most. No one is expected to offer help—except incidentally and in emergencies—to a partner in trade.

The implication of this for the labor market should not be difficult to imagine. Capitalism implies that when workers take jobs, it is their responsibility to choose whether they would work with the risk of hazards, and threats to health and safety, or whether they would prefer to work elsewhere or perhaps not work at all. In pure capitalist economic theory this idea is still well embedded. If the worker does not wish to work without knowing what safety or health hazards are involved, that worker could go elsewhere to sell his or her labor. Capitalism sees workers as essentially equal to employers, only with different values to offer for sale on the market.

Arguments for Political Welfarism

We have now seen some of the ingredients of the moral case for the welfare state, as well as some of the pitfalls of that case. It is clear, however, that from that case political paternalism and government regulation gain their moral support. (No doubt, other support, having to do with unabashed vested or special interest, is also vital for the welfare state to emerge in full swing.)

Let us now look at how certain recent efforts to try to make the moral case in favor of government paternalism and regulation have fared. We will examine three central contemporary ideas, namely, the doctrine of prima facie rights; the doctrine of equal rights to freedom and well-being; and the doctrine of justice as equal resources. The first of these states that there are no absolute (or natural) human rights to liberty and there are competing rights, for instance, to happiness, which sometimes may override the prima facie right to liberty. The second states that individuals actually have a basic human right to both freedom and well-being. The last states that a society must implement a policy of equality concerning the acquisition of resources (income, material goods, and so forth), provided certain conditions obtain in society (which we will explain shortly). The three positions are those advanced respectively by the philosophers Gregory Vlastos, Alan Gewirth, and John Rawls to whom we now turn.

Prima Facie Rights

The Princeton University philosopher Gregory Vlastos advanced a widely studied argument during the mid-twentieth century in support of the modification of the idea of natural rights. He held that although it is true enough that we all possess certain basic rights as human beings, these rights are not absolute or do not really deserve full or consistent protection in the legal system.

Here is what Vlastos's point comes to: As expressed in the Declaration of Independence and in John Locke's theory, each of us is said to have "unalienable" rights. That means these rights—to life, liberty, and the pursuit of happiness—may not be violated or abridged either by our neighbors or by the government. Under no circumstances, therefore, would it be justified to *violate* someone's right to life: Murder is always to be prohibited by the legal system. Similarly with liberty: To kidnap or confine or otherwise interfere with a person's actions against his or her will is always prohibited. And the same goes for the pursuit of happiness: One might seek it through wealth, fame, artistic excellence, scientific discoveries, sex, religion, and so on, and so long as it is peaceful (meaning it does not violate another's rights), it may not be prohibited. And governments are to be established for the purpose of protecting these rights, of resisting any effort to try to prohibit these pursuits.

So understood, these rights are absolute.[28] They are not to be alienated, not even by the individual who has them (thus one may not "sell" oneself into slavery). When one objects that after all one can commit suicide, under some drastic circumstances even permit another to take his or her life, and certainly through criminal action seem to give up the right to life (or at least liberty and property), a confusion makes itself evident. Suicide is an *exercise* of the right to life by the agent. Permitting another to kill oneself is, similarly, the exercise of the rights to liberty and to life. Finally, criminals act in a way that implicitly authorizes others to incarcerate them since they violate the conditions of civilized life and ask to be banished by this action.

In none of these cases do we witness the relinquishing, forfeiting, or surrendering of any rights. Indeed, one reason for the extensive civil libertarian concerns evidenced in our society is that at least in that area many scholars are still concerned with upholding the basic rights of persons, however undesirable and evil they are. (Contrast this to how even in the United Kingdom, let alone innumerable other societies, the state's burden to prove guilt is far lighter. In 1988, proposals were aired to eliminate even the restriction on the British government to forbear coercing testimony from those accused of terrorism. That is clear illustration of the lack of full commitment to the idea of individual rights.)

Despite the link of the doctrine of basic individual rights to the history of the United States, America certainly has never fully lived up to the idea. Indeed, it took a long time before all citizens even gained full legal acknowledgement of their basic rights—that is, until slavery had been abolished and women's rights had been secured (via the Fourteenth Amendment). But the general notion of unalienable rights had been affirmed here more than elsewhere and some of this affirmation had been echoed in the nation's fundamental legal document, the Constitution.

Vlastos argues against such an absolutist conception of human rights. He holds that "We would...improve the consistency of Locke's theory if we understood him to mean that natural rights are subject to justified exceptions."[29] He proposes to speak of human rights as prima facie rights, meaning that "the claims of any of them may be overruled in special circumstances."[30] We must quickly note that Vlastos does not mean to deny the existence of rights: "Prima facie" sometimes is used to mean "on its face" or "apparent." As A. I. Melden, introducing Vlastos' discussion, points out, those who "declare that [a] human right is only a prima facie right....certainly do not mean a right that is merely apparent or presumptive."[31]

Vlastos claims that real as these rights may be, "any of them may be overruled in special circumstances."[32] The reason is simple: clearly we can imagine circumstances when rights must be overridden, as a matter of moral decency. Locke's claim that "government...can never have a power to take...the whole, or any part of the subjects' property, without their consent"[33] seems to him plainly wrong; many instances present themselves when that is just not what morality requires. Vlastos claims that Locke himself appears to have accepted this in his actual political conduct. Locke allowed that governments could punish criminals, which to Vlastos appears to show Locke to be other than an absolutist on the right to liberty, for example.

In the last analysis Vlastos defends prima facie rights on grounds we find expressed by Keynes above: Unless one viewed the basic right to property or liberty as sometimes capable of being overridden, government would have to tolerate some people's flourishing extravagantly while others suffered unbearably. Because this is morally unacceptable— the argument maintains—a different theory must be introduced, one that makes room for occasional relaxation of the prohibition against the abridgement of human rights. Vlastos proceeds to outline a position in favor of a doctrine of "equal welfare-rights and freedom rights" for all.[34] Absolute welfare rights would entitle all persons to being provided with what is required for their well-being, while freedom rights entitle persons to being left alone to live and act as they choose. Thus, if either welfare rights or freedom rights were absolute, they would cancel each other out in virtually all circumstances. An absolute right is a condition that must be fully and invariably respected; for example, if one has the absolute right to be free, then no one may ever take one's freedom. But the welfare of someone is often secured only through another person's productive support; to gain shelter and food, for instance, those who do not have it can get it only if others provide it. If others have an absolute freedom right, it would not be morally justified to obtain such shelter and food without these others' consent. However, if those without shelter and food (welfare, that is) have an absolute right to it, then others would have to, morally and legally, provide it. In practice this would be impossible. One person's absolute right to liberty trumps or cancels another's absolute right to welfare, and vice versa.

A doctrine of prima facie rights appears to solve the problem. Only it does not really. What it does is to leave things pretty much "deuces wild," meaning that it is entirely arbitrary whether the "prima facie" right to liberty or the "prima facie" right to welfare will be protected. Sometimes one may feel that taking one person's liberty so as to house or feed another is morally acceptable, sometimes one may not.

For example, if those who are without shelter and food squander it or fail to be prudent or have never cared about such things until now, then it will seem quite unjust to take these from others who have worked for it. Again, those who have the means to provide welfare nevertheless have their own honorable purposes for the use of these means, such as providing their children with vital medical treatment, giving for charity, improving their artistic talents, or the like. Thus, even when others are in dire need, through no fault of their own, taking from those who have it could easily be seen as quite arbitrary, immoral, or unjust. There may not be enough of the valued things in life for all to have a decent portion. But that may not be used, as a matter of standards of argumentation, to justify taking from those who have managed to obtain some for themselves, even if luck has had something to do with it. It would be wholly unjust to do so.

Clearly, the mere feeling of dismay and concern for the needy will not make such taking a morally good thing. There must instead be a sound moral foundation for such action. (Feelings and sentiments, even righteous outrage, have managed to give rise to policies and conduct that could, with some care, be considered morally objectionable, even outrageous in themselves.)[35]

Human Right to Freedom and Well-Being

We now turn to another defender of the view that gives support to the welfare state. Alan Gewirth, professor of philosophy at the University of Chicago, has defended what he calls the "supportive state" on the basis that each of us possesses the human rights to freedom and to well-being. He holds that we are all equal in possessing generic rights.

> What is of central importance here is not that wealth or property itself is to be equalized but rather that, beyond the minimum required for basic goods, persons have as nearly as possible equal chances for developing and utilizing their own capabilities for successful agency [that is, human action].[36]

How does Gewirth defend this view? He basically says that anyone with good sense who does anything whatever must believe that this is a good thing to do, otherwise he would not freely choose to do it. And then, Gewirth argues, he must view every other person in the same light. So whatever he demands for himself—for instance the freedom and the basic ability to do what he wants—he implicitly demands for others as well.[37] That, in turn, implies that none may rob us of our freedom and that we must be provided, at least when we lack it, with the materials required for action.

But Gewirth is wrong. He has not demonstrated that each of us has a right both to freedom and well-being, only that both freedom and well-being (the ability to act) are necessary for the pursuit of our goals. He has not shown that we have a basic right to well-being so that others must provide us with what we need, only that it is vital for our lives. We often provide such goods for ourselves or have them given to us by others. Rights do not enter the picture, except in so far as government has declared it an entitlement for us to receive such goods. (In a state of nature, surely if someone does not feed us, that is one thing, but if someone abstains from murdering or assaulting us, that is quite another. Then at least we can proceed to try to find our own sustenance.)

The basic right to freedom is different. If others do not "provide" us with freedom, we cannot have it by our own effort. (It surely does not count that we may be able to fend off an assault. We should never have to make that effort and it is clearly an uninvited, undeserved burden.) Without others refraining from assaulting, killing, or stealing from us, we cannot have freedom. But well-being, though also necessary to pursue our goals, is something we ought to produce for ourselves. The only exception to this may be in the case of some drastic emergency or of children, who depend on adults and should be cared for by those who brought them into this world.

Of course, it is at times argued that we can trade our freedom for, say, security, but this is irrelevant. We are discussing the fundamentality of the right to freedom (stemming from our right to life), not freedom itself. Certainly one can contract not to do or to do something, thereby voluntarily foregoing other options—as in a marriage contract. But the right to enter such contracts or not to do so—the right to "trade"—is not relinquishable in this way. (Notice even the phrase, trading one's freedom, assumes the right to trade. If that were also tradable, one would at some point lack the right to trade anything.)

Gewirth's argument for a welfare or supportive state fails because he does not fully appreciate the importance of the distinction between values only others can produce for us—for example, negative freedom, or their abstaining from intruding upon us—and values that almost all adult persons may be expected to produce for themselves—nourishment, shelter, and even wealth or income through free trade—even if sometimes with very great difficulty and on rare occasions only through the generosity of others. Even alone on a desert island, one may well be able to secure the latter kind of values; but it is only with the willing assent of other persons that one can secure the former.

Contrary to Gewirth's repeated insistence, it does make sense that there should only be one basic (negative) human right to life and, derivatively, to liberty and property, from others' invasion of our lives. A right is just the sort of moral condition that must be secured through the assent (respect) of other people and it is the only condition of community life that may morally be secured by force if other people fail to respect it. In other words, we have a right to freedom because it is something that one would always possess were it not for others taking it away. Freedom cannot be given, only taken and then regained. The point of the concept of a basic human or natural right is to identify a value we rightly or justly possess but which could be taken from us only by the actions of others.

Well-being is a different kind of value. We may lack well-being quite apart from what others do or don't do to or for us. Entirely apart from what others do, we may become severely ill, or harmed by natural forces or our own negligence. To claim a right to well-being, then, is to claim something due us from others when they are entirely innocent of any wrongdoing towards us but merely do not contribute to our well-being (maybe for good reasons).

Of course, people can unjustly, wrongfully hurt us. And then they are liable. Theft, assault, murder and such all wrongfully take values from us. We know this from knowing we have the right to life, liberty, and property. That also means others may be thwarted in their efforts to take these values from us. If we had no right to our lives—if it were not for us to decide whether to live or not to live—or to our liberty—if it were not up to us what we will do—or even to our property—if it were not up to us what to do with what we have produced or created in the various complicated ways that can go on—it would not be possible to tell whether these actions would be categorically wrong. If our lives did not belong to us, if we were not the authorized agents of our actions, if we did not own what we produce, then murder, assault, and theft would not be generally wrong and prohibitable actions.

In contrast, if we lacked some value that others were not responsible for taking from us, we could not have a right to this value. It makes no sense to resist rights violations when no one is taking anything from us. It would be impossible. If I am sick because my body was attacked by a virus, my well-being is in jeopardy, my health lost. Need another person have done this to me? No. So how could I be justified in depriving anyone of anything—for example a doctor of time, or my neighbors of income (so that I can pay the doctor)—in such a situation? Just because it may be disastrous for me, even callous for others to not help me, I cannot claim to have a right to the help. Gewirth and other advocates of welfarism do, however, believe that even though persons have done nothing against others—taken nothing from them, injured them in no way, stolen nothing from them—they should be treated as if they had done just these sorts of things.

If I have a right to something, and another takes it, I may take it back or send the police to do this (via the court system). If someone kidnaps me, I may regain my freedom, even by force. That is because I have the right to my life and liberty and no one may deprive me of these. I may file a complaint against someone if I am attacked because I may, morally, regain values I lost through the violation of my rights. But when nothing has been taken from me, no one has assaulted me, no one has kidnaped me or threatened to kill me, I am not morally entitled to forcibly deprive anyone of anything who has not taken from me what is mine. Plainly, any laws that would authorize such conduct would substitute need for justice as the ground of legality.

The value of well-being is undeniable. Sickness, insecurity, worry, and many other things can undermine it. Obtaining relief against these is, then, also immensely valuable. But to regard such relief as a right is a mistake. It imposes on innocent parties legally enforceable duties that they do not have. (There are responsibilities we can have, for example to be honest and careful journalists—if we are in that profession—though the legal authorities have no justification to force us to fulfill them. The same holds for the occasional moral responsibility to help others: no one is entitled to such help, or has a right to it, even though human generosity would often provide it.)

We do not, then, have a human right to well-being. If something is ours by right, it can be compelled from others. Freedom is something we have by right, so it may be compelled from others who would invade it. Any political system that authorizes the initiation of force for any other purpose is most probably wrong, unless defensible from other sources, one of which we shall examine presently.

Others' help may be of great value to us. Indeed, by choosing to live and entangle ourselves in societies we show our desire for a quality community life and may even expect others to help us when in dire straights—usually in quite unexpected circumstances—we are logically and morally (but not legally) committed to be generous. That is the real force of Gewirth's overall theory.

Justice as Equality of Resources

John Rawls has defended the welfare state without extensive reliance on a theory of rights. He argues that unless we are going to contribute to the needy in some exceptional way, we should not be permitted to enjoy greater welfare than others. Inequalities are morally and legally justified if they raise the people who are the worst off to a better station in life. As Rawls himself makes the point,

> Those who have been favored by nature, whoever they are, may gain from their good fortune only on terms that improve the situation of those who have lost out.[38] But why should this be so? Rawls is very clear about that matter as well: The assertion that a man deserves [i.e., it is just for one exclusively to possess and to benefit from] the superior character that enables him to make the effort to cultivate his abilities is...problematic; for his character depends in large part upon fortunate family and social circumstances for which he can claim no credit.[39]

Therefore, of course, as Rawls points out, "no one deserves his greater natural capacity nor merits a more favorable starting place in society."[40] Which is why we must have a system that guarantees equality of resources for everyone in life, unless inequality can be expected to yield welfare improvements for those "who have lost out."

The gist of Rawls's view, then, is that we are all products of forces over which we have no individual control, so that when some of us are better off than others, it cannot be just, or not at least as Rawls understands that concept, namely, to mean "fair."[41] He seems to regard us all as part of a family or team, all aiming for good things, but with some unfortunately left behind the rest as a matter of arbitrary, pure chance. When we view human life in this light, to leave it at that would, of course, be unfair. It would be like favoring some members of a family or orchestra or choir over others, when they are all decent folks, doing their most.

In Rawls's outlook we are really back to what Keynes told us: It is unjust or unfair to leave a society to be governed on the basis of winners and losers. The welfare state is the remedy for this. It does not fully destroy liberty, so with regards to some matters in their lives people are justified in acting autonomously. But they have a right to anything of great value only if by so doing they also improve the lot of the needy.

A few points will suffice to indicate why Rawls's position is unsound. First, it contains a paradox. It denies any merit to individual effort and accomplishment and thus denies the possibility of differential welfare status that might have been earned through such difference of merit. Yet it morally exhorts the merits of a system and places on all of us the moral task of implementing its tenets. On the one hand, then, no one is free to choose and gain moral credit, while on the other we should freely choose (and thus might be credited with) being on the side of justice. Such an inconsistency undermines the theory since it both denies and affirms that we have moral responsibilities the fulfillment of which makes us deserving of certain rewards.

Second, are we really unfree to choose to make something of our lives? The issue here is the traditional problem of free will. There are several reasons to think that we do possess free will, even in the most dire circumstances, in virtue of the kind of beings we are.

1. The very effort to seek answers to questions rests on our freedom to seek and find such answers. It presupposes that we aren't forced to have our prejudices, preconceptions, and simple opinions but that we allow ourselves to fall into them and could well have avoided that trap. This is why we blame people who are prejudiced, who jump to conclusions, who fail to heed good arguments and embrace bad ones. It is why we still trust the jury system in criminal law, taking it that people can choose to pay heed and render a just, objective verdict, even if often they fail to do so.
2. The diversity of human life, the uncanny recurrence of the notion of good and evil throughout it, is explained most comprehensively and consistently by accepting that individuals have substantial control over how they conduct themselves. Even when we hold it against a writer or theorist that he or she has made bad arguments or goes about presenting a case in a confusing matter, we implicitly hold such a person responsible. And that would make no sense if he or she could not have done otherwise.
3. Scientific evidence exists showing that the kind of brain human beings have makes self-generated, self-initiated conduct something that is possible. They, unlike other kinds of animals, are equipped with the mental powers (derived from the structure of their brain) to begin or initiate behavior on their own, without being prompted or forced to do so by factors other than their own initiative. Free will is not a capacity that simply violates science.
4. Self-understanding or introspection gives evidence of personal freedom. We often know ourselves to have failed to do something we know we

ought to have done, and "ought implies can." The very idea that we ought to do this rather than that, or that we ought to have done this rather than that, requires that we be free to choose.[42]

5. The most influential objection to freedom of the will is most probably flawed, namely, that all causes in the universe operate in sequence, one event causing the next, ad infinitum. This idea of causality is reductionist and fails to come to terms with the diversity of kinds of substances in reality, some of which may engage in causal relationships that are different, based on their different nature. We cannot account for much of what goes on in the world by reference to only one kind of causality.[43] And there is good reason to think other kinds also exist. Mozart "caused" his compositions differently from the way an earthquake causes the collapse of a building or a philosopher causes the fallacy of argument.

So we have here yet another failed defense of the welfare state. We will see later how these basic moral considerations about capitalism versus the welfare state bear quite directly on the moral issues surrounding governmental paternalism and regulation.[44]

What is Morally Wrong with Paternalism?

Now that we have considered the most up-to-date arguments for the welfare state, it will be useful to consider the ground of moral opposition to governmental paternalism and regulation. This ground, as we shall see, is an updated version of John Locke's doctrine of natural human rights.

The popular conception of governmental responsibility for economic or spiritual welfare is here rejected. Economic, spiritual, or psychological welfare should not be a primary political goal, although in different situations such equality may indeed be valuable and well fostered by competent protection of human liberty. If welfare and equality are to be primary aims of law, some people must necessarily possess a greater power of coercion in order to force redistribution of material goods. Political power alone should be equal among human beings; yet, striving for other kinds of equality absolutely requires political inequality.[45] The institution of law itself is compromised and corrupted when law is made a tool for the achievement of various special goals by using it to secure nonvoluntary support for them. In plainest terms, the use of force is justified only as a defense against actual or threatened coercion or violation of one's rights, sovereignty or autonomy. The use of coercion to provide welfare or achieve equality is not justified.

The currently prominent belief that such coercion is justified rests, as we have seen, partly on the view that individuals as passive entities driven by circumstances and possessing no free will, are thus unable to initiate any action. The belief that welfare or equality is a primary political goal denies, implicitly at least, the premise that each person is able to be responsible for governing his or her own conduct.[46] It implies that progress is blocked by environmental, biological, or related factors over which no genuine human control can be exerted. This was a central element of Marx's concept of human liberty. It also suggests—somewhat inconsistently, in light of the fact that government is, after all, a group of human beings— that government must eliminate these outside barriers, even if some people's mere bourgeois right to liberty must be infringed.

There is no question that the government has a legitimate role to protect the freedom of its citizens. However, if the concept of "freedom" is used to mean freedom from lack of wealth, ignorance, moral virtue, God's grace, or medical hardship, government becomes not only the peace-keeper but the welfare provider or, in other words, the alleged solution to all human problems.

Of course, not all aspects of the paternalistic conception of the state emerge from the view that human beings are passive entities.[47] Even when the passive view is partially rejected, the perception of a basic deficiency in individual's capacity to progress is used to justify the perpetuation of paternalistic elements in the legal system.[48] These developments in U.S. political institutions are difficult to explain. And I do not wish to pretend that philosophical, ethical, or political ideas alone brought them about. One contributing factor may be that certain paternalistic functions of government emerged from the neglect or deliberate debasement of a system that began with the highest though not fully consistent regard for the capacities of the individual.[49]

The U.S. political tradition is correctly regarded as essentially individualistic. But the philosophical background of this individualism is confused. In U.S. culture, persons have been generally regarded as moral agents with the responsibility to make their own way in life. Nevertheless, within the same tradition, they have also been seen to be motivated exclusively by the desire for material gain. This view has been widely promulgated in economics, for example. These traditions are contradictory, because the existence of moral self-responsibility implies that humans can be motivated by factors other than a desire for material possessions.

The conflict in these views has had an impact on the legal developments of our culture. As an obvious example, restrictions on civil liberties have for a while begun to be lifted, but the demise of substantive, economic due process fosters the idea that individuals are incapable of improving their lives from any point on the economic continuum.[50] Numerous laws and judicial decisions empower the state to regulate the voluntary creative and productive activities of individuals. Indirect control is slowly beginning to be exercised over certain specially guarded areas of human endeavor, such as political and artistic activities, by making financial assistance conditional on various government-ordained requirements. These controls clearly foster greater governmental paternalism and authoritarianism throughout. First, help is offered to "clean up" elections or to "support" the arts; compliance with provisions aimed at achieving various social goals then determines the help contingency.

It may be maintained, of course, that governmental assistance in the form of supervision and endowments provides additional opportunities for personal progress. Yet the price is morally unacceptable. The aid is provided at other people's expense, so some will urge restrictions on those groups who will be able to obtain it. Instead of the admittedly diverse system of private assistance with diverse private "strings attached," assistance today is largely centralized and administered politically, requiring full submission to various federal regulatory provisions.

Some effort has recently been made to allow direct public support of the arts, but still with government help. For example, a lobby group, headed by the late Henry Fonda, made it its special task to urge Congress to enable direct funding for the arts. A bill introduced in 1977 as House of Representatives Bill 1042 aimed at enabling taxpayers to check off some of their tax dollars for specified artistic endeavors. However, those who would support different activities will have to fend for themselves and would be put at a disadvantage by such proposals. In fairness—in the spirit of the Fourteenth Amendment to the U.S. Constitution—all other preferred projects would warrant such state measures.

In fact, regardless of how urgently economic support is desired or needed by some persons, there is no justification for the government of all of the people to become an essentially private collection and dispersal agent for a select group. That just is not the government's proper vocation in a free democratic society.

Admittedly, not all people have an equal opportunity to accomplish their various goals. This is especially true in cases where a person is burdened with genetic defects or is born into a negligent or unfortunate family situation. But even under those circumstances, persons can conduct their lives for better or for worse. In any case, the proper function of law is to make it possible for all individuals to govern their own lives within the broad or narrow limitations afforded by the particular conditions of their individual existence. Anything should be pursued freely, and voluntarily, lest it involve coercive interference with an individual's life and place some people in the position of managers of others' personal and social affairs. This point can be made more directly by discussing the situation of the economically poor.

Certain goals in life are unreachable for people who lack certain resources. For example, some may be less able to obtain proper education than others coming from more favorable economic or intellectual or cultural circumstances. A person with a Hungarian accent will not be able to obtain a job in broadcasting unless he or she works extraordinarily hard at overcoming his "handicap." And those with various physical shortcomings will find it immensely difficult to do certain tasks. And in our time this is considered a reason to justify coercive redistribution of wealth or opportunity in favor of such persons.

The present approach rejects this redistributionist view. Being rich or poor, for a start, is not central to human achievement. A poor plumber can have a far more successful life than a rich movie star. While the news media and our culture in general do not promulgate this point, our personal relationships and private experiences often demonstrate the view's validity. More important, welfare legislation and governmental regulation do not provide people with, and indeed obstruct, what is crucial for leading a successful human life, namely, doing one's very best in his or her own particular circumstances. The law should enhance this only by protecting each individual from those who would interfere with her effort or lack of effort to achieve her individual potential.

Many individuals allege that minimal economic survival requirements, surely crucial for a dignified human life, could not be met by some people if the state did not intercede and provide assistance. This charge ignores economic history. The United States government has exercised relatively less state control over the lives of individuals than any other government in recent world history. This has helped to produce a better general economic life than the ones other societies have, particularly those with extensive government welfare programs and regulation.

A system of governmental paternalism, welfarism, and protectionism necessarily regards the essential dignity or moral self-responsibility of individuals as of less than primary significance. In contrast, a society with the protection of the right to freedom as its primary goal, while it cannot guarantee against poverty—just as others cannot, despite their claims—has repeatedly proven to be more productive (as well as more decent in many other respects). The fact has finally been recognized in those very societies that have had an official ideology rejecting the individualist, free-market tradition of political economy—notably, the People's Republic of China and the former Soviet Union.

As to how soon remedial measures can take effect, that is another question entirely. Free citizens are generally willing to be more productive than slaves or semi-slaves. When relationships between individuals in society are noncoercive, except in retaliation to initiated force, the prospect for all members developing their own innate, individual economic, educational, professional, and other potential is enhanced (although never guaranteed). The protection of the right to freedom as the legal respect for individual dignity can only provide the necessary optimum social conditions for the flourishing of individuals. It is the individuals themselves who are ultimately responsible for their measure of success under such circumstances. While this success may be thwarted by nature or bad luck, that eventuality faces anyone and different people can cope with it differently, depending upon their own willingness to prepare and learn how to.

The Right to Property and the Legal System

In chapter 2 I sketched an argument for private property rights based on the fact that human beings are moral agents in need of a realm of sovereignty. My position is that they ought to pursue their happiness, which is only possible to them as natural beings if they are not prevented from obtaining and holding various items and values that can contribute to their successful living. Moral autonomy and the virtue of prudence necessitate the institution of private property.

A few further conditions may be useful concerning this topic. If law, as I have argued earlier, exists so as to establish a framework within which individuals can develop successfully, the citizenry, government's various branches, and the legal profession must determine what conditions provide individuals the optimum or proper range of action. The way to establish a workable framework is via the right to property. Upholding property rights facilitates and encourages individual self-responsibility, something that cannot be realized without, so to speak, various props.

People are not only conscious but physical (and chemical, biological, social, and political) entities who must act in the natural world. Writers need pencil and paper—nowadays, computers—to exercise their right to freedom of expression. Unless individuals have the right to produce, obtain, keep, and trade their tools, they cannot be free of others' interference. As Francois Bondy explains,

> In a society where everything is nationalized and is the property of the state, anybody can be expropriated and subject to export. The East German Minister of Culture once announced in Leipzig that "*Unsere Literatur gehört uns* [Our literature belongs to us!]" What he meant was that it didn't belong to you, or to some "common national culture of two separate states" (which the DDR's constitution still mentions), certainly not to the shared language of the outside world. In Germany the phrase for chattel slaves or indentured servants was *Leibeigenen*, for the bodies belonged to their owners; now we have the new concept of *Geisteigene*, for minds and spirits are also part of the new social property relations. When a bureaucracy considers itself to be the owner of literature, then it has the absolute personal right not only to cultivate its own garden but also to remove ruthlessly such weeds as it deems harmful.[51]

If the collective and, thus, the government has legal title to the tools needed by a writer, architect, teacher, or plumber to accomplish his or her chosen goals, such a person is dependent on and must seek permission to act from the government. As Bondy notes, in totalitarian states, where the government controls the printing presses and publishing organizations, anyone wishing to state a personal opinion must gain official sanction. (Even under Mikhail Gorbachev's glasnost and perestroika reforms—begun in 1987, prior to the breakup of the Soviet state—the openness and restructuring involved were permitted or instituted by government, rather than being understood as a basic human right that limits the scope and power of the government. Consider also that General Augusto Pinochet's Chile had had a relatively "free" market—that is, a government policy of abstention from heavy-handed economic regulation. Yet its critics will quite rightly refuse to regard it as having been a free country.)

Moreover in countries where broadcasting is government administered, there is no right to telecast one's views or ideas on the airways, only a permission to do so if it suits the state authorities. In contrast, if the right to property is respected, individuals do not have to seek political permission to act, even if they still must earn the opportunity to do so via the free marketplace and in face of natural obstacles.[52]

The right to property is the right to work for, acquire, and hold goods and valuables; it includes the rights of production, trade, and bequest, as well as the right to undertake innumerable actions vis-à-vis the world of ownable items not even conceived of yet. The right to pursue happiness or individual excellence in life, then, requires full support of the right to property.

Private property rights are neither favored nor legally protected in our era and have not been for a long time. Both cultural and legal developments in the last one hundred years have undermined the protection of property rights.[53] The state often acts in a paternalistic fashion toward the citizen's ownership and management of property. It is increasingly willing to usurp mutually agreed-upon contracts.[54]

Nevertheless, broadly speaking, the history of the United States demonstrates that the significant protection of private property rights, despite much compromise and confusion, has a propensity to increase the productivity as well as the self-responsibility of the members of a human community. It contributes to their self-perception as moral agents who cannot expect others to live for them and it fosters their concern for and development toward doing reasonably well in their lives. In short, the right to private property is a required feature of a human community that enhances human flourishing.

Human Dignity and (Natural) Human Rights

Some may still argue that the welfare state does not debase human dignity because it evolved through the democratic process. But use of the democratic process does not justify restrictions on individual rights. Certain decisions may be popular but not morally permissible. The fact that a citizenry does not protest vigorously cannot license government encroachment upon a person's liberty. Similarly, the fact that a welfare state can benefit some people economically does not justify limiting individual liberty via the usurpation of human rights and dignity. Democracy cannot be unlimited in its scope of concern. As an example, in *West Virginia Board of Education v. Barnette* the United States Supreme Court stated:

> The very purpose of a Bill of Rights was to withdraw certain subjects from the vicissitudes of political controversy, to place them beyond the reach of majorities...One's...fundamental rights may not be submitted to vote; they depend on the outcome of no elections.[55]

Any democracy requires constant constraints, lest the democratic process be open to elimination via the democratic method.

The theory that law must uphold human dignity is logically tied to the conception of political justice that rests upon natural rights. Contemporary natural rights theory identifies principles of constitutional or basic law so that each person is understood to be a moral agent whose life, liberty, and property may not be controlled by others. Government control, even of a democratic sort, is justified only if it protects and preserves the rights to life, liberty, and property. Although people sometimes try to vote them away, as if they were granted and revocable by society, government, or the state, these rights are inalienable, even when positive law disregards them. Thus, although slavery was sanctioned by positive law, it was immoral because persons are (by nature) free agents, with their own will to guide their lives, not to be subjugated to the will of others.

All this may, of course, be met with the rejoinder that the entire thesis of this chapter is in error because dignity does not exist or is at any rate of no great importance. Certainly numerous social scientists would concur with the first objection; for them the ingredients of human dignity, if they admit any meaning to the idea, are not freedom of choice or sovereignty of will and action but, instead, security, welfare, safety, a sense of belonging, and so on. And even when some credence is given to human dignity, in the sense discussed in this work, it is at best of minor significance because without some other provisions it simply has nothing much to contribute to a person's life. This sentiment is expressed whenever one hears it said that it does no good for poor, uneducated, underdeveloped, or otherwise unfortunate persons to enjoy the right to liberty when due to their powerlessness they cannot exercise this right to any significant degree.

The first point has already been answered by reference to the fact that nothing in philosophy or science rules out the possibility of something in nature being free, self-determined, and responsible for its actions. Furthermore, there is every reason to think that human beings are precisely such creatures, except when they are crucially incapacitated.

To the second point we need to admit that competing moral ideals will yield competing political and legal ideals and a corresponding recasting of the function of law in society. Thus, if stability is the highest political purpose, there would exist justification for taking measures that normally disregard the dignity of individuals and aim to ensure stability. If, for example, advancing toward communism is crucial, then the terrorism employed and the so-called wars of liberation around the world that were the hallmark of Soviet foreign interventionism, are of greater significance than efforts aimed at protecting the moral autonomy and dignity of the individual.

But, if our society is to give priority to human beings reaching their achievements as a matter of personal accomplishment—if, in other words, we were to have a conception of the human good that prescribes self-government—then legal institutions should support the individualist tradition, which views each person as being individually responsible for leading a successful human life. Human dignity, then, will be of primary significance. And here, of course, it is crucial whether people are still viewed as the crucial agents in their own well- being.

I do not see how this can be coherently denied. Even those who are unfortunate but retain their full humanity intact need to be recognized as capable of governing their lives. Certainly this is still accepted in the context of civil libertarian considerations, so that no private agents are free to rule those who are disabled. But the government seems not to be bound by such restraints and is able to engage in acts of resource redistribution on the behalf of the unfortunate. This is an insult to the disabled and in any case a violation of the rights of those who have other goals they choose to pursue rather than caring for the unfortunate.

Throughout this work I plan to return to the issue of human natural rights as the basic standards of justice in a human community. Since I have discussed the topic in full in several of my books,[56] I will only discuss it briefly in this work, just for the purposes of recalling the basic argument and its relevance to the topic at hand. For now I want to recall that the normative function of such social principles as basic human, natural rights ("natural" meaning derived from their nature) is to ascertain the significance of individual human dignity, the moral nature of persons, within a social context.

But let us explore the oft-defended state paternalism that springs to mind when we are considering this topic. If ever there seems to be plausibility to such a policy it is when people need help.

Human Dignity and Paternalism

Human dignity is crushed by the implementation of regimentation and, more specifically, paternalistic behavior modification techniques in the penal and educational systems of the country.[57] Wherever paternalism sets in, the capacity of individuals to be a decisive element in their own lives diminishes. Yielding to vested interest-group pressures has also produced the denigrated individual human dignity and caused the rapid spread of state paternalism, the consequences of which are extremely regrettable and should immediately be rejected and resisted.

Some, like Steven Kelman, argue that paternalism is justified when people rationally delegate their own authority to others who know more about the subject to be dealt with. Thus government regulation is justified because, by a sort of Rawlsian method, we supposedly know that people would (if they were fully rational) elect to have experts protect them against, say, mercury-poisoned fish instead of try to look out for themselves in such complicated matters.

Yet not only is this Rawlsian method specious; there simply is no universal rationality to be discerned by way of imagining ourselves in a social contract behind the veil of ignorance. There are plenty of other methods beside inviting government to handle such complications of the marketplace. Without the pretense of government's taking care of us in such cases, institutions could easily arise that would serve us with the expertise we need—just as such institutions have arisen when we need them to produce food, clothing, transportation, art, and entertainment. The argument from the alleged shortage of such complex services is shown to be theoretically and practically flawed: first, by the argument of Mises and Hayek against central planning of market services, and second, by the widely admitted debacles of socialist and other collectively planned economies.[58]

Human Dignity and Political Freedom

I have attempted here to outline and defend the value of human dignity and its proper relationship to various features of a legal system. I have proposed that human dignity should be upheld within a good legal system as an essential function of law. Such a function will be fulfilled if the legal system rests on a theory of natural human rights to life, liberty, and property. These rights specify the standards by which each individual's liberty of moral choice can be protected and preserved, thereby achieving valid, nonutopian social justice.

Although the topic of dignity has usually been considered in light of the need to protect civil and political rights, an approach stressing property rights is also needed. When the government has unlimited legal authority to use, dispose of, and expropriate property, the individuals who produce and must depend on property cannot oppose that government's policies and cannot govern their own lives. The tools of pure legal research are inadequate for making basic normative points. Instead, through moral argumentation, one can attempt to establish what we ought to do and hope to influence the basic direction of the political and legal community, a task of every citizen. If the arguments are sound and if people will pay heed to them, policy shifts can be affected and eventually it will be possible to change the direction in which the legal developments of one's society are heading.

I have argued in this chapter that our goal should be a consistent affirmation of human dignity—that is, of the full respect for each member of society as a free and self-responsible being.

Notes

1. Prior restraint is morally and politically objectionable because it treats someone as if he or she had already been proven to have violated the basic rights of others and, thus, could be subjected to punishment or penalties from which free citizens, without such blemish on their conduct, ought to be protected.
2. The concept of *moral* refers to the uniquely human task of choosing between right and wrong conduct in accordance with a standard appropriate to a free and rational agent. Thus, moral issues require making decisions with reference to such a standard. *Moral* does not mean ethically good or right. The concept *nature* here means "essential" or "relating to by definition." Having a *moral nature*, then, involves essentially being required to make choices in accordance with a standard.
3. One need not be a worthy or morally good person to possess human dignity. Merely the capacity to exercise morally significant choices in the performance of human tasks indicates the possession of dignity.

4. B. F. Skinner, *Beyond Freedom and Dignity* (New York: Knopf, 1971). See generally his other books: *The Behavior of Organisms: An Experimental Analysis* (Englewood Cliffs, NJ: Prentice-Hall, 1938); *Science and Human Behavior* (New York: Macmillan, 1953); *Verbal Behavior* (New York: Appleton-Century-Crofts, 1957); *Cumulative Record* (New York: Appleton-Century-Crofts, 1959); *Contingencies of Reinforcement: A Theoretical Analysis* (New York: Appleton-Century-Crofts, 1969); and *About Behaviorism* (New York: Knopf, 1974).

For detailed criticism of Skinner's ideas, see Tibor R. Machan, *The Pseudo-Science of B. F. Skinner* (New Rochelle, NY: Arlington House, 1974); Noam Chomsky, "Review of Skinner's Verbal Behavior," *Language* 35 (1959): 26–58; Noam Chomsky, "The Case Against B. F. Skinner," *The New York Review of Books* (December 30, 1981): 1; Robert Efron, "The Conditioned Reflex: A Meaningless Concept," *Perspectives in Biology and Medicine* 9, no. 4 (1966): 488–513; Ayn Rand, *Philosophy: Who Needs It* (Indianapolis, IN: The Bobbs-Merrill Co., Inc., 1982), pp. 167–197 ("The Stimulus and the Response").

A very good discussion of the mutual benefit to be gained from work in humanistic and experimental psychology is offered by Irvin Child, *Humanistic Psychology and the Research Tradition: Their Several Virtues* (New York: Wiley, 1973).

Such concepts as *purpose* and *intention* sometimes trouble determinist psychologists, but more often than not they simply translate these ideas into forms that accommodate their determinism. See George A. Miller, Eugene Galanter, and Karl H. Pribram, *Plans and the Structure of Behavior* (New York: Adams-Bannister-Cox, 1960). Outside of psychology proper, we also encounter widespread adherence to the behaviorist-determinist-reductionist approach; for instance, in the works of Rorbert Ardrey, *The Territorial Imperative: A Personal Inquiry into the Animal Origins of Property and Nations* (New York: Atheneum, 1966); Konrad Lorenz, *Evolution and Modification of Behavior* (Chicago: University of Chicago, 1965); Konrad Lorenz, *On Aggression*, translated by Marjorie Kerr Wilson, (Chicago: University of Chicago Press, 1966). It is difficult to find explicit discussions of such approaches in the prominent literature because most scholars simply take for granted Skinner's view that science and freedom of free choice are inherently in conflict. It is usually philosophers who discuss the topic explicitly. See Sidney Hook, ed., *Dimensions of Mind: A Symposium* (New York: New York University Press, 1960).

A crucial point to keep in mind is that in the social sciences there are two major aims: explanation and predictions. Explanation is generally taken to involve the showing of what factors preceded an event and made it occur. Prediction is the stating of what the future will be, based on knowledge or estimates of present or past events. The very possibility of free choice is, by many people, either denied outright or regarded as a mysterious—or divinely endowed—feature of the universe. The factors considered relevant to explanations and predictions are usually restricted to the observable material aspects of the world. They therefore exclude choices, decisions, or intentions. Such mental activities have no place in a view of science that excludes from legitimacy any judgment not strictly reducible to or derivable from sensory observations.

Needless to say, this is the extreme version of the position at issue, and many mitigated versions exist. It is fair to hold, nevertheless, that the version of scientism stated above is the ideal being aimed at and wished for by many theorists of human behavior, even though it is sometimes regarded as an impossible ideal.

5. On hospitalization, see, for example, Illinois Rev. Stat. ch. 91 1/2, s8–12 (1975); Massachusetts General Laws ch. 123, s6 (1976); Michigan Comp. Laws Anno. s330.1468 (1975). Psychosurgery is discussed in Jose M. R. Delgado, *Physical Control of the Mind: Toward Psychocivilized Society* (New York: Harper and Row, 1969); and Peter Breggin, *Toxic Psychiatry* (New York: St. Martin's Press, 1991).

6. See, for example, Alabama Code Title 36 s138 (1973); Delaware Code Title 21 s4185 (1974); Florida Stat. Ann. s316.288 (1969).

7. See, for example, 21 U.S.C. s355 (1973); Alaska Stat. s17.20.110 (1972); California Code s26288 (1964).

8. In trying to explain the reason for the emergence and existence of law, numerous writers have introduced state of nature arguments, postulating conditions of natural anarchy and determining that by some quasi-causal process organized community life will emerge. See Thomas Hobbes, *De Cive* (The citizen), chapter 12 in volume 2 of *The English Works of Thomas Hobbes of Malmesbury* (London: J. Bohn, 1839–1845); John Locke, chapter 2, section 15 of *Second Treatise of Government* (Oxford: Blackwell, [1689] 1948); Robert Nozick, *Anarchy, State, and Utopia* (New York: Basic Books, 1974). However, when this approach aims at identifying the basic principles of human community life, not merely at establishing the grounds for enforcing those principles that have been acknowledged to bind everyone, it tends to omit consideration of the fact that even consent or agreement is subject to moral evaluation, so that not everything that may be consented or agreed to ought to be consented or agreed to. A modified social contract focuses on the outcome of what people would have done had they united in seeking their own social survival. In this discussion, since we are considering our best reasons or purposes, not causes, for organized human community life, we arrive thereby at the function law should play in such an evidently valuable endeavor.

9. "Value" for people exists, ultimately, in their choosing to live their lives in accordance with their rational, free, purposeful, and moral nature as fully as possible, given their individual circumstances. See Ayn Rand, *The Virtue of Selfishness* (New York: New American Library, 1964); Eric Mack, "How to Derive Ethical Egoism," *The Personalist*, 52 (1971): 736–743.

10. Tibor R. Machan, *Human Rights and Human Liberties* (Chicago: Nelson-Hall, 1975), pp. 74–77.

11. This ancient explanation for the existence of law is hardly more than a matter of common sense. However, determinists and relativists would have to deny that society and law emerged because of their discovered objective value.

12. This conception of moral goodness has its philosophical background in the Aristotelian tradition of ethics. See Douglas B. Rasmussen and Douglas J. Den Uyl, *Liberty and Nature: An Aristotelian Defense of Liberal Order* (LaSalle, IL: Open Court, 1991). See also, Tibor R. Machan, *Individuals and Their Rights* (LaSalle, IL: Open Court, 1989).

13. For a person to flourish he would have to make the most of what he is: a human individual with the capacity to make choices. Ayn Rand makes a crucial point about this ethical framework in the *Virtue of Selfishness*:

> "Happiness" can properly be the purpose of ethics, but not the standard. The task of ethics is to define man's proper code of values and thus to give him the means of achieving happiness. To declare, as the ethical hedonists do, that "the proper value is whatever gives you pleasure" is to declare that "the proper

value is whatever you happen to value"—which is an act of intellectual and philosophical abdication, an act which merely proclaims the futility of ethics and invites all men to play it deuces wild (29).

Many professional economists sanction psychological hedonism in their support of a free society. Critics of this conception of human community life have charged its advocates with inviting "all men to play it deuces wild." See Daniel Bell, *The Cultural Contradictions of Capitalism* (New York: Basic Books, 1976); Irving Kristol, "When Virtue Has Lost All Her Loveliness," in *Capitalism Today*, ed. Daniel Bell and Irving Kristol, (New York: Basic Books, 1971); and Richard Schmitt, "The Desire for Private Gain," in *The Main Debate: Communism Versus Capitalism*, ed. Tibor R. Machan, (New York: Random House, 1987).

Unfortunately, philosophers have not combined a clear understanding of ethics with a diligent study of the findings of economics. Therefore, while economists have defended liberty with little thought of virtue, philosophers have defended virtue with little regard for liberty. Yet virtue and liberty, as Skinner keenly perceives in *Beyond Freedom and Dignity*, are interdependent: "Goodness, like other aspects of dignity or worth, waxes as invisible control wanes, and so, of course, does freedom. Hence goodness and freedom tend to be associated" (66).

14. Egoism and individualism are usually viewed as amoral and antithetical to morality. This viewpoint may be traced to Plato's conception of the individual as a low-level metaphysical component, something that is inferior to the universal or ideal. Another reason for this view is the general tendency to consider Thomas Hobbes as the advocate of egoistic ethics, even though the Hobbesian conception of human life clearly leaves no room for morality. See two articles by Sherly Robin Letwin: "Modern Philosophies of Law," in *The Great Ideas Today*, ed. Robert M. Hutchins and Mortimer Adler, (Chicago: Encyclopedia Britannica, 1972) pp. 104–153; and "Hobbes and Christianity," *Daedalus* 105 (Winter 1976): 1–21. Subsequent views of ethics, such as Locke's mitigated hedonism and Bentham's full-blown version, along with John Stuart Mill's utilitarianism, fail to qualify as bona fide ethical theories since they tend to deny freedom of the will, thus violating "ought implies can." They do have a theory of value, however, which accounts for their frequent use in economics. Egoism or individualism has not enjoyed much respect as a moral system because of the view that individuals are either inferior beings or ones only inclined to conduct themselves in an antisocial way. As an example of this, consider the following remark: "What is most important is that motives of this sort be distinguished from the typical criminal motive: self-interest." It appears in Jeffrie G. Murphy, *Civil Disobedience and Violence* (Belmont, CA: Wadsworth, 1971), p. 1. For the numerous efforts to defeat Hobbesian egoism, see Kai Nielsen, "On the Rationality of 'Rational Egoism'," *The Personalist* 55 (1974): 398–400; James Rachels, "Two Arguments against Ethical Egoism," *Philosophia* 4 (April-July 1974): 297–314. In all of these discussions egoism is generally construed as the doctrine where each person does (or, rarely, should do) what he or she desires, wishes, or wants. Such hedonistic and/or psychological egoism is indeed deficient, as it provides the acting individual with no standard for determining what is in fact in his or her own best interest. Conflicting alternatives and desires often face us, and we frequently require a standard for deciding what course of conduct to pursue. Eudaemonistic individualism, or classical egoism, offers such a standard in its

reference to human nature. See Rand, *The Virtue of Selfishness*; David L. Norton, *Personal Destinies: A Philosophy of Ethical Individualism* (Princeton, NJ: Princeton University Press, 1976). See also, Tibor R. Machan, *Individuals and Their Rights and Capitalism and Individualism* (New York: St. Martin's Press, 1990). Let me just recall here that the form of egoism I have called "classical" is developed within the Aristotelian eudaemonistic ethical tradition. See David L. Norton, *Personal Destinies.*

15. The conception of law stressed here is normative, and more in the tradition of natural law than positivist conceptions of legality. See Alessandro Passerin D'Entreves, *Natural Law: An Introduction to Legal Philosophy* (London: Hutchinson University Library, 1951). Although the overall influence of positivism and realism has outweighed the natural law tradition in the last century, many writers argue that the U.S. political tradition is related to the natural law stance. See Cornelia Geer Le Boutillier, *American Democracy and Natural Law* (New York: Columbia University Press, 1950); Ernest Barker, "Natural Law and the American Revolution," in his book *Traditions of Civility: Eight Essays* (Cambridge: Cambridge University Press, 1948). The concept of human dignity is individualist rather than collectivist. Within this framework, the individual human being—not the interests of states, nations, or even humanity in general—is of primary concern. U.S. culture tends in our time to balance the individualist and collectivist aspects of the numerous political theories that have emerged. In other parts of the world, only a few elements of the individualist theory are given prominence. In general, however, nothing much of individualism receives respect, let alone legal support, except for the fact that developments in the mid-1980s throughout the world have seen the rise of privatization as a means for economic recovery. (Privatization is the policy of governments to sell off their holdings and to contract out some of their "social" programs and "utilities" to private firms.)

16. Different candidates for the correct (that is, rationally warranted) moral position will yield different conceptions of the proper content and scope of law. When those active in political affairs have particular ethical views, they usually attempt to shape the law to further the purposes they believe to be morally proper. Thus, in predominant religious eras the law tended to serve goals fostered by the dominating religious creeds. See Otto Friedrich von Gierke, *Political Theories of the Middle Age* (Cambridge: Cambridge University Press, 1900). In times that emphasized the primacy of utilitarian goals such as economic prosperity or the equal distribution of wealth, the laws were directed toward these goals. See Edgar K. Browning, *Redistribution and the Welfare System* (Washington, DC: American Enterprise Institute, 1975); Richard A. Posner, *Economic Analysis of Law* (Boston: Little, Brown, 1973); Charles E., Baker, "The Ideology of the Economic Analysis of Law", *Philosophy and Public Affairs* 5 (1975): 3-48.

Even in criminal law, which in most eras focuses on the protection of people from *malum in se* acts, judicial decisions sometimes are governed by consideration of prevailing morality. See Thomas Szasz, *Law, Liberty, and Psychiatry: An Inquiry into the Social uses of Mental Health Practices* (New York: Macmillan, 1963), pp. 218-221. Although *malum in se* statutes usually survive major ideological changes, so that murder, robbery, and assault remain crimes in socialist, communist, monarchical, democratic, or fascist countries, the exact treatment of those found guilty of such crimes changes considerably. Today, the influence of recent theories in psychology and psychiatry on punishment, rehabilitation, and guilt has been evident.

17. A morality or an ethical theory aims to identify the standards by which human beings ought to live their lives. There are numerous proposed ethics or moralities, and a most difficult task it is to identify the best. The correct moral position is one that most successfully serves as a general system of principles to guide conduct for human beings. It must be very general in scope to reach all areas of human existence. The idea of human dignity and the corresponding framework of the just legal order here being defended are based on a detailed ethical theory we may best call individualism or ethical egoism. The idea is that each person's central task in life is to become an excellent human being within the context of his or her own individual situation. The fullest realization of one's own unique human self or ego is the good life for each individual.

18. See Gregory Vlastos, "Justice and Equality," in *Social Justice*, ed. Richard B. Brandt, (Englewood Cliffs, NJ: Prentice Hall, 1962); Samuel Scheffler, "Natural Rights, Equality, and the Minimal State," *Canadian Journal of Philosophy* 6 (March 1976): 59–76. A more recent champion of welfare statism is James P. Sterba, *How to Make People Just: A Practical Reconciliation of Alternative Conceptions of Justice* (Totowa, NJ: Rowman and Littlefield, 1988).

19. There is a very insightful discussion of this point in connection with the kind of thinking that went into the launching of Marxism-Leninism and the Russian revolution in Richard Pipes, *The Russian Revolution* (New York: Vintage Books, 1991).

20. See Tibor R. Machan, "Equality's Dependence on Liberty," in *Equality and Freedom: International and Comparative Jurisprudence*, ed. Gray Dorsey, (Dobbs Ferry, NY: Oceana, 1977).

21. See, for example, *Swann v. Charlotte-Mecklenburg Board of Education*, 402 U.S. 1 (1971). The Swann decision sanctioned extensive busing, limiting the practice only when the transporting of pupils would be detrimental to the educational process or the safety of the students (pp. 29–31). In 1992 the U.S. Supreme Court ruled that such busing may be discontinued in certain cases (for instance, DeKalb County, Georgia).

22. For example, the National Endowment for the Arts (NEA), created at 20 U.S.C. 951 et seq. (1971), bases the award of grants on regulations and criteria set by its chair. A similar matter, involving NEA standards, became subject of a minor national furor in 1990 and 1991 and partly energized the candidacy of Pat Buchanan for Republican Party nominee in the 1992 presidential election.

23. Locke, *Second Treatise of Government*.

24. John Maynard Keynes, *The End of Laissez-Faire* (London: Hogarth Press, 1927), p. 40. Books on the philosophical underpinnings of the welfare state include Nicholas Rescher, *Welfare: The Social Issues in Philosophical Perspective* (Pittsburgh, PA: University of Pittsburgh Press, 1972); D. Marsh, *The Welfare State* (London: Longman, 1970); Noel Timms and David Watson, eds., *Talking About Welfare: Readings in Philosophy and Social Policy* (London and Boston: Routledge and Kegan Paul, 1976).

25. For more on this, see Chapter 10.

26. See Douglas J. Den Uyl, "The Ethics of Advertising: Buyer Beware—Seller Take Care," in *Commerce and Morality*, ed. Tibor R. Machan, (Totowa, NJ: Rowman and Littlefield, 1988), pp. 42–76. Note, especially, Den Uyl's distinction between the "reasonable man" and the "ignorant man", standards by which advertising is often judged.

27. Some may dispute that fraudulent conduct is essentially akin to coercive conduct, and in some respects they are right. To defraud someone does not on its face

involve violating them—inflicting injury on their bodies—as is done in cases of assault, kidnaping, or murder. Fraud does, however, involve extracting from someone goods or services in return for promised payment, goods, or services without making good on the promise. But this is not all: defrauding another also involves sanctioning or inviting their retaliation once the promise has been breached. Fraud, unlike a mere breaking of a promise, is a breach of a promise that officials of governments have been sworn to rectify with the consent of all parties involved.

28. For a modern explanation, see Tibor R. Machan, "Human Rights: Some Points of Clarification," *Journal of Critical Analysis* 5 (Summer 1973): 30–39. For an overview of recent human rights theories, see Tibor R. Machan, "Some Recent Work in Human Rights Theory," in *Recent Work in Philosophy*, ed. K. G. Lucey and Tibor R. Machan, (Totowa, NJ: Rowman and Allanheld, 1983), pp. 227–246.

29. Gregory Vlastos, "Justice and Equality," in *Human Rights*, ed. A. I. Melden, (Belmont, CA: Wadsworth, 1970), p. 82.

30. Ibid.

31. A. I. Melden, "Introduction," in *Human Rights*, pp. 8–9.

32. Vlastos, "Justice and Equality," p. 82.

33. Locke, chapter 11, section 139 in *Second Treatise of Government*.

34. Gregory Vlastos, "Justice and Equality," in *Social Justice*, ed. R. Brandt, (Englewood Cliffs, NJ: Prentice-Hall, 1962), p. 56.

35. For example, racial prejudice is a kind of feeling or attitude, resting not on clear judgments but on sloppy generalizations or "gut reactions." In children it may be excusable, but not in adults. It is interesting that in our time there is a severe criticism of racist and sexist language afoot as well as, at a more philosophical level, a widespread attack on objectivism, the view that some objective reality may be identified and distinguished from popular prejudice or frames of reference. At the most radical point of this latter attack, we find deconstructionists who believe in no common standard for any truth. In short, we have both a trend toward severe verbal propriety or "political correctness" as well as toward cultural relativism. For the latter, see Richard Rorty, *Objectivity, Relativism, and Truth* (Cambridge: Cambridge University Press, 1991).

36. Alan Gewirth, *Reason and Morality* (Chicago: University of Chicago Press, 1978), pp. 198, 209.

37. *Ibid.*

38. John Rawls, *A Theory of Justice* (Cambridge, MA: Harvard University Press, 1971), pp. 101–102.

39. *Ibid.*, p. 104.

40. *Ibid.*

41. That is the central (political) thesis of Rawls's theory of justice, namely, that justice is fairness.

42. As I have noted in several places in this work, while some find fault with this idea, namely, that only if one has a genuine choice to do either the right or the wrong thing can it be meaningful to say that one ought to do the former, there is really no way out for moral systems. Blaming, praising, holding people culpable, forgiving people, feeling guilt, regretting things, etc., all make sense only if the agent is indeed an agent and initiates the conduct involved. Compare with John Kekes, *Facing Evil* (Princeton, NJ: Princeton University Press, 1990).

43. A good discussion of the topic of causality may be found in A. R. Louch, *Explanation and Human Action* (Berkeley: University of California Press, 1966) and Milton Fisk, *Nature and Necessity: An Essay in Physical Ontology* (Bloomington,

IN: Indiana University Press, 1974). See also, Tibor R. Machan, *The Pseudo-Science of B. F. Skinner.*

44. In Chapter 8 I will be examining the case for a federal Occupational Health and Safety Administration (OSHA). We will also see that many of the concrete cases that involve OSHA, or problems to which OSHA is thought to be the best solution, are best understood in terms of a moral and political system that rejects forced welfarism and supports a free labor market as well as free-market solutions to health and safety problems on the job.

45. See Tibor R. Machan, "A Note on Socialism and Elitism," *Intercollegiate Review* 11 (1975): pp. 3–34. Marx recognized this inequality and allowed for it in his theory as merely a temporary political condition. Prior to the emergence of ideal communism a period of dictatorship would be required, one that would take on the form of socialism. Some socialists, such as the late Michael Harrington, have insisted that this could be done in a democratic manner. However, this possibility is dubious, in view of the fact that under socialism proper no private property is permitted—which, however, renders minorities entirely vulnerable to retaliation from majorities, thus destroying the democratic feature of the system. One rare socialist theorist who acknowledges this political problem with socialism is Robert L. Heilbroner. See his *Marxism: For and Against* (New York: Norton, 1980). As Heilbroner puts it, "politics becomes the Achilles' heel of socialism" (164). For more, see Tibor R. Machan, *Marxism: A Bourgeois Critique* (Bradford, England: MCB University Press, 1988).

46. More precisely, those who construe economic, psychological, or related types of well-being tend to view people as (1) moved by forces they do not control, and (2) fully emancipated only when they reach some (unspecified) stage of economic, psychological, or related level of well-being. Karl Marx is the most clear-cut example of those persons adhering to this view. In less basic and more inconsistent fashion, political thinkers such as Rawls, Harrington, and the majority of social scientists making recommendations for social policy agree with this view. In political philosophy, however, the prominent idea today is that the requirement for (the right to) liberty must be balanced with the requirement for (the right to) welfare. See, for example, Gewirth, *Reason and Morality*; and Ronald Dworkin, *Taking Rights Seriously* (Cambridge, MA: Harvard University Press, 1977). See, for a different view, Tibor R. Machan, "Prima Facie versus Natural (Human) Rights," *The Journal of Value Inquiry* 10 (1976): 119–131. See, for a good exchange, Douglas B. Rasmussen and James Sterba, *The Catholic Bishops and the Economy: A Debate* (New Brunswick, NJ: Transaction Books, 1987).

47. For example, some ancient Greek political philosophers envisioned the state as the spiritual father of a community. There is, however, debate about whether Aristotle believed that the state or the civil community should fill the leadership role. If the latter, there is no negation of the dignity of individuals, because the kind of leadership a civil community could offer need not be compulsory, coercive, or otherwise disrespectful of a person's choice and self-responsibility. See Fred D. Miller, "The State and the Community in Aristotle's Politics," *Reason Papers*, no. 1 (1974): 61–69.

48. There is also the idea, advanced mostly by conservatives, that government should support the religions of a community but not the arts, sciences, education, commerce, sports, or secular inspirational organizations. This seems to be in response to the perception throughout much of the culture that there has been a decline in the moral quality of life. See Walter Berns, *The First Amendment and the Future*

of American Democracy (New York: Basic Books, 1976) and James Davison Hunter, *Culture Wars: The Struggle to Define America* (New York: Basic Books, 1991).

49. Several recent commentators have pointed to this paradox in the cultural traditions and elements of U.S. society. See, e.g., Bell, *The Cultural Contradictions of Capitalism.*

50. But consider the demands of certain feminists, especially Catherine A. MacKinnon and Andrea Dworkin, that certain kinds of publications be banned on the grounds that these hurt women by depicting them in demeaning ways. MacKinnon assisted the Canadian Supreme Court in its judgment, early in 1992, to remove free expression protection when it comes to such publications, films, and so on. This could introduce prior restraint not only into commercial but also speech conduct.

51. Francois Bondy, "European Diary: Exit This Way," *Encounter* (April 1981): 42–44.

52. Even in the United States, broadcasting is officially government managed, via the federal government's ownership of the electromagnetic spectrum. Stations lease the airwaves and the Federal Communications Commission grants these leases, sometimes on terms that involve political and ideological considerations such as whether the public is being served fairly or whether controversies deemed important by the state are being covered, etc.

53. Many people believe that the rise of capitalism and the reduction of state control over economic life produced poverty, alienation, and deprivation for millions. At the same time, a class of ruthless capitalists is said to have emerged and wielded enormous power over their communities. The stories of child labor, sweatshops, and robber barons are now common stereotypes in the history of industrial capitalism. For a different view, see Friedrich. A. von Hayek, ed., *Capitalism and the Historians* (Chicago: University of Chicago Press, 1954); R. M. Hartwell, et. al., *The Long Debate on Poverty: Eight Essays on Industrialisation and "the Condition of England"*, 2nd impression, (London: Institute of Economic Affairs, 1974); Wanda Fraiken Neff, *Victorian Working Women: An Historical and Literary Study of Women in British Industries and Professions, 1832–1850* (New York: Columbia University Press, 1929); George Macaulay Trevelyan, *English Social History: A Survey of Six Centuries, Chaucer to Queen Victoria* (London: Longmans, Green and Co., 1942); John Chamberlain, *The Enterprising Americans: A Business History of the United States* (New York: Harper and Row, 1963).

    Respecting the familiar and oft-repeated claim that the unregulated, unrestrained right to private property generates monopolies, predatory pricing, robber barons, etc., see R. A. Childs, Jr., "Big Business and the Rise of American Statism," and Yale Brozen, "Is the Government the Source of Monopoly?" both in Tibor R. Machan, ed., *The Libertarian Alternative* (Chicago: Nelson-Hall, 1974), pp. 208–234 and pp. 149–168.

54. Under the theory of unconscionability, the state can refuse to respect contractual agreements when so-called unequal economic parties are involved. Customers of a department store and the corporation that owns it are regarded as unequal bargaining parties. These state policies clearly undermine a crucial function of a good legal system: respect for the individual's capacity to make proper choices.

    It is sometimes argued that the unconscionability rules are directed against those adhesion contracts which do not allow "meaningful" free choice. However, if men and women form a corporation and invest in it their earnings, work, and time, others do not have a right to force such a voluntary association, i.e., the corporation, to write contracts for the convenience of customers who cannot meet the standard form requirements. Of course, if the standard form contracts hinder the business, the people who use them will not succeed in their business venture. But the individuals standing behind the mistakenly regarded "faceless" corporation should not be forced to succumb to the demands of those who want what the corporation has to offer. Refusing to recognize the liberty of corporations—that is, voluntarily formed economic associations—is no less an affront to human dignity than refusing to recognize the liberty of an individual shareholder.

This situation can be contrasted with certain elements of legislation such as the Truth in Lending acts, which, by requiring accurate information, facilitate choice by protecting against fraud. Similarly, paternalistic legislation and regulation of commerce and industry are often combined with legitimate provisions that protect a person against fraud, extortion, or misrepresentation. What is unjustifiable is that courts are attempting to remedy the failure of individuals doing business or entering contracts to adequately prepare for their lives. Thus it would be possible to plan for future hospitalization and avoid being made the "victim" of unconscionable hospital rules. The same is possible in one's dealings with corporations and their standard forms. The fact that many individuals refuse to prepare for dealing competently in a complex society is no justification for forcing those who have done so to forego their resulting benefits.

Early in their history, U.S. legal institutions put serious limitations on the right to property, including freedom of contract. In 1876, during a time when laissez-faire was at its peak, The Supreme Court, in *Munn v. Illinois*, ruled that business "affected with a public interest" could not be free of government interference. Ten years later, the Supreme Court transferred the regulation of commerce from state to federal jurisdiction on grounds that "the right of continuous transportation from one end of the country to the other is essential in modern times." Subsequently, in this century, we have witnessed the total demise of substantive economic due process and the expansion of the federal and state governments' power to regulate property and business. By now, through judicial interpretation, the commerce clause of the Constitution sanctions the most extensive and pervasive violations of private property rights. Such judicial interpretations and the rejection of economic due process have rendered the Fifth and Fourth Amendments feeble legal measures against government power to violate private property rights and to regulate commercial endeavors.

55. *West Virginia Board of Education v. Barnette* 319 U.S. 638 (1942).
56. See especially, Machan, *Individuals and Their Rights.*
57. For a detailed defense of the compatibility of government paternalism with political autonomy, see Steven Kelman, "Regulation and Paternalism," in *Rights and Regulation*, ed. M. Bruce Johnson and Tibor R. Machan, (Cambridge, MA: Ballinger, 1983). The argument concerning the theoretical unworkability of socialism as an economically efficient system is discussed fully in Don Lavoie, *Rivalry and Central Planning: The Socialist Calculation Problem Reconsidered* (New York: Cambridge University Press, 1985). The current move toward privatization in the East and West gives us the practical support for the theoretical claims of those, such as Ludwig von Mises and Freidrich A. von Hayek who argue that public ownership and administration of resources lead to shortages, misallocation, poverty, etc. For why the economic case against collective economies is insufficient, see Machan, *Capitalism and Individualism.*
58. This point is of interest to our discussion of dignity, because underlying the idea of human dignity is the notion that people can choose to confront issues, follow

arguments, and learn by thinking through the points they may encounter. The assumption here is that ideas have consequences, whereas the assumption in Skinnerism and the bulk of less extreme social science is that ideas are mere products of the environment's action upon the human brain.

4

Should Business Be Regulated?

Zeal is very blind, or badly regulated, when it
encroaches upon the rights of others.

—Quenel

Regulation in Focus

In socialist countries government unabashedly—but honestly—declares its ownership (in the name of the people, of course) of all that human beings value. This, as we have suggested earlier, includes their labor. The Soviet Union and Eastern Germany were classic examples of such systems.

A somewhat different, less honest but no less insidious type of system is one we can only call fascism, whereby government allows individuals and companies to keep legal title to valued items, but regulates nearly all of what they would do with these. We are nearing such a system in the United States and other Western democracies. We might label these systems "democratic fascism." They are characterized by an overwhelming measure of government regulation of people's lives, especially their economic affairs.

The Scope of Government Regulation

The topic of government regulation of business concerns the enforcement by governments (federal, state, municipal) of standards, rules, and practices for the conduct of business. Government regulation has its most direct impact on those who produce, manufacture, sell, advertise, market, transport, and otherwise deal with the country's mostly privately traded goods and services—truck drivers, attorneys, barbers, doctors, pest exterminators, toy makers, fork-lift operators, plumbers, and so forth. Businesses may be regulated in what they may or may not sell, when they may sell some things, how they must manufacture some items, what conditions must be maintained at the workplace, how hiring and firing must be carried out, what may or may not be said in advertisements, what must be worn when traveling on a motorcycle, and so forth.

For example: An ordinance enacted by Westchester County, New York, in 1980 forced two owners to cease the sale of "drug paraphernalia," making it a misdemeanor for "any merchant or other person to knowingly sell, offer for sale or display a cocaine spoon, marijuana pipe, hashish pipe or any other drug-related paraphernalia." A federal appeals court in Manhattan upheld the law, saying it "may constitutionally be applied to prohibit the plaintiffs' sale of certain items clearly within the ordinance's definition of drug paraphernalia."[1]

For example: As of 1975, thirty-three states legally prohibited retail pharmacists from engaging in the advertisement of prescription prices.[2]

For example: The substance instant glue, which can bind human flesh, was used in the Vietnam War in emergency surgery. It is badly wanted by hospitals and often smuggled into the United States from Canada because it is banned by the Food and Drug Administration (FDA). The Minnesota Mining and Manufacturing Company (3M) recently discontinued its testing because the FDA continues to ban the substance.[3]

Government regulations such as these are in force throughout the United States and most so-called liberal democracies or welfare states— countries that are best regarded as mixed economies, combining the ingredients of a laissez-faire market with state planning. These systems tend to accept the institution of private property—or its legal equivalent, private title—in the means of production but do not permit full control of commercial activities along with such ownership and engage in elaborate intervention in the use and disposal of private property when it is related to commerce. Government regulation of business is one facet of such intervention.

There are, of course, different kinds of regulation, some bearing on business affairs more directly than others. But the distinctions are not set in concrete. For example, government regulation of such personal conduct as the consumption of certain drugs has an indirect effect on business because it regulates how such drugs can be sold—for example, by means of doctors' prescriptions. Again, government regulation may involve censorship, yet such regulation can also have a bearing on business, as when the United States Supreme Court held in 1981 that billboard advertising may be regulated, even prohibited, by various governmental bodies, except as it relates to political campaigns.[4]

Generally, in many liberal democracies, commerce and trade are regulated more vigorously than, for example, writing, speaking, and assembly. Still, governments often regulate businesses that engage in publishing, broadcasting, or public entertainment, thus obliterating any supposedly neat division between regulation of business and, for example, regulation of the arts.

It should be noted that government regulation is only one form of government intervention in commerce. Giving various industries like farming and automobile manufacturing subsidies or government loans, and prohibiting competition in some areas, such as utility services, are also forms of intervention. And government regulation often emerges alongside these other forms of intervention. When the numerous public utilities are regulated, part of this is just the price they pay for being protected monopolies.

From the legal point of view, the legitimacy of government regulation of commerce turns on the United States Constitution's commerce clause, which states the "Congress shall have Power.... [t]o regulate Commerce with foreign Nations, and among the several States, and with the Indian Tribes" (Article I, section 8, paragraph 3). The legal interpretation of this clause has varied, however. Walter F. Dodd observes in his widely known textbook on constitutional law:

> The primary purpose of the framers of the Constitution was to prevent state restrictions upon interests and foreign commerce. Our modern economy places an emphasis upon affirmative regulation by the national government.[5]

This means that while most of those who created the U.S. political and legal system wanted to promote the free flow of commerce—by disallowing the separate states of the Union to regulate interstate commerce by means, for example, of trade restrictions, tariffs, or price supports—eventually the federal government turned away from that goal. It will be useful to sketch the history of this change.[6]

A Brief History of Government Regulation

Contrary to popular generalizations, there has never been an era of pure laissez-faire capitalism, even in the history of the United States. Pure laissez-faire capitalism is that economic system in which there exists full legal recognition and protection of private property rights and of the right to trade goods and services owned privately by individuals or voluntarily associated groups (for example, partnerships, corporations). Abstractly conceived, pure laissez-faire capitalism implies unimpeded, absolute individual discretion on the part of property owners to sue, trade, or sell their property without government regulation, even in emergencies, wars, catastrophes, and so forth.[7] That is the form of capitalism we will not find in history. What we do find are more or less impure forms, where governments are not legally permitted to interfere with business, trade, finance, production, manufacture, employment, and other economic endeavors except in such rare and dire circumstances as wars, natural disasters, or civil disorders.

In either its pure or impure form, laissez-faire capitalism lets business do what it wants outside of such criminal conduct as assault, theft, and murder, and precludes the great bulk of government regulatory measures many citizens now take for granted. Policies such as mandatory, government-run unemployment insurance and retirement programs, government-imposed workers' compensation systems, and licensing of such professionals as physicians, psychologists, auto mechanics, pest exterminators—all these are an infringement upon the principles of laissez-faire. (So are, of course, various pro-business and industry measures of government, such as subsidies, price supports, and legally maintained monopolies.) At certain levels of discussion, much debate can ensue about just exactly what may and may not be done by government without upsetting the ideals of laissez-faire. For example, enactment of antitrust legislation has been advocated on grounds that it backs such aspects of laissez-faire as widespread competition. Do mandatory building codes and other measures that aim at safety, such as the requirement that drugs be thoroughly tested before being put on the market for sale, constitute an infringement on laissez-faire, or are they needed measures implicit in the government's role of protecting property rights? If some activities are inherently threatening or dangerous, would not a property-rights-oriented legal system require them to be held in check? (It is usually granted that laissez-faire capitalism would involve laws protecting and preserving the rights of life, liberty, and property, in as much as the last is supposed to either grow out of or indeed encompass the former.)[8]

With all this said, we can accept some portion of the popular idea that the United States enjoyed laissez-faire capitalism for several decades of its early history, especially when we compare it to other societies. Free enterprise is not just Fourth of July rhetoric but a prominent feature of the 1800s, and it still plays a considerable role in U.S. life. While several states have always practiced government intervention, most did so less in the early days of the Republic than either before its birth or in more recent decades—except, of course, with regard to the lives of black slaves and Native Americans, whose property rights were almost completely ignored with full legal sanction in various regions of the United States.[9]

If there is a time when the major legal change involving the instruction of government regulation itself occurred, it must be placed at a point in the spring of 1877. As the historian Jonathan R. T. Hughes tells it, at this time

> the U.S. Supreme Court, still officially sitting in its 1876 autumn term, handed down the fateful decision known collectively as the Granger Cases.... [T]he basic case, *Munn v. Illinois*, concerned the refusal of a Chicago warehouse firm, Munn and Scott, to apply for a state license and to have its service and charges controlled. The Court said that Munn and Scott must comply if they wanted to continue in that line of business.[10]

In the decision, one of the several grounds for government regulation is already clearly hinted at by the phrase "affected with a public interest." Later this and other notions will be discussed more fully, but here let us just note that though the decision marked a departure, even Chief Justice Morrison Waite observed that the power to regulate commerce was very much part of the tradition of government from which the United States emerged. Citing Lord Chief Justice Hale in *De Portibus Maris* (concerning seaports), written two hundred years prior to this ruling, Waite defended the position that "when...one devotes his property to a use in which the public has an interest, he, in effect, grants to the public an interest in that use, and must submit to be controlled by the public for the common good, to the extent of the interest he has thus created." Such control is well established in common law, Waite claimed—that very law "from whence came the [private property] right which the Constitution protects."[11]

As a matter, then, of our nation's heritage in English common law and because of regional practice, governmental regulation had always been a fact of U.S. economic life. Still, the 1877 decision placed on the federal law books a forceful and explicit interpretation of the U.S. Constitution. It is this forcefulness and explicitness, rather than the novelty of the developments of the time, that marks this period as so important in the history of government regulation in the United States.

Following the Waite opinion, matters took a fairly normal turn. Gradually state and federal bodies and agencies were established, such as the Interstate Commerce Commission in 1887. In our time the number of agencies at the various levels of government has climbed into the thousands. With the development of new forms of technology, new application of the various sciences in professional and in manufacturing enterprises, the institution of government regulation grew. Since lawmakers attempt to solve problems and judges sanction these attempts to a large extent on the basis of precedent and perceived need, this growth in government regulation should come as no surprise. Whether more is better in this case will concern us as we proceed.

Many people regard the era of President Franklin D. Roosevelt as the watershed marking the serious demise of laissez-faire capitalism in the United States. Again, this opinion is partly justified. Prior to the 1930s, at least the federal government tended to stay away from extensive government regulation and the U.S. Supreme Court did not accept many attempts at introducing the federal government into market endeavors. But the Great Depression was seen in large measure as the consequence of laissez-faire. At any rate, people were impatient and understandably panicky. Furthermore, the economic theories on the intellectual landscape gave little or no support to the economic wisdom and prospects of laissez-faire, especially as means to rescue the economy from the depression. But without the decisive legal precedent of 1877, and the common-law precedent cited by Justice Waite, the severe federalization of the U.S. economy that legitimized President Roosevelt's policies would not have been likely.

To know some of the history of its development is not yet to come to terms with the various arguments for or against government regulation of business. When a measure becomes law, it is rarely because of some one argument, or even one kind of argument, given in its support. Still, the acceptability of or need for some law, or its repeal, may very well be encouraged by ideas and ideals that can be supported or rejected by purportedly serious moral arguments. For example, the First Amendment, which gives legal protection to free expression of at least political and religious ideas, may have been enacted for various reasons, some of them merely emotional—for example, the fear of persecution. But certain ethical arguments would also be instrumental in giving such a measure backing. The view that truth is more likely to flourish if no ideas are suppressed by the authorities has served to support the First Amendment. This argument alludes to moral consideration by accepting that truth is very important and worthy of support. Anything so important ought to be provided institutional protection, and since free speech fosters the truth, free speech, too, must be given such protection in our basic legal document.

Similar ideas, more or less complicated, can be found backing or opposing various legal measures in the United States and in other cultures. Liberal democracies, as well as fascist, communist, monarchical, and tribal regimes, rest, in part, on people's ethical beliefs. This is true of the part of the U.S. legal system which is our topic, namely, government regulation of commerce.

A Noble Compromise?

The mixed economic systems of the Western world are reasonably viewed as attempts at an equitable compromise. This is to be achieved between the ideals of the right of everyone to individual liberty and a condition of general happiness. The latter is to be achieved by placing stress on regulating economic, commercial, or business affairs, and the former by insisting on a considerable degree of personal sovereignty. Of course, the welfare states of Western-type societies extend their concern for the well-being of people beyond mere "material" benefits, emphasizing the value of art, culture, psychological health, and the like. The attempt to prevent widespread alienation in the workplace, by regulating the employment relationship through such organizations as the National Labor Relations Board, is an example of going beyond mere material concerns. These states also extend the ideal of personal sovereignty to securing a considerable degree of freedom of trade, even while in general they aim at making sure that in an atmosphere of relative freedom of trade and vigorous business no one seriously lacks basic material provisions and some other kinds of support in life.

The ideal of the right to liberty, which the welfare state aspires to uphold, means (roughly) that in the running of one's own life, others must not intrude by the use of physical force or its threat. One's own life includes, variously, one's thinking, talking, and associating with willing others, work projects, commercial endeavors, and the disposal, by sale or by gift, of one's wealth. Classical liberalism, as has been noted already, has upheld the social value of the right to individual liberty, meaning that a person should have authority over his or her life, actions and property. This ideal has supported the promulgation of legal and social institutions that have provided official avenues of protest in cases when individual liberty was threatened.[12]

The most obvious legal exemplification of the spirit of liberalism outside of the idea of economic freedom is the right of a free press or, more broadly put, the right to freedom of personal expression and conscience: "Congress shall make no law respecting an establishment of religion, or prohibit the free exercise thereof; or abridging the freedom of speech, or of the press; or the right of the people peaceably to assemble, and to petition the Government for a redress of grievances." In the United States, the First Amendment is the most forthright restriction on the power of governments.

At first glance no conflict appears between the two ideals. Just one example will illustrate that this impression is not wholly reliable. In advertising their products, people in the business world are subjected to congressional direction—for instance, in the case of cigarette advertisements, which must include a message of warning about the dangers of smoking. Billboard advertising, too, has come under serious regulation by local governments, mainly for aesthetic purposes. In both cases some speech is regulated. And now that some corporations are beginning to include political and ideological messages in their advertisements, the commercial character of some speech is difficult to separate from the political, as ads from Getty, Mobil, Smith-Kline, and Citicorp illustrate. So where no compromise appears at first to be needed, we can see that indeed some very serious compromises could be involved.

Incidentally, one might think that the issue of government regulation could be resolved simply by choosing between the two leading political ideologies presently on the U.S. scene, namely, liberalism and conservatism. Alas, matters are not that simple.

Contemporary liberals, who tend in the main to favor freedom of speech, civil liberties, and intellectual pluralism while also favoring regulation of business have nevertheless often supported government regulation of advertising speech. Again, (modern) liberals have at times not tolerated freedom of expression as when they demanded the removal of the Little Black Sambo figure from front yards and protested speeches of some of their more extreme opponents, such as the late William Shockley and Ambassador Jeanne Kirkpatrick, as well as lobbied for banning pornography that demeans women. Conservatives—who tend to accept the free market as a workable economic order but find it objectionable to allow full personal discretion in areas such as artistic expression, entertainment, education, and sexual relations—have also argued for government regulation of the market in pornography and obscenity. They often disapprove of what to them appears, correctly or not, morally odious free trade—for example, they wish to prohibit prostitution, topless entertainment, and the sale and purchase of "adult" books.

Thus no simple distinction can be made between civil liberties, on the one hand, and economic liberties on the other, and the full range of the problems surrounding governmental regulation spans political ideologies, as is shown by the U.S. legal tradition. Explicit statements of the U.S. Supreme Court and those who are regarded as intellectual supporters of the welfare state, both liberals and conservatives, give clear expression to the idea that what a decent society must do is to reach a compromise between the values of liberty and welfare. (One perhaps should say that liberals are more interested in an economic welfare state, conservatives in a spiritual one, depending, probably, on what realm of life, the economic or spiritual, they regard ultimately as more fundamental.)

This is why the compromise that seems at first to be a relatively amicable one, involving giving up extreme cases of exercising the right to freedom in some areas so as to guarantee some reasonable degree of welfare, turns out to be a more troublesome one, after all. Indeed, in the last analysis—as I argue in this work—the compromise is impossible without very serious breaches of integrity and some other approach is more advisable—to wit, leaving the right to liberty to be fully protected and leave the task of achieving the general welfare to the nonpolitical ("private") sectors of society.

Definitions and Distinctions

To regulate an activity is to adjust and steady its motion at various stages for specific purposes. For example, government regulation aims at the adjustment of people's conduct, and when government regulates business, it aims to adjust people's commercial conduct so as to serve certain ends deemed desirable via the political process. But some regulation involves a crucial ingredient not involved in other sorts of regulation, namely, the use of the threat of force. The Better Business Bureau, the various consumer watchdog groups, and "action reporters" may well attempt and even succeed in the regulation of business. They could influence merchants, manufacturers, advertisers, and the like to do as desired. Governments regulate by issuing legally enforceable edicts.

Government Regulation

Here an initial distinction is important. Government uses or threatens force in many areas, including the criminal law. (Some would hold, of course, that one is being forced to comply when an insurance company withholds its coverage or raises the price for it, but this is sophistry; the government forces one to do things by threatening conviction, fine, and perhaps incarceration. That is the kind of force that is of political consequence.) The difference between plain law enforcement and regulation by government centers on the fact that the latter places limits on conduct deemed generally legitimate. The criminal law makes some things illegal to do. Certain aims are not to be pursued, and the law states these in general terms: the killing of another human being, stealing from others, assaulting them, defrauding them, and so forth. In regulation, however, it is conduct that is generally accepted as quite permissible, such as the manufacture of toys, the sale of cars, the lending of money, the building of houses, and so forth, that is circumscribed by rules and standards, which government will enforce. When we speak of regulation, it is the sort practiced by governments that will be referred to, not what may come about by way of persuasion, boycotts, or self-regulation. Occasional overlaps no doubt occur, as when merely to discuss the possibility of regulating some business leads to the reform of the way that business is carried out. But the distinction is generally sound.

Some Implications of the Definition

Government regulation of people's economic activities involves, essentially, giving legally enforceable guidelines and direction to what are regarded as generally proper, legitimate commercial endeavors in a human community. Gaining compliance with such guidance and direction can involve measures ranging from the suggestive to the compulsory. In the last analysis, government regulation can rely on the legal authority of government to use force to implement its edicts. Whenever the achievement of, or at least the attempt to achieve, some purpose is deemed extremely important, the unique instrument, employed by government with legal authority, is called into service: the use, or threat of the use of force (for example, incarceration, fines, censure). Those who refuse to comply with the law as they carry on with their economic activities can be subjected to arrest, punishment, or forfeiture (being deprived of the right to carry on).

All this is generally expected of legal measures in a society; they will be enforced. Murder, assault, and theft are deemed such serious misdeeds that to discourage them, and respond to them when they occur, severe punishment is called for. Mere verbal rebuke, ostracism, or even concerted boycott would be insufficient in response to such actions. This would be to do too little. On the other hand, if someone fails to honor the mores and traditions of the community, for example, by being crude in personal habits, the behavior may evoke resentment and ostracism, but the individual will not be incarcerated or penalized with severe fines. This would be to do too much.

Government regulation of business is clearly deemed to be a needed official response to some otherwise legitimate activities. Such regulation addresses important social issues, as the more severe type of human response is involved in coping with those who fail to comply: offenders are fined, imprisoned, and so forth. The crucial question for us is whether to allow such regulation to do too much or whether to forgo it would be to do too little. More precisely, is government regulation of business, with its punitive implications, a morally justifiable way to deal with whatever is regarded as undesirable in society's economic affairs?

An historical analogy might make this general question more intelligible. At one time the federal government was enlisted in the effort to stem the consumption and abuse of alcohol. Prohibition was the result and for a while the federal government engaged in the extensive use of its power to accomplish this purpose. It was widely believed to be justified for the government to undertake this task. Subsequently, for various reasons, the government was ordered, via the repeal of the law authorizing its actions against brewers, wine makers, liquor sellers, and so forth, to cease its policy of prohibition. The reasons for believing that government should prohibit alcohol production and consumption are not at issue, only that it was widely believed that it was justified in doing so. But that widely held belief was later rejected.

Perhaps government regulation of people's economic affairs is unjustified, in general, as was true in the case of Prohibition in particular, even though it is widely accepted and believed to be justified. Perhaps the commerce clause of the U.S. Constitution should be repealed. Or perhaps the practice is indeed quite proper, representing neither too little nor too much by way of punitive regulation of commerce. It is to these matters that we will turn in the next section.

Morality and Regulation

It was noted earlier that other possible reasons for government regulation can exist besides moral ones. Historians of business, labor, and law could contribute to our understanding of the issues before us. But here the focus will be on the moral support for and objections to government regulation.

Moral Arguments for Government Regulation

Debates over government regulation sometimes flounder because of a failure to distinguish between what may be called management and regulation. Management can be understood as all those rules and directives that aim at guiding the utilization of public or state properties and funds. For example, in national forests some companies are allowed to engage in mining. But the companies do not own the mines; the public does. And the Bureau of Land Management decides the way the companies must conduct themselves in those areas. When governments administer the rules of highway travel and impose speed limits, place restrictions on the use of cars and motorcycles, forbid the use of bicycles, and so forth, this is not so much government regulation as the management or administration of the publicly owned spheres in a society. When, however, government sets down the rules for the advertising of eyeglasses or the manufacture of toys, no such public spheres and ownership are involved. There is no legal property right that government or the public asserts and has established in the manufacturing plants or the commodities being produced.

This is an important distinction. Ordinarily if someone owns something, that person is understood to have the right of use and disposal over the thing owned.[13] I can give away my tie, my home, or even destroy these if no one else is unavoidably intruded upon as I do so. If I lend you my money, I can put restrictions on its use, conditions under which you are able to obtain it from me, and so forth. When a government lends money to students and requires that this money not be used in such objectionable ways as excluding blacks from enjoying the benefits, it is engaging not so much in government regulation of education as in the management or administration of the public treasury. Most affirmative action programs, whereby a government requires colleges, universities, firms engaged in business with the government, and government bodies themselves to seek to aid members of groups that have suffered injustices in the past, are again not so much cases of government regulation as self-regulation or the adoption of administrative rules for running the government itself and the funds paid into it by all citizens.[14]

True, in popular discussions this distinction is not often made. That is partly because people tend to lump together support for (and opposition to) government taking any sort of jurisdiction over some areas of concern in society, whether government outright nationalizes the area or merely regulates it. But different arguments either support or raise objections to government ownership, on the one hand, and government regulation, on the other. It may be that government should not appropriate many of the spheres that it in fact has appropriated, but that does not prove that it should not regulate these spheres. Perhaps the forests should not be owned by the government, yet it could be true that government should regulate what people and companies do in privately owned forests. As I have noted in an earlier discussion in this work, the Federal

Communications Commission administers the use of the broadcast air-waves—the electromagnetic spectrum. The federal government acquired this realm by senatorial declaration in 1927, and broadcasters such as NBC, ABC, and CBS are merely tenants who must reapply for their leases periodically. They do not own the frequencies on which they operate. And the FCC is charged, by Congress, with the responsibility of administering this public property in the public interest. To speak precisely, therefore, much of so-called "government regulation" of broadcasting is the administration or management of public property for the benefit of the public, "in the public interest." Such measures as the "fairness doctrine" or the "equal time rule," both under constant criticism from broadcasters, amount to what in the law is called restrictive covenants—conditions placed by the lessor on the lessee regarding the occupancy of what is being leased. Questions can be raised whether governments should ever own airwaves, roads, parks, beaches, forests, or the postal system, but these are distinct from questions about whether government regulation of privately owned businesses is morally justified.[15]

The distinction between government regulation and government management or administration is not always clearly manifested. To show legal basis for government regulatory activities, defenders often make their case by reference to (alleged) state interest. For example, in opposition to efforts in the 1980s to compel restaurateurs in California to establish smoking and nonsmoking areas, restaurant owners protested on grounds that this would be an invasion of their private property rights. Advocates of the measure noted, in turn, that restaurants are located on public streets and are licensed by the government. This means that restaurants are unavoidably connected with publicly owned spheres. From this some would infer that regulating them is merely an extension of the government's responsibility to manage its own spheres properly.

However difficult it is to disentangle private from public property, this kind of argument would render the private-public distinction entirely specious. No area of human life could be seen as protected from government management or administration, Bill of Rights or no Bill of Rights, if the justification for government intervention turned on an activity's being connected with a "publicly owned sphere." After all, when a person criticizes the U.S. government, advocates communism or fascism, or rails against the FBI, the CIA, or even the practice of government regulation, that person is probably in a place that can only be reached by driving or walking the public streets.

There is one final distinction that it will be useful to keep in mind. Various government regulatory bodies actually engage in the administration of fairly distinctive judicial disputes as well. Not only the practice of brokerage firms as they advertise their services or trade stocks, but outright fraud and embezzlement could come under the jurisdiction of the Securities and Exchange Commission. Rules against insider trading—taking advantage of special knowledge for personal gain or the advantage of one's clients—are different from outright fraud, yet both are dealt with by the SEC. The Federal Trade Commission, too, has assumed jurisdiction in the handling of commercial fraud alongside its purely regulatory functions, such as setting rules for the conduct of mail-order shopping.[16]

It was important to stress as precisely as possible the question at issue. What needs to be examined is whether any kind of genuine government regulation of any business activity is morally justifiable, at least under normal circumstances. With any social norm there can be exceptions to the most advisable policy in unusual circumstances; we will consider later on whether such exceptions might be morally tolerable even if, in usual circumstances, government regulation of business is unjustified. If some genuine regulation can be morally defended, as the normal policy in the continuing socioeconomic life of a human community, then there cannot be anything wrong in principle with regulating business. On the other hand, if no regulation can be justified as the normal approach to handling problems, then such regulation may well be simply wrong in principle.

Various arguments are available to those who favor government regulation. Though not all of them can be examined here, those that will be are among the most important. All have a common structure, which can be generally characterized as follows:

1. There are certain moral values and principles, these arguments contend, that ought to be respected by a society's economic agents and entrepreneurs.

2. These values or principles, it is claimed, can only be respected if some aspects of a society's economic activity are regulated.

3. Thus, these arguments conclude, some aspects of a society's economic activity ought to be regulated.

Proponents of regulation can differ over what principles or values a society's economic life ought to foster as well as what aspects of this life ought to be regulated. However, all proponents of regulation agree that it is only by having recourse to regulation that the values or principles they favor can be adequately respected. All defenses of regulation thus have both a normative and a practical or factual component. Normatively they insist on affirming that certain values are worth pursuing or that the observation of certain principles is to be made compulsory for moral reasons—even if this requires limitation on liberty, including business activities, by means of regulation. The practical component consists in the claim that, as a matter of fact, these values or principles will be adequately respected only if government regulates business in certain respects.

The strength of any defense of regulation clearly depends on the credibility of both the normative and the factual components. If a given defense fails to make a persuasive case for the values or principles it favors, it will fail as a defense for normative reasons. If, on the other hand, it fails to show that, as a matter of fact (judging by past history and sound theory), regulation is necessary if these values or principles are to be respected adequately, it will fail because of its practical unfeasibility. As we shall see in what follows, the leading defenses of regulation fail sometimes for one, sometimes for the other, and sometimes for both reasons.

Three defenses can be distinguished (although others might also be mentioned): (1) the defense based on ideals; (2) the defense based on utility; and (3) the defense based on rights. Each will be considered, in the order just given.

The Defense Based on Ideals

One of the earliest and most influential defenses of government intervention, including regulation, is offered (as noted in the previous chapter) by the economist John Maynard Keynes (1883–1946). Conceiving, as he did, of a free-market system along lines usually attributed to Herbert Spencer[17]—that is, as a rather crude version of social Darwinism, where only "the strong" survive—Keynes gave the following characterization of laissez-faire. The idea, he said, implies that "there must be no mercy or protection for those who embark their capital or their labor in the wrong direction. It is a method of bringing the most successful profit-makers to the top by a ruthless struggle for survival, which selects the most efficient. It does not count the cost of struggle, but looks only to the benefits of the final result which are assumed to be lasting and permanent, once it has been attained. The object of life being to crop the leaves off the branches up to the greatest possible height, the likeliest way of achieving this end is to leave the giraffes with the longest necks to starve out those whose necks are shorter."[18]

Hyperbole aside, this passage suggests a clear moral argument in favor of abandoning laissez-faire. The moral reason is that the unregulated free market lacks valuable human sentiments, that such a method of arranging a community's economic affairs fosters callousness or insensitivity toward the plight of those who fail in the economic struggle or who, for one reason or another, are unable to take part. A lack of compassion for one's competitors may be acceptable in the jungle but not in human society. Morally, people who are sensitive and compassionate are better people than those who are insensitive and callous. Since these human ideals are destroyed by unregulated business, and since the way to foster them is to regulate it, such regulation is justified.

Does the unregulated free market in fact lack compassion and foster callousness toward those who fail in the economic struggle or who cannot take part? To a large extent, this is a historical claim, one that is not easy to test. Certainly by many popular accounts, whatever version of laissez-faire capitalism existed in England and the United States during the early 1880s did produce vast numbers of hungry, overworked, and disheartened people.

Throughout the markets of these societies there were booms and busts involving unemployment, financial crises, bankruptcies. There was also, in the midst of widespread misery, opulence of such magnitude as to be morally offensive. Granting these large disparities in the quality of life—and ignoring the fact that before the era of laissez-faire began people in general fared much worse and many died before they could experience unemployment and financial crises—it is difficult to determine whether laissez-faire capitalism was the cause.

Serious scholarly disagreement exists on the topic, and Keynes's opinions are not universally shared among social and economic historians. For example, while many attribute the phenomenon of the "robber barons" (monopolistic business tycoons who wielded enormous economic power over others who were economically dependent upon them, such as workers and neighboring small businesses) to laissez-faire, others attribute the robber baron's ascendancy to the fact that laissez-faire was not pure enough.[19]

It was government intervention, not the workings of the free market, that helped these people attain their exclusive economic power. It was government dispensations, in the form of special protection to some against the forces of competition, that gave privileged protection to the barons' wealth and thus enabled them to engage in monopolistic practices, thereby driving competitors to the brink of disaster. The railroads, for example, gained enormous power as a result of the earliest federal subsidy program. This program not only made it unnecessary for the people in the industry to raise their own capital through normal business channels; it also allowed several of the lines to forgo bargaining with landowners for rights-of-way because the government gave the owners money from the federal treasury and exercised the right of eminent domain—taking for public use—on behalf of the railroads. Such government protectionism was, of course, carried out in part because government officials believed that the railroads were doing a valuable public service—building a transcontinental line, for instance. Nevertheless, the prior government intervention distorted the laissez-faire character of the society sufficiently to call into serious question Keynes's picture.

Neither must the hardships often associated with industrial capitalism, especially during its early days—child labor, sweat shops, long working days, unsanitary working conditions, repetitive work, lack of adequate health facilities and safety provisions—be laid at the door of laissez-faire capitalism. Only if it could be shown that government regulation, or some more or less socialized market, would have eliminated or lessened these hardships at that time would there be justice in identifying the free market, even in its compromised form, as the cause, in contrast to simple underdevelopment, scarcity, and the problems inherited from feudal and mercantilist eras. But there is evidence—scholarship, at least—that disputes that early industrial capitalism, with its partial laissez-faire structure, fared worse in these respects than did other social systems at the time and, especially, earlier. And in comparison to existing alternative economic systems in our own time, the more or less free-market capitalist systems of Western industrial societies appear to be in better shape than all others.

Finally, even if it is admitted that laissez-faire will produce some cases of neglect of the helpless and the weak, whether government regulation should be introduced to remedy this depends in part on whether such regulation will in fact produce the needed remedies without producing comparable problems. This point is often expressed by reference to the oft-purported exchange of market failure for political failures. Many economists (for example, Sam Peltzman, Thomas Gale More, and Milton Friedman) claim that on the whole, the measurable costs of government regulation, including the estimated loss of lives, injuries produced, and labor and capital expended, exceed its estimable benefits—greater safety of the drugs actually allowed on the market, better health for the workers who do obtain jobs, more security for investors who do employ brokers, and so forth. Thus despite problems with laissez-faire, government regulation does not offer an adequate solution.

The preceding objections contest the practical elements of Keynes's criticism and suggested alternative. The normative point Keynes makes concerning the moral intolerability of a system that proposes "to leave the giraffes with the longest necks to starve out those whose necks are shorter" may also be contested. Notice, first, that nothing in principle prevents people in a laissez-faire system from lending a helping hand to the unfortunate or the helpless. Because such a system respects the ideal of liberty in general, it respects that ideal in this regard also, and it is highly questionable whether, under an essentially democratic system of government, anything better could be achieved by political coercion. Charity and benevolence, much extolled by Keynes, are not foreign to laissez-faire capitalism, to judge by available statistics.[20]

Notice, next, that Keynes mischaracterizes the "losers" in the marketplace. First, the competition in the market is not like that in a boxing ring, where (normally) there is only one winner and one loser, but rather like that in a marathon race. Between the one at the end and the one up front, there are as many positions as there are participants, many bunched together very close to the front, others a bit behind, some alone in the middle, and so forth. Second, those who do fall far behind are not all "helpless victims." Some are careless, negligent, lazy, slothful, overcome with a greed that sabotages their prudence, or otherwise "victims" of their own character flaws.

The analogy with the jungle makes it appear that in human societies those who are losers do not deserve their fate, because the jungle houses dumb animals who are victims of their fate—their genes, the environment, the comparative physical advantage of their fellow beasts, and so forth. But among human beings another factor needs to be considered. Human beings are capable of making good and bad choices in their conduct, and they are not helpless when they make the bad ones or the good ones. While no doubt some are unfortunate, indeed totally unprepared—for example, those who are severely crippled, utterly deprived, or abjectly mistreated (sometimes by fellow citizens, sometimes by family, sometimes by the government itself)—most others are probably better regarded as capable of making the effort needed for a good showing in "the struggle for survival." Those who can make the effort but fail to do so do not deserve the compassion Keynes seems to believe everyone who fails to succeed deserves. Third, even if it is true that some who fail are helpless and it is the moral responsibility of others to help them, there are serious moral objections against requiring that assistance be given under the threat of force. In morality it is not generally possible that any act of compassion, kindness, generosity, honesty, decency, and so forth be undertaken involuntarily or under coercion. Rather, moral conduct must be undertaken as a matter of conscience and free choice; otherwise the act loses its moral worth.

A society that forces its citizens, under the threat of punishment, to help the less fortunate, is less, not more, compassionate. Even granting, then (in concert with Keynes), that compassion is a noble human trait, it does not follow that coercive regulation of human behavior fosters its development. Indeed, just the opposite conclusion should be reached.

It might also be observed here that a free society does not in the least have to take the shape that Keynes assumes it must. There is no requirement, only the freedom, to engage in constant competition in such a society. Also, while it may be true that competition in the economic realm is valuable—involving, as it does, the seeking of more efficient production of goods and services that human beings need and want—it does not follow that competition needs to or will be exported into other realms (science, art, family life, friendship, neighborliness, and so forth). With sufficient pedagogy concerning this matter, the free society would very likely present a balanced picture concerning competition, not the extreme one Keynes puts forth. After all, human beings are able to keep quite diverse approaches to life in operation as it is. Unless they are motivated solely by the desire to win over others—which is palpable nonsense—there is no reason to think that commercialism will overtake the world with the institutionalization of full free markets.[21]

The Utilitarian Defense

In response to the deficiencies of the defense based on ideals, it might be argued that what matters is what people do, not why they do it. If one person contributes to another out of compassion or generosity, then the presence of these motives makes that person morally admirable, no doubt, but "the virtue of the agent" should be kept distinct from "the virtue of the act"; that is, appraising the morality of what we do (the acts we perform) should be kept distinct from appraising the morality of why we do it (our motives or intention). That much granted, what is crucial to the defense of government regulation of business, it might be claimed, is a standard that evaluates acts, not motives.

The Principle of Utility provides a standard of this kind. The morality of what we do is to be determined, according to this principle, by the overall effects this has on the welfare or happiness of those affected by the outcome. On this view, then, government regulation of business would be justified if such regulation brought about better consequences than would result in its absence. In principle, a utilitarian could argue that government should regulate everything, if this were optimizing (that is, if unchecked regulation produced the best results, all things considered). In practice, however, those enamored of the Principle of Utility take a more selective position, arguing only that some, not all, human activities should be regulated by government. The contemporary economist Kenneth Arrow is representative of this more restricted utilitarian position, and his views may be taken as a working example of the utilitarian defense of government regulation.

Like other economists, Arrow tends to eschew making explicit appeals to normative principles and takes a quasi-utilitarian approach to questions of policy decisions. This approach measures the desirability of any given policy in terms of the contribution it makes to the maximum satisfaction of desires in a society. Since most economists tend to assume that value judgments are meaningful only if they refer to something measurable, the theoretical ideal called Pareto-optimality, after the Italian economist Vilfredo Pareto (1848–1923), looms large in the background of their thought. According to this ideal, a society has achieved maximum satisfaction of desires if no one can be made better off without thereby making someone else worse off, the judgment of "better off" and "worse off" to be determined by consulting the preferences of the individuals involved. That is, each individual is the sole and final judge of what is valuable for that individual. Although no one supposes that this ideal of maximum satisfaction will ever be fully realized, the idea that it should guide public policy is quite prominent. Given this approach, what people value is what they prefer, and because what they prefer is measurable by determining how they behave, statements about what each person values are meaningful and conformable. There is, then, no theoretical objection to the utilitarian standard of Pareto-optimality as a bona fide standard for assessing the moral wisdom of alternative policies. Therefor, all that is necessary to defend government regulation by reference to this standard is to show that regulation will produce results that are closer to achieving Pareto-optimality than the results that would be obtained without it. Arrow evidently believes that this is true sometimes in the case of government regulation. In his essay, "Two Cheers for Government Regulation," he writes:

> For various reasons, it has long been a staple argument among economists that the resulting allocation [in private sector or free market], while efficient in many areas, will fail in some. The most obvious are the goods that serve society as a whole—defense, justice, police, most roads....More broadly, there are...cases in which public intervention, not necessarily expenditure, is necessary to change the way in which resources are used. Take the example of environmental hazards, particularly air- and waterborne pollution. Dumping wastes in a stream may ruin fisheries; this loss should, in a proper economic accounting, be charged against the dumper, but it is impractical to do so. Thus the public must intervene in some way, either by charging the dumper for the costs imposed on others or by regulations. The effects of pollution fall not merely on production but also on comfort, health, and life....I think that while regulation has gone too far or been misdirected in some areas—such as occupational safety—it has probably not gone far enough in those of chemical handling and waste disposal.[22]

When Arrow mentions that the private sector makes efficient allocation possible in many areas but not in others, the measure of efficiency for him is the degree to which Pareto-optimality has been achieved—that is, whether the market, given reasonable estimates, has resulted in greater satisfaction of aggregate desires than would result otherwise. This condition can be reached without coercion in most areas, in Arrow's view, but not in the cases of "defense, justice, police, most roads"; in their cases Pareto-optimality justifies government intervention. And the same is true in cases of "environmental hazards, particularly air- and water-borne pollution."

These defenses of government regulation misfire. Arrow views defense, justice, and police as "the goods that serve society as a whole" and thinks that these goods are better provided by governments than by free enterprise. Though some economists would dispute even this, the central point to notice is that these goods do not appear to be ordinary economic goods at all, even though some economic problems and activities may be associated with securing them.

One simple way to make this clearer is to recall that defense, justice, and police are actually presupposed in the very conception of a free economy; that is, a free market is not possible without those who take part in it agreeing voluntarily to have these goods in place. Defense, justice, and police are not products of the free market, but conditions that make it possible—for example, since that is how property rights are secured and trade is made possible. It cannot be an objection to the free market, any more than it can be an argument for government regulation of business in the market, to maintain that the goods that are necessary for the market are not themselves efficiently supplied by the market.

As I just noted, a free market presupposes a system of private property rights, and thus a system of justice conceived along certain lines (that is, by reference to a given theory of individual human rights). The government of a laissez-faire capitalist society is established in part to uphold this system of justice, to defend it from foreign aggression, and to enforce, via the police, its edicts (for example, to arrest thieves or violators of property rights). Without this system—in other words, the "goods" Arrow speaks of—no free market is even possible (except accidentally).

An objection to Arrow's thesis, then, would be that of course the market is inefficient in doing what it would not even embark on doing since the free market presupposes the doing of that thing for its own operations. (It might be noted that the securing of the goods Arrow lists first—defense, justice, police—is not an economic or commercial but a political problem, a problem, as one might naturally put it, of eternal vigilance.)

But aside from these political "goods," what about "most roads... environmental hazards," etc.? Is it a fact that these goods could not be efficiently produced by the market? Perhaps we cannot really know, though some precedent exists for the idea, both in practice and in theory.[23] Even if roads could not be produced on the scale presently available, however, it is questionable whether the cause of this is something inefficient about the market. Given the massive pollution that automobile travel has created, and given that governments (from local to federal) have built most of the roads, partly as a matter of encouraging automobile travel, the question is not academic. It is entirely arguable that had the free market been left to produce roads without government subsidies—in barring ones needed for law enforcement and national security—while some people might not have been so readily accommodated, on pure Pareto-optimality grounds the result would have been efficient enough.

As to the issue of managing the environment, here we encounter the problem of mixing government regulation with government management of public resources. The air, lakes, rivers, oceans, beaches, and so forth are not privately owned, even where they could be (sometimes because of egalitarian measures intended to redistribute their availability). Free-market-oriented environmentalists have argued that any time private property rights can be legally established, the market is more efficient than regulation would be, although the point is difficult to prove and I will not attempt to do so here. Alternative approaches to regulation, such as tort law, criminal charges for dumping wastes, criminal liability, malpractice law, and similar legal measures, would have to be considered and contrasted with the familiar regulatory mechanisms in order to see whether Arrow's claim about efficiency is true. Where property rights are not feasible—for example, in the atmosphere—Arrow's recommendation seems sound, but not for purely utilitarian reasons. Rather it is because no "proper economic accounting" is possible without some kind of government management in such realms. So-called regulation would in such cases be a mere substitute for desirable but unfeasible judicial handling of problems of allocation, use, usurpation of rights, and so forth. From the utilitarian viewpoint, then, the practical points Arrow offers do not provide compelling support for the ordinary sort of government regulation. Arrow himself seems to notice this when he says, in the passage just quoted, that "regulation has gone too far or been misdirected in some areas—such as occupational safety."

To this point we have confined our criticism of Arrow's ideas to the factual component in his position—the claim that government intervention produces results that better approximate Pareto-optimality than would the result produced by the workings of the free market. Let us now consider the normative component Arrow and many other economists implicitly accept, namely, the utilitarian standard of Pareto-optimality. The attractiveness of this view for social scientists should be clear enough.

What we are to aim at is maximum satisfaction of preferences, with the preferences to be determined by how people behave when they are given the freedom to choose what they want. Public policy decisions, when based on the preferences people reveal through their behavior, give such normative decisions, we are supposed to believe, a basis in fact.

There are theoretical problems at the root of the idea of Pareto-optimality (for example, whether it is meaningful to make interpersonal preference comparisons). We shall not pursue these matters. Here it is enough to observe that, even without an extensively worked-out set of alternatives it seems highly questionable that morality should come to no more than "giving people what they want." Suppose that people prefer to purchase the latest fad items instead of fostering education, medical facilities, the arts, or science? Would it not seem odd for public policy to be directed toward the production of fad items rather than education and health care? Pareto-optimality puts too much trust in the wisdom of individual preference.

In reply it could be said that it is not just what people happen to prefer that is decisive. As Arrow states, "When it come to economic rather than moral goods, there is no legitimate criterion of policy other than giving people what they want, or should want if they are properly informed."[24] Thus, even assuming that most people happened to prefer fad items to arts and letters, it would not follow, given this kind of utilitarian approach to assessing government policy, that the government ought to accede to the preferences of the masses. For though the majority want these things, it is, by Arrow's assumptions, clearly arguable that they would not want them, or should not, if they were properly informed.

But now there is a problem, namely, whether we can possibly measure or establish what people would or, especially, should want if they were properly informed. It looks quite hopeless, judged on the methodological grounds at issue (that is, given the assumption that preferences—values—must be quantifiable and thus measurable, if they are to be meaningful). One looks for a theory to measure "what people would or should want, if..." and finds none. (Even a theory as to what people do want is not as simple as some economists seem to assume—for example, when judged in terms of the notion of revealed preferences, that is, of what people actually do when no one forces them to do anything or restricts their options. Yet there is considerable debate about whether the economist's specification of such "freely chosen" conduct is ever adequate to an understanding of what people want. Some argue, for example, that people may want both a healthy environment and a lifestyle that prevents this, expressing the first via political activism, the second via the market. But what do they want then?)

Moreover, since the one virtue generally conceded to the free market is that it communicates information better than any centralized system of economic management would make possible (for example, between consumers and producers),[25] one must also wonder what more information one could reasonably hope to have so as to provide "proper" information.

Suppose these criticisms could be overcome—for example, by reference to some idea that what individuals "would or should want, if..." can be determined by having experts manage the regulatory process. Such a defense of government regulation based on what people would or should want, if fully informed, is almost certain to open a paternalistic Pandora's box, one with implications that clash with many values and principles that even avid supporters of government regulation of business would not wish to sacrifice, for example, civil liberties that disallow search and seizure or censorship and prior restraint.

Already quite a few government regulatory measures are seen to be a threat to such cherished values as privacy. Banking regulations, for instance, require that financial institutions make a report of any transaction involving checks over ten thousand dollars so that the government may inspect the financial records of citizens who have not committed any crimes. City building inspectors are allowed to enter private property with no need of a warrant to investigate whether a home is built in conformity to the building code. Various businesses are subject to on-the-spot, unannounced inspection by agents of OSHA. And, of course, the concern with drug abuse has led to the most extraordinary measures in police actions against drug dealers and users.[26]

While many supporters of government regulation dismiss such concerns as alarmist, it is quite arguable that such powerful tools in the hands of government are always a strong temptation for abuse and should not be placed at the disposal of governments in the first place.

The Defense Based on (Positive) Rights

A utilitarian defense of government regulation of business, as we saw in the preceding paragraph, has implications that clash with well-considered beliefs about the worth, integrity, and autonomy of the individual. These notions—individual worth, integrity, and autonomy—are allied, both historically and logically, with the idea that people have basic moral rights, including, for example, the rights to life, liberty, and the pursuit of happiness. None of these ideas are simple, and the philosophical case for recognizing the validity of the worth of persons and individual rights is not simple either. I shall have more to say on these matters later.

The essential point to note at this juncture is how the idea of the worth and rights of the individual simply cannot find a place in the standard utilitarian cost-benefit analysis favored by many economists. Benefits, according to this approach, are to be measured by what people prefer (or would prefer, if properly informed), while costs are reducible to what people would prefer to do without or avoid if they were properly informed. The kind of value (or worth) individuals have, however, is not just one benefit competing among other benefits. Your worth as a person is not reducible to whether you happen to be the object of my preference, or of anyone's preference. Your value as a person, in other words, is not to be thought of in terms of whether you are liked, admired, wanted, or valued by anyone. As a person, therefore, the kind of value you have is not reducible to the preferences of others, so that your value will not and cannot show up in any cost-benefit analysis.

The public policy scientist—and former Federal Trade Commission staffer—Steven Kelman has been a persistent critic of cost-benefit analyses for this very reason. (He is, however, a defender of government regulation based on the kind of purportedly justified paternalism we have considered in the previous chapter.) Consider the case where some people are injured or harmed by others. "Since the costs of injury are borne by its victims," Kelman contends, "while its benefits are escaped by its perpetrators, simple cost-benefit calculations may be less important than more abstract conceptions of justice, fairness and human dignity."[27] Developing this theme more fully, Kelman writes as follows:

> We would not condone a rape even if it could be demonstrated that the rapist derived enormous pleasure from his actions, while the victim suffered in only small ways. Behind the conception of "rights" is the notion that some concept of justice, fairness or human dignity demands that individuals ought to be able to perform certain acts, despite the harm to others, and ought to be protected against certain acts, despite the loss this causes to the would-be perpetrator. Thus we undertake no cost-benefit analysis of the effects of freedom of speech or trial by jury before allowing them to continue.[28]

The introduction of the ideas of individual dignity and rights in place of cost-benefit analysis means that government regulation of business, if it is morally proper, cannot be justified in the way utilitarians assume. Might it be justified if human rights and dignity are taken into account? Kelman, for one, thinks so, as does Joan Claybrook, former National Highway Transportation Safety administrator: "What about the rights of individuals to breathe clean air, to drink clean water, to secure drugs or food that do not have unnecessary side effects or cause illness, to have a job that does not foster cancer, to drive an automobile without unnecessary exposure to death or crippling injury? These are rights of the citizenry which regulation is designed to defend."[29] In other words, if an unregulated market would violate these rights of the citizenry, then the market should be regulated. And the market should be regulated, not because doing so will bring about better consequences for everyone affected by the outcome (the utilitarian cost-benefit approach), and not because such regulation will foster certain preferred human character traits (the defense based on ideals approach), but because regulation is necessary to ensure that consumer rights are not crushed under the wheels of unbridled free enterprise.

Two questions jump out at us here. The first is whether people have the sort of (positive) rights championed by those who argue for regulation based on rights—the right to "jobs that do not foster cancer," for example. The second is whether, assuming that they have them, there is any reason to believe that an unregulated market would violate these rights, or violate them to any greater extent than a government-regulated market. This latter question is a question of fact—though a difficult one. The former is a normative question. Thus, our assessment of the rights defense of regulation parallels the structure of the earlier discussions of the utilitarian and ideal defenses. The factual question will be examined first.

Does the marketplace violate individual rights? The answer depends on what rights individuals in fact have. Kelman and Claybrook seem to hold that individuals have rights to be spared all sorts of mishaps and protected against all manner of risks. This doctrine of positive rights— rights to be provided with benefits by others—is highly disputable, a point explored more fully below. However, even if they are correct in supposing that we have such rights, it is unlikely that government regulation is the best way to protect them. In general, there is no reason to assume that the motivations of people in government, from legislators to those who implement and enforce policy, are any more free from vulnerability to temptations than are the motivations of market agents. The "profit motive" is often said to induce great predilection for negligence and lack of care. But are there not equally powerful motivations operating on politicians and bureaucrats to engender "gross abuses"? And since politicians and bureaucrats have at their disposal not only the freedom of the marketplace, as do people in business and industry, but also the legal use of punitive force or its threat, it is arguable that, all things being equal, gross abuses of government power would violate more rights than would the free market. Thus, even if the rights claimed by Kelman and Claybrook are accepted as among the rights that individuals posses, there is serious reason to doubt that government regulation could on the whole provide more or better protection for individual rights than the protection offered by a free market.

In response it might be claimed that since people are selfish and greedy,[30] erecting an economic system run by "the profit motive" merely plays into the hands of selfishness and greed, with the predictable result that an unregulated market will violate many more rights than a government-regulated economy. For example, greed is likely to engender recklessness, negligence, even cruelty and callousness. What is called the public interest or the common good is also threatened by such a system, and individual rights as conceived by Kelman and Claybrook will be violated with abandon.

But this defense of regulation dies by its own hands. If people are selfish and greedy, as this defense contends, then their selfishness and greed will merely show up at a different place in a regulated market— namely, in the offices of politicians and special interest groups. If persons are selfish and greedy as a general, persistent trait (instead of merely now and then, off and on, depending on goodwill that is just as probable as its opposite), it does not appear that this could be eradicated by passing regulatory statutes and by creating government agencies. Indeed, the law and economic and public choice schools of economic analysis make exactly this point: Starting with their assumption that all human beings are essentially utility maximizers, they show that this implies that in the public sector people carry on just as they would in the private sector—aiming to fulfill their own desires or vested interests. And that certainly undermines the view that such persons would guard the marketplace instead of seek whatever economic advantage they could get by their role as such guardians.

But assume for a moment that this objection could be met and somehow the conduct of politicians and bureaucrats could be made safe from the sort of abuse claimed to be widespread in the marketplace. Defenders of government regulation would still be obliged to explain why business should be regulated, in the name of protection of rights, but not other human institutions (for example, religion, the press, art, and even family life, all of which are vital features of human social life). If, as defenders of regulation maintain, people have a right to have their welfare protected against "gross abuses that the marketplace does not correct," why does this same protection not extend to government regulation of news reporting, novel writing, movie making, and so forth? Why should someone who chooses plumbing or toy-making as a profession be subjected to various government edicts, inspection procedures, and so forth, while those working in the printed news media or publishing are exempt?

One answer might be that the professions of news reporting or publishing are special. Indeed, since these professions involve perhaps the most delicate and precious faculty of human living—namely, the creative mind—and carry out some of the most highly prized human activities, such as the search of truth and the creation of beauty, these activities should not be subjected to coercive political direction. This line of defense of discrimination in favor of some profession is probably based on the time-honored tradition, with roots in ancient Greece, according to which the human mind, spirit, or intellect is often viewed as something special, something extraordinary and unique to human life, and, as befits its uniqueness as the priceless jewel in the crown of our humanity, as a power meriting special consideration in its various manifestations. Thus are we allowed to regulate business, which is "material," but not art and letters, which are "spiritual."

It is important to note, first, that this argument could just as well support more rather than less political control of the press, arts, and publishing. Such paternalistic politics would suggest that if the search for truth is so vital, it should be guarded or regulated even more carefully than making toys or barbering. But even if we accept that a vital human activity requires greater liberty for those who engage in it, the view that the spiritual, mental, or intellectual aspects of human life are more important than what some regard as the more mundane aspects, such as production, trade, or advertising, is open to challenge. Human beings are, let us agree, unique in being intelligent, rational beings, with minds (or spirits, if you will). But they are, also, living, biological entities. That fact is no less important, even though not unique. Without ample regard for medicine, housing, psychological and sexual welfare, and so forth, human life would be at least as impoverished as it would be without adequate concern for pure science, literature, philosophy, and the arts. It is arguable that the tradition of separating human beings into two parts, the mind and the body, celebrating the former and denigrating the latter—for example, in treating people's sexual desires as something base and degrading throughout much of Western history—wrought ill not only for the body but also for the mind.

Instead of accepting the elitist view that some aspects of human life (namely, those having to do with the mind, intellect, or spirit) are more noble than the rest and so should be above government regulation, a less cumbersome and humanely democratic or egalitarian view recommends itself. This is to regard human beings as integrated, whole beings, important through and through, a view that requires a consistent regulatory approach to all human professions in place of the selective regulation of only some professions that characterizes present democratic free markets. If business is to be regulated, why not ballet?

In reply it might be claimed that some human endeavors are so important that government regulation is necessary. Consumer health often is touted as such a concern, as witness Claybrook's claim that people have a right "to secure drugs or food that do not have unnecessary side effects or cause illness." Claybrook's view is not eccentric. Studies referred to by Kelman verify that people are overwhelmingly in favor of government regulation and inspection in the areas of food and drugs.[31] But majority sentiment can be mistaken, and it often has been, prompting such political scientists as the Founding Fathers to guard against unlimited power for majorities. So let us ask whether the public's legitimate interest in consumer health warrants government regulation of food and drugs.

To consider this point we must ask, first, whether it is true that the marketplace fails to eliminate significant health risks. A full answer would require extensive statistical work, more difficult even than might be supposed initially. This is because for years government has promised to reduce the risks in the marketplace, and the marketplace—that is, the system of interacting firms, corporations, factories, business executives, foremen, shop stewards, carpenters, exterminators, and others involved in commerce—may well have accommodated itself to that promise. Regulation may well have preempted the efforts of those who would have been ready and willing to help reduce significant health risks on their own. It is arguable and quite plausible to suppose that when government, with considerable political hoopla, goes on record guaranteeing some service or goods—safety of fast foods, social security—there will be less market-oriented demand as well as market-oriented supply of these. The common sense idea that those who believe that they can gain what they want as a matter of right rather than having to obtain it with effort will prefer the former approach. Whether they would have tried to obtain it through effort had they not been told it was theirs by right, is difficult to demonstrate with precision. Certainly the strict empirical approach is not going to work here; one must make do with comparisons and inferences.

For instance, even today some businesses are regulated via the market so as to avoid unnecessary risks. For one, that is a condition for getting better insurance rates. When banks refuse to serve walk-up customers at their drive-up windows, the risk of accidents between pedestrians and cars is reduced; banks that observe this policy in turn receive lower rates from insurance companies as a reward. Such nongovernmental regulation does reduce significantly the risk of material health impairment.

But when governments take over the field and promise to achieve the same thing, the incentive to do this via the marketplace clearly diminishes. True, if government regulation managed to achieve what it set out to, its record would probably be impressive, but the "cure" for government regulation is very frequently worse than the "disease" it is called upon to treat. For example, a Brookings Institute study has demonstrated that scientific findings are ignored in all of the five cases of government regulation the authors selected for scrutiny.[32] Are we seriously to suppose that the public's concern about health is served by regulatory mechanisms that ignore the scientific assessment of regulation's implications?

Aside from the difficulty of assessing the success of government regulation, there is evidence that what government regulation achieves in the way of risk reduction can be achieved by way of a combination of

(1) market services for this purpose, and (2) the judicial system, with its ex post facto rather than preemptive approach to actual product liability, pollution, and work safety cases.[33]

The second question we must consider concerns what rights individuals have. Kelman and Claybrook seem to have more than a fair share of confidence about what rights people have, including rights to innumerable deeds and services—for example, not to suffer because of their own mistakes, and protection from risks involved in contemporary life. Kelman argues this explicitly when he says that "if a person gets sick or injured, or if he dies, because he purchased an unsafe product, clearly his action in buying the product had external effects [that is third party adverse impact] on friends and loved ones."[34] The suggestion here is that when these effects are untoward, the friends and loved ones should be viewed as having been deprived or harmed unjustly. Kelman even believes in the duty to render Good Samaritan aid, or so it appears, when he claims that "the person who sees a fire starting in a building and goes on his way without calling the fire department is hardly in a position to say that his failure to act had no external effects."[35] Indeed, Kelman and Claybrook seem to assume that others have a right, which ought to be enforced (judging by what Kelman and Claybrook infer from their assertion of this right), to the services of such a bystander.

This line of reasoning appears very promising at first. Consider, however, that Kelman assumes, without argument, that all of us have enforceable duties or legal obligations not only to help other people, but to prevent others from suffering adverse consequences of their own risky associations with others who may also wish to enjoy risk-free associations but failed to guard against risk. But do they have a right to a life in which they risk less regardless of their risky choices? As long as no contract to avoid risk has been entered into, human associations will have to forego the security government is asked (by Kelman) to provide (against mishaps, and even against negligence) as a matter of the individual rights of the citizenry. Some kind of "external effect" can be associated with virtually any action we take, especially when we have close personal ties. Kelman himself notes that "if I choose to patronize one business, my action has an effect on other businesses that lose my patronage."[36] But this "effect" is quite ambiguous. The mere truth that I could have gone to the other business but did not is taken by Kelman as having produced an effect. By that line of reasoning any action anyone takes in some respect deprives those who would have benefitted if another option had been taken. But, of course, someone else would have been deprived if another option had been selected. Are we to suppose that we violate someone's rights no matter what we do—or don't do? Such a view is preposterous. In the kind of case Kelman seems to have in mind, such as not patronizing some business, no injury is done. No one's rights are violated for the simple reason that no one has the rights Kelman seeks to defend.[37]

It is true, of course, that Kelman could fall back on some moral theories, both recent and ancient, to claim some support for holding that we are all bound together by enforceable duties. His view in fact seems to take to the extreme the doctrine of justice-as-fairness made prominent by John Rawls.[38] There is some suggestion in that doctrine that, if several ethnic restaurants are available for patronage in one's neighborhood, one's choosing to eat only at one of these is unfair and should be regulated so as to promote justice. But it is very likely that this view flies in the face of the equally plausible doctrine that each person has exclusive jurisdiction over his or her own life, a life that is unavailable, as a matter of morality, for others to make use of as they would wish. Given the plausibility of the extreme priority of personal moral autonomy—the view that persons are ends in themselves, not means for the promotion of others' well-being (and certainly not by force)—the Kelman-Claybrook defense of regulation, that an unregulated market violates individual rights, no longer carries conviction. If we had the rights they claim on our behalf there is no good reason to believe that a free market would violate these rights more often than one that is regulated. And since there is no good reason to believe that we have such extensive rights, a defense of regulation based on their position is worse than no defense at all.

Why Government Regulation is Wrong

I wish now to propose that government regulation of business is morally wrong, despite some very appealing grounds given in its support. If I am right, deregulation should commence. At any rate, in coming to grips with the issue of whether business should be regulated, the following reflections should be taken seriously.

The points I will raise are, as in the Kelman-Claybrook approach, related to a consideration of human rights. When we appreciate what rights there are, including various types of rights, we should conclude that government regulation is an impermissible violation of people's most basic rights. We might also come to the point of conceiving of solutions to the problems such regulations aim to solve, solutions that would otherwise seem remote and tenuous.

There are three distinct types of rights: natural, special, and acquired, each with distinct moral implications for human life and institutions. Natural rights are entitlements to liberty (from other's intrusion or forcible interference), which, if we have them, are possessed simply because we are beings who can act autonomously, independently, of our own free will. Such rights are not created by the law. On the contrary, a just society will base its legal system on these rights and establish the means for their protection and preservation. Special rights are almost as firm but obtain selectively, holding, for example, between parents and children. Given the special characteristics of children as more or less young human beings, and given how they came into the world—by virtue of the voluntary actions of their parents—certain rights and duties emerge when children are born, involving both parties to the relationship. Such special rights may perhaps extend to other members of families; thus, one may have duties to next of kin that one may not have to others (for example, to care for them when they are sick). In general, then, special rights arise because of the special relationships we have to some people. Acquired rights differ. They arise because of various choices adults make. When I promise to meet you for dinner, you acquire a moral right to my showing up, a right you would not have if I had not chosen to make the promise. Again, if I agree to sell something to you, you acquire the (moral) right to the merchandise if you meet my conditions, a right you would not have if I had not agreed to sell it.

Each of these types of rights calls for different ways of handling violations. Violation of a natural right warrants the most severe response, beyond mere verbal rebukes or social ostracism, since respect for natural rights is the minimum requirement for a just society. Without such respect for the autonomy of other human beings, one fails to recognize them as human beings. Violation of special rights comes close to this, especially in the case of the parent-child relationship. But the choice of bringing a child into the world, however explicit or tacit, is presupposed, so it is not basic like natural rights. Acquired rights, in turn, are quite a risky business. My promise does commit me, and if I break it for frivolous reasons, I certainly am morally condemnable. But no one is justified in taking punitive action in retaliation. Some type of ostracism or rebuke is as much as justice allows.

The one type of right that stands apart from all these is a legal or positive right, one created by contract or legislation and justified by reference to rights discussed above. It is possible for someone to have a legal right to aid, even though this right would be morally wrong to enforce. Legal rights and contractual rights may or may not be morally well-founded. In any case, such rights presuppose the establishment of government or some third (enforcing) party, apart from those who are subject to the laws or who have entered contracts. Unlike a promise, the minimum parties to a contract are three: the two who contract promises, and the third who is hired, invited, or otherwise empowered to enforce, supervise disputes about, or otherwise stand watch over the terms of the contract. A legal right, in general, involves enforceability and presupposes the institutions required to enforce it, whereas the existence of other rights, though not their protection, is independent of these considerations. One's natural right to be free, the special rights of children and the acquired rights of promises do not depend on third-party enforcement for their reality or existence.

Now, the marketplace does in fact leave room for all these rights to be respected and protected. Government regulation assumes, however, that all types of right must be like legal or contractual rights, subject to enforcement. And that is the heart of the matter. Our natural, special, and acquired rights do not presuppose the third-party enforcement assumed by legal rights; government, serving the entire public, ought to be appointed to enforce just those rights—namely natural rights—that have the widest scope. No doubt it is a good thing that the products you produce and I purchase prove to benefit me, just as it is a good thing that a father takes his daughter to the show as promised. But no one who respects individual autonomy would assume that the elaborate punitive machinery of the law should be enlisted to coerce the father to keep his promise. In the absence of compelling argument to the contrary, why should we regard the role of the law any differently when it comes to ensuring the quality of the products you produce and I purchase? Only if solid moral justification is at hand should we allow natural rights—to life, liberty and property—to be overridden. Such justification is difficult to come by, and though it is arguable that in certain exceptional cases our natural right would have to be overridden (for example, when we face circumstances in which social life is impossible, as on a life raft or desert island), exceptional cases are not the rule.[39] Our day-to-day commerce does not take place in a state of emergency.

For reasons already advanced in the section headed *Definition and Distinctions*, the major sorts of justification of government regulation (ideals, utility, rights) fail. Ought we to oppose it, then? This argument places the burden of proof on those who would promote the regulation of business. The value of individual liberty is so great that it ought not to be limited in the absence of very strong moral arguments (as is true, for example, in the case of the criminal law). Arguments for government regulation lack the necessary strength. Therefore, they fail to meet the burden of proof. The free market may not be perfect but it is one that largely respects the basic, natural rights of individuals (while it also places considerable responsibility on everyone to fend for himself—"caveat emptor"). In the absence of compelling reasons for overriding individual rights as they find expression in the free market, restrictions should not be accepted. Lacking adequate argument to the contrary, we are right to view government regulation of business as wrong, based on the existence of the right to property I have defended in chapter 3, as well as the wrongfulness of prior restraint and other violations of negative individual rights.

Should Business Be State Regulated?

Should business be regulated by the government? I have presented sketches of arguments that reach an affirmative answer to this question and I have myself offered a negative reply. But the issue is very complicated, involving as it does matters of economics, morality, politics, law, considerations of human nature, the psychology of commercial relations, and so forth. Nevertheless, what has been presented here should provide an opportunity for enterprising minds voluntarily to enter into commerce with one of the most active normative public policy issues of our time. In a democratic society everyone is called upon to help decide what the government will do. And it is clearly better if the decision rests on as clear a conception of what government should do as possible. The politicians who run to gain our votes, the bureaucrats who wish to be appointed by these politicians, and the whole array of officials of the various levels of government in a democracy depend on us all for moral guidance. That is what government by the people, of the people, and for the people amounts to. The present discussion has been conducted with this fact in mind.

Notes

1. *New York Times* August 19, 1981.
2. John F. Cady, *Restricted Advertising and Competition: The Case of Retail Drugs* (Washington, DC: American Enterprise Institute, 1976), p. 1.
3. David A. Mathisen, "Whatever Happened to Human Body Glue?" *Reason* (May 1980): 20-27.
4. *Metromedia, Inc. v. City of San Diego*, 101 S.Ct. 2882 (1981).
5. Walter Fairleigh Dodd, *Cases and Materials on Constitutional Law: Selected from Decisions of State and Federal Courts* (St. Paul, MN: West, 1954), p. 390.
6. For a full treatment, see Bernard Siegan, *Economic Liberties and the Constitution* (Chicago: University of Chicago Press, 1981).
7. My own fuller exposition of the nature and justification of this system is in my *Human Rights and Human Liberties* (Chicago: Nelson-Hall, 1975). See also, for a diverse selection of support and development of the laissez-faire idea, my *The Libertarian Alternative* (Chicago: Nelson-Hall, 1974) and *The Libertarian Reader* (Totowa, NJ: Rowman and Littlefield, 1982), both edited to cover all major questions.
8. The exception is libertarian anarchism, as represented by Murray N. Rothbard, *Man, Economy, and State: A Treatise on Economic Principles* (Los Angeles: Nash, 1970).
9. Interestingly, however, the strongest support for slavery came not from defenders of the market economy but from socialists. See George Fitzhugh, *Sociology for the South; or the Failure of Free Society* (New York: Burt Franklin, [1854] 1965); and *Cannibals All! or Slaves without Masters* (Cambridge, MA: Harvard University Press, 1960), both republished after about ninety years.
10. Jonathan R. T. Hughes, *The Governmental Habit: Economic Controls from Colonial Times to the Present* (New York: Basic Books, 1977), pp. 3-4.
11. Quoted in *ibid.,* p. 111.
12. When I refer to this ideal, I may not always qualify it by calling attention to the right to liberty, but that is what I have in mind. Liberty or freedom per se, rather than the right to it, is not so much at issue. Clearly, one can trade in one's freedom to do *X* by deciding instead to commit to a different course, *Y*, that may involve more security—as happens in marriage, for instance, or taking a long-term job. What one is not deemed to be doing in these cases of trade-off is trading one's basic right to life or liberty—this is generally deemed unalienable. For the best sense of the concept "unalienable," see Tibor R. Machan, "Human Rights, Some Points of Clarification," *The Journal of Critical Analysis* 5 (July/October 1973): 30-39. See also, Tibor R. Machan, *Individuals and Their Rights* (LaSalle, IL: Open Court, 1989).
13. As noted earlier, Norman Malcolm tells a story about Ludwig Wittgenstein that illustrates the point about property rights. "On one walk he 'gave' to me each tree that we passed, with the reservation that I was not to cut it down or do anything to it, or prevent the previous owners from doing anything to it: with those reserva-

tions it was henceforth mine." He calls this one of Wittgenstein's "deliberately absurd or extravagant remarks," in Norman Malcolm, *Ludwig Wittgenstein: A Memoir* (London: Oxford University Press, 1958), pp. 31–32. What the story points up is the absurdity of owning anything that has numerous restrictions placed on it as regards its peaceful use.

14. Of course, one might still object to such governmental edicts on the grounds that education suffers when they are imposed or that they counter the spirit and letter of existing law. But that is not to challenge the government's proper authority to intervene.

15. See my *Human Rights and Human Liberties*, and Chapter 2 of the present work. An earlier and less complete version of that chapter appeared under the title "Rational Choice and Public Affairs," *Theory and Decision* 12 (September 1980): 229–258.

16. Henry G. Manne, "Insider Trading and the Law Professors," *Vanderbilt Law Review* 23 (1970): 547. Manne's are mainly economic objections to laws prohibiting insider trading. In cases other than those involving fraud or violation of fiduciary duty, prohibiting insider trading violates the rights of individuals to the liberty to act in their own interest with information they have obtained honestly without violating anyone's rights. The motivation behind such laws is the ideal of fairness, a procedural principle that ought never to supersede basic human rights.

17. Herbert Spencer, *The Principles of Ethics* (Indianapolis, IN: Liberty Classics, [1892–1893] 1977).

18. John Maynard Keynes, *The End of Laissez-Faire* (London: Hogarth Press, 1927), p. 40.

19. Yale Brozen, "Is the Government Responsible for Monopolies?" in *The Libertarian Alternative*, pp. 149–168.

20. Robert Bremner, *American Philanthropy* (Chicago: University of Chicago Press, 1960); Alfred de Grazia and Ted Gurr, *American Welfare* (New York: New York University Press, 1961); Frank Greene Dickinson, *The Changing Position of Philanthropy in the American Economy* (New York: Columbia University Press, 1970); and Arnaud C. Marts, *The Generosity of Americans: Its Source, Its Achievements* (Englewood Cliffs, NJ: Prentice-Hall, 1966).

21. Arguably, however, the very recent experience with utter poverty everywhere, including the United States, as well as the opportunity, perhaps for the first time in human history, to focus on avoiding such a fate, has caused many people to exert considerable effort at securing for themselves economic well-being, often to the detriment of other objectives and even of the system itself (which makes such exertion of effort possible). I would speculate, based on elementary psychology, that when people are afraid of something, they try to avert it and then can go overboard in their eagerness to do so. That tendency and not the right to free trade and free markets would seem to me a more important explanation for commercialization. Freedom to do *X*, after all, does not cause one to do *X*, but simply leaves that option open.

22. Kenneth J. Arrow, "Two Cheers for Government Regulation," *Harper's Magazine* (March 1981): 20.

23. Robert W. Poole, Jr., ed., *Instead of Regulation: Alternatives to Federal Regulatory Agencies* (Lexington, MA: Lexington Books, 1982). For the idea of a free market in roads, see Walter Block, "Free Market in Roads," in *Libertarian Reader*, pp. 163–184.

24. Arrow, "Two cheers...," p. 19.
25. Thomas Sowell, *Knowledge and Decisions* (New York: Basic Books, 1980). This is the idea that had been pitted against Marxist-Leninist socialism, and because of which the socialist economist Oscar Lange of Poland wanted to erect a memorial to the economist Ludwig von Mises, who advanced it in his *Socialism: An Economic and Sociological Analysis*, trans. J. Kahane, (Indianapolis, IN: Liberty Classics, 1981), as early as 1920. Friedrich A. von Hayek received the Nobel Prize in part for his development of this thesis, namely, that without the price system that efficiently communicates fluctuations of demand and supply, the allocation of resources in a society will be misguided. In my *Capitalism and Individualism* (New York: St. Martin's Press, 1990) I argue, however, that all of these objections to socialism presuppose the value of accommodating the needs, wants, and desires of *individuals* in society, whereas in socialist systems that is definitely not the goal of public administration.
26. For a very instructive discussion of the impact of the drug war on various aspects of our legal system, see Superior Court Judge James P. Gray, "We Cannot Win the War Against Drugs—A Legal Brief for Decriminalizing Use of Heroin, Cocaine, and Marijuana," *Orange County Register*, April 10, 1992, sec. B.
27. Steven Kelman, "Regulation that Works," *The New Republic* (November 25, 1978): 19.
28. *Ibid.*
29. Joan Claybrook, "Joan Claybrook Responds," *Regulation* (March-April 1979): 4.
30. This view is inherited from Thomas Hobbes and forms a substantial premise of much of neoclassical economic theory. For a historical sketch, see Albert O. Hirschman, *The Passions and the Interests, Political Arguments for Capitalism Before Its Triumph* (Princeton, NJ: Princeton University Press, 1977). See also Machan, *Capitalism and Individualism*.
31. Seymour Martin Lipset and William Schneider, "The Public View of Regulation," *Public Opinion* 2 (January 1979): 11.
32. Robert W. Crandall and Lester B. Lave, eds., *The Scientific Basis of Health and Safety Regulation* (Washington, DC: Brookings Institution, 1981). Perhaps the most grievous fault of the bulk of government regulations in this area is the assumption underlying them that the mere possibility of harm to consumers or users of merchandise or services (from children's nightwear to breast implant procedures) justifies restraining trade in those items or services. This amounts to prior restraint: even though nothing untoward was done to anyone, someone is being penalized. Though many protest this approach in the criminal law—so that, for example, the use of profiles is frowned upon even though the percentage of success may be high—the same is accepted in government regulation of market processes.

Perhaps what accounts for this attitude, in part, is that what markets achieve for us is deemed too trivial for us to accept serious risks. In the case of the furor over the serious risk in market transactions associated with silicone breast implants, some critics expressed dismay about risking so much for merely improving one's looks. First, why would such an objective have to be trivial? And second, why should anyone make the decision for others as to what kind of risks they may assume? (Where is the outcry about women owning their bodies in this case?)

33. Poole, *Instead of Regulation*; and Michael S. Baram, *Alternatives to Regulation: Managing Risks to Health, Safety, and the Environment* (Lexington, MA: Lexington Books, 1982).
34. Steven Kelman, "Regulation and Paternalism," in *Rights and Regulation: Ethical, Political, and Economic Issues*, ed. M. Bruce Johnson and Tibor R. Machan, (Cambridge, MA: Ballinger, 1983), p. 241.
35. *Ibid.*
36. *Ibid.*
37. In addition, the moral significance of acts is diminished if not totally obliterated when they are performed under compulsion alone, as in government-regulated conduct. See Douglas Den Uyl, "Freedom and Virtue," *Reason Papers* 5 (1979): 1-12. There is, of course, the oft-repeated idea that government regulation is a matter of collective decision, something that is the essence of democratic government, so no coercion is involved. But democracy has to adjust to the principles of basic human rights. An individual who is born into society may not be subjected to policies that undermine or violate his or her basic rights. Thus democracy may not extend beyond that point; indeed, in a constitutional system it is generally confined to matters the government is authorized to care for, such as the administration of justice. For more on this, see Tibor R. Machan, chapter 7 of *Individuals and Their Rights*.
38. John Rawls, *A Theory of Justice* (Cambridge, MA: Harvard University Press, 1971).
39. See my "Prima facie versus Natural (human) Rights," *Journal of Value Inquiry* 10 (Summer 1976): 119-131; I develop the points in my *Individuals and Their Rights*.

5

Further Normative Aspects of Deregulation

*Government is not reason, it is not eloquence—it is
force! Like fire it is a dangerous servant and
fearful master; never for a moment should it be left
to irresponsible action.*

—George Washington

I have thus far discussed some of the normative problems that pertain to the issue of government regulation of business. This time I am concerned, however, with certain more specific issues. I want to focus on one main problem of government regulation. This has to do with government regulation's violation of a basic principle of a free society, a violation that makes its appearance very clearly in the criminal laws of such societies but has not managed to be exported into some other regions of government-citizen relations. I have in mind the violation of the prohibition of prior restraint. The idea I wish to explore is that free men and women may not be treated as if they had already been proven guilty of violating the law before proof of the same has been established in line with just criminal procedures or due process of law.

The Problem of Prior Restraint

Although this issue of prior restraint usually comes to attention in connection with legal proceedings and may be deemed a mere legal principle, my aim is to call attention to its underlying moral components and justification. The reason it is wrong to restrain someone—that is, to hinder or prohibit his or her action—is that unless some basic principle of human interaction has been violated demonstrably by the agent, that agent is every bit as free to act, as are others, without restraint. The basic

sovereignty of individuals is at stake. For example, even when law enforcement authorities are extremely eager to combat crime, which is an
admirable, vital goal, they may not do so by treating some persons as if
they had been proven guilty when in fact they have not.

My central concern here is to point out that government regulation of
business undermines this basic moral principle which is so well recognized in the context of concern about due process in the criminal law.

Economics and Regulation

Throughout the last several decades economists have amassed evidence about the effects of government regulation of people's economic
affairs.[1] The general consensus among scholars is that, by the standard
economic measure of cost and benefit, the government's regulatory policies and actions have failed. In a number of studies it has also been
shown that the avowed goals of regulation have not, in fact, been achieved
by regulation. Comparative analyses show, on the other hand, that in the
absence of regulation those same goals are being attained.[2]

Despite the wide acceptance of the methods employed in these studies, the results have not produced the deregulation that they would appear to warrant.[3] In view of the lack of significant progress in that
direction, some have advanced theories aiming to explain why deregulation is not proceeding. Henry G. Manne, for example, originally proposed that bureaucrats were acting in pursuit of their self-interest, which
resulted, in part, in their refusal to institute deregulation measures. Having revised his theory in some measure, Manne later proposed that, in
addition to the bureaucrats, the managers of regulated firms were acting
in pursuit of their self-interest too.[4] So both regulators and the regulated,
acting from economic self-interest, promoted regulatory activities in the
face of evidence showing the failure of these in terms of costs and benefits or of their avowed purpose.

Several other economists and legal theorists have also focused on the
issue of why deregulation is not proceeding.[5] I will not attempt here to
summarize the findings or theories of these economists but merely note
that the method of analysis employed by them draws heavily from the
standard "economic man" model of human behavior. For example, Professor Milton Friedman uses this model in a recent nontechnical article
when he claims that "every individual serves his own private interest. . . .

The great Saints of history have served their 'private interest' just as the most money-grubbing miser has served his interest. The private interest is whatever it is that drives an individual."[6]

I want, instead of scrutinizing the economic approach to the problem of regulation and deregulation, to propose a different explanation for why, despite the economists' findings, there is no serious move toward deregulation. One of the laments expressed about the so-called Reagan Revolution by friends of the market economy is that despite its rhetoric it did not involve significant cutbacks in the state's involvement in the economy, nor in the tax and regulatory burdens shouldered by the American people. Even in the face of substantial privatization, the absolute level of economic statism has constantly increased.

The fact is that proponents of deregulation are not presenting a powerful and persuasive moral case. As economists and political operatives, they tend to argue solely from the "efficiency" perspective—and they argue from this perspective because they ultimately deny the ability of human beings to know moral truth. As one author of an economic textbook maintains, "as an economist, it is not his job to spit out a bunch of 'I believe,' but rather, 'the implications will be thus and so.'"[7] The implications, however, of the "economic man" (or "utility maximization") model of human action, for purposes of understanding the conduct of regulators, either preclude any consideration of motivation based on moral or political convictions; they subsume such motivation within the more general idea that we all are driven to serve our private interest.

Both the rejection and subsumption of normative motivation effectively eliminates the possible additional significance of normative considerations for understanding such public affairs as the future of government regulation of the economy. Indeed, both of the major advocates of the free market economy, although they approach economics from somewhat different theoretical frameworks, reject either the possibility of moral truth (Friedman)[8] or the appropriateness of normative consideration in this context (Hayek).[9]

On the other hand, those who reject the free-market economic system, including those who advocate numerous vigorous government regulatory measures, do base their recommendations on various ethical principles that, they believe, override the call for efficiency and, therefore, economic liberty as advocated by the economists. Accordingly, they also have an argumentative edge in the general public debate about the free versus the planned economy and, in particular, about the issue of whether to deregulate or to continue, even increase, government regulation.

For example, Ralph Nader, John Kenneth Galbraith, and numerous political thinkers and leaders of both Left and Right clearly accept that we can arrive at conclusions about what is right and wrong for governments to do apart from what is efficient or expensive. Others, such as the late influential democratic socialist Michael Harrington, advance an entire philosophical theory in support of their call for government control, not just regulation, of the U.S. economic system.[10] Again, such philosophers as John Rawls, Thomas Nagel, Thomas Scanlon, and George Kateb make no secret of their view that we can identify some basic ethical principles of justice and equity that should guide us in forging government policy.[11]

In regard, particularly, to government regulation we find, for example, Roger Noll commenting in a discussion about whether to establish an agency for consumer advocacy:

> My conclusion, after reading what everyone else has said about the consumer advocacy agency, is that I cannot understand why people are so strongly opposed to it or so strongly in favor of it. If I were forced to vote, I would vote for it—because I accept the principal argument for it—that the consumer advocacy agency will promote justice and fairness.[12]

Ralph Nader, too, states that "it is important to look at regulation issues in terms of the needs of society.... we should ask ourselves what human purposes regulation fulfills, whether it is just or unjust."[13] It will be worthwhile, then, to continue to consider whether outside the economists' case (showing the inefficiency of government regulation) there might not be a more forceful (nonskeptical) argument in support of freedom in general and deregulation in particular. Let us try to find out if there is a theoretical basis not only for the economic discussion but for the ethical and political discussion.

It is no secret that among those supporting deregulation, economists dominate the discussion. The modest aim of this discussion is to examine some themes that would, at least, balance the discussion outside the economic framework or, at most, make a case for the moral and political priority of liberty within the context of public policy. None of this is to dismiss entirely the usefulness of economic explanations of why deregulation is not proceeding. When concern for ethical issues and political justice seems to support regulation, it is not unlikely that many will join in support of such a policy who are in fact simply seeking to preserve their vested interests by giving lip service to such concerns, provided that the normative ideas promulgated are never challenged head-on. In addition, the intellectual climate itself discourages fundamental changes in the moral perspectives of influential people in society and government, partly because of the very method that economists employ to oppose government regulation.[14] In view of the apparent influence of some normative considerations as well as the recent theoretical concern to arrive at rational social policy via the "economic man" model, it will be useful to consider some of the ethical and political (normative) ideas that might indeed give support to the free society and, thereby, to deregulatory efforts.[15]

It will be useful for our purposes to consider some normative dimensions of economic and political life that are pertinent to the possibility that government regulation is wrong or improper public policy. I will be invoking and reiterating a moral case for the value of political liberty, that is, the political basis of the free-market system and of deregulatory policy.

The Normative Case for Freedom

Within a very plausible framework, as we have already seen, and one that is certainly familiar within the U.S. philosophical and political context, it can be shown that government regulatory activities are wrong, improper, indeed immoral. By this I mean that they fall within the class of activities, policies, or institutions that can rationally be considered as unjustified on grounds that a standard or principle of human conduct is being violated. The idea is not that such practices are legally unjustified, of course, if by "legally" we mean only that the legislative and judicial practices of our society have been adhered to more or less faithfully. But it is possible, in a different sense of "legal" or "lawful," to regard some established public policy as lawless, if, that is, we mean by "lawful" an adherence to fundamental conditions of human community life (as this term is used within the tradition of natural law legal and political theory).[16]

Instead of a concern with legality, which is today mostly conceived along lines of legal positivism, the present discussion will focus on the extralegal question of what kind of public policy we should follow. The issue is not whether the kind of policy that we should follow may be followed ineptly, unprofessionally, or incompetently; the most appropriate of policies (for instance, the military defense of a country) can be mismanaged by governments or other groups of people. The point is whether government, as a certain kind of agency in a human community, should assume certain functions, such as the regulation of the economy.[17]

With these preliminaries mentioned, let us consider what may be good reasons, from the normative point of view, to oppose government regulation and to support deregulation. We can admit at the outset that the goals that are pursued in our day via coercive government regulation can be important, even if we would conclude that such coercive methods are not the proper means by which to pursue them. Such goals are certainly of value to some members of a human community, even though one would probably have to challenge their frequent characterization as public goods or as being in the public interest.[18] For example, meeting health care needs is valuable for those who have such needs, preserving the wilderness is valuable for those who are inclined to enjoy the outdoors, and fostering the arts is valuable for art lovers. Even more, securing safety in food and drug manufacture would probably benefit everyone.

There are other morally crucial matters to be considered, however, aside from the admitted value some of these goals have for various members of the community. As an example, consider the principle of justice whereby, when accused of a wrongdoing, a person's guilt must be demonstrated before penalty or punishment is imposed. In the ordinary criminal proceeding such considerations fall under the legal principle of due process. This principle is usually conceived as specifying the need for the state to follow the law, including the portion of it that requires that an accused be proven guilty before any action is taken that can be construed as punishment. The normative underpinning of this idea is, generally, that without a demonstration that the accused is indeed guilty of having wronged someone (or violated a law that stands to protect the rights of the members of a society), there is no justification for placing burdens upon him, such as for depriving him of liberty or property.

Of course once some laws are in effect, all the state needs to do to satisfy the due process requirement is to demonstrate that these laws have been violated. Yet there is a more stringent way of understanding the idea of due process, one that is not so widely considered, even by legal theorists, in our times. Sometimes it may be argued that inherent in certain types of legislation we find an abridgement of due process, at least if this idea is understood to involve considerations of justice that are extralegal and not merely statutory. (In tyrannies or dictatorships we can observe due process if by this we mean only that statutes are followed consistently; but we may argue that certain statutes should never have been permitted to become part of the legal system, and we may insist that their having become part of the system is itself a violation of due process, that is, an abridgment of the proper domain or limits of governmental action.) If, for example, the constitution or legal code of a just human community should prohibit statutes abridging freedom of speech or contract or trade, then any legislation or related procedure that has in fact established such statutes must be construed as undue.

It is in this broad, substantive, instead of procedural, sense of the idea of due process that it can be argued that various statutes of our legal system fail to respect the principle of due process. But whatever the term "due process" may be used to mean—admitting that today it is far from being used in this sense—the idea is clear enough. Governmental regulatory practices have led to the result that prior to anyone's having caused any injury to others, members of various industries, professions, and other commercial association are made to suffer burdens. True, these burdens are required by legally well-founded statute,[19] but this can be said, as noted above, of the burdens that tyrannies or dictatorships impose on the members of the communities they rule by brute force. This brute force is "backed" by law of a certain kind. It is not at all impossible that various less drastic impositions on the members of our society constitute merely less brutal but still unjust exercises of force, backed by unjust legal measures.

The upshot of these remarks is that there is a firm and well-developed moral objection to the bulk of government regulation, namely, that such regulation declares the regulated parties guilty and deserving of numerous burdens without it having been demonstrated that those burdened are guilty of violating anyone's rights and, therefore, deserving of shouldering the imposed burdens. The point is, to stress the matter again, moral, not legal. The toy maker, dress manufacturer, barber, or restaurateur who is forced by the state to meet various requirements set by a regulatory agency, and thus forced to incur expenses, hardships, even ruin, simply has not done anything wrong to another person.[20] It is true, any one of these individuals or groups of individuals might do (is capable of doing) such harm. Yet it is also true that anyone might murder (is capable of murdering) someone, but this does not seem to be regarded as sufficient grounds for government imposition of antimurder regulation. It seems sufficient, and certainly more just, to make murder illegal. Would it not seem comparably sufficient and just to regard various forms of injury to others illegal, so that once some manufacturer has engaged in conduct injurious to others—or is regarded as being probably engaged in such conduct (within the framework of the idea of probable cause or clear and present danger)—the manufacturer is liable to criminal charges? This admittedly cumbersome procedure, due to citizens in numerous other circumstances, is shortcut by way of government regulation of manufacture, and the like.

Let me illustrate how the above considerations have a bearing on arguments for government regulation based on moral consideration. The following points are raised by Ralph Nader in support of such government policy (although Nader, as most other advocates, is not an unqualified champion of the various regulatory agencies):

> As you know, there are too many useless drugs in the market-place. The National Academy of Sciences documents this. Many of these drugs should be taken off the market. I think if you read the Senate Small Business study of the assertion ["for every case you can bring up of a drug that slipped by the Food and Drug Administration and has been harmful to some people, you can bring up dozens of cases of the Food and Drug Administration going too far"], you'll see that they simply are not supported by the evidence. What we do know is that fortunately our Food and Drug Administration stopped the drug Thalidomide, which caused 10,000 deformed births in Western Europe and Japan, from coming into this country. I really think that what we have to ask ourselves in this discussion is, to what extent can these agencies reflect the value system of a population by operating openly, accountably, and subject to citizen or consumer participation?[21]

Nader and others accept the view that useless drugs (as well as ones that might have some side effects that are harmful, but by standard testing procedures do not indicate such a probability) "should be taken off the market," that is, their manufacture and sale should be legally prohibited. He is not speaking of what manufacturers should do themselves, as a matter of their moral responsibility, but what should be forced upon them. And he calls this approach justified because he believes that "these agencies" of prohibition should "reflect the value system of a population", even though it is certainly very doubtful that the exercise of force is the means by which the value system of a society should be reflected. It is of the essence of a virtuous citizenry that it should practice its virtues voluntarily.

Nader is also convinced that government should act to prevent individuals from injuring themselves and other individuals from participating in the self-injury of others, not for purposes of prevention (that is, acting so as to forestall risks and hazards of living) but for purposes of protection and retaliation (that is, the valid purposes of a government of a free society). This preventive conception of proper government policy is well illustrated by the late Senator Jacob Javits's reply to a question regarding the alleged need for regulation of Vitamin C production, sale, and consumption: "While we protect the right of the individual to buy vitamins, we must at the same time safeguard him and those individuals who may not be aware of the dangers of potential over-use of vitamins against the possible hazards."[22]

To these sorts of arguments, the present normative perspective supplies the following reply. Individuals have as their responsibility in life to pursue their well-being while at the same time refraining from interfering with the similar pursuits of others. The desire to "help" others by directing their lives may be strong, but to yield to this desire is to undermine the very human dignity of the person who is being benignly coerced. In a society that accords with the principles based on the political theory of natural human rights to life, liberty, and property (with government assigned the role of serving its members by protecting and preserving these rights), paternalism is not authorized. Where such paternalism is legally authorized, the laws should be changed. Deregulation of the economic system is a species of the kind of change that will accomplish bringing the legal system into accord with the crucial normative principles at issue; ergo, deregulation should be pursued.[23] To put the matter differently, in line with the points raised as to placing burdens on people only after they have been shown to have violated the rights of others, deregulation should be pursued because government regulation of the kind we have discussed is a violation of the basic rights of individuals, derived from all persons' responsibility to pursue success, well-being, and overall excellence in their particular lives.

Of course, the foregoing normative approach will not accord with the normative approach presupposed in the argument Nader and others have advanced.[24] But here the issue is at least being faced at the level at which the relevant discussion has occurred, namely, the normative validity of government regulation in general. And, in addition to the relatively narrow normative point raised above—based, however, on a broad normative framework—some other objections may be mentioned concerning the practice of government regulation. Regulatory policies are inherently redistributive; that is, they involve the seizure of earned income for purposes of allocating this income in ways the government's policymakers believe are more important than do those whose income has been seized. By not allowing the people to live with the choices they have made, the government is engaging, via the redistribution of funds, in the assignment of priorities against their expressed choices (a good example is the widespread opposition of the public, as indicated by public opinion polls, to enforced and costly school busing programs).

I have also been arguing that it is improper for government to spend funds for purposes other than providing the protection and preservation of the rights everyone in the society possesses. The latter purposes, such as national defense, maintenance of judicial and policy provisions, and the related technical services, are to everyone's objective benefit, and so do not involve any policy of income redistribution.

But this is not the case with the kind of public interest theory to which Mr. Nader and his friends adhere. The following exchange between Nader and Ronald Reagan, when he was Governor of California, brings to light the problem with Nader's conception of the public interest, as well as with some aspects of government regulation:

> REAGAN: I would join any propaganda or public relations campaign to urge motorcyclists to wear helmets—since I happen to think anyone is foolish to ride a motorcycle at all and very foolish to do so without a helmet. But I don't think government has any business telling a person he has to wear a helmet . . . a person who wants to ride a motorcycle without a helmet is only endangering himself, and I don't think it is any of government's business...
>
> NADER: Of course, if a motorcycle operator who is not wearing a helmet is in an accident and is sprawled on the highway, you would expect a police car, taxpayer-paid, to drive the victim to a tax-payer hospital; and you could expect the risk of secondary accidents to increase with the motorcycle driver sprawled on the highway unconscious—which he wouldn't be if he were wearing a motorcycle helmet. It isn't that simple. If you are on your own private road on your farm and you don't want to wear a motorcycle helmet, fine, I agree with you...[25]

First, Nader evidently has a point, but only because the "public" domain today includes virtually any domain of society. Virtually everyone gains some benefits from taxes, that is, from political redistribution of people's wealth. Thus virtually everything is *public* in some measure. So in line with this argument there really should be very few domains, if any, left to private choice.

One might wonder, for example, whether Nader supports freedom of speech, since most speech is performed on property that comes under some kind of government jurisdiction. Broadcasting news, for instance, is carried on the public airwaves. Newspapers are distributed on public street corners. Art shows are presented in public museums. Books are mailed through the public mails. Even such areas of life as sexual activity and religious worship cannot be regarded as private since they, too, tie in at some point with state-funded projects—schools, hospitals, roads, airports, and so on.

There are those who would bite the bullet and declare all aspects of our lives subject to public—albeit democratic—scrutiny. Benjamin Barber's book *Strong Democracy* (1984) advances such a thesis, at least by implication. Democratic socialism sides with this position. Marxism, which sees all of us as species-beings—that is, as parts of the larger "organic body (or whole)" of humanity—also accepts these implications.

But from an individualist frame of reference, one that I have been invoking and outlining here (and have defended elsewhere), none of these basically coercively collectivist positions is warranted. And that should be interesting news to those who really do not wish to accept much of the substance of the socialist choice—ACLU liberals, welfare statists who champion civil libertarian ideals, etc. For them, the analysis I have been presenting should accentuate the imperative not only to commence deregulation but to disengage the various levels of government from the numerous private and voluntary social spheres that they now invade.

Regulation, furthermore, involves, as noted already, the practice of prior restraint, since those regulated by government are prevented from freely choosing their courses of conduct prior to having done anything wrong to anyone, prior to having violated anyone's rights. In the ordinary criminal law in our system it is impermissible to punish or restrain by force the conduct of those who have not been proven guilty of a crime or who are not engaged in conduct involving clear and present danger to some innocent persons. Unless there is probable cause to believe that a crime will be committed, a person may not be restrained in his or her choice. Government regulation flatly contradicts this honorable individualist principle of our legal tradition.

As to what remains, properly, within the jurisdiction of government, this is not regulation but public management or administration. Because today there is no principled distinction between the private and the public spheres of life in the United States, not to mention in other countries, the issue of deregulation needs to be considered carefully enough to observe that what seems to be government regulation is in fact government management or administration. Yet the confusion that exists in view of these considerations should not be permitted to obscure the virtue of proceeding with deregulatory efforts where they apply. Ronald Reagan's answer to Nader's argument did not heed this point, so that he simply admitted that he found "it very hard to determine what exactly victimless crimes are" and that "there is a gray area in all of these things."[26] He also said that a person in a motorcycle accident "is going to be somewhat disabled and will end up lying on the highway with or without the helmet," to which Nader responded by citing studies allegedly showing that what the Governor said was "not true."[27]

That is not the way to discuss these issues, but when those party to these discussion lack the moral frame of reference from which to object to what they vaguely perceive to be unjustified government intrusion into the lives of individuals, one cannot really expect better results.

Justice and Government Regulation

The thesis of this chapter is that government regulation of people's commercial activities is wrong because it violates various provisions of justice derivable from the theory of natural rights (à la John Locke) and the underlying ethics of individualism.[28] Some of the points raised in support of the free society and deregulation can be expressed in the language of law, provided we recall that it is not simply positive law but law conceived as a system of justice that is being referred to. Thus reference to the concept of *due process* or *prior restraint* should be understood simply as an attempt to stress the possible connections between the idea of justice that this concept gives expression to, on the one hand, and some existing legal system that is intended to abide by this idea of justice, on the other. (The point is most clearly discussed in connection with the debate about whether the U.S. legal system is committed to substantive or merely procedural due process, especially in relation to economic or commercial aspects of human conduct.)[29]

It is not the thesis of this chapter that if these normative considerations are heeded and make their way into our legal system, there will be perfect attainment of the goals now sought via government regulation. Nor does my argument rest on the view, held by some, that all government regulation must be inefficient; on occasion regulatory measures taken by government can have overall beneficent results. In the particular instance of Thalidomide, which is often cited, it was not such regulation that helped most. The argument here does not reject the research that has convinced many economists of the economic inefficiency of government regulation; it merely rejects the idea that such economic arguments suffice to make the case for deregulation. Economic arguments must be supplemented by normative arguments. Or, to put it somewhat differently, the moral import of an economic argument, focusing as it does on the best means for achieving prosperity in a community, simply is not decisive; it could be trumped by a competing moral consideration. With the economic and the moral objections both well-developed and well-grounded, however, the case for the ever-widening network of government regulation and coercive economic control reveals itself to be extremely weak.

Notes

1. See Nicholas Askounes Ashford, *Crisis in the Workplace: Occupational Disease and Injury: A Report to the Ford Foundation* (Cambridge, MA: MIT Press, 1976); Lee Benham, "The Effects of Advertising on the Price of Eyeglasses," *Journal of Law and Economics* 15 (1972): 337–352; John F. Cady, *Restricted Advertising and Competition: The Case of Retail Drugs* (Washington, DC: American Enterprise Institute, 1976); Rita Ricardo-Campbell, *Drug Lag: Federal Government Decision Making* (Stanford, CA: Hoover Institution Press, 1976); H. J. Levin, "Federal Control of Entry in the Broadcast Industry," *Journal of Law and Economics* 5 (1962): 49–67; Thomas Gale Moore, *Trucking Regulation: Lessons from Europe* (Washington, DC: American Enterprise Institute; Stanford, CA: Hoover Institution Press, 1976); Sam Peltzman, "An Evaluation of Consumer Protection Legislation: the 1962 Drug Amendments," *Journal of Political Economy* 81 (1973): 1049–1091; Richard A. Posner, *The Robinson-Patman Act: Federal Regulation of Price Differences* (Washington, DC: American Enterprise Institute, 1976); Lynne B. Sagalyn and George Sternlieb, *Zoning and Housing Costs: The Impact of Land-Use Controls on Housing Price* (New Brunswick, NJ: Center for Urban Policy Research, Rutgers University, 1973); Murray L. Weidenbaum, *Government-Mandated Price Increases: A Neglected Aspect of Inflation* (Washington, DC: Ameri-

can Enterprise Institute, 1975); Murray L. Weidenbaum, "Reducing Inflationary Pressures by Reforming Government Regulation," in *Contemporary Economic Problems*, ed. William Fellner, (Washington, DC: American Enterprise Institute, 1976). Further work on safety, trucking, airline, and other regulation has also been published by the institute.

2. See Ashford, *Crisis in the Workplace*, p. 13; Benham, "The Effects of Advertising..."; Cady, *Restricted Advertising*; Peltzman, "An Evaluation..."; Weidenbaum, "Reducing Inflationary Pressures..." pp. 274–280.

3. See Milton Friedman, *An Economist's Protest: Columns in Political Economy* (Glen Ridge, NJ: Thomas Horton, 1972); George J. Stigler, *The Citizen and the State: Essays on Regulation* (Chicago: University of Chicago Press, 1975); Yale Brozen, "Wage Rates, Minimum Wage Laws, and Unemployment," in *The Libertarian Alternative*, ed. Tibor R. Machan, (Chicago: Nelson-Hall, 1974); Manuel S. Klaunser and Robert Poole, Jr., "Working within the System: An Interview with Sam Peltzman," *Reason* (June-July 1972):

4. Henry G. Manne, *Capitalism: The Impossible Dream?* Business, Education, Media Series (Malibu, CA: Pepperdine University, 1974).
    Manne's position is, of course, the application of the now famous public choice theory, for which James Buchanan was rewarded with the Nobel Prize in 1986. My own reservations about that theory are advanced in Tibor R. Machan, *Capitalism and Individualism* (New York: St. Martin's Press, 1990). The problem is that public choice theory fits public administration in a welfare state in which no distinction between private and public affairs is possible—all public affairs are, in fact, politicized private affairs. In a limited government context, however, public choice theory may find that the bona fide public service need not degenerate into the pursuit of vested or private objectives. See Chapter 2 for more on this.

5. See Stigler, *Citizen and the State*; Sam Peltzman, "Toward a More General Theory of Regulation," *Journal of Law and Economics* 14, no. 2 (1976): 211–290; Paul W. MacAvoy, ed., *The Crisis of the Regulatory Commissions: An Introduction to a Current Issue of Public Policy* (New York: Norton, 1970).

6. Milton Friedman, "The Line We Dare not Cross," *Encounter*, November 1976, p. 11. This is perhaps one of the clearest statements of the position.

7. Augustus J. Rogers, III, *Choice: An Introduction to Economics* (Englewood Cliffs, NJ: Prentice-Hall, 1971), p. 2.

8. Joe Cobb, Tibor Machan, and Ralph Raico, "An Interview with Milton Friedman," *Reason* (December 1974): 5.

9. Tibor R. Machan, "Economics, Politics, and Freedom: An Interview with F. A. Hayek," *Reason* (February 1975): 11.

10. For example, in Michael Harrington, *The Twilight of Capitalism* (New York: Simon and Schuster, 1976). Harrington's *The Other America* (New York: Macmillan, 1962), helped to launched the "war on poverty." It is noteworthy that some neo-classical economists, such as the late George Stigler, held the view that it is not ideas but expressions of economic self-interest that exert a decisive influence on politics. The impact of Harrington's writing is a clear refutation of that thesis. For a detailed analysis of the Stiglerian thesis, see my "Politics and Ideology: Do Ideas Matter?" *Mid-Atlantic Journal of Business* 28 (1992): 159–167.

11. John Rawls, *A Theory of Justice* (Cambridge, MA: Harvard University Press, 1971); Thomas Nagel, *The Possibility of Altruism* (Oxford: Clarendon Press, 1970), Thomas Scanlon, "Preference and Urgency", *Journal of Philosophy* (November

6, 1975): ?-??; George Kateb, "The Night-watchman State," *American Scholar* (Winter 1975-1976): 816-826.

12. Roger Noll, "The Dilemma of Consumer Protection," in *Regulatory Reform*, ed. W. S. Moore, (Washington, DC: American Enterprise Institute, 1976), p. 44.

13. Ralph Nader, Ronald Reagan, et. al., in Eileen Shanahan (moderator), *Government Regulation: What Kind of Reform?* AEI Roundtable, September 11, 1976 (Washington, DC: American Enterprise Institute, 1976), p. 2; see also David Ferber, "The Case Against Insider Trading," *Vanderbilt Law Review* 23 (1970): 622; Edwin M. Zimmerman, "The Legal Framework of Competitive Policies Toward Regulated Industries," in *Promoting Competition in Regulated Markets*, ed. Almarin Phillips, (Washington, DC: Brookings Institution, 1975), pp. 367-383.

14. For a criticism of this method as a general approach to the study of human action, see A. R. Louch, *Explanation and Human Action* (Berkeley, CA: University of California Press, 1966); Isidor Chein, *The Science of Behavior and the Image of Man* (New York: Basic Books, 1972); Tibor R. Machan, *The Pseudo-Science of B. F. Skinner* (New Rochelle, NY: Arlington House, 1974). See also Machan, *Capitalism and Individualism*, for an extensive discussion of the economic versus ethical justification and analysis of capitalism.

15. Two prominent examples of influential formal arguments critical of the very possibility of policy making from within the empiricist-utilitarian perspective are Kenneth Arrow, *Social Choice and Individual Values*, 2nd ed. (New York: Wiley, 1963) and Amartya Sen, *Collective Choice and Social Welfare* (San Francisco: Holden-Day, 1970).

16. I develop a more detailed argument than it is possible to reproduce here in "On Petty Tyrannies: Morality and Government Regulations," in *Rights and Regulation*, ed. Tibor R. Machan and B. M. Johnson, (Cambridge: MA: Ballinger, 1983), pp. 259-288. The general framework for the present discussion is developed in my *Human Rights and Human Liberties* (Chicago: Nelson-Hall, 1975) and in *Individuals and Their Rights*. See also my "Recent Work in Ethical Egoism," *Americana Philosophical Quarterly* 16 (January 1979): 1-15, for a discussion of the varieties of ethical egoism and their strengths and weaknesses.

17. By concentrating on government economic regulation I do not wish to give the impression that I consider other coercive governmental practices above criticism. Government regulation of religion, the arts, entertainment, or any other human activity also falls victim to arguments based on individual rights.

18. For a detailed examination of the concept of *public*, see chapter 2 of the present work. For a discussion of the public interest, see my "Some Considerations of the Common Good," *Journal of Human Relations* (Fall 1970): 979-994. See also Robert F. Sasseen, "Freedom as an End of Politics," *Interpretation* (Winter 1971): 105-125. For a clear statement of a contrary, welfare statist position see Thomas C. Grey, "Property and Need: The Welfare State and Theories of Distributive Justice," *Stanford Law Review* 28 (1976): 877-902, and Nicholas Rescher, *Welfare* (Pittsburgh: University of Pittsburgh Press, 1975).

19. For historical accounts of the developments of legal trends favoring government regulation, see Jesse S. Rapheal, *Government Regulation of Business* (New York: Free Press, 1966); Posner, *Robinson-Patman Act*, pp. 17-34; William Letwin, *Law and Economic Policy in America* (New York: Random House, 1965); William Letwin, ed., *Documentary History of American Economic Policy* (Chicago: Aldine, 1962); Jonathan R. T. Hughes, *The Governmental Habit* (New York: Ba-

sic Books, 1977). Some legal precedents for the full legitimation of federal government economic regulation include *United States v. E. C. Knight Co.* (1895), and *National Labor Relations Board v. Jones and Laughlin Steel Corp.* (1937).

20. Generally when regulation of business is discussed in the popular media, or even in economic and philosophical journals, no consideration is given to the question whether such regulation might not have untoward consequences for those involved. Since such consequences tend to be gradual and thus are unavailable for purposes of presenting a sensational picture, they are generally treated as nonexistent. Yet there is evidence that government regulation often produces severe hardship for those touched by it. See, for example, Raymond D. Walk, "Analysis of Shipment Trends and Foundry Closings in the U.S.," *Modern Castings Market Insight*, publication no. 739, March 31, 1975. See also "CPSC Mistake Leaves Company Clinging for its Life," *Industry Week* (November 4, 1974): 54. For more detailed discussion of these matters, see Murray L. Weidenbaum, *Business, Government, and the Public* (Englewood Cliffs, NJ: Prentice-Hall, 1977), and Kenneth Chilton, "The Impact of Federal Regulation on American Small Business," (occasional paper, prepared for the Center of the Study of American Business at Washington University in St. Louis, MO, 1978).

21. In Shanahan, *Government Regulation*, p. 7. It was, however, private citizen Mrs. Sheri Finkbein who started the crusade against the drug.

22. Personal communication on U.S. Senate letterhead, November 1, 1973.

23. Machan, *Human Rights and Human Liberties*, and *Individuals and Their Rights*; see also Douglas B. Rasmussen and Douglas J. Den Uyl, *Liberty and Nature, An Aristotelian Defense of Liberal Order* (LaSalle, IL: Open Court, 1991), for more details pertinent to this general framework.

24. See note 11, above, for list of relevant works.

25. Shanahan, *Government Regulation*, pp. 3–5.

26. *Ibid.,* p. 5.

27. *Ibid.*

28. See chapter 2 of this work as well as Machan, *Individuals and Their Rights*.

29. See, for example, Robert G. McCloskey, "Economic Due Process and the Supreme Court," in *The Supreme Court and the Constitution*, ed. P. B. Kurland, (Chicago: University of Chicago Press, 1965); William Letwin, "Economic Due Process in the American Constitution, and the Rule of Law," in *Law and Liberty, Essays on F. A. Hayek*, ed. R. L. Cunningham, (Lubbock, TX: Texas Tech. University Press, 1978), pp. 22–73. See, also, J. Roland Pennock and John W. Chapman, eds., *Due Process* (New York: New York University Press, 1977); Rodney L. Mott, *Due Process of Law* (Indianapolis, IN: Bobbs-Merrill, 1926).

6

Ethics and the Regulation of Professional Ethics

...nothing that is learned under compulsion stays with the mind.

—Socrates

I wish here to continue developing the thesis defended in this work, namely, that obtaining a coherent conception of the public realm requires taking a normative approach to human social affairs. I want to show at this time the scope of ethics and its relationship to that sphere of social concern known as "professional ethics."

Markets involve diverse moral and legal relations. They may be governed by various principles of conduct. The breach of these principles may, in turn, deserve nothing more from us than rebuke or ostracism, perhaps boycott. Others may invite legal action, including legal prohibition or punishment. For example, ordinary promises may not be enforced but breaching them could warrant rebuke, even ostracism. Betraying friends should also be handled along such lines.

Contractual obligations, however, may be enforced by government or some private agency in accordance with due process of law. Violations of basic human rights may be resisted or punished by government. And there may be a substantial area of indeterminacy regarding whether, for example, advertising or marketing a product or service should be construed as involving a legally binding promise, so that violation of it could be taken as not mere moral deception but fraud.

In our time professional ethics is one prime realm of social life that many believe must be placed under stringent public scrutiny. The professional conduct of those who carry out tasks that many members of the public are concerned with or have an interest in—bankers, brokers, television repairers, dentists, psychologists, real estate brokers, doctors, broadcasters, and many others—are to be regulated by the government. And such regulation and licensing are merely taken further by the various federal government agencies that set standards for innumerable professions.

I argue here that a clear understanding of what ethics involves and how it bears on professional ethics does not justify the kind of governmental supervision many in our society deem desirable and even necessary.

The Role of Ethics

Many philosophers, as well as others, accept the view that ethics or morality concerns how we should treat other people. They believe that such a system of principles involves a set of coordinating rules with the goal of guiding human interaction so as to avoid conflicts among the various goals people pursue. When several individuals have wants or needs that cannot fully be satisfied without somebody taking steps to prevent another from realizing his or her goals, morality or a code of ethics must serve to provide for everyone's just due.[1] Otherwise, without such a code, power and might and shrewdness would be the sole means for regulating human interaction.

This view is quite plausible. It is undeniable that at least one use or purpose of any moral position is to provide guidelines for decent conduct toward others. And since when we air our moral concerns to each other these concerns tend most often to bear on problems of human interaction, the appearance is created that the central element of morality is to give us guidance in interpersonal relationships. But is this really the primary or central purpose of ethics?[2]

Philosophers, and others who are systematically concerned with morality, have tried numerous ways to discover how we should conduct our lives, that is, what basic principles should guide human living. I think the best way to discover the answer requires, first and foremost, considering what human beings are. This approach applies to any inquiry where one wants to distinguish between doing well or badly. The growth of a pine tree, the progress of a baseball game, the quality of a ballet performance, and even a discussion of ethics would have to be evaluated by reference to what is known of the subject matter at issue. In some cases, however, choice is involved, and some of those choices have to do with basic human questions. At this point the concern begins to focus on doing morally well or badly. But even here the beginning point has to be a consideration of the nature of what is being evaluated, morally praised or blamed, or given moral direction. Morality involves doing well at being a human being, when this is a matter of choice.

It has to be noted that morality as a distinctive field of human study concerns us because, unlike other animals, we lack instincts or drives that automatically guide us to behave properly. We are the only known living beings that can choose between alternative courses of conduct and can go wrong in our choices. To say that someone should or ought to act in a certain way is already to assume that the person could refrain from so acting. The very idea of morality presupposes that human beings can make free choices, that they possess freedom of the will. To turn it around, it is this freedom to choose that gives rise, in part, to the question of morality.

The other factor that gives rise to morality is that in life some ways of acting have consequences that are good, while others have bad consequences. Morality is the principled and self-determined concern with good consequences where the choice to adhere to or violate principles is a real possibility. (Of course, even when principles are adhered to, unforeseen factors can produce bad consequences, but since these are out of the agent's control, they are morally irrelevant.) Unless some good purpose can be served by conducting oneself in certain ways, right conduct cannot be distinguished from wrong. (I will here ignore various Kantian objections because in my view Kant's approach to morality presupposes radical skepticism about future objectives of either the particular or the general kind.)

In line with the ethics of classical egoism or individualism I have argued for elsewhere, morality need not be confined to social matters. Being a human being and doing the best at this task can occur, and most often does occur, in publicly relevant contexts. But numerous private and personal tasks face us to which the concern with whether we act rightly or wrongly is equally and perhaps even more intensely applicable. Indeed, since the existence of social life is for each person a matter of considerable choice—we could withdraw from others and many of us do to a sizable degree—and since this choice could itself be a right

or wrong one, ethics must be applicable to each of us individually before it concerns us as social participants. While human beings are social
in the sense that they are most likely to realize their full potential in the
company of others (when others are not a severe threat to them), their
individuality is always present as a fundamental fact of their existence.

Professional Ethics

Although it may appear that my view of morality differs drastically
from what others hold, this is not really so. The main difference is that I
regard morality as essential for personal conduct, while others tend to
see it as irrelevant there but applicable only in guiding conduct among
members of a community. The reason is that many have held that when
it comes to personal and especially prudential action, human beings carry
on pretty much instinctively or naturally and only vis-à-vis their social
interactions do they require principles to guide them. But I do not share
this view and, indeed, have argued that it is false.[3]

Still, we all realize that ethics concerns standards of good conduct
applicable to individuals in various professions—law, medicine, business, education, and so forth. A rough but accurate illustration of a standard by which professionals should conduct themselves may be given in
the context of education. A professor should conduct herself by reference to standards that emerge from an understanding of what it is to
teach. When a professor, therefore, uses her classroom to expound on
some theme irrelevant to her subject matter, or, with certain fields, uses
it to single out just one view of the subject matter, then she is violating
professional standards, doing what as a professor she should not do. The
same may be illustrated by reference to the manner in which baseball
umpires can subvert their professional responsibilities, namely, by ruling in favor of people for personal or political reasons, ignoring the
evidence relevant to the rules of the game.

These are just some illustrations of how professional ethical considerations arise for us. But what we want to know is why there is anything
wrong with such conduct. So what if a professor manages to get tenure
and uses her classroom to achieve tasks in conflict with education—
indoctrination, for instance, or searching out a date? What, in short, binds
anyone to her or his professional standards?

It is commonplace to speak of people's obligations, as for instance
their obligation to keep promises, to obey laws that come about in ap-

propriate fashion, to provide a decent upbringing for their children, and so forth. But such commonplace ideas are not without their challenges in professional, intellectual, and lay circles. Why should we keep our promises?

Now, it may appear that the very idea of a promise involves the commitment to fulfill what is promised, but why? Perhaps this is just a myth, a cultural quirk. Some serious people consider any law a mere imposition, with but a facade of obligatoriness, promulgated by those who want their edicts obeyed. Other equally serious people believe that if a parent does not desire to bring up his or her child, the child may be abandoned since there is nothing that binds us to giving our children a decent upbringing. While one may regard such views as contentious and odious, this needs to be demonstrated. Those who object will surely include some very sincere believers, and on the basis of mere disagreement we would merely have a standoff, not a resolution of a controversy.

To put the matter more in terms of professional ethics, why are doctors of medicine who haven't bothered to keep up with developments in their profession irresponsible? Maybe the reward for having stuck it out in the field by cleverly hiding one's incompetence is to be freed of responsibilities? And when one is found out, that's just bad luck, something that befalls both conscientious and irresponsible people in a profession. Unless some ground of a binding nature is identified for professional standards, all talk of professional ethics becomes mere wishful thinking on the part of those concerned with performance and good conscience in the workplace. What this would then come to is nothing more than the pleading of the "case" for one faction in a sort of Hobbesian state of war among various social groups.

Earlier I sketched an argument in support of ethical egoism, the idea that every human being who wants to live is by choice committed to conducting life by certain standards that will help ensure his or her excellence as the person he or she is. The standard most basic to guiding human life is, of course, derived from the nature of such life as understood from what we know of human nature and the world in which people must live. It is possible, however, to extend this very general point of ethics to more specific areas of human life.

If a person makes a free choice to become, say, a medical doctor, lawyer, or salesman, from an ethical standpoint this should have been a choice made in good faith, conscientiously. Ethical egoism does not sanction sloppy choices about one's life goals; they are not choices that bear merely on playing games. Some no doubt take on tasks for the sake of social rewards or other ulterior motives. When such people carry out their work in irresponsible ways, they should either reform their resolve or withdraw from the field. Barring such disorientation, a choice to pursue medicine, for example, must be taken to have been made in good faith and the person who made it is bound by what follows from such a choice. As a growing field of practice, something any ordinary person can recognize, with discoveries coming into play in rapid succession, a medical professional is committed, by his or her own choice, to keeping abreast of the relevant developments. The choice to become a doctor does not imply various specific and particular requirements such as becoming an expert at some particular skill, or learning how to use some tool. It does, however, point to the range of concerns a doctor should attend to. The very understanding of the ordinary concept "medicine," which anyone who chooses this field in good faith should clearly comprehend before making the choice, will involve the realization that to practice medicine competently constant attention to its facets is necessary.[4]

The point applies to all professions. Concerning the specifics, philosophers as philosophers can say very little, but from the philosophical ethics of egoism it is possible to appreciate the general rationale for professional ethics as such. The binding character of professional standards stems from the personal resolve that should accompany a bona fide, freely made or voluntary choice of one's profession. And the standards are binding even when one is tempted to depart from them in line with some strong desire to pursue some competing end.

But this is just the start. What lends greater firmness to the binding nature of one's professional standards is its promissory character. In service professions, such as medicine, a person is not merely committed to some private course of conduct but has gone on record for all to notice that one will do this kind of work. A prediction as to what one is has been announced, as it were, and others, as with honest advertising, have the moral right to expect that this person, free to choose a course of conduct, will do what he knowingly set out to do and make known to others he would do. Among human beings communication is one way to report on facts, plans, and prospects. Honest communication is something someone is rightfully reliant upon, regardless of the fact that under some circumstances, as in talking with Nazis, it may go wrong. So from the moral perspective alone, one's own resolve and one's announcement of this resolve creates a commitment of a binding character. The precise nature of this commitment depends upon the specifics; becoming a taxi driver and becoming a medical doctor carry different implications, but both carry some. And in view of what "taxi driver" and "medical doctor" mean by the standards of reasonableness applied in most civilized legal systems, the announcement of such intentions puts rational expectations before others to whom this is announced who may count on them whenever the choice is free choice.

Of course, the moral commitment alone to standards of professional ethics may not carry the kind of implications one may desire from human interactions, namely, enforceability and penalty for failure of fulfillment.[5] Here is where contracts strengthen the bonds. In short, if when someone offers a service for sale, those who wish to obtain it insist that the service be performed in accordance with certain standards, this insistence can be made enforceable by involving a third party—government or some private arbitration and even enforcement agency. (In some respects, of course, these private agents will be bound by certain legal standards of due process and not left to their exclusive discretion.)

A contract is an enforceable agreement. It requires at least three parties, the two of whom agree on what will be done and how, and the third who is employed to see to it that the terms of the agreement are met. This is a rational approach to securing values and guarding against misspent trust and investment. Other approaches are, of course, available, such as the purchase of insurance against nonperformance or nondelivery.[6]

In cases where persons choose to certify their agreements and to obtain protection against failure to abide by them, the parties involved choose not to rely solely on their information about each other and each other's good record—in other words, they do not wish to depend solely on trust. Where, on the other hand, it is a simple enough matter to institute caveat emptor measures, such enforceability provisions would probably be too involved and costly, and one is often going to be willing to take the risk of having agreements or promises broken, or of being the victim of misunderstanding.

The Role of Force Without Coercion

The point of view I have been taking here is somewhat unusual because it is my contention that when one partakes of market transactions and exchanges, one is not naturally entitled to the agreed-upon performance—that is, it is not one's basic right to have another's mere promise kept. It may be one's special moral right to be treated with consideration, but promises and agreements—and even contractual market transactions and exchanges (i.e., ones legally protected, with terms explicated)—always involve the risk that someone will default. Morally speaking, the fault involved in such noncontractual default in promising or agreeing, as distinct from cases of the violation of legal contract, is more on the order of a self-betrayal than anything else. Deception but no fraud, which is open to legal remedy, is involved. That is, one has chosen to undertake a task and then broken one's word—gone back on this choice or commitment. And the results of such self-betrayal are already considerably adverse. One's self-esteem is undermined, one's reputation suffers, one loses the confidence to make future commitments and promises based on a poor record. So there is no need for enforcement to take place, unless express provisions are made for it.

There are those—I would think the majority of people concerned with the issue in our time—who think that when a moral commitment involving others is breached, punitive measures may be taken; so government may inject itself into the transactions and exchanges between various parties regardless of whether the parties have given their consent. The reasoning underlying this view differs from one ethical perspective to another. Some think this is justified because all transactions and exchanges have a public dimension; so the public interest might then be involved, which could trigger the need for "public" supervision via government. Others contend that each such interaction contains reference to a natural duty. For instance, if I make a promise to another, that promise becomes enforceable because another has acquired a right to fulfillment of the promise; since government enforces rights, government may enter the interaction not only after the event to have the promise fulfilled (or punishment meted out for nonfulfillment), but ahead of time, via extensive government regulation, to prevent nonfulfillment.

The view I have been developing rejects this extensive legalization and judicialization of transactions and exchanges among individuals and groups, unless they expressly invite it in the form of entering into contractual relations. The position I take depends, of course, on a particular conception of the function of government and the relationship between some administration carrying out that function and the individuals' choices. It depends on the kind of delimitation of the public realm developed in chapter 2. In using the familiar terminology, the consent of the governed to have their rights protected provides government with its just powers. More cannot be agreed to, since one has no authority to agree to, say, having another's wealth confiscated or someone else conscripted for military service. So we need to consider the just powers of government, and the criteria for consent.

If adult individuals interact with each other without asking for supervision via contract, to impose regulations upon them would be to subvert their independence as moral agents. If one desires a contract and if the party to the possible transaction agrees, government may be made part of the arrangement. This does not violate the provision for the consent of the governed.

There are complications to this distinction between noncontractual transactions and contractual ones, and some are worth mentioning. When one purchases a ticket to a motion picture showing, does one enter into a contractual arrangement or simply embark upon an exchange? (The famous case of yelling fire in a movie house, incidentally, has little to do with freedom of speech but a good deal to do with whether that is what buying a ticket to see a movie entitles one to do). When prices are advertised for a dozen tomatoes and one pays the price, and the tomatoes are in poor shape—green, rotten—is there anything beyond refusing further trade with the merchant that may be counted on? What is involved in announcing publicly, "A dozen tomatoes for 59 cents"?

In the former case several alternatives could be available, depending on what a ticket is used for. It might be a certificate that is backed by government or some private group designed to arbitrate such conflicts; or it might simply be a convenience for distinguishing those who will be admitted from those who will not be. Before one assumes anything about tickets, one might wish to ask or read them. In the latter case the announcement seems to be no more than a promise, which one may either trust or wish to investigate. Thus, taking a look at the tomatoes would be an alternative open to a person. (In the case of written and published advertisements there may be good reason to hold parties responsible for more than is implied by a mere promise, although this is questionable and it seems to me that common law is not a reliable guide to how we should understand the moral dimensions involved. Suffice it to note that, as I argue in chapter 9, advertising is improperly conceived as primarily an information-conveying practice. It is, rather, an attention-getting device.)

Ralph Nader, at a conference on government regulation at Hillsdale College, Michigan, in April 1976, contended that there is a difference between purchasing apples, whose quality is easily perceived, and purchasing an automobile or a bottle of hair dye, something that requires an expert to evaluate it. He said that in the former case there would be no justification for government regulation by inspection, but in the latter there would be. This point was developed more fully by Steven Kelman, in his important essay "Regulation and Paternalism,"[7] so as to give support to the view that in certain circumstances governmental paternalism is of a permissible type, one that the majority of the people would prefer, were they ever asked about it.

Nader and Kelman are mistaken. One has the responsibility to be more careful in the latter case. This greater care could issue in numerous complicated yet still nonpolitical measures, such as accreditation firms, stamps of approval, insurance, and so forth. Moreover, even if the majority would opt for such paternalistic regulation, they have no moral justification to impose it on others.

The greater complexity does not change the principle involved; a promise made need not be accepted by anyone, so there is nothing that is imposed upon a purchaser against his or her will. If the purchaser chooses to enter into the transaction without requiring a contract and without taking precautionary actions, that is something he or she is at liberty to do. To interpose government between the transacting parties would be to destroy their moral autonomy, their status as choosing agents. It would also preempt for them what their priorities in life should be.

Extensive checking of merchandise is costly. And if the parties wish to invest in other tasks rather then spend their wealth on safety and caution, that is something they ought to be free to do. They ought not to be coerced into risk-free policies because from the outside it is possible to discern that the risk may be too high even for them. They ought not to have their right to be wrong violated.[8]

Of course, they might very well be right. There are no general principles pertaining to what in any particular case is right for various people to do or which of the innumerable alternative values one should seek out more or less vigorously. This does not contradict the validity of general moral principles or virtues, however; it simply acknowledges that how they are to be applied by individuals cannot be simply foretold. Indeed, an individual human being gains moral credit precisely for whether and how he or she implements general moral principles in particular circumstances. The individuality of human beings, their special circumstances, talents, goals, and so on, will play the role of making it rational, for example, for some to invest in safety and for others in ease or higher income.

These are very abstract ways of referring to complicated and multifaceted matters. Basically, I have argued that human beings should live by seeking their happiness in life, which involves some very general and some possibly highly idiosyncratic principles of conduct. Choosing one's job or profession or career would optimally constitute a step in one's pursuit of one's happiness. The choice would also be a commitment to do what one has chosen to do. Thus professional ethics arise from one's pursuit of one's happiness in life, not from some obligations one has to others (after all, some professions such as being an artist or a scientist, need involve no service to others, yet one can default on them, which could be immoral). The commitment to act in accordance with the ethics of one's profession is made firmer by the additional act of going on record for the benefit of informing others of what one is prepared to do. Both the particular requirements of the profession and the general condition of human communications, namely, honesty, involve morally binding elements.

Nevertheless, professional ethics as such, independently of contractual provisions, imply only moral responsibilities, not yet legal obligations to others. The performance of service or delivery of goods is a matter of one's doing what one morally should; others have only a moral, not a legal, right to expect fulfillment—unless, of course, in the course of the relationship such a legal obligation has been agreed to. That means that official or governmental punitive measures are inappropriate, except insofar as they exercise the client's or costumer's right to protest, picket, boycott, blacklist, or refrain from further transactions with the defaulting party.

Of course, provisions are available for a more binding relationship than what is involved in simply offering services and goods. They involve making one's transactions contractually binding. To this end one may be persuaded to enter into contractual arrangements, whereby agreements are enforceable and nonperformance or malpractice legally actionable.[9]

Generally, the viewpoint I have presented takes professional ethics very seriously but resists the attempt of governments to make them a matter of coercion.[10] As a result it implies a free-market approach to professional ethics. It also opposes licensing of professionals. Indeed, it is arguable that professional codes maintained by acts or threats of enforcement really are not a matter of ethics at all, that is, not a matter of (voluntarily) choosing to do the right thing. Yet this view does not deny that professionals owe certain obligations to customers, and there is nothing in what was presented above that precludes post facto litigation based on claims of fraudulent practice, product liability, and so on. What is ruled out is the preemptive government regulatory approach that imposes burdens on members of professions simply for being such members, something that amounts to the practice of prior restraint or, put in the vernacular, extortion.

A final point. The distinction between coercion and voluntary interaction can get hazy in certain regions, especially when the legal mechanism has not had the chance to explore an area of human action and to develop the criterion for peaceful versus hostile interaction. For instance, in the 1920s people had just started to utilize the radio electromagnetic spectrum and it was unclear what constituted imposing on another's sphere, that is, violating property rights in the airwaves. Today the area of videotaping poses a similar problem. Furthermore, often it is difficult to tell in concrete cases whether someone was forced to do something by circumstances no one may be held responsible for—bad health, natural catastrophe, the condition that others have certain rights that bar one from calling upon them at one's own discretion—or was coerced by policies and actions others could have avoided, as when negligence releases toxic fumes and impairs someone's health, or someone loses a job because another business has succeeded through impermissible government protection of an unjustified exemption.

The main thing to remember, in connection with the innumerable and constantly changing interactions, transactions, and exchanges, is that imposing known burdens on others is not justified unless it has been demonstrated that they have harmed someone without justification. In short, in a civilized community, human beings are entitled to be treated as not guilty unless otherwise demonstrated. While government regulation of trade, manufacture, farming, transportation, and other fields breach this provision by imposing burdens on people at large without showing that anyone has earned this imposition, it is quite possible to demonstrate, in courts of law, that some people in the course of performing in their chosen profession have indeed earned it. The onus of proof, however, is always on those who want the imposition. And the hazy areas, where it is unclear if a professional or merchant has done something fraudulent or simply inept, must be subjected to case-by-case scrutiny, however impatient we might get with such laborious proceedings. That is, to put the matter plainly, the price of living in a free society.

Notes

1. For one classic and one routine example of a moral system with an altruistic bent, see respectively, Kurt Baier, *The Moral Point of View* (Ithaca, NY: Cornell University Press, 1958); and Richard Taylor, *Freedom, Anarchy and the Law* (Englewood Cliffs, NJ: Prentice-Hall, 1973). But see the criticism of this outlook in W. D. Falk, "Morality, Self, and Others," in *Morality and the Language of Conduct*, ed. H. N. Castaneda and G. Nakhnikian, (Detroit, MI: Wayne State University Press, 1965), pp 25–67.
2. I will only suggest here why the mainly social conception of morality is in error. For more on this see Tibor R. Machan, "Recent Work in Ethical Egoism," *American Philosophical Quarterly* 16 (January 1979): 1–15; *Individuals and Their Rights* (LaSalle, IL: Open Court, 1989).
3. See, Tibor R. Machan, *The Pseudo-Science of B. F. Skinner* (New Rochelle, NY: Arlington House, 1974).
4. The foregoing presupposes a type of essentialism about such concepts as *physician, teacher, philosopher,* and others that are used to thinking about and refer to various professions. These fields are not so indefinite or ambiguous as to make it impossible for us to have some criteria by which to tell what constitutes practicing them and to use the criteria to tell how well someone practices them given the particular circumstances that he or she faces.
5. This is clearly the most controversial aspect of the present conception of professional ethics. Yet the very idea of morality when applied to practicing one's profession would require that how one performs must not be a matter of compulsion or coercion, lest the performance become void of moral significance. Ought implies can, and if the proper way of carrying on in one's chosen profession becomes a matter of behaving as one is told, surely nothing morally commendable would be evident in what one is doing. However awful it might be that a professional has, through incompetence, helped injure a trusting client, that client was not coerced into associating with the professional but chose him or her freely (or as a result of earlier failure to prepare for emergencies). (But see, also, note 9 below.)
6. Some of the legal permutations of the approach presented here in ethical and political terms may be gleaned from Peter Huber, *Liability* (New York: Basic Books, 1988).
7. Steven Kelman, "Regulation and Paternalism," in *Rights and Regulations*, ed. Tibor R. Machan and M. B. Johnson, (Cambridge, MA: Ballinger, 1983), pp. 217–248.

8. Tibor R. Machan, "Is There A Right to Be Wrong?" *International Journal of Applied Philosophy* 2, no. 4 (1985): 105–109.
9. The common-law tradition will, of course, develop various nuances to pay heed to verbal contracts, implied contracts, etc. Provided this does not contradict the point that legal enforcement may be involved only when contracts (of some kind) have been formed, these approaches to offering services and products are entirely consistent with what is being proposed here. Some say libertarian theory cannot sustain the view that fraud violates rights because, e.g., fraud is only words and we all have the right to speak and write freely. So if one contracts to hand over a car but then delivers a lemon, so what? The buyer has no right to have the seller give over information and the state should not protect people "from their own market mistakes." This would amount to "cutting back the domain of the principle of self responsibility." (James W. Child, "Can Libertarianism Sustain a Fraud Standard?" *Ethics*, Vol. 104 [July 1994], p. 737–8.)

   Libertarianism—which is only a political, not a full philosophical or even moral system—does not spell out fully what fraud involves. Violating a contract—a written and sometimes spoken commitment to deliver goods or services in return for compensation—is legally actionable because it is a performance with indicative meaning created by the performer. Those for whose benefit this is done may normally (without making a "mistake") except delivery and when enforcement has been agreed to (*via* signature, oath, or the like), thos in default may be made to suffer suitable losses to be transferred to the defrauded. In a way the reaction to fraud is justified akin to the way reaction to threats (uttered or written) can be. No "cutting back" of libertarina principles is involved at all. Consenting, after all, has to be done is some fashion.
10. For several interesting discussions of the normative aspects of government regulation of business see Johnson and Machan, *Rights and Regulations.*

7

Occupational Health and Safety by the State

...isn't it lawlessness if a tyrant does not use persuasion, but instead enacts measures and forces the citizens to carry them out?
—Alcibiades

The purpose of this chapter is to explore in some detail, vis-à-vis a special and hard case, how the classical liberal or libertarian natural rights perspective would respond to the welfare statist position that the market morally requires government regulation. I will look at one of the main regulatory agencies of the U.S. federal government, the Occupational Health and Safety Administration (OSHA), and try to determine whether it is morally proper and needed. I will argue that it is not, intuition and argument to the contrary notwithstanding. And in this way I will show that in one of the most plausible instances of its applicability, government regulation of the economy is morally unjustified and should be abolished. In general terms this means that, once again, I will have vindicated the thesis of this work, namely, that public policy ought to be restricted to matters that are of genuine, bona fide public concern—of concern to all citizens as citizens—not to matters that are of special (albeit worthwhile) interest.

Corporations and Government Regulation

In our day, corporations are subject to extensive government regulation. The firms that produce, market, transport, and otherwise help make available all the goods and services we want to have, are regulated by a myriad of municipal, county, state, and federal regulatory agencies. Is the most recent philosophical and moral case for one of these regulatory

175

measures, OSHA, sound? I do not believe so and that is what I plan to argue here.

OSHA is probably one of the most widely supported regulatory agencies of the federal government because it deals with safety and health measures in the workplaces of the United States. Thus it should prove to be a fair test case of the soundness of government regulation in general.

Among the innumerable regulatory bodies, OSHA has managed to acquire a special place. It has often been singled out for its bureaucratic zeal. Members of the business community have frequently "lost their cool" about its conduct, more so than about other federal regulatory bodies such as the Federal Trade Commission (FTC) or the Interstate Commerce Commission (ICC).

OSHA inspectors have been frequent targets of complaint, usually about their unannounced visits to factories or mines to catch firms unaware and find them guilty of some infraction of one of OSHA's thousands of rules. Major court battles have ensued, with OSHA charging business with violating standards and with reckless conduct, and with businesses responding with attempts to squelch the attack.

I will examine the moral dimensions of government regulation, a vital institution of the welfare state—with special attention to OSHA— which should help us decide whether the corporation in a free society is in need of the severe restrictions that some critics (for example, Ralph Nader and Melvin Belli) advocate. My task, in short, is to take a close look at whether the sort of activities OSHA carries out vis-à-vis many corporations is something governments should be engaged in. Some questions surrounding government regulation bear on science, but not on whether hospitals, research centers, space exploration institutes, and the like ought to be run by the state. Neither is ours, then, a scientific question.

The Moderate Complaint Versus the Radical Challenge

There are two prominent opinions afoot regarding OSHA, the first typical of the thinking that supports the welfare state, the second not so supportive. One holds that this agency is a vital and long-needed but only belatedly established protective measure against the recklessness and greed of the business community. As Jonathan Alter remarked, it doesn't take an industrial psychologist to know that the urge [to cut corners on health and safety] gets stronger if businessmen know there's no real threat of getting inspected. There is nothing sinister in this; it's simply a by-product of American capitalism. Indeed, to expect a business to take care of these matters itself on all occasions is to expect it not to behave like a business.[1]

It is the widespread view that corporate commerce is inherently inconsiderate of people's welfare, health, and safety. This has encouraged the emergence of a strongly paternalistic government in our culture. Steven Kelman of Harvard University expresses the view that helped precipitate this development, when he says that "there are frequent occasions when regulatory officials are justified in requiring that consumer products meet certain standards or even in banning them."[2]

Such thinking in the United States is not new by any means, as is shown by what Woodrow Wilson noted almost a century ago:

It was no business of the law in the time of Jefferson to come into my house and see how I kept house. But when my house, when my so-called private property, became a great mine, and when men went along dark corridors amidst every kind of danger in order to dig out of the bowels of the earth things necessary for the industries of the whole nation, and when it came about that no individual owned these mines, that they were owned by great stock companies, then all the old analogies absolutely collapsed and it became the right of government to go down into these mines to see whether human beings were properly treated in them or not.[3]

The other prevalent view is not so harsh about corporate commerce but simply asserts that government regulation has during the last several decades gone overboard. And it is the view of the advocates of this group that OSHA has done so more than the rest of the regulatory agencies.

But this is not a fundamental disagreement, only one about how much is too much. In this discussion we are concerned with a more fundamental issue: is regulation itself morally just? We are concerned with the more basic question about government regulation, and about the welfare state. Specifically, we will argue that government regulation is morally wrong, unjust, and not merely a nuisance from which corporate commerce ought to be rescued.

Those holding this more radical viewpoint would readily admit that problems in the business community exist that might sometimes be solved by OSHA-type organizations. But they deny that there is compelling reason, ultimately, for introducing such an institution, and affirm that there are morally compelling grounds for rejecting OSHA and similar efforts. In the last analysis this position rests on a general argument for the human right to individual liberty and freedom of trade, especially in the labor market. But it is not the familiar economic defense of laissez-faire that will carry the point here. Rather, at the heart of our discussion lies the question of whether a free-market economic system or a welfare state is more just.

The Case for Individual Natural Human Rights

What general, human rights do we all have? I have been alluding to these basic human, natural rights throughout this book and at this point I wish to discuss them only very briefly, (for a detailed treatment, my book *Individuals and Their Rights* would be more appropriate.[4])

Individual natural human rights would be ones we are morally justified to secure by using (organized) physical force—such as an established government—because our human nature requires that in communities other persons treat us as sovereign moral agents. Any government program that would violate these rights would itself be open to moral rejection and opposition.

Our natural rights are absolute, unalienable, and universal because: (1) within their scope, namely, social relations, no excuse legitimatizes their violation or infringement; (2) no one can lose these rights, although some actions a person might take can lead to having to exercise them in very restricted ways (for example, in jail); and (3) every human being has these rights, even when they are not respected by others; (4) having such rights confers upon us the authority to resist, forcibly if necessary (but without undue force), attempts by others to violate or infringe upon them.[5]

Many people want to protect another kind of human right to "freedom," different from the one that is at the heart of the above viewpoint. They wish to have government protect so-called *positive freedom,* meaning the ability (rather than the freedom from others) to flourish in one's life as a human being. In plain terms, many people want government to secure for us not just the right to freedom from other people's violence against us, but also freedom from other hardships we face in life, sometimes as innocent casualties of acts of nature, sometimes because of our own misdeeds or negligence. Yet such a right to positive freedom can only be secured via the full protection of the right to negative freedom. This is because only when the latter is fully secured are human beings going to be most willing and able to provide both for themselves and for others—including the specially needy—the values for our lives. Our right to negative liberty is best secured by the identification and implementation of the human rights doctrine I have just sketched. It is, moreover, the primary requirement of human social life that each person's moral nature be protected and everyone be left free by others to govern his or her life.

Property Rights in Focus

Woodrow Wilson's point that property rights are irrelevant in these days of industrial empires and multinational corporations must be denied. A fundamental principle applicable to human life does not stop being applicable simply because human life becomes more complicated. Theft is theft, whether a cow or a complicated industrial formula has been stolen. Trespassing is trespassing, whether on another's backyard, ranch, or electromagnetic frequency. Clearly, we may come to express the particular form of wrongfulness somewhat differently as the contexts of its manifestation multiply and we find it useful to develop concepts that express the wrongfulness linked to such manifestations. Deception is a form of lying, as is slander, but they communicate more detailed information. Industrial theft might be reconceived and new terms might be found for it as matters get complicated—indeed, I am sure the law has developed innumerable nuances that are not part of ordinary discourse. But the basic principle that stealing is wrong, if correct in the first place about human life in this world, seems to have lasting value. (Only some kind of magic transformation of the world, so that people will stop wanting to have for themselves and their loved one's some of whatever is scarce, could change that—as Karl Marx clearly realized.) In short, the principle of private property rights is basic to human social life whether simple or complex. It is required because all individuals must have a sphere of personal authority wherein they know they have the liberty and responsibility to make right choices and wherein they can succeed or fail in this task. Garrett Hardin's—and Aristotle's—idea of the "tragedy of the commons," which we considered in chapter 1, applies here precisely: If there is no specified individual or voluntarily assembled group with a common chosen purpose to whom a valued item belongs, then the valued item will be mismanaged.[6]

The natural right to private property supports a legal system that assigns freedom—defined as the right to exclusive power of decision or choice—to each individual within some range of alternatives. Individuals, in turn, have the right to pursue their happiness as they see fit, including use of their property to gather into corporations and hire experts to manage these for their mutual benefit. The right to private property creates, in Robert Nozick's terms, the "moral space" we all must have to live life in dignity, without losing our moral autonomy. We may have more or less of such space. The crucial point is that whatever our moral space, it must be clearly identified. The effort by anyone to violate anyone else's moral space is not to be tolerated.

This is the only efficient way to preserve morality in human community life—the only way, too, that individual human beings can exercise personal moral responsibility. The abolition of private property rights will destroy the possibility of bourgeois virtues, as Marx knew very well. His dream of a global commune simply could not promise a better alternative, as indeed Aristotle already noted in his criticism of Plato's similar sketch of such a dream in his *Republic*.

Worker's Rights

What does all this imply for rights in the workplace? (It implies a great deal about rights anywhere else, of course—at the schoolhouse, in the science laboratories, at newspaper and magazine publishing houses, even in the bedroom,) essentially, workers are individuals who intend to hire out their skills for whatever they will fetch in the marketplace. Workers have the right to offer their skills in return for what others, usually called employers in these discussions, will offer as compensation. In short, the framework of human rights sketched here implies free trade in the labor market.

Any interference with mutual trade would violate the rights of the workers as well as their trading partners. It would abridge freedom of association. Workers also have the right, as do others, to organize into groups, with willing associates, and to authorize selected people to represent them in trade negotiations. Defenders of workers' rights believe that employees possess special rights as employees, for instance, rights to occupational health and safety. In general, proponents of such special workers' rights hold that aside from negative rights, workers are owed the (positive) right to be treated with care and consideration on the job.[7] But workers' rights in this sense is an unjustified doctrine and, ultimately, a harmful idea. Failure to be treated with care and respect can be open to moral criticism. When values such as safety and health provisions are neglected by employers, some crucially important features of the work situation could be missing. And there are numerous effective avenues to remedy for this. What is not such a remedy is the idea that workers have a fundamental right to have certain things done for them by employers or "by society."[8] The general value of such provisions is categorically different from that of enforceable positive rights.

Adults have no rights to have benefits provided for them by unwilling others, including their employers. To believe the opposite is to adhere to the doctrine of involuntary servitude. Employers or members of society who would be required to provide for the workers what they need are, indeed, free agents whose conduct should be guided by their own judgments unless they encroach upon someone's natural rights. To believe in, for example, the right to health care for workers is to believe, by implication, that there are persons who are to be forced to provide for the health of these workers—even if they would want to do something else with their lives. Not even the very wealthy or ingenious, for whom it may be nearly an effortless task to provide for others, lack the rights that bar others from treating them as if they were natural resources to be exploited.

Only negative basic rights exist. (There can, of course, exist some positive rights—special ones, for example, and contracted ones in the case of children, and professional services.) There is no basis for the belief in and enforcement of natural or basic positive rights or duties among adult human beings, a belief that is not very different from holding that slavery, serfdom, and other forms of subjugation of some by others "by nature" is morally proper.[9]

Having one's basic, natural (human individual) rights respected is a primary requirement of human life in an organized community and as such merits no special gratitude; one need not thank others for not murdering or assaulting or robbing one. Whereas having benefits provided, however crucial to one's well being, is something that can, in the case of otherwise unrelated individuals, always be taken as an act of charity or generosity.

I should note here that having one's benefits provided by another can, of course, be a function of various moral duties arising out of moral relationships. A physician friend may have a moral responsibility based on friendship to provide certain benefits. Relatives, pals, and even professional associates develop moral ties among themselves which if they went unheeded would merit moral criticism, rebuke, and even condemnation. Even among strangers, certain needs people may have should not go neglected. When a person who has plenty is aware of another in dire need, help would ordinarily be commendable.[10]

This point extends to the employment relationship so that the refusal of some companies to install adequate safety measures and provide adequate protection against health hazards could be open to moral criticism. This is, however, something that can vary from situation to situation, depending on numerous factors that cannot be subjected to some general rule. Although, as one observer has put it, risk is "ubiquitous and inescapable," generalized "regulation may impede risk-reducing change, freezing us into a hazardous present when a safer future beckons."[11]

Many workers' rights advocates claim that a free labor market can lead to horrid experiences such as child labor or hazardous and health-impairing work conditions. However, it is far from true that a free labor market has to imply child labor and rampant neglect of safety and health in the workplace. Children are, after all, dependents. Hence parents owe enforceable duties to children. To subject children to hazardous, exploitative work, to deprive them of normal education and health care, could be construed as a violation of their individual rights as young dependent human beings. Similarly, knowingly or negligently subjecting workers (who have not accepted this condition) to hazards in the workplace constitutes a form of fraud and assault and comes under the prohibition of the violation of the right to liberty and even the right to life. Thus it should be actionable in a court of law and workers, individually or organized into unions, would be morally justified, indeed well advised, to challenge it.

Justice Applied to OSHA

This viewpoint on the nature of a just human community can serve as a basis for examining some of the concrete cases with which OSHA type institutions concern themselves.

Of course, various political systems have been advocated and few of them have ever been fully tried. Socialists and capitalists understandably protest that so-called socialist and capitalist countries are a travesty, nothing like what real socialism or real capitalism would be. The free society, with its authentic capitalist freedom of trade (which gains neither support nor opposition from the state), has never been fully tried. Yet, substantially capitalist systems—England, the United States, West Germany—have done remarkably better for workers than all other types of economic systems, especially socialist ones.

To conclude this discussion of the moral foundations of a system that stresses negative liberty as its primary legal principle, we need briefly to respond to Keynes's observations about the market economy. Contrary to Keynes, there is a much better metaphor at hand for depicting capitalism than his, which has the tall giraffes starving out the short ones. This metaphor is, as I hinted earlier, the marathon race with its friendly yet fierce competitiveness.[12]

In a marathon race thousands of very different people, differently motivated, differently equipped, and generally characterized by multifaceted diversity, all try to do what they believe the race deserves from them. As the race keeps going, the positions of the competitors keeps changing with but a few exceptions. Of all the participants, only one or two take their place up front and only a few are way behind; the bulk keep running in what makes up the huge middle. There are winners and losers, but they don't remain in that position for long. And most people are neither winners nor losers but manage to be more or less successful survivors. Instead, of living lives of quiet desperation, most live lives of modest glory and frequent exaltation, with, of course, some moments of dismay, anxiety, and fear.

This, in the main, seems to me a far more honest and accurate depiction of what a free, capitalist society means to most of us. The combative imagery projected by Keynes's vision is really quite unfair. True, now and then, as in marathon races, cheating occurs. Some participant will trip another or, more subtly, spike another's breakfast orange juice. Some people would like to but either are unable or haven't prepared themselves sufficiently so as to compete. And maybe when, here and there, someone trips through no one else's fault, not everyone will stop to help. But usually some (even without the spectators) will think it more important to help than to keep running. A fair rendition of capitalism is quite possible, provided one is not being guided by some utopian conception of what members of society must be made to conform to.

To try to socially engineer human goodness is a futile task. There is no political solution to the problem of human folly and evil. Making others good by force is impossible and to try is wasteful and insulting. It will also be resisted with black markets, mobs, tax evasion, draft dodging, and the like.

Safety and Health the OSHA Way

OSHA was established mainly through the initiative of Robert Hardesty, a speech writer to President Lyndon Johnson. Hardesty's brother worked for the Bureau of Occupational Safety and Health at what was then the Department of Health, Education and Welfare. This connection led to Hardesty's mention of health and safety concerns in the president's speeches. The speeches, along with some concurrent events, such as reports in 1967 of high lung cancer rates among uranium miners, precipitated the effort that eventually produced OSHA. Hardesty's initiative, the special-interest support of labor unions, the need for issues on the part of the president, and the 1968 Farmington, West Virginia, mining disaster (which took seventy-eight lives), led Congress to pass the Occupational Safety and Health Act (the vote was 534–5 in the House and 83–3 in the Senate). President Richard Nixon signed the bill on December 29, 1970.[13]

OSHA was established so as "to assure so far as possible every working man and woman in the Nation safe and healthful working conditions."[14] With respect to safety, the degree of protection to be provided by the regulations had been left pretty much unspecified by the Act of 1970. OSHA's regulations originate with initial recommendations from the National Institute for Occupational Safety and Health, a research organization located in the Department of Health and Human Services (HHS), originally known as HEW. Then an advisory committee is appointed, including representatives from labor, business, and the "public"—someone from "Nader's Raiders," in other words. Concerned "outsiders" frequently get a chance to be heard at open meetings. Then a proposed regulation is published in the Federal Register, representing "an initial consideration of the technical evidence and of the deliberations of the advisory committee."[15]

These initial procedural specifications were supplemented by others in executive orders from presidents Gerald Ford and Jimmy Carter. OSHA regulations now must be accompanied by environmental and economic impact statements (that is, by some kind of cost-benefit analysis and inflation projection). After public hearings on the proposed regulation (and other minor procedure), the regulation is published in the Federal Register in its final form, accompanied by a "statement of reasons." OSHA's decisions can be challenged in court.

The Occupational Safety, and Health Review Commission

Some of the details about one of OSHA's most important branches will be useful here. It is fairly typical of the mechanisms of the welfare state. With a 1982 budget of $8 million and a staff of 168, the Occupational Safety and Health Review Commission—which is but a branch of OSHA—is charged with the responsibility "to rule on contests initiated by employers or employees subsequent to a workplace inspection by OSHA." Established in 1971, "the Commission acts as a court to rule on alleged job safety and health violations cited by OSHA that are contested by employers or employees after a workplace inspection."[16]

A typical subject under OSHA's jurisdiction is the noise level to which workers may be exposed on the job and how workers must be protected against levels above the permissible ones. As Kelman notes:

> Reducing exposure to health hazards (such as noise or chemicals) by engineering controls is often horrendously expensive, especially when the new controls must be fitted onto existing machines at existing plants with fixed layouts. By contrast, personal protective equipment—earplugs, earmuffs, and respirators—costs a tiny fraction of what engineering controls cost.[17]

OSHA urges engineering controls, mainly because "workers do not like to wear [earmuffs, earplugs, etc.]."[18]

To do otherwise would put the burden on workers, not on employers. OSHA prefers such engineering controls also in view of their efficiency. "Once engineering controls have been installed, the problem is basically solved. OSHA inspectors can observe whether the controls have quieted the work place down to the threshold-limit value and thereby establish compliance or noncompliance."[19] However, if the burden were placed on workers, they could just put on their uncomfortable earplugs when the OSHA inspectors came around and take them off later. That would make OSHA's inspections entirely ineffective. Industry guidelines also point to engineering controls as preferable to personal protective equipment.[20] Professional hygienists find the personal protective approach a kind of "paste-over, a Band-Aid."[21] Once such professionals assume control of what is to be done in the workplace, it is expected that the personal protection approach will be rejected by the inspectors.

OSHA has been enforcing its edicts and getting fairly consistent success in court rulings when challenged by various firms. Courts have also ruled against challenges to OSHA's power of imposing fines. The claim that this violates the constitutional right to a jury trial was dismissed. In one case, however, the court ruled that OSHA inspectors must obtain warrants before inspecting a firm. They made this burden very light by spelling out rather liberal criteria for the granting of such warrants.[22]

OSHA's Record

Even if we were to question OSHA's legitimacy merely on the basis of its effectiveness, by many accounts its success in reducing injuries at the workplace has been doubtful, since "the BLS [Bureau of Labor Statistics] found that after a three-year decline, on-the-job fatalities among employers with 11 or more workers were 20 percent higher in 1977 than in 1976."[23] A study by *Business Week* magazine offers a similar picture. It appears that the less money OSHA has available, the more efficient its work—that is, the less there is of OSHA's budget, the lower becomes the national injury rate in the workplace. *Business Week* went so far as to report that the correlation of coefficiency, for ten years, "tells us that increasing OSHA outlays predicts a higher (accident) rate and decreasing them predicts a lower rate."[24]

Figure 7.1 further supports doubts about OSHA. It shows that, at least for a given period of time, OSHA measures had little beneficial influence on workplace fatalities. Of course, to learn precisely of OSHA's influence, one would have to carry out research that would control for all other possible influences—technological innovation, normal improvement in health protection based on ordinary experience and learning, and so forth. Yet, given that the federal government is satisfied with this kind of data, it should suffice for us to indicate that OSHA is no guarantee of improved health protection in the workplace.

There have been different accounts of OSHA's record, as well. We can by no means contend that any of these is conclusive concerning

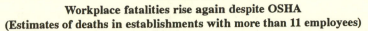

FIGURE 7.1
Workplace fatalities rise again despite OSHA
(Estimates of deaths in establishments with more than 11 employees)

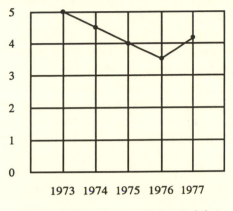

1973 1974 1975 1976 1977

● = thousands (Data: Bureau of Labor Statistics)

FIGURE 7.2
Workplaces Become Safer
(Workplace injuries or illnesses per 100 private full-time workers)

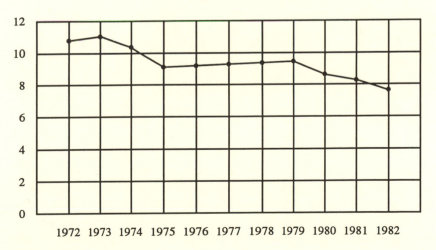

1972 1973 1974 1975 1976 1977 1978 1979 1980 1981 1982

Data: Bureau of Labor Statistics

OSHA's failure or effectiveness as regards the fulfillment of its goals. Figure 7.2 gives a mixed picture. A "preliminary Labor Department analysis" has reached the conclusion that OSHA's rule to limit workers' exposure to inorganic arsenic has cut their risk of developing lung cancer about 98 percent. Thorne Aucher, OSHA's chief in early 1982, explained that OSHA's first formal finding of "significant risk" shows that the agency's arsenic standard greatly reduces the risk of job-related cancer for the workers who face the most serious exposures.[25] The study determined that if current OSHA standards had prevailed for forty-five years, "only" 10 out of every 1,000 workers exposed would die of lung cancer, but that at the level permitted before 1978 the rate was between 375 and 465 for every 1,000 workers exposed. Robert S. Smith, in a study of OSHA's performance, notes that no one denies that effective health and safety regulations have benefits.

> The benefit of a lower speed limit is the reduced risk of injury every time one drives; the benefit of dust control in a coal mine is a decreased probability of a miner's contracting black-lung disease; and the benefit of lower noise levels in factories is a reduction in the risk of hearing impairment. Safety and health are goods in the sense that they enhance welfare....For greater safety or health to benefit society, the value of the reduced risk must exceed the value of the resources used to obtain it.[26]

There are also the more partisan records of OSHA's recent efforts. The U.S. Chamber of Commerce, for example, has been keeping track of just how well OSHA's regulatory activities have done in reducing injuries in the workplace. Here is the chamber's analysis:

> Statistics show that employers and employees respond better to reasonable enforcement policies, unlike the regulatory extremism of the past. Through better targeting, increased incentives and increased responsibility for employers and state people and less cost to taxpayers, American workers are better protected to the advantage of all concerned parties. Beyond the statistics, the business community is now convinced of the legitimacy of OSHA's purpose and the role to be played by the federal government in occupational safety and health efforts.[27]

The chamber is simply claiming, in effect, that moderate regulation is better than extreme regulation, leaving it unclear how the distinction is to be determined. In one of its news releases the chamber explains that during the "most stringent and adversary" periods of OSHA's regulatory activity, "the period 1976–79, the rate of serious injuries and illnesses rose 22.9%, their severity rate rose 12.7%, and workplace fatalities rose 30.6%"[28] Furthermore, reports the chamber, comparison of the first full year of the Reagan Administration (1981) versus the worst performance year of the Carter Administration (1979) in occupational injury statistics shows that incidents rates per 100 full-time workers dropped: (1) in total injuries from 9.2 to 8.1; (2) in lost workday injuries from 4.2 to 3.7; (3) in nonfatal injuries without lost workdays (minor injuries) from 5.0 to 4.4; and (4) in total lost workdays from 66.2 to 60.4.[29]

Peter Huber observes that "regulation may impede risk-reducing change, freezing us into a hazardous present when a safer future beckons."[30] By their very nature laws and regulations must be generalized, and they last until the democratic process repeals them.[31] Moreover, OSHA-type regulations sometimes contradict others that aim for different objectives. For example, certain chemicals seem to do harm only to women, some only to men. Dibromochloropropane, a soil fumigant, is suspected to cause sterility among male workers, while polyvinyl chloride seems to be harmful to female workers.[32] The idea that general standards can be established by OSHA or the Food and Drug Administration for the use of chemicals, for the consumption of food additives, or for exposure to noise seems to be undermined by enormous individual differences, as well as group differences between races, sexes, etc.

Clearly, then, government regulators are sometimes willing to proceed with haste and thus do not pay close enough attention to the scientific evidence underlying the problem that they are supposed to solve.[33] There is evidence that OSHA has relied in the past on flawed studies[34] so as to set new regulations.

Comment on the Numbers

Statistics bearing on matters involving value (especially moral) considerations are always a bit suspect. They usually record correlations, not even causal relationships, and that itself poses difficulties when it comes to laying blame on various parties and drafting punitive legislation and regulation. It is furthermore possible that OSHA's longevity does not suffice to prove its effectiveness. And effectiveness itself is a complex issue since one cannot judge it without first determining what the goals are or should be. In the last analysis all the data about OSHA's effectiveness must be assessed in the light of the general moral framework. One might best appreciate this point by considering that censorship might improve news reporting, even literature and scientific writing. Such censorship might then be regarded as effective, and studies could be developed to demonstrate as much. Yet we should discount this on grounds that there are other values to be preserved by a free press.

OSHA's occasional effectiveness need not be disputed. Despite occasional desirable results, and even if OSHA's overall contribution to our society exceeded its enormous cost (which will be considered shortly), the institution is in such fundamental discord with basic values of human social and political life that it must be rejected. Instead of looking to OSHA for the relief, we must explore other alternatives.

"Right-to-Know" Laws

What are right-to-know laws? They aim to compel companies to inform workers of the risks they face at the job. They often require firms to make information available to workers about toxic substances being used in the workplace. Some require that the public in the vicinity also be provided with such information.

Right-to-know legislation and resulting regulation rest on the belief that when certain information can benefit workers or consumers, those who have this information should be legally required to provide it to those who might benefit from it. Right-to-know provisions are motivated, in part, by the moral conviction that workers and consumers, who are not expected to be experts on such matters, should not be burdened with having to discover whether the workplace or the goods and services being sold on the market are hazardous to their health and safety.

There are complicated matters at issue here. Under right-to-know laws, firms would very often divulge trade secrets by informing workers or consumers about possibly hazardous materials. They might very easily frighten workers and consumers about either their work conditions or their products. It would also be costly for them to provide the information, a matter that could influence prices and wages.

It is also arguable that workers could learn of any hazards, if they wanted to, by asking about them. They are free not to work for companies that refuse to divulge information about hazardous substances. Consumers, in turn, maybe in a similar position. They could ask about the products they are interested in—even support businesses that look into these matters, such as Consumers' Union—or they could abstain from purchasing these products and go where their wishes are better satisfied. Both workers and consumers could organize to exert influence upon firms to provide information, as well as take legal action in cases where a firm's refusal to divulge relevant information might constitute a kind of deceit or even fraud—for instance, where the job description failed to reveal hazards, or where there were products that might cause harm (or where the risk of causing such harm was significant) and this information was not provided. Some kinds of hazards may be inherent in a certain line of work, and if in hiring workers this information is suppressed, that would be fraudulent employment practice.

Right-to-know legislation and regulation is a mixed bag and often requires divulgence that goes beyond what may be warranted. The law on providing information has not really been necessary in the large chemical companies. As one Du Pont Company worker observed in the early 1980s, "The large chemical companies aren't the ones this is aimed at. We worry about the little plants and the nonunion plants. Why shouldn't everyone be entitled to get this information?"[35]

The "right-to-know (or right-to-be-informed)" type of legislation often associated with the workers' rights movement is fully applicable to cases of the kind where the work entails discernible hazards for workers as such. But it may not be applicable in cases where hazards face only those with special characteristics. Yet in the former case, the protection of such a right would follow from provisions against fraudulent employment or trade, rendering regulation superfluous and an example of prior restraint.

Comment on Right to Know

Plainly, to many of the workers the knowledge at issue would be of considerable value. But is it the kind of value that is owed to them by their employers? Based on the "reasonable man" doctrine of the law— which rests the determination of responsibility on whether the parties charged with nonperformance created an expectation of such performance within the context of the situation—it does seem that when workers are placed into situations that, unbeknownst to them, pose hazards to their health and well-being, they are being unjustly victimized. Were one to invite guests into a home contaminated by a serious disease, they would surely be owed knowledge of this fact before being given the option to enter. Or suppose that a workplace is such that those working there will encounter extreme physical hazards of a more familiar sort, such as the danger of falling off scaffolds or being swept away by waves on the open seas. Surely they are entitled to a job description that contains these features of the job they are being offered. It is a matter of being told what they are being hired to do and that the job may include certain costs to them in addition to the time and energy they are expected to exert. It would be quite rational to interpret the failure to provide this information as a kind of fraudulent or negligent conduct on the part of firms. Of course this is not a matter that can be handled without complications. Some workers probably would suffer from exposures to substances that would not do harm to others. Sometimes women may suffer from exposures that do not hurt men, blacks from ones that do not hurt whites, youngsters from ones that do not harm adults, slightly built people from ones that do not bother more bulky ones, and so on. In short, there are individual variations.

But even here matters are not simple. If some line of work is known to be hazardous to certain types of persons—women, twenty-five year olds, those with emphysema—withholding this knowledge from them should be legally actionable. Here the law would have to be developed, probably through several court cases. But government regulation, such as the kind produced by OSHA, preempts this legal process and muddies the waters of justice.

There is a basic responsibility to identify hazards to human beings as such. Employers, for example owe workers up-to-date information about contact with substances—or significant risk of such contact—that are poisonous to any human being. Is anything else owed to workers? Is it the employer who must discover the particular vulnerabilities of employees and then make sure they know of the likelihood of being hurt because they will be exposed to certain substances that hurt them but not others? There are people with allergies who would suffer terribly from working in the wild at certain times of the year, while others are unaffected. Must employers inform these special individuals of what would harm them?

A basic right to be informed about what generally harms human individuals goes with the basic right to be told about what the job is that one is hired to do. Again, failure to inform would be a type of fraudulent employment practice or trade. That is part of the governing system of a free market in labor, as in any other commodity: not informing parties to the trade of the significant, crucial facts involved in the trade is fraud. It is (or should be, in a just legal system) an actionable misstatement of the conditions of the trade, made in the course of establishing conditions of employment. Beyond that no justification for demanding additional information appears to exist.

In any case, OSHA has little to do with the question of any right to know about hazards in the workplace. That is one reason why its recent "gutting" of "a 'right to know' rule that would have required employers to identify hazardous substances to workers exposed to them"[36] cannot be construed as morally objectionable. The right-to-know is a matter of contract law and fraud. OSHA regulates the workplace, whereas right-to-know rules are standards of the employment relationship, so that when violations of the standards are brought to the attention of the authorities, prosecution could ensue.

A wholly free, pure, unregulated market economy is one that may very well have laws on the books protecting certain derivative rights in various areas of human life, among which the right to be informed of adverse work conditions could be included. Civil rights, political rights, and various other special and contractual rights are precisely the subject of legislative action. But these would not generate government regulation, merely laws on the books in accordance with which criminal, civil and administrative suits could be brought against offenders.

The crux of the difference between such laws and government regulation is that the laws exist as standards of behavior and when someone is suspected of having broken such laws and acted in violation of such standards, he or she may be prosecuted. In the case of regulation, however, there is prior restraint, whereas in the case of prosecution the onus of proof of lawbreaking is on the authorities. Furthermore, in government regulatory action the agency, such as OSHA, imposes various burdens on people, supervises their actions, and inspects their property, despite no proof of any violation of rights by the individuals who are so burdened.

Right-to-know—or right-to-be-informed—legislation merely establishes a more detailed specification of what rights individuals have in society. With such laws on the books, it is easier to identify rights violations. The basic human right in need of protection, in case of the right-to-be-informed laws, is the right to life or liberty. And the special area of protecting this right is in the sphere of commercial interaction involving labor. Obtaining value from a worker without truthfully explaining that the worker will very probably lose something crucial in the process—for example, so many years of life due to the high probability of lung cancer that goes with the job—would be, if done either knowingly or negligently, a violation of the worker's rights to life and liberty. There are of course "judgment calls" in matters that cannot be handled without full knowledge of the context, even in what aims to be a coherent and complete system of rights. Because the spheres of application of the protection of rights constantly change, especially in highly technical areas such as those OSHA is concerned with, this is bound to be so. But a basic distinction between information "everyone should be entitled to get" and information that serves a special purpose of the particular worker needs to be kept in mind. If I sell someone a car unfit for human use and still maintain it is a car, I am perpetrating fraud. If I sell someone a car with seats especially harmful to those with back trouble, I am not doing anything wrong, even if this person does have back trouble. Here caveat emptor is fully applicable.

This is not a point of law but of morality and legal theory. We are talking about which laws serve justice and which thwart it. The points just made accordingly bear on our investigation of OSHA by making clear that OSHA's power goes beyond what a just system of laws warrants when it is legally authorized to regulate the workplace concerning what needs to be told by employers to employees. A just system would regard it a matter of mutual agreement whether employer informs employee about various possible hazardous or dangerous facilities, materials, processes, etc., in the workplace. What is not optional under such a system is describing accurately the job to be done by the employee. And if such a job inherently causes harm to normal human beings—for instance, to the lungs, liver, heart, or other vital organs of any person—then employees are owed a report of this when they are told what job they are being offered. The reason is that a failure to identify the job as inherently destructive of some element of human life—that is, normally harmful to workers—would amount to fraudulent conduct. And fraud, that is, trading goods or services falsely identified, is a violation of the rights of the party getting value delivered.

What I have argued here, in connection with right-to-know laws or legal provisions, is that any OSHA type regulation requiring that workers be properly informed about the nature of their jobs would be redundant. OSHA is not needed for this purpose. What is needed are well-crafted laws on the books in terms of which workers can file complaints.

Unfortunately, often when regulators begin to be active in an industry, they assume jurisdiction over genuine unjust lawless conduct. For example, the Securities and Exchange Commission (SEC) has a fraud division. Aside from handling such matters as what brokers may or may not say and to whom and when, the SEC is also involved in prosecuting cases of plain fraud. Yet such cases should be handled within the judicial branch of governments, not under any kind of regulatory authority, which is unjust. In the course of approaching these kinds of disputes within the framework of adjudication, rather than regulation, the needed care can be taken so that due process of law is observed and no prior restraint or imposition of undeserved burdens occurs.

This example also brings up the general problem of arguing about the activities of many other regulatory agencies. Among them is the SEC, an agency that handles many cases belonging within the judicial branch of government, which is largely based on the wording of the U.S. Constitution, with its Bill of Rights. Thus the SEC is much closer to fostering justice in some cases than are other federal regulatory agencies. When regulatory agencies begin to do what prosecutors of rights violators are supposed to do, they acquire credibility. From the moral point of view, what they do, for example, in combating fraud is perfectly proper. It is difficult to credibly oppose them when, aside from the unjust things they do, they also carry out some perfectly just policies, such as prosecuting perpetrators of fraud.

As John Locke (as well as the Declaration of Independence) noted long ago, we will tolerate a lot from government merely to remain stable. The petty tyrannies of government are wrong but not unbearable. Much more evil has been endured in human history than such petty tyrannies amount to.

Social Cost-Benefit and OSHA

In a welfare state largely committed to a (social) scientific approach to government, social cost-benefit considerations loom prominent. This means that when governments set out to implement their agendas, they try to determine whether their plans enhance or thwart the overall measurable welfare of the membership of the community.

The best, yet very controversial, information available on OSHA's value to our society as a whole during the 1980s can be appreciated when one considers that complying with OSHA costs about $35,000 annually for companies that have from 1 to 100 employees, $75,000 for ones with 101 to 500, and $350,000 for those with 501 to 1,000.[37] These figures are, as Robert S. Smith observes, possibly "biased upward in an attempt to persuade the government to adopt a go-slow approach to job safety and health."[38] The estimates are supported by the fact that the thirty-three businesses that obtained loans from the Small Business Administration for the purpose of compliance with OSHA needed, during the early 1980s, an average loan of $200,000.[39] While admitting that the general approach of calculating the social costs and benefits of OSHA type regulations is troublesome, some observers hold that the method is valid for certain limited purposes. To ensure a one-in-one-thousand reduction in the risk of death (so that the risk will fall from two out of every 1,000 each year to 1 out of every 1,000), certain calculations are available: "[T]he cost per worker for this kind of risk reduction is as follows for several recent standards: inorganic arsenic: $1,000 to $9,000; coke-oven emissions: $4,000 to $158,000; vinyl chloride: $5,00 to $10,000; deep-sea diving: $15,000 to $39,000."[40] But, as Smith makes clear, the entire calculation depends upon "the value workers place on being provided with a one-in-one-thousand reduction in the risk of death."[41] If OSHA has incorrectly assessed workers' judgments in these matters, it "may be mandating that resources that are very valuable to people in some alternative use be employed in a manner that does not produce benefits of comparable value."[42]

John Mendeloff argues that OSHA costs far more than it benefits our society.[43] Still, Mendeloff maintains that although pressure on OSHA to quantify is desirable, ignoring or belittling the uncertainty [that's involved] is not, because it diverts attention from the need to devise ways to reduce uncertainty and to decide how its presence should affect the choices we want regulators to make.[44]

Others find little hope in the cost-benefit approach. As observed earlier, Steven Kelman, who has argued against taking it too seriously, observes that "simple cost-benefit calculations may be less important than more abstract conceptions of justice, fairness, and human dignity."[45] We saw in chapter 3, however, that the welfare statist idea of justice fails. Its main proponents—Vlastos, Gewirth, and Rawls—have not fared well in their arguments.[46]

Kelman himself has relied to a large extent on the Rawlsian framework, in preference to cost-benefit analysis. He is among those whom Kristin S. Shrader-Frechette calls advocates of "the deficiency argument." In her guarded defense of risk cost-benefit calculations, she maintains that such analysts appear to ignore the value of admittedly flawed, systematic approaches (such as RCBA [risk cost-benefit analysis]), and prefer nonsystematic, nonanalytic approaches (such as intuition and open discourse). Thus, proponents of the deficiency argument underestimate the benefits of using RCBA. Likewise they appear to overestimate the possibility of rational policy making when no analytical procedure is part of the process.[47]

What this means is that we really should not complain about the problems associated with cost-benefit analysis or risk cost-benefit analysis if we have nothing else as a substitute. As Schrader-Frechette puts it, "any decisive argument against RCBA ought to explain why the known flaws of this technique are more significant than the flaws of other approaches, and why rational policy making appears more likely in the absence, rather than the presence, of RCBA."[48]

Shrader-Frechette explains forthrightly the problems with RCBA:

1. there is no widely accepted theory of rationality, yet such a theory appears necessary if one is to take RCBA seriously;
2. the democratic process, not some mathematical-economic theory, ought to determine public policy;
3. RCBA ignores factors such as the equity of distribution and the incommensurability of various parameters;
4. RCBA's data base is inadequate;
5. RCBA experts disagree fundamentally among one another;
6. RCBA cannot take account of various political, ethical, and religious attitudes.[49]

Based on these observations, we must—within the framework of the social cost-benefit analysis debate—agree with the kind of results that John Mendeloff found, namely, that OSHA is more expensive to us than we can afford. In other words, given our best estimates of the value of goods and services, our society appears, from the evidence, to value alternatives to OSHA more than OSHA itself.[50] It means that what we now pay for OSHA regulation could obtain more of what we actually value, if we could make the choice to spend it on something else.

All this does not show OSHA to be of no value. That is, it does not show that OSHA's efforts and achievements are not valued. Neither does it prove that OSHA should not exist.

When we judge matters not on the basis of their propensity to produce desired goals but whether they are morally and politically appropriate, some policy or institution could fail to be cost-effective and yet be quite appropriate. One need only think of the constitutional protections of the rights of the accused and criminals to appreciate this fact. One does not even ask the question whether it is cost-effective to protect the rights of the accused. It is a matter of justice, not of utility.[51]

Comment on Cost-Benefit Analyses

Can it be shown that some policy or other will produce quantitatively specifiable betterment for society, as against alternative policies? There are several controversies associated with the social cost-benefit approach. There is the issue of whether any quantitative standard of betterment exists at all—and of whether such a standard exists for society as a whole. There is also the question of whether some central decision-making process, carried out by government, is suitable for calculating overall social cost-benefit.

Put in plain terms, is it possible to tell whether we are well off in terms of some numbers—whether we have so much money, such and such a degree of health, so many friends, so much productivity, or whatnot? And if it is possible to do this for individuals, is there some way to calculate the matter for society at large? Is there a quantifiable social good?

The problems associated with social cost-benefit analysis are notorious and they are widely discussed in the literature of public choice.[52] We cannot treat the matter here in detail but we can report on some general results and add some reflections on how these apply to the topics with which OSHA is primarily concerned. Mainly what we need to note is that OSHA is one among many agencies of our government that costs taxpayers considerable money, labor, opportunities, and possible opportunities. Does what OSHA accomplishes compensate for these losses? And how would we tell? One of the elements of this problem lies in calculating the value of life and limb. Mendeloff observes that although OSHA acknowledges in its cancer policy that risk assessments may be useful, it has never done any, asserting that solid bases for making such estimates do not exist. However, others have used data OSHA has gathered to suggest that the coke-oven standard would prevent workplace cancer deaths at a cost of anywhere from $500,000 to $150 million per death prevented. Richard Wilson estimated that OSHA's 1 ppb [parts per billion] benzene standard would cost $300 million per death prevented. It was also estimated that the 2 ppm [parts per million] acrylonitrile standard would cost $3.5 million per death prevented. A study of the asbestos standard adopted in 1972 suggested that the costs had probably been $250,000 or less for each death prevented.[53] Nevertheless, Shrader-Frechette is not impressed with the skepticism about RCBA. As she notes in the statement already quoted, unless we have something better to offer, we cannot complain about this admittedly flawed approach to public policy determination.

But do we have a better alternative? Is there a more appropriate way of judging public policy than social cost-benefit (risk) analysis? This question has two different senses: It may uncritically assume that at least some kind of decision-making procedure is going to be required, and so even a flawed one is better than none. But it may also raise the question of whether we should accept that some kind of decision-making process must be invoked. Perhaps we should take the unavailability of a method for making decisions concerning these problems as a clue that some sets of problems should not be a part of public policy.[54]

If one wishes to stick to making decisions concerning matters that should not be subjected to public decision making, one will of course seek out some systematic, analytic process, regardless of how flawed it may be. But we should go into the matter more in depth and ask this question: When ethically neutral modes of inquiry come up with conclusions doubting the rationality of some methodology, can we really accept that the subject matter at hand is the province of proper public policy-making?

Shrader-Frechette herself mentions a plausible (and, by many, highly preferred) alternative to RCBA, namely, participatory democracy with a moral foundation. What this approach would accomplish is to make the policy that arises from the use of RCBA morally proper. But Shrader-Frechette regards the introduction of such moral constraints as unrealistic because they include measures that are difficult to satisfy. Among them, most importantly, all the persons who are affected by such policies would have to be "noncoerced, rational, accepting of the terms of the procedure by which they seek agreement, disinterested" and so forth.[55]

Shrader-Frechette's point is that in the case of institutions such as OSHA, in a political climate that tolerates petty tyrannies, it is difficult to approach public policy in a principled fashion. But we may also conclude, more constructively, that what we learn from all this is that some matters are not to be left to public choice, period.[56] Indeed, once a suitable set of moral constraints has been found, it will help us determine whether some realm of human life ought to be subjected to politics in the first place.

Various analytic problems about regulation give concrete expression to what has been argued by scholars at a more abstract level:

1. Government planning for a democratic society must involve irrationalities.[57]

2. Wholly, centrally, or even democratically planned, economic decision making will necessarily fail.[58]

3. A necessary condition of morality, namely, the right to private property, is undermined in the welfare state.[59]

I will not rehearse these matters here but simply note them. It is more important now to consider what responses have been offered to the criticisms. How then should one respond to the theoretical problems that confront such institutions as OSHA? Some have argued that we must muddle through, whatever the theoretical problems. A good example of this is Jerome Rothenberg, who has argued that despite these difficulties we must proceed with the welfare state the best we can.[60] As Samuel Scheffler puts it: "In political theory as in life one can't always enjoy all good things together. All too often we must sacrifice one to save another."[61]

With this attitude by defenders of the welfare state, it is difficult to see why they do not begin with accepting the kind of sad but unavoidable situation described by John Maynard Keynes in his lopsided metaphor of capitalism as mirroring the case of the lucky giraffe versus the unlucky animals unable to reach their nourishment. But, assuming that Keynes's picture of capitalism is correct, it seems that the welfare state, introduced precisely to set matters straight, simply fails to make sure that the humanitarian values alluded to by Keynes will be properly served.

Rothenberg's and Scheffler's suggestions amount to nothing less than capitulation to what for them must appear as gross injustice.

In contrast, we could view the situation along lines spelled out by another philosopher, Ranford Bambrough, who has noted that "it is self-defeating to attempt to impose a requirement which must necessarily fail to be satisfied by every conceivable attempt to provide a justification."[62] Which is to say, we are entitled to question a theory of a good and just society that fails as both a matter of abstract theory and in practical implementation.

Within the framework of the individualist approach the constraints on public policy are such that only very limited areas of human community life can be left to politics.[63] This emerges from moral and political theory itself, directly, as well as from attempts to produce a rational account of the welfare state's public decision-making processes. When we consider that some of the concepts proposed turn out to make no sense, that is, do not refer to what could in fact exist in reality, then we can see the force of the criticism of social cost-benefit analysis.

None of this makes cost-benefit analysis irrelevant to the decision-making processes of individuals and voluntary groups. Once everyone's consent has been obtained, the viability of such procedures as cost-benefit analysis changes considerably.[64] And of course within the moral theory I have outlined earlier in this work, consent is one of the primary ingredients of moral social relationships.

Practical Versus Moral Issues in Focus

Moral considerations override pragmatic ones; indeed, it is not possible to know what is ultimately effective or workable without first determining what ought to be done. This is the first point to be made in connection with any discussion of OSHA's record and the methodology employed in implementing its policies. One cannot assess the value of an institution such as OSHA on the basis of quantitative analysis. The performance of OSHA can produce benefits to some. It is clear that these benefits will involve costs. But even if it were possible to benefit society more than to harm it by establishing an agency such as OSHA, it could still be argued that we ought not to sacrifice certain basic societal principles for the sake of such benefits.

I have already indicated that even if it could be shown that a regulated press were more productive—more relevant, accurate, honest, frugal, and so forth—than a free one, the principle of human autonomy demands foregoing the benefits obtained through censorship. We know also that without constitutional restraints we could probably apprehend some criminals who can roam freely in light of those restraints. Yet we insist that in the process of pursuing commendable goals such as crime prevention we adhere to moral principles and refuse to violate the rights of the accused.

OSHA's benefits to society, even if they could be calculated adequately, would not by themselves justify maintaining this institution on our political scene. Moral objections aside, OSHA's measurable value is questionable. The most sensible conclusion I can come to based on looking at OSHA according to the numbers is one articulated with eloquence and precision by Peter Huber:

> It is commonplace to observe that risk is ubiquitous and inescapable. Every insurance company knows that life is growing safer, but the public is firmly convinced that living is becoming ever more hazardous. Congress, understandably enough, has been more interested in the opinion polls than in the actuarial tables. A bountiful crop of federal health and safety regulation, most of it of recent harvest, reflects the popular concern.[65]

It is worth adding to this Robert S. Smith's observation, that because safety and health are goods, it is natural that we value them, but that at some point a lower speed limit, lower dust levels, or reduced noise levels simply are not worth the cost to us.[66] These observations are made by individuals who take the cost-benefit approach seriously, who find the numbers if not decisive at least impressive, and who regard it as imperative that we calculate and estimate how best we can help those in the workplace who may suffer unnecessary harms. In short, these individuals are against OSHA not in principle but in consequence of their belief that OSHA is not doing the work it was set out to do. What if we considered these individuals' approach short-sighted, even callous?

What if we turned to the points raised by Steven Kelman, namely, the "more abstract conceptions of justice, fairness, and human dignity"? In the following section we will do exactly that. We will look at some cases from the standpoint of common sense morality and politics.

OSHA Case Studies: Justice and the Welfare State

Many of the measures that emerge in the welfare state are the result not of elaborate utilitarian cost-benefit analyses but rather of widespread moral impressions and the resulting public mobilization in favor of such measures. As we learned from the account by Steven Kelman, OSHA itself was established when some influential individuals found conditions in the workplace intolerable and made it their task to enlist the federal government to do what they deemed appropriate to remedy matters. In a democracy public opinion and instigation, fueled by moral perception, will often give rise to public policies and institutions.

This source for public policy determination has lately gained considerable support from within moral and political philosophy. That our public policies should be determined by a system of coherently arranged prevailing moral intuitions—that is, widespread moral sentiments that have been coordinated to form a consistent frame of reference—is now the most prominent contender for how our moral and political judgments should be grounded. It is remarkable how many prominent papers in journals dealing with the philosophical aspects of public policy begin with laying down as the groundwork "our considered moral judgments." And in the main, in our time, those who claim to be reading these judgments correctly have held that what follows is a policy of balance between the values of individual autonomy and [negative] liberty on one hand, and those of well-being, welfare or happiness, on the other.

The beginning point of a framework of policy determination, according to the intuitionist line of analysis, must be concrete moral situations. That is to say, some paradigm cases of moral evaluation must be found. Once it is clear what our intuitions are with reference to these, we can get on with harmonizing our intuitions and deriving public policy from them. In connection with assessing OSHA's moral legitimacy, then, what we need, by such an intuitionist approach, is some clear cases of moral problems, involving safety and health provisions at the workplace. If it turns out that these cases—albeit somewhat tedious in a general philosophical discussion—issue in considered moral judgments that lead to a public policy of the type that OSHA exemplifies, then the case for OSHA will have been well paved.

We can, of course, argue with the wisdom of this approach to laying the ground for public policy. But, in my view, it will be useful to take a close look at a few cases that may elicit the moral intuitions that serve as the ground of OSHA type public policy. Even a policy resting on perfectly accurate moral intuition can leave serious and reasonable doubt about its wisdom.[67] The following examples, despite their appearance and publication in forums unsympathetic to the market approach, will demonstrate this point.

Threat of Sterility

A detailed television interview conducted by CBS News in 1979 introduces us to our first OSHA case. We learn that some workers were found to be sterile at Occidental Chemical Company. "Oxy" was assumed to be responsible. When one of its officials was asked, "What was your initial feeling when you first found out that these men were sterile?" he answered: "Shock. We had no idea. I had no idea at all that we had any kind of process here in our plant operations that could do such a thing to a human being." The interviewer reminded the official of "a study...done by Dow Chemical back in 1961 that indicated DBCP [1,2 Dibromo, 3 Chloropropane] did cause sterility in rats." Occidental's official replied that the study "showed...that with very high doses of DBCP you could get testicular atrophy, if you will, the shriveling up of the testicles. I've talked to two scientists who are familiar with the work, and they both say, 'Heck, we just didn't draw the conclusion that there'd be sterility from the fact that the testicles were shriveling up....'" *Mother Jones*, the magazine from which this report was taken, continues by noting that at this point one of the workers from "Oxy" came on camera and said: "Large corporations are in business to make money, you know, regardless of what happens to my life or Jack's life or anybody else's life, and their number-one priority will still be money until somebody puts their foot down." Another worker, however, observed, "We have safety stuff. It's our choice whether to use it." When asked "Does anyone use it?" the reply was that yes, "Joe uses it. He goes by the book." and "Joe's a pain in the ass." The rest of the workers seemed to agree that working "by the book" is an impossible situation and would "slow things down." One added that "Hans, the plant's owner, would lose profits, and the men would lose some of their profit-sharing...."[68]

Mother Jones's own editorial comment follows the transcript:

After the furor broke out, the union forced the company to put a new ventilation system in the Ag-Chem department. Oxy agreed to pay for semi-annual physical exams, with results going to the union's doctor. The men who became sterile slapped Dow Chemical, Shell Chemical, and the University of California with a civil suit, alleging negligence based on DBCP research done at the university and funded by both companies. They also filed workers' compensation suits against Occidental. But beyond that, making the plant really safe seems an awfully steep hill to climb.

This account creates the kind of moral revulsion that intuitionists will call upon to support public policies requiring OSHA-type intervention in the workplace. We shall shortly examine whether serious moral reflection will show the same results. First, however, we will look at some other cases.

Farm-work Safety

The Los Angeles Times for August 11, 1978 recounts a Stockton, California, hearing "mobbed by 200 growers" where the issue of language and safety intersected: [Ralph] Lightstone [attorney with California Rural Legal Assistance] said CRLA investigators called 17 agricultural commissioners. Speaking only in Spanish, the investigators asked what to do if they were poisoned by DBCP, but no one in [ten of] the offices could speak Spanish. At that point, someone in the hearing audience yelled, "This is America, not Mexico. . . ."

Arguing in 1978 before the FDA, Lightstone sought to show that various county agricultural commissioners are unwilling and/or unable to protect the largely Spanish-speaking farm workers who must work with DBCP in the fields. Here the idea is that surely with workers who are unable to speak English one may morally expect government interference in the employer-employee relationship, especially where considerations of health and safety are at issue. Any morally aware individual would accept this conclusion—or so the intuitionist approach would have it.

The next cases are different since OSHA had already been involved in them. The results are meant to indicate OSHA's weak-kneed approach to health and safety issues at the time.

Workplace Fatalities

Some adjudicated cases have received wide publicity for fatalities on the job. In each, OSHA charged violations of safety rules. Five of them involved noncompliance with construction rules. One of these concerned

Research-Cottrell Inc., a New Jersey company, charged in the deaths of fifty-one employees when scaffolding on a cooling tower collapsed in Willow Island, West Virginia. Another of the companies was Rollins Environmental Services's subsidiary in Bridgeport, New Jersey. This company was under investigation in connection with an explosion that killed six employees. The others were Youngstown Sheet and Tube (a division of Jones and Laughlin Steel, Pittsburgh); Warner Plumbing, of Washington, D.C., and S. O. Jennings Construction, of Fairfax, Virginia. Here is how *Business Week* reported the handling of these cases:

> Philip B. Heymann, Assistant Attorney General for the Criminal Div. [U.S. Dept. of Justice], makes clear that the new attention to criminal sanctions for OSHA violations is part of an overall Administration push against white collar crime in health and safety. "My own view," he says, "is that if there are flagrant violations of safety regulations—in food and drugs, the environment, workers' safety and health, and mine safety and health—we ought to take it seriously." ... Two corporate officials were convicted in connection with the four cases involving deaths and in others, involving Die Construction Co., of Colorado Springs, and Turcone Co., of Millard, Nebraska; the companies were fined $3,500 and $5,000 respectively, "for failing to secure the sides of a trench, resulting in a collapse and a worker death."[69]

In the case of a company that failed to provide safety nets for workers who operated more than twenty-five feet aboveground, the company was found not guilty since the worker who died was provided with the line but did not use it. *Business Week* reports that "in the fourth case, Crosby and Overton, of Long Beach, Calif., and its president and vice president pleaded no contest to charges of failing to provide properly functioning respirators. The executives received a suspended sentence and were placed on probation for four years."[70]

The OSHA-Benzene Case

This is formally known as *Industrial Union Dept., AFL-CIO v. American Petroleum Institute et al.*[71] OSHA had issued an emergency temporary standard that limited worker exposure to benzene to no more than 1 ppm, as against the previous standard of 10 ppm. The ruling was precipitated by a report from the National Institute of Health (NIH) in 1977. OSHA responded to the findings of NIH, which indicated noticeably large numbers of leukemia deaths related to benzene, by requiring that exposure be kept to the lowest technologically feasible level. This level could be maintained only at considerable cost—estimated to be in the hundreds of millions of dollars.

No one disputed that benzene is a carcinogen, especially in animals. (OSHA has followed the widespread policy of understanding findings related to cancer in animals to be applicable to humans as well. Of course, there is extensive disputation about this extrapolation within the scientific community, but public policy has not taken much notice of that.)[72] What interests OSHA and its supporters is that "workers can be seriously affected by" benzine; they base this on the studies that extrapolate from animal reaction to benzine or any other substance tested.[73] They conclude that "OSHA therefore has a legitimate interest in the regulation of industrial manufacture involving benzene.[74] This rests, in part, on the allegation, based on animal studies, of the possibility of such a causal relationship, not on established causal links between benzene exposure and (human) leukemia.

The U.S. Supreme Court eventually ruled that the benzene ruling was too strict, but it went on to confirm OSHA's statutory authority to regulate:

> The [Occupational Safety and Health] Act delegates broad authority to the Secretary [of Labor] to promulgate different kinds of standards. The basic definition of an "occupational safety and health standard" is found in P3 (8), which provides: "The term 'occupational safety and health standard' means a standard which requires conditions, or the adoption or use of one or more practices, means, methods, operations, or processes, reasonably necessary or appropriate to provide safe or healthful employment and places of employment." 29 U.S.C. P652 (8). Where toxic materials or harmful physical agents are concerned, a standard must also comply with P6 (b) (5), which provides: "The Secretary, in promulgating standards dealing with toxic materials or harmful physical agents under this subsection, shall set the standard which most adequately assures, to the extent feasible, on the basis of the best available evidence, that no employee will suffer material impairment of health or functional capacity even if such employee has regular exposure to the hazard dealt with by such standard for the period of his working life...." 29 U.S.C. P655 (b) (5).[75]

Despite OSHA's general authority, in this case the Supreme Court did not believe that grounds existed for setting this particular standard. It held that a mere possibility that certain deaths were related to benzene exposure did not justify OSHA in this particular action: "The Agency made no finding that the Dow study [which found a possible connection between benzene exposure and leukemia deaths], any other empirical evidence or any opinion testimony demonstrated that exposure to benzene at or below that 10 ppm level had ever in fact caused leukemia."[76]

The Lubricating Gun Case

The following account is provided in a prominent business ethics text:

> At a Shell location not too long ago, a refinery employee nearly lost an arm while using a high-pressure lubricating gun. The incident began harmlessly enough when the worker inadvertently got his forearm in the way of the spray jetting from the gun's nozzle. He wiped the grease off, unmindful of the serious injury he had sustained. Later the arm swelled and became painful, and surgery was required. For a while surgeons thought the arm would have to be amputated.[77]

What had happened? Grease propelled at a high velocity can penetrate the skin. In this instance the grease penetrated the skin, depositing foreign material up to the worker's elbow. The material, insoluble in blood, could be removed only by surgery.

Was this a bizarre, remote occurrence? Not exactly. With the widespread use of a similar tool, the high-pressure airless spray-paint gun, such incidents have become common enough for concern. Indeed, a recent survey by the Consumer Product Safety Commission's Bureau of Epidemiology indicated that an estimated 847 surgeons and hand specialists have treated at least one injury caused by injection from high-pressure grease guns or airless spray-paint guns. Ninety-six percent of the patients were professional painters.[78]

In the next section I will examine whether these cases support what advocates of the welfare state believe they clearly support, namely, supervision of the labor market by government regulatory bodies. My approach will be to raise familiar questions and argue for some suggested answers and their foundations. Then we will see which of the answers makes the best sense, when taken within the context of the problem and related problems we face in human community life.

A Closer Look at Cases

On the face of it, all the above cases give some good reasons why we do indeed need OSHA. But in morality as in law, due process should be employed. The consequences of public policy are every bit as serious and severe as those of law, and since the moral judgments involved in the cases we have recounted often help determine whether someone is going to support or oppose certain public policies and institutions, we should pay close heed.

Comment on Sterility from Work

The sterility case, as we saw, concerns the treatment of workers by Occidental Chemical Company. Specifically, workers experienced sterility at the time of working for the company and eventually sued it, charging culpability for contracting the ailment that caused such sterility.

As we noted earlier, critics of the company made reference to the 1961 Dow Chemical Company study that showed sterility in rats. Dr. Torkelson's study showed that "with very high doses of DBCP you could get testicular atrophy." Officials of Occidental did not assume that sterility would be a possible corollary.[79]

Does this really condemn Occidental from the moral point of view? Even if in the end culpability for criminal negligence could be laid at Occidental's feet, does this give support to OSHA-type government action as against, for example, straightforward legal prosecution based on the laws of wrongful death or injury? (If someone is given poison at a restaurant, or by a friend at home, the law is not helpless but can supply the framework for forceful response.)[80]

Intuitions to the contrary notwithstanding, testicles can shrivel up for many reasons. Furthermore, studies showing that very high doses of DBCP cause testicular atrophy in rats may well have no bearing on what will happen to human beings, despite widespread assumptions to the contrary. Certainly this has been argued by enough scientists to leave one with reasonable doubt when charges are based on such studies.[81]

But there is the far more important moral issue to be considered. Workers are not and should not be thought of as helpless creatures in these circumstances. Labor organizations could insist that their members work in safe and healthy workplaces. Once it is recognized that employers may not and should not be primarily concerned about their employees' well-being, it would be logical and morally sensible to consider the well-being of workers mainly the responsibility of workers themselves and their unions. Since corporate managers owe it to shareholders, both legally and morally, to do as well as possible for them economically, they cannot serve their employees equally well. This is no different from how we understand the relationship between clients and attorneys or patients and physicians. If the latter had to serve first of all their secretaries or technical staff, they could often face divided loyalties.

One might ask why corporations have a primary responsibility to shareholders rather than to employees. Shareholders own the corporation and managers have committed themselves to administering this property in a productive, profitable fashion. Employees, on the other hand, have chosen to trade with the corporation with the unambiguous objective of making this primary purpose possible. Any detraction from that purpose, except perhaps in emergencies or with the consent of the owners, would be a violation of trust.[82] That the law does not always acknowledge this point in our day is not germane to the present argument. What is germane is that no convincing case to the contrary has been made by those who have tried to defend the law—as we saw in chapter 3 in our examination of three major figures whose theories have been aimed precisely at doing so.

Interestingly, when one of the Oxy workers mentioned the other who uses "safety stuff," the group of workers being interviewed reportedly scoffed at his insistence on going "by the book." They called him "a pain in the ass" and said that doing what he did would "slow things down" so that the plant would lose profits and the workers would lose some of their profit sharing. They seemed to be aware of the inadequacies of these regulations, despite their immediate, intuitive gain from them. It would appear then that the workers quite freely, out of concern for their own and their firm's economic prosperity, chose to forego some of the safety measures of which they were clearly aware and which they could have followed had they so chosen.

Why is anything like this morally suspect to some people? Mainly because the idea that workers would freely choose to trade their safety for prosperity seems almost impossible. Workers must be exploited in the process of making such a trade-off. And that really means, to most of us, that workers lack the freedom to choose; they are stuck with their jobs and must accept what is offered them. If anyone ought to sacrifice anything of value in keeping a firm prosperous, it is unheard of for many people that it should include the workers. Surely, business corporations can afford a few million, can't they, to provide workers with the maximum amount of safety that is technologically feasible?

But the idea that workers have a basic right to be provided with this rests on views we have already shown to be flawed, as well as on the general belief that workers are not really free to choose and thus need government protection against the adversities of the labor market. This is demeaning to workers. Surely workers—who are not permanent members of some inferior species—are able to plan for the eventuality that a company is not mainly going to look out for their interest. When we see that the union finally did produce the desired changes in safety provisions, this shows that thinking of workers as unimaginative in regard to their well-being is insulting and unjustified.

Finally, it would be naive to entirely ignore workers who participate in the creation of the myth of worker impotence, ones who resent that they are not running the corporation, or at least reaping its benefits. Envy is not an unknown sentiment in the marketplace, and some people would take any such envy as a statement about one's helpless circumstances. Yet it need not be that. It could be a culpable resentment of other people's relatively better lot. But because of the generally favorable moral response to workers' demands, this sentiment is often overlooked or mistaken for righteous indignation.

Many people do in fact forego opportunities in early life and so are left in economic circumstances that are difficult, perhaps impossible, to escape from later, especially once they have started families, and so on. These choices can hound one across life. Attempts at evading responsibility for them and substituting some doctrine of how one is really the victim of exploitation is a handy measure for trying to escape the results.

To believe that workers are incapable of such moral culpability is again to demean workers, fundamentally, as something other than human moral agents. This view would have them all back in a position of serfdom, as the peasants and their offspring found themselves several centuries ago. This attitude lay in back of Kipling's famous notion of the white man's burden. There is nothing morally objectionable about ordinary compassion for individuals who face hardship and misfortune in life. It is quite another thing, however, to assume the role of life-supervisor and guardian over such individuals. Such paternalism has no moral basis.

Workers showed their own self-reliance when they "slapped Dow Chemical, Shell Chemical and the University of California with a civil suit, alleging negligence based on DBCP research done at the university and funded by both companies." This is clearly, unambiguously indicative of the workers' ability to stand up for their own interest and rights. If indeed the companies were guilty of negligence in failing to inform workers of the hazards to them associated with their work—if the "reasonable man" doctrine applies here so that the companies could be shown to have dealt fraudulently with the workers by not informing them of these hazards—courts of a just legal system should be the forums where such guilt is established and in line with due process of law. Once companies have been found guilty in the course of such a just process of demonstration, a clear precedent will have been established so others will be alerted to how they should behave.

In short, government regulation is really superfluous. What is needed are active workers' organizations aiming at substantive improvement of the workers' employment situation (as distinct from advocating featherbedding, economically impossible job security, and the like) as well as a sound judicial system. Anything else constitutes an unjustified invasion of a domain of human interaction. If one hopes to make "the plant really safe" there is no reason to believe that bureaucratic supervision and inspection will solve the problem without destroying more fundamental values such as human liberty and moral autonomy. These, in the context of social-political life, require primary protection, not health, safety, or similar concerns.

Comment on Agricultural Hazards

In the effort to upgrade the safety of agricultural work, Ralph Lighthouse complained about the fact that agricultural commissioners spoke no Spanish during discussions of DBCP. Someone's outburst, "This is America, not Mexico," might in turn be regarded as morally insensitive. More significantly, I want to address the concern that because it is "largely Spanish-speaking farmworkers who must work with DBCP in the fields, stronger safety measures need to be imposed."

It is not true that Spanish-speaking farm workers "must" work with DBCP in the fields. If the growers fail to inform the workers of their use of DBCP and if DBCP is actually hazardous to human health and safety, then this case can also be handled through the courts. The criminal and civil law, not government regulation, are the far more promising means for remedying such matters.[83] Unions, legal-aid societies, and similar organizations, supported by vigorous fundraising efforts, should be in a position to help workers sue those employers who are suspected of being negligent or fraudulent.

Of course, because the case already involves government supervision at the county and state levels, it does not support the usefulness of any further governmental activity, such as might be expected from OSHA. There is no reason to think that government is any more (or less) just at the federal than at the local level. Admittedly, at any time it could turn out that some locality is far more corrupt than some other, or that the administration, indeed even the government's ideals, at the federal level are more just than those locally. But as a rule, there is no justification for assuming that government regulation, locally or federally, does more good than judicial resolution of conflicts that may arise at the workplace.

Raising the issue of a linguistic handicap is also open to criticism. Mexican Americans are no less able and obligated to learn English, than have been Jewish, Japanese, Chinese, Polish, or Hungarian Americans, all of whom chose to immigrate to the United States which as a whole has an English-speaking tradition and culture. Here again we find a kind of condescension toward some people that under other circumstances would be described as racism.[84] Hispanics, no less than others, are capable, if need be, of acquiring the skills required to cope with conditions that make prospering in a new society possible.

Comment on Fatalities

In our next example, all the cases under consideration involve "flagrant violation of safety regulations." Why should this be the point? After all, deaths were involved. It completely understates the issue to label this a mere violation of safety rules. The main point is surely that the companies may have caused or contributed to the deaths of almost one hundred people?

The judicial approach to these kinds of cases could be far more strict and just, precisely because the judiciary would not focus on violation of rules, which bring relatively minimal punishment in response. As one commentator observes, "The imposition of the full costs of accidents on dangerous industries would no doubt be unpopular, but the consequences of not doing so are serious."[85] Furthermore,

> a study...compar[ing] accident rates in the construction industry between Ohio and Michigan, the former highly regulated and the latter not, showed...no significant difference. [It] did, however, find a more positive attitude toward safety on the part of management as the parties themselves assumed more of the responsibility for safety.[86]

Careful attention to white-collar crime in health and safety would not so much counsel government regulation but prosecution of perpetrators of actually unjust harmful acts toward workers.[87] Such an approach would also avoid the harassment of people in the business world who are not reasonably suspected of having unjustly harmed anyone. Instead of a concern with safety rule violations—and charges brought against firms on grounds of allegedly neglecting them—the focus would center on actual, consequential rights violations. This would preserve one of the most crucial and deservedly prized elements of recent Western legal tradition, namely, the refusal to impose burdens on individuals unless they have been proven to have committed wrongs against others.

In the cases at hand, however, some of the companies had to prove themselves innocent, for example by showing that the safety lines had been provided and that the employee who fell to his death did not use them. In a just system there would be no prosecution in the first case without some reasonable ground for assuming that the company had been negligent or fraudulent in its relationship with the employee. The burden of proof would have been on the prosecution, consonant with the doctrine of individual rights.

Comment on OSHA-Benzene

We find in our next case how well entrenched OSHA's legal powers are. Moreover, we also see that the fact that "workers can be seriously effected by," benzene, for example, imposes the legal obligation on firms not to make use of benzene or expose workers to it at work. Indeed, here the idea is that even if workers are aware of their exposure to benzene and the hazards this entails, it might be something OSHA can prohibit at certain levels. Yet the U.S. Supreme Court's "finding" that "OSHA therefore has a legitimate interest in the regulation of industrial manufacture involving benzene," does not establish that OSHA is a morally proper institution. "Legitimacy" is a statutory warrant, not a moral one.

Furthermore, the terms "reasonable" and "feasible" have significant roles in describing what OSHA legally should do and require of others. But, as noted before, what is reasonable or feasible is impossible to determine on a society-wide basis. This is because of all the pitfalls of cost-benefit analysis, planning, determining values for people in a human community, and so forth. The determination of values must often be left to individuals in their voluntary relations with each other. The idea of assessing what people should do (produce or forego) on a collective, social basis is extremely problematic, even meaningless.[88] Interference by OSHA, then, cannot help determine what is "reasonably necessary or appropriate to provide safe or healthful employment and places of employment."

Nor is the Occupational Safety and Health Act the most efficient, let alone ethical, way to achieve what Congress wants, namely, delegating "the broad authority...to promulgate [and to] set the standard which most adequately assures, to the extent feasible, on the basis of the best available evidence, that no employee will suffer material impairment of health or functional capacity." This is not even efficient legislative policy.

Comment on the Lubricating Gun

In the Shell case we can raise other questions: Should workers be responsible for making sure that their exercise of a skill be carried out safely? When someone professionally uses a high-pressure lubricating gun, is that individual responsible for learning about its hazards? Certainly no "inadvertent" placing of one's own or another's forearm in its path should occur. It is out of place here to even bring in the firm involved. If anything is clearly a case of worker responsibility, it is to know how to make the best and safest use of tools vital to one's profession. Were a plumber, who comes to fix one's sink, to be injured by misusing a tool, the homeowner may not be justly blamed. The information concerning the hazards associated with the use of the lubricating gun were available. Workers involved could (and should) have taken precautions. Why is there any need to bring OSHA into the picture? The case shows what irresponsible conduct by workers and/or employers can do to. To imagine that this general state of affairs could be avoided by introducing OSHA is to suppose something plainly wrong.

It appears, then, that even if we take seriously the idea of basing some of our decisions as to what public policy should be on the examination of key cases, such an approach still will not support OSHA and the kind of legislation that gave rise to it and to numerous similar government agencies. When we add that powerful moral objections exist to attempts at remedying socioeconomic problems by way of such preemptive governmental methods as OSHA represents, the moral case for OSHA has to be regarded as extremely weak.

The Welfare State Does Not Measure Up

When it comes to the basic alternatives connected with the moral issues surrounding the welfare state and OSHA in particular, there are two choices available to people: They can either work to make sure they are as well off and safe as is reasonable for them to be; or they can take risks but demand better pay for this from their employers. The welfare state and OSHA are not genuine moral alternatives since they violate individual rights. Establishing a bureaucracy such as OSHA is, accordingly, not morally and politically permissible. It is, rather, to intrude on the moral spheres of authority of other people.

Furthermore, OSHA and the welfare state amount merely to a pretense of providing protection. In fact they introduce a new source of mistakes committed by their officials, managers, and whoever else is involved. As has become so clear in connection with the far more drastic cases of human slavery and serfdom, liberty is not only a requirement of human dignity but also turns out to be a better means, all things taken into account, for securing beneficial results to all concerned. No doubt there are market failures that make the welfare state appealing. In the end, however, welfarism proves to be a certain political failure.

Believing otherwise—namely, that OSHA-type agencies can really solve problems of well-being, health, and safety—reveals an unwarranted bias in favor of the inherent wisdom and efficiency of government coercion and bureaucracy. It shows the error of thinking that market failures, even if thought of in the broad sense of what the market should but does not do, can really be remedied by political means. That completely overlooks the far greater hazard of political failures, based on the problems we have outlined earlier: rights violation, paternalism, inefficiency.

Not only is the political process unsuited for handling problems that arise in the marketplace, but there is every reason to think that political workers, managers, and the rest—in short, bureaucrats—are every bit as capable of failure, corruption, haste, greed, and other vices that produce harm to people as are those who own and work in the workplace and in executive suites. The belief, expressed earlier in this work by Jonathan Alter, that capitalism is especially geared toward tempting people to evade responsibilities is, of course, crass prejudice. But if there is something to it at all, there can be no reasonable doubt that the political process offers temptations toward vices of its own. That those who work for OSHA should escape such temptations is one of the tragic myths human beings are beset by and deserves to be contested at every possible turn.

As a final *Gedankenexperiment*, or "thought experiment" let us imagine a society in which one has been asked to morally evaluate the Ministry of Poetry.[89] Such a governmental body should not exist, but perhaps some excuse could be found for it. The ministry's failures and achievements are recorded and it is found that some of the poets have improved, some have obtained grants to keep working, some abandoned the nonsense they wrote before, and others quit because their work has been withdrawn from circulation (they have been found inappropriate for aesthetic consumption). The ministry's work has both advanced and hindered poetry, yet no clear quantitative advantage related to its existence or nonexistence can be identified.

What should one do? Censorship undermines a basic value of a good human community. The work of the ministry must, therefore, be abolished. Despite what Irving Kristol says, namely, that "no reasonable person is in principle opposed to all government regulation,"[90] there is no essential difference between opposing OSHA and opposing such a ministry. The significance of creative and productive liberty when applied to poets is the same as when applied to engineers, miners, chemists, pharmacists, and others regulated by OSHA. Furthermore, OSHA's people are not inherently more virtuous than those they regulate. Thus Herbert Spencer's comment is most apt: "The ultimate result of shielding men from the effects of folly is to fill the world with fools."[91]

Notes

1. Jonathan Alter, "Reagan's Regulatory Report Card," *Washington Monthly* (November 1982): 13.
2. Steven Kelman, "Regulation and Paternalism," *Rights and Regulation: Ethical, Political, and Economic Issues*, ed. Tibor R. Machan and M. Bruce Johnson, (Cambridge, MA: Ballinger, 1983), p. 218. Kelman argues that it is to provide people with greater choice that government regulation is required. He believes that people choose at times to give up some of their choices so that they can secure greater safety, security, health, and so on. He also holds, however, that occasional paternalism is permissible. But the idea that people choose to give up the right to choose is muddled. If people commit themselves, say, to being treated by a doctor, that is not giving up the right to choose but is itself the exercise of that right. If, however, they democratically impose some alternative on others, that is not choosing to give up one's own rights but depriving others of theirs.
3. Woodrow Wilson, *The New Freedoms* (New York: Doubleday Page, 1913), pp. 23-24.
4. Tibor R. Machan, *Individuals and Their Rights* (LaSalle, IL: Open Court, 1989).
5. Here, briefly, is the argument in support of these four points. Human beings are rational animals, with the moral responsibility to excel as such. A good society requires standards of social relations among human beings, standards that are constituted by these rights. Living in human dignity requires, at least for adults, that persons govern themselves and guide their own lives. And it requires that they are not dealt with (by other persons, who should know better) as if they were not who they are, namely, persons with a moral nature, with dignity. It is this requirement of the right to freedom from the willful invasion of others (what is called "negative" freedom) that is stated within a framework of basic human rights within relatively large human communities. And it is only so as to secure these rights that governments are justifiably established in society; any other goal for government is either itself rights violating or superfluous. I discuss the topic of emergency cases in Tibor R. Machan, "Prima Facie v. Natural (Human) Rights," *Journal of Value Inquiry* 10, no. 1 (1976): 119-131. Sometimes basic rights may be disregarded, namely, when the conditions of peace are impossible.
6. Recall the way Aristotle put it: "That which is common to the greatest number has the least care bestowed upon it." Hardin states the point somewhat differently: "Freedom in the commons brings ruin to all." See chapter 1, notes 21-22.
7. See most of the contributions in G. Ezorsky, ed., *Moral Rights in the Workplace* (Albany, NY: State University of New York Press, 1986). For a contrary view, see James Chesher, "Employment Ethics," in *Commerce and Morality*, ed. Tibor R. Machan, (Totowa, NJ: Rowman and Littlefield, 1988), pp. 77-93. See, also, Tibor R. Machan, "Rights and Myths in the Workplace," in Ezorsky, *Moral Rights...*, pp. 45-50.
8. For a detailed elaboration of such a view, see Ronald Dworkin, *Taking Rights Seriously* (Cambridge, MA: Harvard University Press, 1977). See also Henry Shue, *Basic Rights* (Princeton, NJ: Princeton University Press, 1980).
9. For the full story on this, see my *Individuals and Their Rights*.
10. This relates to the current discussion of what, if any, exchanges ought to be blocked by law—whether, for instance, surrogate mothering for pay, selling blood or organs, or selling sexual services ought to be banned. In these cases, too, what is

morally right is not universal and treating it as such is a mistake. Yet, even if it were always wrong, for example, to sell blood or sex, banning the practice forecloses the opportunity to resist the temptation to do it. The same does not apply to banning murder, kidnaping, assault, or robbery, since the conduct involved is directly intrusive and violates basic rights (or sovereignty), thus rendering another morally incapacitated.

11. Peter Huber, "Exorcists vs. Gatekeepers in Risk Regulation," *Regulation* (November-December 1983): 23.

12. It is confused to think that because such competitiveness reigns in the economic domain, the attitude must begin to infuse all of society. If one competes in the workplace, it does not have to follow that the same attitude will be cultivated for church, play, childraising, friendship, or love.

13. Huber, "Exorcists vs. Gatekeepers...," p. 23.

14. Steven Kelman, "Occupational Safety and Health Administration," in *The Politics of Regulation*, ed. James Q. Wilson, (New York: Basic Books, 1980), p. 266. Kelman's is a very succinct and informative discussion of OSHA's political development. The quotation above is from Kelman and Ronald J. Penoyer, *Directory of Federal Regulatory Agencies* (St. Louis, MO: Center for the Study of American Business, May 1981).

15. Kelman, "Occupational Safety...," p. 266.

16. *Ibid.*

17. *Ibid.*

18. *Ibid.*

19. *Ibid.*

20. *Ibid.*, pp. 251–252.

21. *Ibid.*, p. 252.

22. *Ibid.*

23. See *Atlas Roofing Co. v. Occupational Safety and Health Review Commission*, 430 U.S. 442 (1977); *Marshall v. Barlow's Inc.*, 436 U.S. 307 (1978). For other significant rulings, see *Industrial Union Dept., AFL-CIO v. American Petroleum Institute et al.*

24. "Accident Statistics That Jolted OSHA," *Business Week* (December 11, 1978): 62. The story reports that Administrator Eula Bingham, herself a toxicologist, blames some of those figures on "increases in employment and other factors."

25. "Behind Gains in On-the-Job Health, Safety," *U.S. News and World Report* (June 11, 1984): 79.

26. Robert S. Smith, "Protecting Workers' Health and Safety," in *Instead of Regulation: Alternatives to Federal Regulatory Agencies*, ed. R. W. Poole, Jr., (Lexington, MA: Heath, 1982), p. 319; U.S. Chamber of Commerce, news release, November 18, 1982. All the figures are based on data provided by the U.S. Department of Labor, Bureau of Labor Statistics.

27. U.S. Chamber of Commerce, news release.

28. *Ibid.*

29. *Ibid.*

30. Huber, "Exorcists vs. Gate Keepers," p. 23.

31. *Ibid.*, Considering how rarely laws are repealed, the probability of bad laws and regulations remaining on the books is very high.

32. "The Dilemma of Regulating Reproductive Risks," *Business Week* (August 29, 1977): 76-78.

33. Robert W. Merry, "OSHA's Action Plan on Cancer," *Wall Street Journal* (October 11, 1978).

34. See, in this connection, the rather technical discussions in Robert W. Crandell and Lester B. Lave, eds., *The Scientific Basis of Health and Safety Regulation* (Washington, DC: Brookings Institution, 1981); Edith Efron, *The Apocalyptics: Politics, Science and the Big Cancer Lie* (New York: Simon and Schuster, 1984). See also Marjorie Sun, "OSHA Reviewing Cotton Dust Standards," *Science* 217 (September 24, 1982): 1232–1233. The study in question here is one conducted by the National Academy of Science in 1982. The general thrust of the critics of the study is that the academy failed to note stronger links between exposure to cotton dust and respiratory illnesses.

35. Quoted in Frank Allen, "Battle Building Over 'Right to Know' Laws Regarding Toxic Items Used by Workers," *Wall Street Journal* (January 4, 1983): 20.

36. Robert Love, "Indecent Exposure: Reagan Guts the Rules on Cancer Protection," *Rolling Stone* (June 7, 1984): 9.

37. Smith, "Protecting Workers' Health...," p. 319.

38. *Ibid.*

39. *Ibid.*

40. *Ibid.*

41. *Ibid.*

42. *Ibid.*

43. John Mendeloff, *Regulating Safety: An Economic and Political Analysis of Occupational Safety and Health Policy* (Cambridge, MA: MIT Press, 1979).

44. John Mendeloff, "Reducing Occupational Health Risks: Uncertain Effects and Unstated Benefits,"*Technology Review* (May 1980): 73.

45. Steven Kelman, "Regulation That Works," *New Republic* (November 24, 1978): 19. See also his article "Cost-Benefit Analysis, An Ethical Critique," *Regulation* (January-February 1981): 33–40.

46. See, for a detailed discussion of these proponents, Machan, *Individuals and Their Rights*.

47. K. S. Shrader-Frechette, *Science Policy, Ethics, and Economic Methodology* (Boston, MA: Reidel, 1984), p. 47.

48. *Ibid,* p. 47.

49. *Ibid,* p. 33.

50. This is not the same as saying that people who vote for elected officials do not believe in OSHA-type measures. But their concrete expressions of preference would contradict their expressed opinion.

51. I would argue, however, that no conflict need arise between these considerations.

52. For a survey of work on this topic, see Dennis C. Mueller, *Public Choice* (London: Cambridge University Press, 1979). For a technical assessment of the status of the controversies involved, see Amartya Sen, *Choice, Welfare and Measurement* (Cambridge, MA: MIT Press, 1982). For a very pessimistic assessment of the results of the work in this area, see Edward I. Friedland and Stephan J. Cimbala, "Process and Paradox: The Significance of Arrow's Theorem," *Theory and Decision* 4 (1973): 51–64. In chapter 2 I outline a way that a constitutionally limited, classical liberal polity would avoid the social choice paradox.

53. Mendeloff, "Reducing Occupational Health Risks...," p. 73.

54. One implication of the familiar metaethical slogan, "Ought implies can," is that if no solution to a problem can be found, no imperative can be valid requiring that

we act in line with some solution. Some deny the validity of "Ought implies can," mainly on grounds that at times we regret having done something we could not avoid doing or having not done something that we could have done. See, for a critical discussion, John Kekes, *Facing Evil* (Princeton, NJ: Princeton University Press, 1991).

55. She cites Norman S. Care, "Participation and Policy," *Ethics* 88 (July 1978): 316–337.

56. This much is already suggested by the discussion in chapter 2.

57. Kenneth J. Arrow, *Social Choice and Individual Values*, 2nd ed., (New York: Wiley, 1963). The argument is complicated but comes down to showing that given the standard conditions of liberal democratic societies, such that people can try to get the government to satisfy their preferences, there is no way that government can make consistently rational choices, for example, by ranking collective preferences. See, for more, chapter 2 of the present work.

58. Don Lavoie, *Rivalry and Central Planning: The Socialist Calculation Debate; Reconsidered* (Cambridge, UK: Cambridge University Press, 1985); Don Lavoie, *National Economic Planning, What Is Left?* (Cambridge, MA: Ballinger 1985); Trygve J. B. Hoff, *Economic Calculation in the Socialist Society* (London: Hodge, 1949). This debate was begun by members of the Austrian school of economics—Ludwig von Mises, F. A. Hayek, and others. They replied to socialists and welfare statists who argued that central planners can determine what to produce and how much of it even without the price system of an exchange economy. Socialists and welfare statists have never been able to answer the charge that without the exchange of "information" in the market-place, misallocation of resources must result.

A point might be added here. If socialists maintain that they know that, morally speaking, individual wants, preferences, and desires are to be ignored and only certain supposed general human needs should be served, their case becomes somewhat stronger. For example, Jon Elster, *Making Sense of Marx* (Cambridge: Cambridge University Press, 1985), argues that the central goal of securing for everyone a direct role in organizing labor in society (which secures self-development and esteem) is what vindicates the Marxian idea of collectivism. Only if it is shown that individuals have a natural right to seek to have their wants, preferences, and desires satisfied—meaning, they have "the right to the pursuit of [individual] happiness"—does the argument against collectivists succeed. See my "Toward a Theory of Natural Individual Human Rights," in *The New Scholasticism* 61 (1987): 33–78; see also "A Reconsideration of Natural Rights Theory," *American Philosophical Quarterly* 19 (January 1979): 61–72. For more, see my *Capitalism and Individualism* (New York: St. Martin's Press, 1990).

59. Tibor R. Machan, "Property Rights and the Decent Society," in *Ideology and American Experience*, ed. J. K. Roth and R. C. Whittemore, (Washington, DC: Washington Institute Press, 1986).

60. Jerome Rothenberg, *The Measurement of Social Welfare* (Englewood Cliffs, NJ: Prentice-Hall, 1961).

61. Samuel Scheffler, "Natural Rights, Equality, and the Minimal State," *Canadian Journal of Philosophy* 6 (March 1976): 76.

62. Renford Bambrough, *Moral Scepticism and Moral Knowledge* (Atlantic Highlands, NJ: Humanities Press, 1970), p. 109.

63. See chapter 2.

64. See chapter 2.
65. Huber, "Exorcists vs. Gatekeepers...," p. 23.
66. Smith, "Protecting Workers" Health...," p. 319.
67. I develop this point further in "The Petty Tyrannies of Government Regulation," in *Rights and Regulation: Ethical, Political, and Economic Issues*, ed. Tibor R. Machan and M. B. Johnson, (Cambridge, MA: Ballinger, 1983), pp. 259–288; see also Chapters 4 and 5.
68. Daniel Ben-Horin, "The Sterility Scandal," *Mother Jones* (May 1979): 52ff.
69. "An OSHA Crackdown on Job-related Deaths," *Business Week* (August 20, 1979): 25.
70. *Ibid.*
71. Tom L. Beauchamp, "The OSHA-Benzene Case," in *Case Studies in Business, Society, and Ethics*, ed. T. L. Beauchamp, (Englewood Cliffs, NJ: Prentice-Hall, 1983), p. 185.
72. For a detailed discussion, accessible to lay readers, see Efron, *Apocalyptics*, especially chapter 7, "The Bridge to the Regulatory World."
73. Beauchamp, "The OSHA-Benzene Case," p. 188.
74. *Ibid.*, pp. 185–186.
75. *Ibid.*, p. 189.
76. *Ibid.*, p. 188.
77. Vincent Barry, ed., *Moral Issues in Business* (Belmont, CA: Wadsworth, 1983), pp. 129–130.
78. *Ibid.*
79. Ben-Horin, "The Sterility Scandal," p. 56.
80. But the degree of swiftness some desire will not be available in a system of justice that demands due process. It is interesting that very often the same individuals who advocate strong safeguards against "swift" justice in the criminal courts—for instance, by insisting on *Miranda* protection and by considering legitimate the use of legal "technicalities" to protect even known murderers—will be very impatient when it comes to the lack of swiftness due process of law would precipitate in connection with dealing with the accused in the business community. For the development of the law that has led to this double standard, see Normal Karlin, "Substantive Due Process, A Doctrine for Regulatory Control," in *Rights and Regulation*, pp. 43–70.
81. Efron, *Apocalyptics*, passim.
82. For a discussion of an individual rights approach to understanding the nature of corporations, see Robert Hessen, *In Defense of the Corporation* (Stanford, CA: Hoover Institution Press, 1979); Roger Pilon, "Corporations and Rights: On Treating Corporate People Justly," *Georgia Law Review* 15 (1979): 1245–1370. Pilon's argument differs from the sort advanced by those who think that individuals possess natural rights, natural rights in the sense familiar from John Locke's doctrine and those following Locke. See above, note 77. Barry, *Moral Issues in Business*.
83. See Michael S. Baram, *Alternatives to Regulation* (Lexington, MA: DC Heath, 1981); J. C. Smith, "The Processes of Adjudication and Regulation: A Comparison," in *Rights and Regulation*, pp. 71–96.
84. Since I immigrated to the United States from Hungary and English is my third language, I suppose I may be regarded as somewhat biased in how I view this. Certainly there may be some for whom retaining their native language as their primary means of communication would be more suitable than learning the lan-

guage prominent in their new homeland. I do not mean to imply some universal formula here, only that when people make certain choices in their lives, such as moving to another country, we ought to believe that they are able to cope with the consequences.

85. Paul E. Sands, "How Effective Is Safety Legislation?" *Journal of Law and Economics* 5 (1976): 165.

86. *Ibid.*

87. Smith, "The Processes of Adjudication..." Adjudication, rather than regulation, is the only way to secure due process. For a discussion, see Sanford H. Kadish, "Some Observations on the Use of Criminal Sanctions in Enforcing Economic Regulation," *University of Chicago Law Review* 30 (1963): 423; Harry V. Ball and Lawrence M. Friedman, "The Uses of Criminal Sanctions in the Enforcement of Economic Legislation: A Sociological View," *Stanford Law Review* 17 (1965): 197.

88. F. A. Hayek argues that for this reason the concept of social justice is meaningless. See his *Law, Legislation and Liberty*, vol. 3 (Chicago: University of Chicago Press, 1978). His thesis is probably an overstatement, based on the unavailability or lack of prominence of a conception of social justice that is individualistic. Individualism rejects the idea of collective purposes or goods that supersede the individual's moral responsibility for self-government but it does not preclude concern for just social relations.

89. This imaginary case is a reality in some societies. According to Yakou Smirnoff, the ex-Soviet comedian, the GPU had a department of jokes.

90. Irving Kristol, "A Regulated Society?" *Regulation* (July-August 1977): 12.

91. Herbert Spencer, "State Tempering with Money Banks," *Essays* (1891).

8

Pollution and Political Theory

*For besides other considerations, everybody is
more inclined to neglect the duty which he expects
another to fulfill...*
— Aristotle

The concept of pollution is problematic from the start. Dictionaries differ as to what it means. One says pollution (created by people) is "the act of defiling or rendering impure, as pollution of drinking water."[1] Another states that it "occurs when materials are accumulated where they are not wanted."[2] Yet another says that to pollute is "to corrupt or defile," and identifies pollution with "contamination of soil, air, and water by noxious substances and noises."[3] In the end, a sensible definition of pollution will have to cover harmful air and water contamination from materials, nuclear particles, radiation, noise, light, and anything else that is the result of human activity and can be shown to cause harm to another human being or damage to property. Such a definition would preclude anything like "natural" pollution. Nature may render things impure, but only human beings can pollute.

The Pollution Problem

The central problem associated with pollution, as far as the general public is concerned, has to do with the difficulty—perhaps even the impossibility—of confining harm to particular people and places. For example, air pollution occurs when people dump materials into the air that harms others or puts them at risk of harm. Were it possible to confine these materials in some definite location, the agent doing the dumping could release them without inflicting the pollution on others. But as

225

things are now, in many familiar circumstances, pollution is not controllable—or, at any rate, deemed too expensive to contain—in this way. The airborne contaminates from Birmingham's smokestacks can end in New England's lakes—can, indeed, "kill" those lakes by sterilizing their waters.

It is by no means clear just how permanent or inescapable this problem is. Those with a robust sense of reality are not likely to be optimistic on this score, however, and, in any event, the kind of problem it is—a kind of public evils problem—could well be a permanent one. It is important, therefore, to examine what different political theories say with respect to handling pollution, important both because their answers might help us understand how best to cope with this problem, and because their approaches to it might help us choose which one among them, all things considered, is the best.

There is a further point to be made, before preceding. In our day-to-day life there is an understandable inclination to focus attention upon particularly noxious examples of pollution such as Love Canal or the nuclear fallout from early atomic testing in the U.S. Southwest. Convinced that a grave injustice has been done, we are unlikely to ask about the grounds of justice themselves. And yet a moment's reflection should direct our attention in this more theoretical, though not less important, direction. Particular acts, laws, or practices are unjust. Their injustice consist of failing to meet certain standards by which human beings evaluate conduct and institutions.

But what are these relevant respects? That is a question that must be answered by thinking about those particular acts we judge unjust, not merely by issuing our judgment that they are. Thus arises, not by a philosopher's trick or ruse, the need to think about the nature of justice generally—its grounds and scope. Indeed, once we feel the logic of the pull of ideas, we soon realize that questions about what is just in particular cases will lead us, if we will but follow, to questions about the nature of a just social order. The question about how to deal with the problem of pollution justly, therefore, cannot and should not be answered in a theoretical vacuum. If we are to command a clear view of the problem, we must see it against the backdrop of competing visions of a just society.

Although virtually every known and distinct political theory is in force to some degree somewhere on our globe, we will concern ourselves only with those operative in the more powerful, influential societies.

These societies provide the effective leadership in matters of problem solving, including how the problems created by pollution are approached worldwide. Though selective, we are not arbitrary in limiting our attention to these political alternatives.

Two distinct political theories will concern us. These are capitalism— or, as some of the more consistent defenders of the system refer to it, libertarianism—and the welfare state. (I have dealt with two others, socialism and fascism, in the essay from which the present chapter is drawn.) We shall examine each with special reference to the problem of pollution. But we shall also want to assess their respective merits (or lack of them) at a deeper level.

The Welfare State

Of all the political systems dealing with human community life, the welfare state is perhaps the most familiar to us today. It is also that system in which some of the main faults of the more remote but often-championed systems of democratic and central planning socialism might find an effective remedy.

As our previous discussions of the welfare state have already noted, two widely embraced goals are generally taken to be the objectives of this political and economic system, namely, the right to liberty and the right to happiness, or well-being.[4] The welfare state is the political attempt to do justice to both of these widely supported values—both to human happiness and to human liberty. It is, therefore, something of a delicate balancing act, an attempt to keep some ideal proportion between a concern for individual liberty and welfare. This is fairly evident in the United States. Neither of the two major political parties, for example, can discount the ideal of liberty or the ideal of well-being, at least for the needy, as a political objective the government must pursue.

But just what kind of balance is to be pursued by the government of a welfare state? On some interpretations, we must look to the U.S. Constitution to answer this question. The Constitution stresses both the right to negative liberty and the right to welfare. Whether this stress is placed in such a way as to be more in line with those political thinkers who favor negative liberty above well-being, or vice versa, we can imagine that one way to attempt to strike a balance is to let the Constitution be our guide: As a matter of law, Congress may not do certain things but also must do others. Legally, that is, various powers are kept away from the state as far as the U.S. Constitution is concerned, but the government is constitutionally empowered to go to work on certain matters where, it is felt, other elements of our society fail. Still, the Constitution does not hand us a blueprint regarding how much liberty and how much welfare should emerge from government action. Instead, this is a matter of procedural interpretation, usually guided both by the democratic process of voter participation and by extensive delegation of authority to experts—for example, departments of the government, government regulators, and license bureaus. Depending on whether a welfare state is more democratic or more republican—meaning, depending on whether law making and law interpretation is carried out more by the people themselves or by various selected political representatives—more or less direct participation of the members of the community in the political process determines what balance will be struck between liberty and well-being as governmental objectives. We might say that the welfare state places a good deal of faith in the wisdom of the electorate and in those the voters choose to represent them.

But now we can ask what we did before in connection with other systems, namely, what standards should be invoked in forging public policy and what standards should voters, especially, invoke as they participate in the political decision-making process? Most generally put, the welfare state assumes, alongside democratic theory itself, that the majority (or plurality) is authorized to have a final say in public matters, guided by the needs and wants, whether similar or dissimilar, of the individuals who comprise the whole community. Unlike a pure democracy, however, it is impossible to maintain a welfare state without some checks or restrictions on the popular will. And the individuals involved will know, more or less clearly and precisely, what those checks are—for example, forced labor is prohibited, striking is a human right, the press may speak its mind almost without reservation, people may associate with each other as they choose.

According to familiar welfare state theories—some of which have already been explored in this work—the main legal restriction on democratic power is the right of individuals to a wide scope of self-expression and self-determination. Welfare for all is pursued by getting the input of all, and by following the mandate of that input in the most practical way possible. But there is a limit, namely, when such pursuit threatens to thwart, to an unacceptable degree, the personal will and initiative of members of society. Liberty is protected, in turn, by not subjugating individuals to anyone's authority beyond what is required for maintaining a decent, respectable standard of living for all. This may involve some "forced labor" by requiring, for example, that all who are able should contribute some portion of their earnings to the public treasury. Although such labor as is used for public purposes is extracted often without explicit or even implicit consent of the actual members of a community, advocates of the welfare state argue that it is nonetheless obligatory and may be extracted by the government in order to respect the (positive) right of all citizens to a minimally decent standard of living. In essence, then, a welfare state accepts that individuals have a (negative) right to liberty and a (positive) right to a reasonable standard of living just by being members of the society. The recognition of these rights limits what governments can and cannot do, and also instructs government as to its obligations. The state is not to overdo its intrusion upon people's lives. At the same time, it is empowered to hold people legally responsible to furnish those in need with essential goods and services just because they are members of the community.

The main difference between the welfare state and socialism concerns the scope of legitimate government intervention in the lives of its citizens. In the welfare state, government is restricted in its efforts to direct people's lives toward the pursuit of certain goals, such as economic progress and the security of the people in their health. Not so in a socialist state. In the welfare state even if some wish to use their liberty frivolously, they have the right to do this, but again, not in a socialist state. Moreover, even if some do not earn any wealth by productive effort, thereby failing to express their (Marxian) human nature or neglecting themselves due to incapacity or unwillingness, they are entitled simply as members of the community to some wealth—that is their positive right—although they are not entitled to as much as they may claim is needed for them to live very well. A socialist state would have little patience with such appeals to "positive rights."

Welfare State and Pollution

How can the welfare state approach the problem of pollution? In a welfare state the vehicles of both criminal law and government regulation are available for handling the pollution problem. In other words, in this system, individuals possess rights, the violation of which by way of pollution is a legally actionable offense. Both the criminal and the civil law offer remedies against such violation. The welfare state also engages in the regulation of production, via the political process, which may lead to the establishment of government regulatory agencies. Acceptable levels of pollution may be set and members of the community are required both to observe these levels as they engage in production and to tolerate them as they experience the side effects of production.

In a recent ruling by the U.S. Supreme Court it was made clear that various governmental bodies are not fully authorized to impose pollution on the citizens by permitting others to engage in production processes that inevitably pollute the environment. On the other hand, no legal obstacles that would make it illegal to pollute, say, lakes, rivers, or the air have been placed in the paths of various municipal, county, state, and federal boards that issue permits to private and public corporations, especially utility companies, and that themselves, via such production facilities of their own as municipal electric companies or federally run power plants, produce pollutants.

It is probably fair to say that, from the point of view of the welfare state, the problem of pollution should be handled just about the way it is handled today in the United States, the United Kingdom, West Germany, Japan, Canada, and other democratic industrial countries. Besides the democratic process, these countries rely also on their basic legal traditions to adjudicate disputes that arise within community life. To the extent that those who pollute and those who are thereby harmed can be identified by the courts, considerable reliance on criminal law is possible. To the extent, however, that those who cause pollution are difficult to identify and the victims are linked rather loosely to the perpetrators, one must rely mostly on political regulation and some version of a utilitarian cost-benefit approach. The government of a welfare state has rather extensive powers to place constraints on individual liberty, though less extensive than those of a socialist system. Whenever some feature of community life is publicly administered, managed, and regulated, it is not possible to introduce considerations of individual rights as the sole determinant of public policy. Thus it is rarely a matter of whether pollution will be allowed, but rather a question of how much of it, where, and under what conditions. From the perspective of the welfare state, the answers call for public policy decisions that depend in part on basic rights, and in part on general goals that express the public interest, including an estimate of the tolerable risks to which people may be exposed.

A Critique of the Welfare State

The welfare state is often defended on the grounds that it is a buffer against extreme elitism and statism. Nevertheless, it seems that the system is exposed to the charge that the majority can still rule in some cases to the detriment of minorities and, especially, of individuals.

If, for example, the majority of the people in the United States believe in the promise of nuclear power generation, the government would be justified in encouraging the construction of nuclear plants, even if this meant acting contrary to the perceived interests of opponents of nuclear power by spending their funds, collected through taxation, to subsidize the nuclear industry (for example, in the way of limited liability in case of nuclear accidents, so that insurance costs could be kept low). True, consideration is given in the welfare state to the rights of individuals, but, as in democratic socialism, the consideration is largely procedural—one that permits individuals to take part in the forging of decisions. Once some majority or plurality has won the day, supposed rights to be free from constraints on, and intrusions in, one's liberty by others often are, and, under this theory, often should be, allowed.[5]

Since the welfare state does not limit wealth accumulation in principle but merely taxes the wealthy a bit more—and is perhaps neglectful of the possibility that the wealthy are also better equipped to take advantage of legal loopholes—great discrepancies in economic power are possible within this system. As a result, with politics being much entangled with commerce, the wealthy are in a position to exert considerable influence on political decision making, for example by fielding candidates who are able to wage expensive campaigns. In this way captains of industry can (and do) acquire large shares of political power, placing themselves in a position to guide the system toward a public policy that can (and sometimes does) disregard the interests of those who cannot wield similar power. The implications of all this for dealing with the problem of pollution are not difficult to appreciate. The owners and managers of industry can encourage public policy in such a way that their polluting production processes would be allowed—for example, the appointed regulators would license their plants and issue permits to allow considerable waste emission into lakes, the air, and rivers—while they themselves can afford to live far away and not be harmed. Moreover, to wage court fights against such policies is a costly endeavor, well beyond the means of most individual citizens, and even with the welfare state's policy of defending some of the rights of individual members of the community through the court system, not all rights of every citizen can be defended in this way. One has only to take an honest look at the living conditions of the citizens of, say, Gary, Indiana, to see how well the welfare state works when it comes to pollution. Many citizens are constantly exposed to air pollution, mainly due to their inability to leave the areas where they reside, while the more affluent have the ability to live in places very little affected. Finally, the government of the welfare state must provide for the well-being of all, including the rich and powerful, yet, because it must respect the liberty of all, it must more or less accept people's own conceptions of their welfare. Hence, those who favor short-term wealth over reductions in pollution may legitimately demand that this preference be given some weight in public policy.[6]

It is often argued that the welfare state is a kind of halfway house between extreme statism and anarchy, but this is not so. Anarchy is in fact the absence of any rules or principles enforced on the members of a human community. In anarchy there is no government at all, or so the theory would maintain. The problems with anarchy are not our concern here, but if there is a midway point between anarchy and full statism or totalitarianism, it may well be capitalism, in which a role for government does exist, but a severely limited government, one to protect the (negative) liberty of each citizen, neither more nor less. It is possible that this system can handle the problems of pollution more successfully, when consistently implemented, than any other we have considered thus far.

Capitalism

Although this system is mostly discussed in economic terms, especially when it comes to considerations of environmental or ecological facets of contemporary life, advocates of capitalism as a socioeconomic system have usually tied its features directly to certain specific political and legal principles. Accordingly, capitalism is best described by reference to those of its features that have emerged from the tradition of political philosophy associated with the thought of John Locke, whose views are briefly summarized below.

The Priority of Individual Rights

Capitalism is the socioeconomic arrangement of human communities that aim to preserve, enhance, and protect natural rights, primarily because, proponents believe, it is only with such a system in force that it is possible for human beings to both live in dignity and fully pursue their happiness. The basis of capitalism, namely, the right to private property, serves as a policy of concrete determination and protection of every individual's realm of personal authority, sovereignty, or jurisdiction. It enables a community's membership to know and work within a framework that treats human beings as individual moral agents.

This view of capitalism is different from another possible approach, one that argues for it on utilitarian grounds. This latter defense emphasizes the practical value of capitalism, that is, the system's supposed utility as an effective means for achieving the goals of those partaking in it, regardless of what those goals are. Like the Lockean defense, the utilitarian one involves certain values, even though most of those who advance it like to de-emphasize the fact and insist that they are advancing a "value-free" defense. But, unlike the Lockean approach, the utilitarian locates the standard of right and wrong in the value of the consequences rather than in respect for the individuals and his or her rights. In this latter view, the autonomy and independence of individual human beings should be affirmed and protected in a human community, something that requires recognition of private property rights. If there is a legally protected sphere of personal authority, specifiable by reference to the limits of each individual's legitimate autonomy or independence—in Robert Nozick's words, "moral space"—then individuals will be at liberty to make choices concerning their lives within those limits, either enjoying the benefits or shouldering the liabilities of their free choices. For example, if John's life destiny is for him to govern and a certain sphere of authority is acknowledged and protected for him, then, were John to choose to be a bum, which leads to his poverty, others should not interfere "for his own good," or for the good of others (for example, John's wife) who have chosen to associate themselves with John. On the other hand, if John chooses to be a productive person, thereby acquiring various valuable items through his productivity and prudence, he is to be protected from any interference with his use and disposal of these items, provided only that he does not violate the rights of others in the process. In a capitalist system, if a person neglects her health and shelter, then she and no one else is to blame, while if she takes care of her health and shelter, then she and no one else (unless there is mutual agreement to the contrary) deserves to have the benefits of her labor.

Some people argue that by its own tenets the capitalist system must make room for quite a large public sector since in advanced industrial states persons have rights to being provided with numerous goods and services, at least when they cannot provide for these themselves. So-called positive rights—for example, to health care, welfare, education, and employment—would, if they existed, require governments to do much more than capitalism might appear to allow. One reason suggested for this is that the individuals who are destitute would not benefit much from just having their right to liberty protected and preserved. It would be meaningless for them to be free from others' intrusion if they could not advance on their own, so they must be provided with some initial help by society.

While some destitute people no doubt exist in any society, the issue really is whether this is a political matter at all. People need not be destitute because of any interference by others, so to make it obligatory for others to help them—that is, to regard others' help as a right—would be to impose on others unearned punishment. And though not obligatory, basic human decency and charity would probably cause people to reach out to these destitute folks anyway. If people failed to help, there is no reason to suppose that governments would do any better at the task of securing for the needy what other people refuse to provide. But the bottom line is that there is no basic right to welfare, since lack of well-being is not a uniquely social problem but rather a problem of living itself. Poverty requires solutions from individuals, by themselves or in voluntary cooperation with each other. The only basic rights that make clear sense are ones specifying limits of social interaction, that is, ones that specify what people in society may not do to each other.

Capitalism and Pollution

What is the implication of this for our topic? In plain terms, capitalism requires that pollution be punishable as a legal offense that violates individual rights. This may appear to be a rather peculiar thing to say if one considers the United States and other Western democracies capitalist societies. In fact, however, none of these human communities is capitalist in the strict sense of that term, but only in the sense that, more than ever in previous times and places, individual rights, including the right to private property, have gained substantial, though sporadic, legal recognition in them. (Of course, neither was, for example, the Soviet Union a fully socialist society; plenty of low-key capitalist endeavors prevailed there and were, indeed, not only legally tolerated but encouraged. Nor are such semisocialist systems as those in Norway and Sweden free of capitalist features.) Still, a fledgling capitalist nation such as the United States provides some clues as to how a purely capitalist political and economic system would enforce the legal proscription against polluting. For example, in the United States polluters are often sued, under what are called tort or nuisance laws, for harm done to the polluted.[7] And the U.S. Supreme Court has held that when pollution occurs, merely considering the overall public cost of preventing it cannot be construed as an adequate determinant of whether to allow that pollution to continue. In other words, existing law is largely committed to resisting rape or assault regardless of the expense and inconvenience involved to the system and the perpetrator. (Of course, even in the most principled approach to crime, cost considerations will arise—the size of the police force, for example, and the quality of the equipment used for crime prevention.)

Let me just take a brief detour here because some may telescope the above discussion by interpreting it in the most pessimistic vein, namely, as leading to the undoing of the industrial revolution. This would be a mistake, although drawing back from certain widely established practices, such as industrial dumping, may require reorienting some industrial processes. For example, it may involve, as economists would put it, the full internalization of the cost of production—full cost pricing of services and goods that arise from such production, and so on. But there is nothing in this that would require undoing the fruits of technology, excepting those rare cases that would render internalization impossible (some types of transportation, for instance, might have to be abandoned). Viewed from the perspective of pure (that is, private-property-rights-respecting) capitalism, most Western democracies treat pollution on an overall cost-benefit, not a prohibitionist basis. For example, whether Lake Erie can be polluted with chemical discharges from the factories and power plants surrounding Buffalo, New York, and Cleveland, Ohio, is mostly a matter of some alleged cost-benefit calculation pertaining to the overall well-being of the region's population (including, perhaps, members of future generations).[8] Still, there is evidence that individual property rights are sometimes treated by the courts as inviolate, as they should be, given capitalist theory. Dumping—the act of deliberately or negligently causing the intrusion of harmful wastes upon another's domain—is generally regarded to be a crime in the United States. Pollution, in turn, is a type of dumping, namely, one that occurs in connection with the public realm, as when a chemical firm pours harmful wastes into a public lake or the atmosphere.

Under capitalism any pollution that would most likely lead to harm being done to persons who have not consented to being put at risk of such harm would have to be legally prohibited. As with people who have a contagious disease, so with processes of production that involve pollution, so long as the harmful imposition upon others occurs, without the consent of the victims, the process may not be carried out. This may lead to an initial and often temporary increase in the cost of production or to the elimination of some production process, and, in either case, to increased unemployment and related hardship. Yet, just as there were avenues of productive farming in the U.S. South once slavery had been abolished, so there may well turn out to be perfectly adequate means for providing for our needs and wants by way of technology after dumping has been prohibited.

In any case, prohibition of dumping would be the consistent way to apply the capitalist principle in the legal system. The intentional or negligent violation of individual rights, including the rights to life, liberty, and property, must be legally prohibited. To permit this type of production to continue on grounds that it will sustain employment would be exactly like permitting the continuation of other crimes on grounds that allowing them creates jobs for others.

More generally, pure capitalism rejects, in principle, the use of social risk and cost-benefit analysis as a legal basis for the redistribution of pollution. Even if some region of the country were to experience an extensive economic downturn as a result of the prohibition of air or water pollution, for example, that is no reason to allow such pollution. No one has a right to benefit from acts or practices that violate the rights of others. Just as the sexual needs of some potential rapist do not justify raping someone, so the economic needs of some potential polluters do not justify pollution.

An even better analogy might be that of a person with a contagious disease who wishes to carry on his daily activities in public, the members of which would be exposed to harmful germs if he did as he desired. Such a person would not be permitted to go on about his activities, according to capitalist thought, although it would be the responsibility of the officials of the legal system to prove that his activities cause the violation of others' rights. (The onus of proving a criminal wrong-doing is on the prosecution, since without such proof untoward and restrictive actions would easily violate individual rights.)

Unlike a rapist, who intentionally assaults a particular person to satisfy his needs or desires, the person with a contagious disease may not intend any harmful results to befall members of the public. However, the activities of this person could harm others, or put them at grave risk of serious harm, without their consent. We need not be able to tell who in particular will contract the disease before we can justify limiting this person's liberty. The fact that exposure to someone with the disease would harm some indeterminate number of the public, or place them at risk of significant harm, without their consent, suffices to invoke a quarantine against this person.

In a similar fashion, although the polluting agent may not intend to harm anyone, and even granting that we are unable to say which individuals will be harmed by the actions of the polluter, the fact that the agent's actions produce pollution suffices to justify prohibition of those activities that produce it (unless the production can be carried out without the polluting side effect).

The Moral Superiority of Capitalism

Several of the problems facing the previous theories would be tractable if restated in capitalistic terms, although some would remain to be solved. First, if the natural rights theory that underlies the capitalist political economy has solid foundations in moral theory, and if the moral theory supporting it is itself rationally superior to its competitors, then the system is clearly superior to its alternatives, all things considered. Natural rights theory rests, essentially, on the idea that it is possible for us to understand human nature and to derive from this understanding, together with our knowledge of the world in which we live, what would be the proper conditions for human social life. Although much controversy exists concerning these matters, the crux of the capitalist claim— or at least one line of reasoning advanced by defenders of capitalism about these matters—is that knowledge of human nature is no more difficult in principle than knowledge about the nature of other things we encounter. That knowledge includes the recognition that persons are the sort of beings that have a moral dimension to their existence, a moral worth or dignity, which then must be taken into account in the formulation of human social institutions, including legal systems. We have already mentioned the results of the natural rights theory.

Whether this is ultimately a successful endeavor cannot be fully explored here. But at least the theory avoids the most glaring deficiencies endemic to the welfare state. Unlike fascism, capitalism does not allocate special powers to an "inspired" leader, and unlike pure democracy or democratic socialism, pure capitalism will not allow the interests of the majority to override the rights of the individual. Moreover, while central planning socialism rests on a very dubious metaphysical theory about the gradual but revolutionary development of the human species, with little guidance as to what we should do at present, libertarianism involves a theory about the dignity and worth of human persons here and now and, as we shall see shortly, offers specific guidance regarding current problems calling for public action. Whereas the welfare state is, one might say, of two minds about the values it aims to advance, what with liberty and welfare always in potential conflict and with no clear way to resolve that conflict, capitalism, by contrast, proclaims the ultimate moral significance of the lives of individuals, lives to be led by the individuals themselves, and it proposes a social order in which the negative rights of individuals are the primary guidelines for public policy. It does not concern itself with some widely touted values, such as, for example, universal equality, absolute fairness, or unbreachable moral duty to lend help where it is needed. It does not reject anyone's efforts, alone or in concert with others, to pursue such values, but it rejects making the general welfare a basis for setting public policy, since that can, and likely will, lead to violations of individual rights. So neither the tyranny of some hero leader nor of some majority threatens individual rights. Within the confines of a capitalist system each person would be completely free of others' uninvited intrusions or could count on legal sanctions when such intrusions occur. But the rest is up to individuals acting in voluntary groups, establishing uncoerced institutions, or doing whatever is necessary to secure what they value.

This conception of capitalism may not hold out the promise of some environmental or ecological utopia, where full ecological rationality is guaranteed by government. Nor does this approach pretend to guarantee something less ambitious, namely, a reasonable level of environmentally sound living conditions for all. The system succeeds in comparison to alternatives, not in comparison to some fantastic ideal the attainment of which is impossible. It is in the effort to reach such impossible ideals that the more modest but realistic objective of a manageable environment, with the least likely unwanted harm to anyone from others' mismanagement, will occur. Promises of anything more are unfulfillable anyway. Capitalism is offered, instead, as a plausible vision of a just social order.[9]

Problems of Implementation

How could the pure capitalist apply capitalist theory in practice? This is of course the crux of the matter for this system. If it is to make good its claim to being the most adequate political theory, all things considered (and granting that not everything will be fully satisfactory in it), capitalist theory must be applicable in the real world, and then in difficult, not only in easy, cases. To show a theory's application to the problem of pollution is by no means easy. Thus it provides an interesting, important test case for assessing capitalism's theoretical mettle. How, precisely—or at least in fairly rigorous outline—could the capitalist position regarding pollution find expression in a system of law? The following observations are meant to explain, at least partially, how the ideal of a capitalist political economy might find a home in the real world of law and public policy as regards the subject of environmental management.

Pollution Defined

We may treat as pollution any form of objectively unwanted harmful by-product of human action that is not confined to an area or location but is dispersed so it may intrude on unidentifiable other persons. (Toxic waste, for example, is not pollution until it harms someone who did not choose to be harmed.) Economists call such substances uninternalizable negative externalities, although the term "uninternalizable" is somewhat of a hyperbole, since in many cases these substances are in fact simply very expensive to internalize—that is, keep from spreading throughout some occupied region.

Controlling Pollution

Stationary sources of pollution contained within the boundaries of the polluter's private property present no insurmountable problem to capitalism. Toxic as well as nuclear wastes, for example, can be identified as polluting, and if owners of firms dealing with these would act in a proper fashion, they would have to confine their operations to areas where others are left unharmed. Any breach of this requirement would meet extremely severe penalties—that is, the punishment would have to fit the crime. If the operations of such firms would be impossible without pollution—that is, without causing emissions that are harmful to others who have not consented to suffer such harm—then the operations would have to be shut down. Thus, if any people were harmed, they would be those who contractually gave their informed consent to run the risks associated with pollution. Workplace pollution would raise the issue of workers' rights, but in a capitalist framework these, too, would be recognized and protected by contract law, including laws regarding fraud and "assumption of risk." Essentially, then, any stationary source of pollution would be dealt with in the way familiar to us in connection with the operations of the free-market system of economic and legal affairs—that is, the system of individual private property rights would guide the conduct of members of the society.

Aside from the problematic nature of the "rights" of nonexisting (future) persons—rights that would not be invoked in the capitalist framework since a mere potential, nonexisting person cannot have actual, existing, and binding rights—future owners of private property could manage the problems of contained "pollution" under contract law—for example, by deed covenants running with the land. There would be some problems with abandoned property (which no one consents to take over) and with bankruptcies (where the owner is simply incapable of meeting liabilities). (Such a society would not carry the ridiculously lenient policies on bankruptcy now afoot virtually everywhere, policies that engender wholesale irresponsibility in business and industry.) In such cases one could rely, in part, on insurance provisions that might in some cases be legally mandated, given the problems reasonably anticipated with the property in question.

Some Difficulties

Stationary sources placed on (or nonstationary sources that move to) other property with the consent of the owner (whether private person or public entity) seem to present the same contract considerations and difficulties as were mentioned under the heading "Pollution Defined." For instance, automobiles are nonstationary sources that move from property to property, but that may do so if the property owner's permission has been obtained (perhaps for consideration, perhaps gratis). Barring that, however, and barring the continued availability of space within the atmosphere, so that no pollution threshold has yet been reached, automobile exhaust fumes (containing carbon monoxide) would constitute pollution and should be internalized or prohibited. Chemical wastes dumped on stationary sources might, in turn, seep out and contaminate other places than those on which they had been dumped, so once again arrangements with owners would have to be made to gain permission. If that were unfeasible—if, for example, the seepage led to the contamination of the commons, or public spheres—internalization or prohibition would be the only legitimate capitalist alternatives.

Again, it can be argued that the government of existing societies, where the problems of pollution are most pronounced, have throughout the last several decades given their implicit (and often quite explicit) permission to have the public's property—lakes, parks, forests, the atmosphere—polluted. To correct this would require some drastic measures, including, first, and foremost, the privatization of public properties, where that is possible, and total prohibition where no privatization is possible (recalling the quarantine analogy). To the objection that it may be too late, the capitalist would have to reply that indeed it is better late than never, because to allow current practices to continue is to simply exacerbate the existing pollution problems. As to seepage and similar movements, here the development of law of trespass and strictures against dumping could again be used to address the problems. But these fall into our category of difficulties.

Stationary sources placed on others' property or nonstationary sources that move to others' property without the consent of the owner form the most difficult category. For example, air traffic, factory waste emission, automobile emission on (so-called) public property , and so on, are examples of the kind of harmful emissions that others would suffer without their consent, whether explicit or implicit. This sort of pollution might be handled, first of all, through what we might call preventive market measures—for example, insurance premiums against the possibility of court suits for liability, or liability bonds. Here there is ample room for reflection, but it seems that the earlier mentioned policy of quarantine could be employed to handle the most troublesome cases.

Wherever activities issuing in pollution cannot be carried out without injury to third (nonconsenting) parties, such activities have to be prohibited as inherently in violation of the rights of members of the community. (This would not include trade in pesticide-treated fruits, for example, where the risk of harm from eating such fruit is lower than or equal to normal risks encountered in everyday life.)

When pollution occurs at threshold levels, so that only once so much emission has occurred could the emission be actually called polluting (that is, harmful to persons) rather than simply a nuisance, a system of first come, first served might be instituted, so that those who start this type of production first would be permitted to continue, while others, who would raise the threshold to a harmful level, would not. This may appear arbitrary, but in fact numerous areas of human life, especially commerce, make good use of this system, and human ingenuity could well be expended toward making sure that one's firm is not a latecomer.

A word about thresholds. The earth—as well as any part of the universe where life support is reasonably imaginable—can often absorb some measure of potentially injurious waste. (This can be expected, since life itself produces waste.) Most toxic substances can dissipate up to a point. Arguably this is no different from the simple observation that within a given territory only so much life can be supported by the same means, after which the quantity and quality of life must be lowered. Barring the privatization of hopelessly polluted areas, so that they can be kept apart and separated from others, a judicially efficient management of toxic substance disposal must take into consideration how far disposal can continue before the vital point, beyond which the waste can no longer be harmlessly absorbed and dissipated, is reached. Technical measurements would need to be employed and correlated with information about the levels of human tolerance for the toxic substance in question. Risk analysis would need to be performed so as to determine whether the risk of falling victim to toxic substance disposal corresponds with or exceeds expected risks not produced by human pollution.

The Natural Rights Approach

It is important to state that the natural rights capitalist standard of tolerance might very well be far lower than even those who support it would imagine. Many free-market advocates favor a social cost-benefit approach here, based on the utilitarian idea that what ultimately matters is the achievement of some state of collective satisfaction. This is not the approach that flows from the idea that individuals have natural negative rights to life, liberty, and property. If we assume the soundness of the natural rights stance, it may be necessary to prepare for some drastic life-style changes, so that some past abuses can be rectified. For example, whereas automobile wastes have been poured into the atmosphere with an understanding that from a utilitarian perspective it is worth doing so (based on social cost-benefit analysis), from the natural rights capitalist viewpoint it would be necessary to insist on the full initial cost being borne by automobile drivers and owners, thereby at least temporarily prompting a considerable rise in the prices of vehicles. (That the overall cost may be borne more widely, since more expensive manufacturing and transportation processes will prompt more expensive goods and services, is not relevant here. The issue is what persons can chose to do or avoid doing in light of their understanding of what may harm them.)

Certainly, a capitalist political economy's government would not have the authority to rely on the utilitarian notion, used by many courts today in their refusal to enforce "public nuisance laws," that those harmed by pollution have to "pay" since the benefits of industrial growth outweigh the costs of pollution. Instead, the principle of strict liability would apply: The polluter or others who are bound by contract with the polluter, such as nuclear utilities that may have a pact to share insurance premiums and liability resulting from accident at one member's plant, would be held liable. Benefits not solicited cannot be charged for if one respects the individual's right to choose, as the capitalist system is committed to do.[10]

International Sanctions for Pollution

Of course, there are environmental problems to which solutions are difficult just to imagine. Even if one particular country has managed to institute the legal-constitutional measures that would best handle environmental problems—according to our hypothesis, a system of strictly observed and enforced basic private property rights—the international arena will still remain unmanaged. Various problems of judicial inefficiency, the tragedy of the commons, deadlocks of public choice, and the like, will continue to permeate the international public realm.

The destruction of the ozone layer is a threat to virtually everyone, yet it is at present uncertain whether human beings are responsible for this destruction; the main cause appears to be volcanic eruption. If it should turn out that certain kinds of human activities cause this damage and if harm to human beings will be the result, once again, provided this is all demonstrated—in other words, if due process is followed—those activities may be curtailed or even prohibited. After all, no one may place poison in the atmosphere with impunity, and the problem with the ozone layer is not unlike that: the destruction of something vital that is not anyone's private property and thus no one's to destroy at will, while its destruction, nonetheless, serves to do harm to individuals.

Another type of problem to which it is difficult to construct a solution without plenty of specific and relevant scientific evidence is illustrated by the destruction of the Amazon rain forest, in this case by persons who own it. (We leave it aside for now whether the ownership was come by in a fashion consistent with individual rights.) Here, too, the only point that can be made is that if it is demonstrated that this destruction will produce a result that is injurious to others who have not consented to be so treated, the process must be legally stopped. The reason is, once again, that if one even unintentionally but knowingly violates the rights of others by depriving them of life, liberty, or property—that is, if one does not set out to do this but one's actions can be known to result in it—the action can be a kind of negligent assault or even homicide. The more accessible model might be one building a very tall but weak structure near another's home in a high wind region. Since the structure is very likely to invade the other's sphere of jurisdiction, or private property, there is reason to forbid its construction; the strong probability of causing such invasion is a justification for prohibition. If, then, cutting down trees in the Amazon could be shown to uniquely result in the destruction of the lives and properties of others, this could be cause for legally prohibiting it.

Of course, when there are no proper institutional instruments—no constitution of natural human individual rights—to guard against such actions, it is difficult to suggest where one should turn. The most effective approach in these kinds of cases would be to tie various diplomatic negotiations—including military cooperation, bank credit, and cultural exchanges—to terms that would effectively express the principles of private property rights. The quid pro quo approach might be utilized on numerous fronts, including the drafting of treaties. Once the principles and terms have been firmly entrenched, various more or less vigorous diplomatic measures need to be taken when environmental destruction occurs at different degrees of magnitude. Consider that if Brazil wishes to maintain friendly relations with the International Monetary Fund, the United States, or neighboring countries, such friendly relations would have to be manifested in part by Brazil's complying with their private property rights systems. This would apply even if Brazil itself did not adhere to such legal measures within its borders. This would be no different from other international agreements in which countries commit themselves to legal measures vis-à-vis citizens and organizations of other countries that they do not observe within their own borders. Trade agreements, contract laws, and numerous economic regulations bind foreign nationals in their interaction with a given country's population, even if within the foreign national's country these do not apply. The same kind of restrictions could be achieved on the environmental front.

Justice and the Environment

We may now return to the more general implications of the private property rights approach to managing environmental problems. For one, we must acknowledge that in some cases protecting the rights of individuals, or groups of individuals, in this strict manner may lead to their not enjoying certain benefits they might have regarded as even greater than the benefit of not suffering the harm caused by, say, pollution.

But this is not relevant. The just treatment of individuals must respect their autonomy and their choice in judging what they think is best for themselves, even if and when they are mistaken, so long as this does not involve violating others' rights. Paternalism and consistent capitalism are incompatible political ideals. The system of rights that grounds the legal framework that supports consistent capitalism is sound, if it is, precisely because as a system of laws it is the one that is most respectful of individual rights—because, in other words, it rests on acknowledgment of the sovereignty of individual human beings.

Such acknowledgement implies equal respect for every person who embarks on social life, and it is this equal respect for all combined with awareness of threats to it, that justifies the establishment of government for all, even if such a system does not guarantee that everyone will in fact make the most of its provisions. Nor does the resulting polity guarantee that all values sought by members of human communities would be best secured; technological progress in outer space travel, for example, might be enhanced by not paying heed to the strict liability provisions of the natural rights capitalist legal system.

In short, the ultimate objective of such a system is a form of justice—not welfare, not progress, not equality of condition, not artistic advancement. The justice at hand pertains to respecting every person's status as a being with dignity, that is, as a being with the freedom and the responsibility to achieve a morally excellent life in his or her own case.

What Is Done Is Done

One must be careful not to expect something impossible of a certain field of inquiry. For too long demands placed on the fields of morality and politics have been unjustly severe. Final, irrefutable, timeless answers were sought, and in response to the inevitable failure to produce these a cynicism about the prospects of workable answers has gained a foothold throughout the intellectual community, as well as among members of the general public. As a result, it is now part of the received opinion of the day that no solid intellectual solution to any of the value-oriented areas of human problems can be reached. The best we can expect is some kind of consensus that vaguely represents the tastes and preferences of a significant number of the concerned population. Yet this "consensus" is a house of cards. Tastes and preferences are unstable, flexible, and so indeterminable that the only thing to emerge has been some kind of arbitrary public policy produced either by bureaucrats or by dictators, whether official or unofficial.

In morality and politics, and thus in public policy too, there can be some very general answers that are stable enough, ones that apply to human life, so long as there is such an identifiably stable phenomenon as human life. Human life and human community involve certain lasting considerations. And innumerable changing problems that emerge in them can be approached reasonably fruitfully by taking into account some of these considerations. The several political systems we have canvassed in this discussion appeal to such basic factors with a view to dealing with one of the more thorny problems of the present epoch of human community life: pollution. Pollution is a relatively recent problem, one that proves to be an important, difficult test of the older political theories considered above: fascism, socialism, the welfare state, and capitalism. We saw that fascism would gauge the justice of the state by reference to the inspired leadership of a hero leader. Pollution problems would be managed differently, depending on the different inspired visions of different hero leaders. Science, economics, and other methods would all be available for use by such a leader, if the leader's intuitions led her or him to approve of these methods. Otherwise, they would be dispensed with.

The welfare state is designed to balance the widely acknowledged values of individual liberty and well-being, as a matter of governmental, public policy. In such a system each person would be guaranteed some measure of liberty, regardless of any overall public benefits that might be lost, as well as some measure of well-being, regardless of individual liberties that might for that purpose have to be sacrificed. Pollution, in turn, would have to be handled by reference to whether these two basic human rights could be secured through producing more or less of it.

Capitalism, in turn, stresses the ultimate importance of the rights and value of the individual, gauging the acceptability of public policies by their success in protecting individual human rights, even where other values, such as progress in science and technology, might have to be set to one side.

This discussion by no means exhausts the treatment of the pollution problem, nor does it enter into great technical detail concerning this quite essentially contemporary topic. These details could not be dealt with in relation to particular problems, ones encumbered by counter-charges; claims and counterclaims involving harm or injury by way of pollution would be at issue. (Those are best dealt with in the judicial system where they can receive proper and full attention, just what is needed to settle such claims.)

Nor can it be claimed that capitalism will always manage everything smoothly. Nevertheless, it has been argued that the capitalist approach to handling the problems of pollution accords most fully with that prime objective of human community life, namely, human justice. Ironically, it appears that this approach to problems with the environment and ecology often yields stricter measures than those championed by most environmentalists.

In any case, the arguments and theories advanced herein should serve as a useful starting point to consider some of the more particular problems of the environment as they emerge in the actual, day-to-day affairs of individuals living in communities and on the globe.

Notes

1. *Blakiston's Gould Medical Dictionary*, 4th ed., (New York: McGraw-Hill Book Company, 1979), p. 1073.
2. Richard B. Steward and James F. Krier, *Environmental Law and Policy*, 2d ed., (Indianapolis, IN: Bobbs-Merrill, 1978), p. 3.
3. *Black's Law Dictionary*, 5th ed., (St. Paul, MN: West, 1979), p. 1043.
4. Tibor R. Machan, "Pollution and Political Theory," in *Earthbound*, ed. Tom Regan, (New York: Random House, 1984).
5. For presentation of this position, see the discussion in Chapter 3 of the views of Gregory Vlastos, Alan Gewirth, and John Rawls.
6. John Ahrens (personal communication, August, 1990) brought this point to my attention.
7. See Robert K. Best and James I. Collins, "Legal Issues in Pollution Engendered Torts," *Cato Journal* 2 (Spring 1982): 101–136.
8. See Joseph P. Martino, "Inheriting the Earth," *Reason* (November 1982): 30–40, 46.
9. For the kind of "utopia" promised by capitalists or libertarians, see Robert Nozick, "Utopia," part 3 of *Anarchy, State, and Utopia* (New York: Basic Books, 1974). Oddly, even some of those who are very sympathetic to the classical liberal or

libertarian system lament its alleged failure to produce a theory of community. See Richard Cournell, "New Work for Invisible Hands," *Times Literary Supplement,* (April 5, 1991): 4-6. The point of the liberal theory of community is to call attention to the plurality of possible communities that individual human beings in voluntary association with one another are going to develop, based on their varied (though often equally meritorious) purposes. A good approximation to this is the history of the United States, with its overlapping as well as coexisting communities in religion, the arts, athletics, and recreation.

10. For a discussion of the pervasiveness of the violation of individual rights on grounds that people should not benefit without paying, see chapter 11.

9

Advertising: The Whole or Only Some of the Truth?

They know enough who know how to learn.

—Henry Adams

There are numerous reasons for the advocacy of government intervention. We have looked at some of these in the abstract, with reference to some illustrative examples. But I want now to consider an argument that will give us another kind of reason why government regulation is advocated, especially vis-à-vis the profession of business—the human activity of commerce. This argument illustrates how readily some persons—most of them teachers of our young people at colleges and universities—disparage the moral underpinnings of trade, marketing, and advertising. Once the moral standing of these activities has been called into question, it is easy to argue that government ought to be especially attentive to these untoward but perhaps necessary human endeavors.

What is especially remarkable about the kind of moral case that is advanced below by the critic of advertising is that if the argument succeeds, advertising becomes a "public concern." If there is a fundamental obligation for merchants to help the public, and if the customers have a right to this help, then surely the government must make certain the obligation is fulfilled and the customers' rights protected. Rights protection, as we have already noted, is the quintessential public purpose. So it will be useful to see whether the argument aimed at broadening the public realm succeeds in this instance. It will be evident from what follows that we can handle community problems without the invalid expansion of the concept of *public* that is prevalent in our time.

251

When commercial advertising is criticized, often some moral assumption that surfaces that should be explored more fully. I have in mind in particular the hidden premise that advertising is first and foremost a means for conveying information. Another assumption that lingers in the background of criticisms of advertising is that ethics requires that those who sell goods and services should first of all help customers.

My first goal here is to defend the approach to advertising that does not require of merchants that they tell all. So long as merchants are honest, and do not mislead or deceive, they are acting in a morally satisfactory manner. It is not good for them—and there is nothing in morality that requires it of them—to take up the task of informing consumers of the conditions most favorable to them in the marketplace, or to aid them in their efforts to find the best deal. Then I will consider an aspect of advertising that bears more directly on politics, namely, whether cigarette advertising should be banned, in light of the plausible contention that smoking is harmful to the smoker. (I merely touch on the issue of harm from secondary smoking, that is, when one inhales another person's smoke. I will briefly deal with that topic in the second section of this chapter.)

The following passage will help introduce us to the topic. It illustrates the kind of views that many philosophers who work in the field of business ethics seem to find convincing. Merchants and producers have many ways of concealing truth from customers—not by lying to them, but simply by not telling them facts that are relevant to the question of whether they ought to purchase a particular product or whether they are receiving full value for their money.[1] The author goes on to state that "it is certainly unethical for [sales representatives and business owners] to fail to tell their customers that they are not getting full value for their money."[2] He cites David Ogilvy, a top advertising man, as admitting that "he is 'continuously guilty of suppressio veri, the suppression of the truth.'"[3] In other words, what advertisers do that is ethically or morally wrong is to fail to tell the whole truth when they communicate to others about their wares, services, goods, products, or what not.

Yet there is something unrealistic, even farfetched, about this line of criticism. To begin with, even apart from advertising, people often enough advance a biased or partial perspective about themselves, their skills, their looks, and so on. When we go out on a first date, we tend to dress ourselves in a way that highlights our assets and diminishes our liabilities. When we send out résumés in a job search effort, we hardly tell all. Even when we dress for the normal day, we tend to choose garb that enhances our looks and covers up what is not so attractive about our whole selves.

Burton Leiser, the critic we have been using to illustrate the prevailing view of advertising, is not wholly unaware of these points. Leiser continues with his quotation from Ogilvy, who says: "Surely it is asking too much to expect the advertiser to describe the shortcomings of his produce. One must be forgiven for 'putting one's best foot forward.'" At this Leiser exclaims: "So the consumer is not to be told all the relevant information; he is not to be given all the facts that would be of assistance in making a reasonable decision about a given purchase."[4] Nevertheless, Leiser does not tell us what is ethically wrong in such instances of *suppressio veri*. In fact, the claim that in all advertising one must present the whole truth, not just be truthful about one's subject matter, presupposes the very problematic ethical view that one ought to devote oneself primarily to bettering the lot of other people. What commerce rests on ethically, implicitly or explicitly, is the very different doctrine of caveat emptor ("Let him [the purchaser] beware"), which assumes that prudence is a virtue and should be practiced by all, including one's customers. I will argue here that the merchant's ethical stance is more reasonable than that of the critics.

The Vice of Suppressio Veri

Leiser and many others critical of business and sales practices assume that in commercial transactions persons owe others the whole truth and nothing but the truth. This is why they believe that merchants act unethically in failing to tell their customers something that customers might ask about if they would only think of everything relevant to their purchasing activities. Leiser gives a good example:

Probably the most common deception of this sort is price deception, the techniques some high-pressure sales representatives use to sell their goods by grossly inflating their prices to two, three, and even four times their real worth. Again, there may be no "untruth" in what they say; but they conceal the important fact that the same product, or one nearly identical to it, can be purchased for far less at a department or appliance store.[5]

Before I discuss the ethical themes in these remarks, a word, first, about the alleged simplicity of learning whether some item for sale by a merchant is in fact available for purchase "for far less" elsewhere. The idea is, we may take it, that the customer will indeed obtain what he or she wants by purchasing this item from some other seller. This ignores the fact that it may be quite important for customers to purchase some items in certain places, in certain kinds of environments, even from certain types of persons (ones with good manners, for instance). Sheer accessibility can be crucial, as well as atmosphere, the merchant's demeanor, and so on. If it is legitimate for customers to seek satisfaction from the market, it is also legitimate to seek various combinations of satisfaction, not simply product or price satisfaction.

Let us, however, assume that a customer could have obtained all that she wanted by going elsewhere to purchase the item at a price "far less" than what it costs at a given merchant's store. Is there a responsibility on the merchant's part, if the merchant knows this, to make the information available to the customer? Or even more demandingly, is it ethically required that the merchant become informed about these matters and convey the information to potential customers?

The answer depends on a broader ethical point. What are the standards by which human beings should conduct themselves, especially in their relationship to others? If something on the order of the altruist's answer is correct, then, in general, suppressio veri is wrongful. Telling the whole truth would help other people in living a good human life. Altruism here means not the ideal of equal respect for everyone as a human being, advocated by Thomas Nagel.[6] Rather, it is intended in the earlier sense of having as one's primary duty advancing the interest of others.[7] A merchant need not be disrespectful toward her customers if she does not inform them of something that perhaps they ought to have learnt in the first place. By volunteering information that quite conceivably a customer should, as a matter of his personal moral responsibility (as a prudent individual) have obtained, a merchant might be meddling in matters not properly her own, which could be demeaning.

But an altruism, in terms of which one is primarily responsible to seek and obtain the well-being of fellow human beings, would render suppressio veri morally wrong. Such an altruism is certainly widely advocated, if not by philosophers then at least by political reformers. For example, Karl Marx states, in one of his earliest writings, that "the main principles...which must guide us in the selection of a vocation is the welfare of humanity...," and that "man's nature makes it possible for him to reach his fulfillment only working for the perfection and welfare of his society."[8] Here he states precisely the morality of altruism initially espoused by August Comte, who coined the term itself and developed the secular "religion" by which to promote the doctrine.[9]

Only by the ethics of altruism does it follow unambiguously that a merchant who does not tell all "is certainly unethical." Neither the more common varieties of utilitarianism, nor Kant's theory, as it is often understood, implies this. If we are to live primarily to do good for others, then when we have reason to believe that telling the truth will promote others' well-being (without thwarting the well-being of yet some other person), we morally ought to tell the whole truth to this person. So when a merchant has reason to believe that telling his customer about lower prices elsewhere (for goods which he sells at higher prices) will benefit his customer, he ought morally to do so.

But for it to be established that this is what a merchant ought morally to do for any customer, and that not doing so "is certainly unethical," the sort of altruism Marx and Comte defended would have to be true. No other ethical view point seems to give solid support to the above claim about what "is certainly unethical."

Still, might one perhaps be able to show the whole-truth thesis sound by other means than depending on a strong altruistic moral framework? Not very plausibly. Intuitionism, as generally understood, would not override the well-entrenched belief that when one embarks on earning a living and deals with perfect strangers, one should not promote one's weaknesses, or volunteer information detrimental to one's prospects. I doubt anyone would seriously advise job-seeking philosophers to list on their curricula vitae rejected articles and denied promotions; that would be counterintuitive.

It is also doubtful that most versions of utilitarianism would support a very strong general principle of self-sacrifice from which it could be shown that it is "certainly unethical" not to tell the whole truth. There could be many good utilitarian reasons to support at least a substantial degree of caveat emptor in the marketplace. For example, if the classical and neoclassical defenses—and the Marxian explanation of the temporary necessity—of the unregulated market of profit-seeking individuals have any merits, it is for the utilitarian reasons that the competitive, self-interested conduct of market agents should be encouraged. From a utilitarian perspective on what maximizes the good of society, which in this case would be wealth, businesses should not give away information free of charge.

Even a Kantian deontological ethics, as generally understood, advises against taking over what is very plausibly another person's moral responsibility, namely, seeking out the knowledge to act prudently and wisely. The Kantian idea of moral autonomy may not require seeking one's personal happiness in life, as the Aristotelian concept of the good moral life does, but it does require leaving matters of morality to the discretion of the agent. Meddling with the agent's moral welfare would conceivably be impermissibly intrusive. By reference to the Kantian categorical imperative it is difficult to imagine why one should invite commercial failure in one's market transactions, a failure that is surely possible if one is occupied not with promoting one's own success but with the success of one's potential customers.

It seems, then, that the altruistic ethics that make it everyone's duty to further the interests of other people is indeed the most plausible candidate for making it "certainly unethical" to suppress the truth in commercial transactions. Yet, of course, troubles abound with altruism proper. Specifically, the altruism that might be the underpinning of the criticism of advertising ethics, as illustrated above, should be thought of more along Rawlsian lines. According to this view, we owe help to others only if they are found in special need, following the lead of Rawls's basic principle: "All social values—liberty and opportunity, income and wealth, and the bases of self-respect—are to be distributed equally unless an unequal distribution of any, or all, of these values is to everyone's advantage."[10]

But this form of moderate egalitarianism no longer supports the prevailing idea of proper business ethics.[11] In complying with this principle the merchant should, in the main—except when informed of special disadvantages of potential customers—put a price on products that will sell the most wares at the margin, that is, reaching the largest number of customers. Such behavior is also exactly what economists, who assume that merchants are profit maximizers, claim merchants engage in. And this is the kind of conduct that the merchant has reason to believe will ensure the equal distribution of values, as far as she can determine what that would be. The reason is that from the perspective of each merchant qua merchant it is reasonable in the course of commerce to consider potential customers as agents whose status is equal to the merchant's own and who are interested in advancing their economic interests. From this, with no additional information about some possible special disadvantage of the customer, merchants must see themselves as having equal standing with customers and legitimate motives for furthering their own interests.[12]

Thus, the Rawlsian egalitarian moral viewpoint will not help to support the doctrine that merchants owe a service to customers. Only the robust form of altruism we find in Marx and some others is a good candidate for the morality that, for example, Leiser assumes must guide our merchant. Ethical views other than altruism might support the view that the merchant ought to be extra helpful to special persons—family, friends, associates, even neighbors—but not to everyone. Even a narrow form of subjective "ethical" egoism can lead merchants to regard it as their responsibility to be helpful toward some other people. For instance, a merchant might consider most of his customers close enough friends that the morality of friendship, which need not be altruistic and may be egoist, would guide him to be helpful even to the point of risking the loss of business. Or, alternatively, were it the case that having the reputation of being helpful leads to increased patronage from members of one's community, then in just such a community such a subjective egoist would properly engage in helping behavior, including now and then informing customers of more advantageous purchases to be had in other establishments.

The Morality of Caveat Emptor

In contrast to the assumption of altruism, I wish to suggest a form of egoism as the appropriate morality in terms of which to understand commerce. I have in mind a form of egoism best called "classical" because, as I have argued elsewhere,[13] it identifies standards of (egoistic) conduct by reference to the teleological conception of the human self spelled out in the works of classical philosophers, especially Aristotle.[14] I have modified these standards, in line however, with an individualism that arises from the ontology of human nature. The idea, briefly put, is that each individual should seek to promote *his interests as a human being and as the individual he is*. This is not the psychological egoism of Hobbes or the extreme subjective egoism of Max Stirner, usually criticized by contemporary moral philosophers.[15] Classical egoism regards the individual person as the ultimate, though not sole, proper beneficiary of that individual's own moral conduct. The standards of such conduct are grounded on the nature of the individual as a human being, as well as the particular person he or she is. Thus in a moral universe that is coherent there need be no fundamental conflict between the egoistic conduct of one person and the egoistic conduct of another.

Accordingly, in the case of our merchant, he should abide by the basic moral principle of right reason, and the more particular implication of this, namely the virtue of honesty, as he answers the questions his customer puts to him. He might, for example, even refuse to answer some questions instead of either giving help or lying. It is a person's moral responsibility to promote his rational self-interest. And taking up the task of merchandising goods and services can qualify, for various individuals with their particular talents and opportunities in life, as promoting one's rational self-interest. So a merchant could be acting with perfect moral propriety in not offering help to a customer with the task of information gathering (especially if it were clear that competing merchants were doing their very best to publicize such information as would be valuable to customers). The responsibility of merchants is conscientiously to sell their wares, not to engage in charitable work by carrying out tasks that other persons ought to carry out for themselves.

It might be objected that if someone asks an informed merchant, "Is this same product available for a lower price somewhere else?" no other alternative but letting the customer know the answer exists, because it could be rather strained to refuse to answer. But there are many ways to deflect answering that do not mark someone as a deceiver. Smiling at the customer, the merchant might even quietly put a question to the customer: "Well, do you actually want me to help you to take your business elsewhere?" Should it be clear to a merchant that the customer is not going to be satisfied with the wares available in his or her establishment, it would make perfectly good sense to offer help—as indeed countless merchants do frequently enough. Thus, when one looks for shoes, one frequently finds that one merchant will guide a customer to another where some particular style or size is likely to be available. Both good merchandising and ordinary courtesy would support such a practice, although it is doubtful that any feasible ethical system would make it generally, morally obligatory.

In terms of the classical egoism that would seem to give support to these approaches to ethical issues in business, it does not follow that lying, in order to avoid putting oneself at a competitive disadvantage, would be acting properly. One's integrity, sanity, reputation, generosity, and one's respect for others are more important to oneself than competitive advantage. Yet neither is prudence merely a convenience, and seeking a competitive advantage in the appropriate ways would indeed be prudent.[16]

Of course showing that this morality is sound would take us on a very long journey, although some work has already been done to that end.[17] As I have noted already, in numerous noncommercial situations human beings accept as perfectly proper the form of conduct that characterizes ordinary but decent commercial transactions. In introducing ourselves to people we have never met, for example, we do not advance information that would be damaging to the prospects for good relations. We do not say: "I am John Doe. When I am angry, I throw a fit, and when in a bad mood I am an insufferable boor." When we send an invitation to our forthcoming party, we do not say: "While this party may turn out to be pleasant, in the past we have had some very boring affairs." Innumerable noncommercial endeavors, including professional ones, are characterized by "putting our best foot forward," leaving to others the task of making sure whether they wish to relate to us. The fields of romance, ordinary conversation, political advocacy, and so forth all give ample evidence of the widespread practice of putting our best foot forward and letting others fend for themselves. We do not lie to, mislead, or deceive others by not mentioning to them, unsolicited, our bad habits, our foibles. As suggested before, we are not lying or misleading others when in sending along our résumés or curricula vitae we do not list projects that have been rejected.

The exceptions to this are those cases in which we have special obligations arising out of special moral relationships such as friendship, parenthood, collegiality, and so on. In these—as well as in contractual relationships, where the obligations arise out of explicitly stated intent instead of implied commitments and promises—one can have obligated oneself to be of assistance even in competition or contest. Friends playing tennis could well expect one another to lend a hand when skills are quite uneven. Parents should not always allow their children to fend for themselves, with limited information, as the children embark upon various tasks. And in emergency cases it is also reasonable to expect strangers to set aside personal goals that ordinarily would be morally legitimate.

Commercial relationships usually take place between strangers. The only purpose in seeking out other persons is for the sake of a good deal. Even here, sometimes further bonds emerge, but those are essentially beside the point of commerce. So the moral aspects of personal intimacy would not be the proper ethics for commercial relationships, anymore than they would be for sports or artistic competitions.

Some, of course, envision the good human community as a kind of large and happy family, the "brotherhood of man," as Marx did (not only early in his life but, insofar as his normative model of the ultimately good human society was concerned, for all of his career). For them the fact that some human beings interact with others solely for "narrow," "selfish" economic purposes will be a lamentable feature of society—to be overcome when humanity reaches maturity, perhaps, or to be tolerated only if out of such selfishness some public good can be achieved.[18]

But this alleged ideal of social life cannot be made to apply to human beings as they in fact are found among us. That vision, even in Marx, is appropriate only for a "new man," not the actual living persons we are (in our time). For actual human beings this picture of universal intimacy must be rejected in favor of one in which the multifaceted and multidimensional possibility of pursuing personal happiness is legally protected. For then commercial interaction or trade does not place the fantastic burden on the parties involved that would be required of them if they needed to "be forgiven for putting one's best foot forward."

I have tried to offer some grounds for conceiving of trade in such a way that the unreasonable burden of having to tell others the whole truth, blemishes and all, need not be regarded as morally required. None of the above endorses cheating, deception, false advertising, and the like. It does recommend that we look at the practice of commercial advertising—as well as other practices involving the presentation of oneself or one's skills and wares in a favorable light—as morally legitimate, justified, even virtuous (insofar as it would be prudent).

Product Liability: Some Caution

One line of objection that has been suggested to the above approach is that failing to tell all about the features of a commercial transaction on the part of those embarking on it is like not telling someone about a defect in a product. When a merchant sells an automobile tire, if he is aware that this tire is defective, the mere fact that his customer does not explicitly inquire about defects does not appear to be, on its face, sufficient justification for suppression of the truth of the fact. But is this not just what my analysis in the previous section would permit, on egoistic grounds? And would that not be sufficient ground, as James Rachels argues in another context against egoism, for rejecting the argument?[19]

Without embarking on a full discussion of the topic of product liability, let me point out some possible ways of approaching the issues that are consistent with the moral perspective I have taken on truth telling. First, as in law, so in morality there is the "reasonable man" standard that can be appealed to in considering personal responsibility. After all, a merchant is selling an automobile tire and it is implicit in that act that he is selling something that will, to the best of available knowledge, function in that capacity when utilized in normal circumstances.

One problem with this response is that it comes close to begging the question. Just what the reasonable expectation is in such cases of commercial transaction is precisely at issue. If it is true that caveat emptor is justified, then why not go the full distance and make the buyer beware of all possible hitches associated with the transaction?

The answer to that question introduces the second approach to handling the product liability issue. I have in mind a point that introduces some difficult metaphysical and epistemological elements into this discussion. I am thinking here of the need for a distinction between what is essential about some item and what is incidental or merely closely associated with it. And when we are concerned about truth telling—and I have not tried to reject the requirement of honesty, only that of telling everything that one knows and that may be of help to the buyer—it is more than likely that in the very identification of what one is trading, one commits oneself to having to give any information that is pertinent to the nature of the item or service at hand. Concerning automobile tires, their function as reliable equipment for transport on ordinary roads is a good candidate for an essential feature. So not telling of any defect in tires pertaining to this feature would amount to telling a falsehood, that is, saying one is trading x would render whatever is identified as x a fake—something that would in the context of commercial transactions open the party perpetrating the misidentification to charges of fraud.

This is not to claim that what is essential about items must remain static over time. The context has a good deal to do with the determination of essential attributes of items and services, and convention and practice are not entirely inapplicable to that determination. Here is where a certain version of the theory of rational expectations would be useful and may indeed already function in some instances of tort law. As J. Roger Lee puts it,

> I have rights. They do not come out of agreements with others, being prior to and presupposed by such agreements. But standard relations with others, which I will call "rational expectations frameworks," fix the criteria of their application to situations in everyday life. And rational expectations frameworks are a guide to those criteria....For example, if I go into a bar and order a scotch on the rocks, then it is reasonable to expect that I'll get what I order and that neither it nor the place where I sit will be booby-trapped. There are countless examples of this.[20]

But a detailed explication of this theory would lead us far afield, into the thorny problems of identity and essence as regards human artifacts. It suffices for my purposes that a distinction may well be available to handle the objection I have been considering. It is possible to show that from a robust or classical ethical egoist standpoint, the truth about an item or service being traded should be told. But this does not mean having to tell the whole truth, including various matters associated with the buying and selling of the item or service in question such as its price elsewhere, its ultimate suitability to the needs of the buyer, or its full value. This perspective, in turn, does not imply that defective products or incompetent service are equally suitable objects of trade in honest transactions.[21]

Banning Some Speech?

We may at this point explore further an aspect of government regulation, namely, whether something that is possibly harmful may be sold and advertised in a free society. At the outset I wish to recall a point made by the U.S. Supreme Court, one that fully accords with what I have been advancing as the moral thesis of the present work. The Court, at one point, said:

> The very purpose of the Bill of Rights was to withdraw certain subjects from the vicissitudes of political controversy, to place them beyond the reach of majorities and officials, and to establish them as legal principles to be applied by the Courts.

One's right to life, liberty and property, to free speech, a free press, freedom of worship and assembly and other fundamental rights may not be submitted to a vote; they depend on the outcome of no elections.[22]

We have noted that there are many who would eagerly expand the public realm. But it might be thought that this is least likely to succeed, even within the ranks of modern liberals, when it bears on the activities of speaking and writing.[23] Does not the First Amendment to the U.S. Constitution make clear that such activities are none of (at least the federal) government's business? Actually, there are prominent arguments that disregard that plain fact. Here, I wish to concentrate on whether those who argue that position have something to offer. Should advertising even a controversial product come under public jurisdiction? It seems to me that that would only be justified if this activity would violate someone's rights. But let us first see how the argument goes. Then we can examine its merits.

Among others, the American Medical Association (AMA) has been calling for a ban on the advertising and promotion of all tobacco products. A new wave of debate on constitutional questions and on the nature of advertising is sure to follow and, indeed, has already begun. I intend to focus in our discussion of this proposal on some of the basic moral and political values that are involved. While I realize that the public debate will be conducted in terms of legal precedent, I regard the main problem to be the manner in which the issue relates to basic values in a free society. Let us stipulate here that the main values embodied by the U.S. Constitution are basic moral-political values. Central among these are citizen sovereignty or democracy, limited government, and natural or human rights. Of course, our particular issue here is commercial speech and whether it deserves protection under the First Amendment. But tobacco is merely an example of the principles we wish to explore.[24]

A prominent argument for why the First Amendment does not protect anything other than political speech may be found in the following passage:

Although the prohibition in the First Amendment is absolute—we see here a restraint upon Congress that is unqualified, among restraints that are qualified—the absolute prohibition does not relate to all forms of expression but only to that which the terms, "freedom of speech, or of the press" were then taken to encompass, political speech, speech having to do with the duties and concerns of self-governing citizens. Thus, for example, this constitutional provision is not primarily or directly concerned with what we now call artistic expression or with the prohibition of obscenity. Rather, the First Amendment acknowledges that the sovereign citizen has the right freely to discuss the public business, a privilege theretofore claimed only for members of legislative bodies.[25]

I do not accept this argument for the following reasons. I regard the unqualified character of First Amendment restrictions on regulating free speech to imply that the provision must be read strictly. Some suggest it must be interpreted by reference to what is called original intent. I regard the wording of the amendment as the result of debate, and it is within the debate that the original intent appears. The result of the debate expresses the resolution of the debate, which does not qualify speech by such terms as "political" or "public business." Rather, the result is "free speech, or of the press," the meaning of which is unambiguous, covering, by the logic of the terms involved, all kinds of speech and all subjects that are dealt with in the press.

Ours may be termed the strict constructionist interpretation, rather than what has gained designation as the original intent interpretation of the First Amendment. But I would also like to call attention to the fact that the original intent interpretation omits from serious consideration a reading of the Declaration of Independence, the document that presages the manner in which the Bill of Rights should be interpreted. It is my view that the more radical Declaration of Independence puts on record the political philosophical ideals that would serve as a clear clue to the reading of the Constitution—and so to original intent. And the Declaration refers to certain "truths" that are held to be "self-evident," namely, "that all men are created equal, that they are endowed by their Creator with certain unalienable rights, that among these are Life, Liberty and the Pursuit of Happiness. That to secure these rights, Governments are instituted among Men, deriving their just powers from the consent of the governed." Therefore, the reading of the Declaration counters the restrictive interpretation of the First Amendment, because the Declaration speaks broadly of the "unalienable" rights to life, liberty, and the pursuit of happiness, suggesting that the liberties that these rights secure for us reach beyond the narrow liberty of political participation.

Finally, let me quote a very telling criticism of the narrow interpretation:

Under such an approach, while government authority could not silence direct criticism, they could exercise an almost unlimited power to control other kinds of speech in order to gain support and discredit opposition. For example, though the government could not directly silence critics of a planned weapons system, it could suppress publication or broadcast of any scientific discussion that related to its feasibility. Though the government could not directly silence critics of its economic policies, it could suppress any words about economic issues that had a bearing upon those policies. Though the government could not ban opposition political parties, it could exert a rigid control over the expression of political philosophies which might provide a broad intellectual foundation for organized political opposition. [Anastaplo's and] Judge Bork's approach would thus drastically weaken the First Amendment as a safe-guard against government abuse of power.[26]

I do not wish to argue why, independent of constitutional interpretation, commercial speech ought to be given the protection already provided by the First Amendment of the U.S. Constitution. Instead, I will advance a moral-political rather than jurisprudential argument. Even if the case based on how the constitution should be interpreted does not suffice to defend a legal verdict in favor of commercial and other speech, the argument here ought to support efforts to change the constitution to provide for such broader protection.

A Basic Error

Virtually all attacks upon citizenship sovereignty, or political liberty, rest upon a basic moral error. This is the confusion of basic rights with what is right. Attempts to regulate commercial speech so as to ban tobacco products is one of the purer examples of this error.

If we assume, for the sake of argument only, that it would be right for all people to stop smoking, we have, as yet, said absolutely nothing about the basic *rights* related to the case. It may turn out that forcing people to quit smoking, as well as restricting their access to tobacco products or information about such products, violates basic rights that deserve constitutional protection. The paradox here is that in the pursuit of something right, one would violate a basic right and do what is politically wrong. The reason for the paradox is that the particular way in which the correct course or good conduct in question is pursued conflicts with another correct course, a more basic one, that upon analysis takes moral priority, namely, respecting others' moral autonomy or free will.

It is another matter what to do about harm from secondary smoking. If it is demonstrable and takes place in a "public" sphere—that is, a sphere now under government jurisdiction, regardless of whether it has to be—than it may be prohibited. If it takes place on private property and those who enter are forewarned, there is nothing legally objectionable about the practice. It may, of course, be rude, but that is not the province of the laws of a free society.

Let us begin now with the issue of banning cigarette advertising. Some moral principles are more fundamental than others. And what is characteristic of rights is that when we consider their role in interpersonal moral circumstances we can see that they are, almost by definition, foundational. Other socially relevant moral principles or values must give way to them in cases of conflict.

We can detect this throughout ordinary discourse. It makes perfect sense to say, "It may not be right for me to do (or believe) this, but I have every right to do so."[27] And it makes perfectly good sense to both criticize some conduct—bad writing, shoddy argumentation, theoretical confusion, obscenity or pornography, prostitution, drug abuse, the greedy pursuit of wealth, or yellow journalism—as well as defend it against those who would want to prohibit or ban it. This is indeed one of the functions of the First Amendment of the U.S. Constitution. We realize that most people favor some of these types of conduct over others, so that they will say that one has the right to carry on with that type but not with another—pornography but not excessive greed, or the greedy pursuit of wealth but not prostitution. The point for now is that we can see the conceptual priority in social morality or politics of having a right to do many things that are not the right thing to do. Rights are prior to obligations, it seems, as principles of citizenship sovereignty and, derivatively, democratic government. If this were not so, then democracy itself, the participation of citizens in the formation of their political institutions, could be overridden by some higher political duty, one that might be imposed upon the people against their will by anyone.

But before this can be discussed more concretely, we need to turn briefly to just what basic rights we have. Some rights seem to be dictated by common sense. The "right" not to be harmed seems to be one of these rights. If this is a right, should not tobacco products, or information about such products, be restricted or banned?

Common sense is not always a definitive clue. There is in fact no basic "right not to be harmed." The reason for this is twofold: people can voluntarily undertake risks, and people can have their rights violated without being harmed. In the first case, people voluntarily pursue dangerous activities all the time. They take on dangerous jobs, pursue dangerous sports, drive cars, and so on. What we expect in such situations is that the people involved have some conception of the risks they are undertaking—not that they be free from harm. On the other side, if the government restricts my freedom to speak on behalf of a cause I do not believe in, I have not been harmed, but my rights have been violated. In the end, then, rights and harms are not necessarily connected.

In a similar vein, rights and government have no necessary connection. Some philosophers believe that rights are what the government allows us to do. But if this were true, it would make no sense to say that governments can violate people's rights, something they in fact do quite often. Since, as the Declaration of Independence so clearly notes, we are "endowed . . . with certain unalienable rights," we can possess rights that were not given to us by government and that government cannot legitimately take away. The first ten amendments to the U.S. Constitution were included so as to protect U.S. residents, at least, from government infringement of rights that all persons were said to possess "by nature."[28]

The Amendment that concerns us here is the first; but the principle behind all of them is the same: People have basic rights independent of governments. This principle further supports our claim that a fundamental error occurs when one confuses basic rights with what is right. For what one discovers about basic rights is that they represent liberties, and liberty implies the possibility of choosing a "wrong" course of action as much as a "right" one.

This point is clearly evident in speech cases where many wrongheaded causes are allowed to have their say with the same degree of legitimacy as those that are closer to the truth. Our basic rights, therefore, must be understood as essentially liberties; and these liberties are given political expression through constitutional guarantees against state interference. This is at least what underlies the theory of civilized government wherein the law is available for all to consult, that is, where law is objective and not arbitrary—in the sense of its being both morally well founded and clearly evident.

The lurking issue in the present context—namely, where the welfare state is a serious challenge to a state that regards citizens as sovereigns—is whether people can have their liberties restricted in the name of "paternalism." This means using the power of government as parental authority is used over children, that is, to protect citizens from themselves.

This is a complex matter and we will not discuss it in full. If paternalism has a place at all in a free society, it would arise only in cases where information about alternatives was unavoidably lacking. As we shall see, such is not the case with tobacco products and their use, even if at times their use may correctly be regarded as a wrong. Of course, we are not arguing or conceding here that smoking is a "wrong" that might generally justify paternalistic protection from the government, although something else might qualify, such as exposure to ultraviolet rays normally expected to be shielded by the ozone layer. Whether someone's smoking is wrong conduct is certainly not a simple matter to decide. Even if in some cases it is clearly wrong to smoke, there can be many others when it is not. Consider that for some individuals the preservation of their health may not be a primary value at all, not given the context of their lives; a nervous novelist, for instance, or terminally ill scientist, or even someone with special preference for the sensation of tobacco smoke might be justified in not considering his health as a primary matter of concern. (We are not here discussing the infliction of smoke on others in public places.) Some certainly regard smoking in this way; and it is useful to recognize that even if one concedes the point about the "wrongfulness" of smoking, no foundation has yet been laid for waiving basic rights or Constitutional protections.

Commercial Speech and Constitutional Principles

In an important case, the Federal Trade Commission (FTC) charged R. J. Reynolds Tobacco Co., Inc. with running a false and misleading "advertisement" (titled "Of Cigarettes and Science")[29] on the health effects of smoking cigarettes. The FTC believed the "ad" to be "deceptive" because Reynolds had interpreted a government study on the causes of heart disease to show that smoking was not detrimental. The FTC lost the case because the judge ruled that the "ad" qualified as noncommercial speech, since no prices or brands or products were mentioned. Had such things been mentioned, the FTC would have had the power to "regulate" the advertisement under the limited First Amendment protections granted to commercial speech. The question arises, however, as to why Reynolds would not have enjoyed full First Amendment protection even if it had mentioned its own products.

In the last few years the courts have given commercial speech secondary status with respect to First Amendment protection. Although the courts clearly protect the right to advertise,[30] they nevertheless subject advertisers and producers to a myriad of government regulations. The secondary status of commercial speech is the inevitable result of trying to reconcile free speech with a regulated economy. But this reconciliation is conceptually unstable. It assumes, on the one hand, that economic activities can be divorced from communications and information about such activities. Since these two cannot be separated, the value of free speech is compromised in an attempt to retain the government's power to regulate voluntary economic transactions. On the other hand, the reconciliation assumes that the rights of free speech apply to some categories of speech and not others. Commercial speech needs to be wrenched from other forms of speech to make this argument fly.

The main way of trying to separate commercial from noncommercial speech is to argue that the latter is "public" speech while the former is "private" because it serves some private interest.[31] This distinction is used to argue that the courts have gone too far in allowing First Amendment protection of commercial speech.[32] The First Amendment, these critics claim, was meant to cover cases of public speech, not private. They would agree with us that it is incoherent to grant commercial speech only partial protection; but their solution is to afford commercial speech no First Amendment protection at all.

It is our view that the distinction between public and private speech is simply not viable. Paradoxically, it is typical for those who object to First Amendment protection of commercial speech to also fail to object to government regulation of the economy. But if economic matters were purely private, the government could have no "public" interest in regulation, and it is the supposed public interest of government in economic regulation that refutes the claim that commercial speech is a purely private affair.

Then, also, speech acts are never disinterested as the concept of *public* would lead us to believe in the present context. Groups that have causes to advance in the name of the *public interest* have at stake various goals and objectives, exactly as corporations do in their advertisements: organizational growth, jobs, visibility, competitive advantage (relative to other groups with a cause), and the like. Although these may not be fully captured by labeling them commercial or economic, it is a far cry from claiming that they are disinterested.

Individuals, too, seldom make disinterested public pronouncements, especially on such controversial issues of public policy as taxes, zoning changes, and so on. If the First Amendment is not designed to protect speech, motivated by self-interest or vested interest, there is precious little that it does protect.[33] Finally, speech is, by its very nature, public, because it is addressed not to particular individuals, but to unknown members of the public. We should abandon the distinction between private and public speech. Does it now follow that advertisers can make any false or fraudulent claim they wish about their products? The answer here is no, because there is a significant moral difference between making a promise and expressing a belief. The informational components of advertisements can plausibly be construed as an initial statement of terms between seller and buyer. This is why it is legitimate to hold advertisers accountable to some degree for the truth of their advertisements. Expressions of belief, on the other hand, do not function like promises, because no one is called upon to deliver a good according to stated terms.[34] No one has the right to defraud another. But to say that hardly justifies intrusive governmental regulation of commercial speech.

If the Reynolds advertisement had included accurate product information, the advertisement should not have been held morally culpable. The court should have ruled in Reynolds favor (even if they had included product information as part of the advertisement). The court's attempt to dodge the issue by calling the Reynolds advertisement "noncommercial" may have been convenient, but it leaves commercial speech vulnerable to attack by foes of liberty. And in this respect, the U.S. Supreme Court has strayed even wider of the mark in its recent ruling in *Posadas*.[35]

It is true that the First Amendment does not unequivocally grant protection to commercial speech, but it certainly does not bar such protection either. We should recall here the Ninth Amendment which says that "the enumeration in the Constitution, of certain rights, shall not be construed to deny or disparage others retained by the people."[36] This constitutional provision can only be understood as extending protection to many matters not explicitly mentioned or foreseen by the Founders. So when the First Amendment is coupled with the Ninth, one must assume that commercial speech is still speech and hence constitutionally protected. When we also add to all this that the Fourteenth Amendment requires that "no State shall...deny to any person within its jurisdiction the equal protection of the law," it becomes clear that a ban on any kind of honest advertising would constitute a form of discrimination against people in business vis-à-vis other professions, activities, and forms of speech. In short, the principles embedded in the Constitution clearly favor the argument for full Constitutional protection of commercial speech.

It is now commonplace to hear the argument that cigarette advertising is inherently deceptive; yet of all the products we can think of where the charge of deception is most inappropriately applied, it is to cigarette advertising. No product carries a more visible, repeated, and blanket warning about its use than do cigarettes. Nor can I think of any product that has been subjected to so much counteradvertising. Nevertheless, the argument persists. It is a simple one. Cigarettes are "lethal" products, while the images conveyed by cigarette advertisements in no way convey this danger—indeed, the opposite message is conveyed.[37] The consumer is therefore deceived into believing that cigarette smoking is acceptable, attractive, or without risks and hazards. This argument is, however, nothing but a version of the shibboleth that advertising itself is inherently deceptive.

Advertisements are said to be inherently deceptive because they "selectively emphasize" certain features of a product to make the product appear more attractive. Since this technique ignores or deemphasizes other features, the consumer is deceived. The moral conclusion many draw is that since advertising is deceptive, and deception is morally wrong, advertising is morally wrong. But the case for "generic deception" depends upon there being something wrong with presenting something in a positive light, and upon the likelihood that people are unaware of the type of message being delivered. Neither condition can be satisfied for adults.

There is nothing wrong with presenting something in its most attractive light.[38] We do it all the time. In our personal grooming we take care to look attractive and hide our "flaws." As to the nature of the message, what is (generic) to advertising is precisely the effort to present something in its most attractive light. Since attractive presentation of information is virtually the meaning of advertisement, it is nonsensical to claim generic deception when one confronts an advertisement. Selective emphasis does not violate the canon of truthfulness per se, because the basic truth about advertising is that when you see it you should expect to see the item portrayed in its best light.[39] And surely there are (some) attractive people, like those presented in cigarette advertising, who use tobacco products, just as we sometimes engage in conversations about mouthwash or toothpaste, however inane it sounds when dramatized in a commercial.

Since cigarette advertisements cannot be charged with generic deception, the only remaining alternative is that they deceive in specific ways about health risks. But this claim also fails, given warning labels and counteradvertising. As such, no advertisements are less deceptive than cigarette advertisements. And if truthful advertising deserves constitutional protection, then no product is more deserving of that protection than cigarette advertising, since no product more truthfully displays the risks and benefits of its use.

No Exceptions

After examining basic moral and constitutional values, one is forced to conclude that the tobacco industry is on the side of principle in its opposition to the AMA. It is obvious that banning or restricting commercial speech about tobacco products would ignore basic rights and liberties and open the door to further coercive control of speech.

What is perhaps less obvious is the damage already done. That Congress and the media could take a proposal like the AMA's seriously, and indeed that well-educated medical professionals could be so completely ignorant of the meaning of liberty, signifies a national crisis in the understanding of our own heritage. Furthermore, the ad hoc attitudes of the present courts concerning commercial speech offers little hope that this crisis will be remedied from this quarter. Yet in the end, what is most disturbing is how insulting all this is. Despite continual subjection to claims about the "evils" of tobacco, we are being told we are too incompetent to make up our own minds about these products. The damage that has already been done is reflected in the fact that we take such insults on a daily basis. Let us reverse the trend and identify the insult as just that. It is a first, but necessary, step—recalling Herbert Spencer's insight—in preventing the world from filling with fools.

Notes

1. Burton Leiser, "Deception Practices in Advertising," in *Ethical Theory and Business*, ed. L. Beauchamp and Norman Bowie, (Englewood Cliffs, NJ: Prentice-

Hall, 1979), p. 479. Leiser's rendition of this view is perhaps the most extreme. Others have put the matter more guardedly, focusing more on the kind of suppression that conceals generally harmful aspects of a product rather than on the failure to inform the public of its comparative disadvantage vis à vis similar or even identical substitutes. Yet the general statements of the ethical point, in contrast to the examples cited, are very close to Leiser's own. See, for example, Vincent Barry, chapter 8 of *Moral Issues in Business* (Belmont, CA: Wadsworth, 1983). Barry chides advertisers for concealing "a fact...when its availability would probably make the desire, purchase, or use of the product less likely than in its absence" (p. 278).

2. Leiser, "Deception Practices...," p. 479.

3. *Ibid.,* p. 484.

4. *Ibid.,* p. 479.

5. *Ibid.,* p. 481.

6. Thomas Nagel, *The Possibility of Altruism* (Oxford: Clarendon Press, 1970).

7. This is the sense of the term as it occurs in the writings of August Comte (1798-1857), who reportedly coined it. Thus under "altruism" the *Oxford English Dictionary* (Compact Edition, 1971) says that the term was "introduced into English by the translators and expounders of Comte," and quotes one of them, George Henry Lewis, who remarks, in his *Comte's Philosophy of the Sciences* (1853): "Dispositions influenced by the purely egotistic impulses we call popularly 'bad,' and apply the term 'good' to those in which altruism predominates."

8. Loyd D. Easton and Kurt H. Guddat, eds., *Writings of the Young Marx on Philosophy and Society* (Garden City, NY: Anchor Books, 1967), p. 39. See, for a recent statement, W. G. Maclagan, "Self and Others: A Defense of Altruism," *Philosophical Quarterly* 4 (1954): 109-127. "'Altruism' [is] *assuming* a duty to relieve the distress and promote the happiness of our fellows.... Altruism is to...maintain quite simply that a man may and should discount altogether his own pleasure or happiness as such when he is deciding what course of action to pursue." (pp. 109-110). As presented in ordinarily, by ministers or priests or in fiction, altruism means ranking looking out for others in first place in one's list of moral duties.

9. Wilhelm Windelband, *A History of Philosophy*, vol. 2, (New York: Harper Torchbooks, 1968), pp. 650ff.

10. John Rawls, *A Theory of Justice* (Cambridge, MA: Harvard University Press, 1971), p. 62.

11. Because of the intimate association of ethics and altruism (self-sacrifice), some defenders of the value of commerce or business have settled for a total disassociation of business and morality. See, e.g., Albert Carr, "Is Business Bluffing Ethical?" in *Ethical Issues in Business*, ed. Thomas Donaldson and Patricia H. Werhane, (Englewood Cliffs, NJ: Prentice-Hall, 1979), pp. 46-52.

12. This point about the compatibility of Rawlsian egalitarianism and the market economy has been argued in James Buchanan, "A Hobbesian Interpretation of the Rawlsian Difference Principle," *Kyklos* 29 (1976): 5-25. Buchanan points up the fact that Rawls's beginning point, prior to the generation of the hypothetical social contract behind the veil of ignorance, is not significantly different from Hobbes's, involving, as it does, self-aggrandizing individuals.

13. Tibor R. Machan, "Recent Work in Ethical Egoism," *American Philosophical Quarterly* 16 (1979): 1-15. See also Chapter 6.

14. Aristotle *Nicomachean Ethics* 1169a12. "Therefore the good man should be a lover of self (for he will both himself profit by doing noble acts, and will benefit

his fellows), but the wicked man should not. Artistotle's egoism is stressed in W.F.R. Hardie, "The Final Good in Aristotle's *Ethics,* "*Philosophy* 40 (1965): 277.295.

15. For more on this see my books: *Individuals and Their Rights* (LaSalle, IL: Open Court, 1989) and *Capitalism and Individualism* (New York: St. Martin's Press, 1990).

16. For more elaborate development of these points, see chapter 3 of my book *Human Rights and Human Liberties* (Chicago: Nelson-Hall, 1975) and *Individuals and Their Rights.* For a detailed examination of the topic, see Douglas J. Den Uyl, *The Virtue of Prudence* (New York: Lang, 1991).

17. See., for example, Eric Mack, "How to Derive Ethical Egoism," *The Personalist* 52 (1971): 735–743, as well as my *Individuals and Their Rights.*

18. The entire tradition of classical economics embodies this point, made most forcefully by Bernard Mandeville's *The Fable of the Bees* and Adam Smith's *An Inquiry into the Nature and Causes of the Wealth of Nations* (1776). Mandeville's famous motto, "Private vices, publik benefits," captures it poignantly. See Den Uyl, *Virtue of Prudence* for a detailed scrutiny of this tradition, as well as my *Capitalism and Individualism.*

19. James Rachels, "Two Arguments against Ethical Egoism," *Philosophia* 4 (1974): 297–314.

20. J. Roger Lee, "Choice and Harms, " in *Rights and Regulations: Ethical, Political, and Economic Issues,* ed. Tibor R. Machan and M. Bruce Johnson, (Cambridge, MA: Ballinger, 1983), pp. 168–169.

21. For more on product liability, see Richard A. Epstein, *A Theory of Strict Liability* (Washington, DC: Cato Institute, 1980). See also Tibor R. Machan, "The Petty Tyranny of Government Regulations," in *Rights and Regulations,* pp. 259–288.

22. U.S. Supreme Court in *West Virginia State Board of Education v. Barnette,* 319 U.S. 624 (1943).

23. In the area of pornographic or obscene expression, which for a long time had been eagerly protected by modern liberals in the name of the First Amendment, some (but by no means all) feminists have argued that no protection should be forthcoming because such materials—books, magazines, videotapes, movies, plays—violate the civil rights of women by demeaning them. See Catherine A. MacKinnon, *A Feminist Theory of the State* (Cambridge, MA: Harvard University Press, 1991). But see Tibor R. Machan, "The Right to Privacy vs. Uniformitarianism," *Journal of Social Philosophy* 24 (1993): 76–84. The assumption underlying this development, precipitated by feminist theory, had been rejected when advanced by religious opponents to pornography. It was that such materials had a bad influence on persons. The grounds for the rejection were, mainly, that no one is forced to believe anything by some people's expressing themselves in these ways—"Sticks and stones may break my bones," etc. The other type of defense offered is that no one can make a precise enough distinction between pornography or obscenity and bona fide art. (It is interesting that these developments in feminist thinking come at the same time that many in the intellectual community have embraced deconstructionism and pragmatism concerning the way in which meaning is to be determined, suggesting that no universal meaning is available for any word, including what some deem to be pornographic or obscene.)

24. With respect to advertising, the theory that advertising increases aggregate demand in mature industries has been refuted so often that belief in the theory is on

a par with belief in astrology and palm reading. Even the FTC appears to agree. A letter to Congressman Thomas J. Bliley, Jr., from FTC Chairman Daniel Oliver, August 1, 1986, once again affirms the point.

25. George Anastaplo, *The Constitutionalist: Notes on the First Amendment* (Dallas: Southern Methodist University Press, 1971), pp. 15-165. For a very similar argument, see Robert Bork, "Neutral Principles and Some First Amendment Problems," *Indiana Law Journal* 47 (1971): 20ff.

26. Robert F. Landerson, "Scientific and Technical Information, National Security, and the First Amendment: A Jurisprudential Inquiry," *Public Affairs Quarterly* 1 (1987): 10.

27. See J. Roger Lee, "Choice and Harms," in *Rights and Regulation*, pp. 157-172.

28. See Jeffrie Murphy and Jules Coleman, eds., *The Philosophy of Law* (Totowa, NJ: Rowman and Allenheld, 1984), p. 87.

29. As in *Virginia State Board of Pharmacy v. Virginia Citizens Consumer Council, Inc.*, 425 U.S. 748 (1976).

30. *FTC News* (June 16, 1986).

31. See, for example, E. Baker, "Commercial Speech: A Problem in the Theory of Freedom," *Iowa Law Review* 62 (1976): 1, 3.

32. See Gerald J. Baldasty and Roger A. Simpson, "The Deceptive 'Right to Know': How Pessimism Rewrote the First Amendment," in *The First Amendment Reconsidered*, ed. Bill F. Chamberlin and Charlene J. Brown, (New York: Longman, 1982), pp. 66-88, esp. pp. 77-82. For a refutation, see M. H. Redish, "The First Amendment in the Marketplace: Commercial Speech and the Value of Free Expression," *George Washington Law Review* 429 (1971): 39ff; M. H. Redish, "The Content Distinction in First Amendment Analysis," *Stanford Law Review* 34 (1981): 113-151.

33. The claim that there is little or no disinterested speech in no way implies that there are little or no true propositions spoken. Most of science, for example, is motivated by very clear concerns and interests, yet truth is an essential goal of scientific work.

34. Even here it is important to realize that advertisements are not actual promises, but only analogous to promises. Morally, the restrictions on advertisements would have to be less than we would apply to actual promises.

35. *Posadas de Puerto Rico Assoc. v. Tourism Co. of Puerto Rico*, 54 U.S.L.W. 4956, 4961-62 (U.S. 1986).

36. For a discussion of this amendment see Thomas E. Towe, "Natural Law and the Ninth Amendment," *Pepperdine Law Review* 2 (1985): 270. For a defense of one possible right of the people, see Tibor R. Machan, "Is There a Right To Be Wrong?" *International Journal of Applied Philosophy* 2 (1985): 105-109.

37. See, for example, the testimonies of William J. McCarthy, a research psychologist at UCLA, and Henry Paul Monaghan, Professor of Law, Columbia University, given before the House Subcommittee on Health and the Environment, U.S. House of Representatives, July 18, 1986 and August 1, 1986 respectively.

38. This is not to say that this is the only thing generic to advertising, communication of information is also inherent.

39. See the testimony of Barry W. Lynn, legislative counsel, American Civil Liberties Union, before the House Subcommittee on Health and the Environment, August 1, 1986.

10

Some Philosophical Aspects of National Labor Policy

This chapter is about the way ideas manifest themselves in, and often have influence on, legal and political developments and history. In our age the labor market is under extensive government regulation. It is thought by most people that that is as it should be. And such regulations are on the increase—mandated health insurance, maternity and paternity leaves, child-care centers, plant closing notification, protection from foreign competition, and so on, all constitute an intrusion into the free contractual agreements between market agents. How did all this come about in a country that still finds many of its leaders giving at least lip service to liberalism—that is, to the political outlook once clearly associated with the concepts of individual liberty, free trade, and limited government?

The Case of Labor

There is much confusion, still, about the reasons behind the particular history of labor law in the United States. Most of the explanations offered exclude an important factor, namely, moral convictions, as having significant influence. Indeed, some economists favoring the market system—the Nobel laureate George Stigler, for instance—hold that ideas cannot influence economic and political developments. Instead such variables as demographics, economics, ethnicity, race, and positive law are offered as sufficient grounds for understanding developments in economic affairs, including national labor policy.

To focus on such factors alone is to ignore a very significant feature of human life: human beings are moral agents who make choices about the alternatives they face, with some standard guiding these choices, implicitly or explicitly. The most basic standard is provided by morality. And there are different moral positions that have been influential in different periods of human history, as well as in different places on the globe. Moral convictions may often be rejected in favor of other considerations, even if they should not be. But often they do guide people's behavior. And even when they do not, various ideas play a role in rationalizing their absence.

It will be useful to take an initial look at what moral considerations have had a bearing on the development of national labor policy, including judicial and legislative development.[1] I will not provide a complete treatment of this topic but will offer for consideration a general hypothesis concerning some of the major philosophical and ethical influences on labor policy in the United States. An important aspect of the history of moral influences is that individuals play a very crucial part in this history. It is individuals who make moral choices; even those choices that concern broad trends, such as national ones. It is individuals who have the power of thought and volition—committees, juries, legislatures, and regulatory bodies do not, as such, possess that power, and when speaking of them as having views and making decisions, we are speaking loosely. This chapter thus accepts the notion that to understand developments in some field such as labor policy, it is necessary to consider the moral beliefs that guide people's decisions and conduct. And it also accepts the view that even when people are motivated by factors other than their moral beliefs, they will often make an attempt to explain what they want and what they do in terms of those moral beliefs they regard as sound and respectable.[2]

It should be noted at the outset that the findings of this inquiry will not be very surprising. They confirm, in the end, what has been noted by many commentators in general terms, namely, that constitutionalism, based on the political theory of natural rights and individualism, has been eroding and has been giving way to unlimited democracy throughout the last one hundred years or more, a democracy that is undermining itself by delegating increasing powers to a centralized state bureaucracy. This is indeed what has occurred in national labor policy.

Early Developments in Labor Law

Although this work is mainly concerned with the philosophical underpinnings of recent and current national labor policy, it will help to consider briefly early developments in labor law in the United States. The reasoning in pivotal court cases, as well as the courts' application and interpretation of such legal concepts as "the police power of the state" and "due process," provides the context in which a national labor policy eventually developed.

Early Cases: The Legality of Concerted Action

During the early part of the nineteenth century, most labor disputes were adjudicated within the court systems of the several states, with only a few of these cases reaching the Supreme Court; the state cases yield what may loosely be construed as national labor policy.

The earliest of such cases is *Commonwealth v. Pullis* (1806),[3] commonly referred to as "the Case of the Philadelphia Cordwainers."[4] It involved conspiracy charges against a group of shoemakers. As Falcone relates the case: "These workers had been charged with the following activities: (1) Agreeing among themselves that they would work only in those shops where the employees were all members of the group or combine. (2) Agreeing among themselves that they would not work for any wage below the wage scale established by the group,"[5] In charging the jury, Recorder Levy relied on "the volumes of the common law" and authorities on the criminal law, Hawkins, Blackstone, and Lord Mansfield, who held that "an act innocent in an individual, is rendered criminal by a confederacy to effect it."[6] Thus, it was argued that, although individuals may ask for higher wages than those they are receiving, withhold their work (quit) if not satisfied, request that others obtain minimum levels of pay, withdraw work if not satisfied in this, etc., they engage in criminal conspiracy if they combine into groups and act in concert for such purposes. Likewise, it was held that, by agreeing among themselves not to work or board or lodge with a newcomer to the trade who would not join their group, the workers "compel [the newcomer] to become a member."[7] The point was not to single out as forcible certain methods of leading newcomers to become members of the group; rather, it was to characterize concerted efforts as instances of compulsion.

Essentially the same judgment was reached in 1809 in *People v. Melvin*.[8] As Falcone observes:

> In the case the court was quite sympathetic with the desire of the workers to improve their wages and felt that they might properly have sought this end individually, but when they combined for the purpose of attaining this lawful end the means were disapproved. Anther point of interest in this case is the attempt on the part of the workers to organize closed shops so as to establish a uniform wage scale. The court held that the closed shop was an unlawful means.[9]

The point of the Cordwainers and Melvin decisions is that actions that are permissible for an individual—say, promising to leave work should some (itself permissible) action not be performed—can be wrong when taken by individuals in concert. What lay behind this distinction? As Levy argued in the *Cordwainers* case, "it is proper to consider, is such a combination consistent with the principles of our law, and injurious to the public welfare."[10] Citing the common-law tradition and the belief that such concerted conduct "exposes [the commerce of the city] to inconveniences, if not to ruin," he found it inconsistent with the law and "against the public welfare."[11] And the conspiracy doctrine in the common law, as Falcone notes, was itself based on "a general acceptance that a combination of persons possess a power to commit serious wrongs which individuals as such do not have."[12] In the case of trade unions, Falcone goes on to note the wrongs threatened were "the impoverishment of the nonunion workers" and the fact "that prices would naturally rise and the general public would suffer."[13]

The reason concerted actions are to be proscribed is that, through such actions, others are probably going to find it impossible to achieve their economic goals (employment, trade, and consumption at wages, terms, and prices that would obtain in the absence of this concerted effort). We may infer from this the general position that the pursuit of economic advantage is impermissible if such pursuit, even without force or fraud, would hinder the satisfaction of the desire of great numbers of people. One has the right to act in one's economic interest only to the extent that one is not using means that are likely to hamper the desires, goals, or expectations of others to any substantial degree. The law seems to affirm, by implication, both individual liberty and majority will with respect to individuals' noncoercive action. It is left to the judge or the jury to decide how much exercise of this liberty is too much or how much satisfaction of majority will is too restrictive of liberty. Conflicting judgments are clearly possible where such weighting of conflicting principles is a necessary part of the system.

Such a view is neither coherent nor consistent. But it is not unusual for individuals and their communities to be guided by conflicting standards, striving toward mutually exclusive goals. The attempt to balance such standards or goals, to establish a mixed system, is often thought to be the art of political administration. It is important to note, however, that in its earliest days the U.S. legal system had such built-in conflicts. Subsequent developments may be better understood with this in mind.

In 1842 a somewhat different direction was taken. In *Commonwealth v. Hunt*,[14] Justice Shaw of the Massachusetts Supreme Judicial Court argued:

> Suppose a class of workmen, impressed with the manifold evils of intemperance, should agree with each other not to work in a shop in which ardent spirit was furnished, or not to work in a shop with any one who used it, or not to work for an employer, who should, after notice, employ a journeyman who habitually used it. The consequences might be the same [as if workers agreed not to work for a person who employed a journeyman who was not a member of their society]. A workman, who should still persist in the use of ardent spirit, would find it more difficult to get employment; a master employing such a one, might, at times, experience inconvenience in his work, in losing the services of a skillful but intemperate workman. Still it seems to us, that as the object would be lawful, and the means not unlawful, such agreement could not be pronounced a criminal conspiracy.[15]

It is widely acknowledged that this judgment marked a turning point in the development of labor-related law throughout the several states (with the exception of New Jersey). What does this judgment indicate? What general framework is implicit in the wording?

First of all, Justice Shaw rejected the view that, by refusing to work for an employer (Wait) who hired a nonmember (Horne) of their society, the workers had in any of the crucial respects compelled another's actions. As Shaw pointed out:

> If this is to be considered as a substantive charge, it would depend altogether upon the force of the word "compel," which may be used in a sense of coercion, or duress, by force or fraud....If, for instance, the indictment had averred a conspiracy, by the defendants, to compel Wait to turn Horne out of his employment, and to accomplish that object by the use of force or fraud, it would have been a

very different case; especially if it might be fairly construed, as perhaps, in that case it might have been, that Wait was under obligation, by contract, for an unexpired term of time, to employ and pay Horne....But whatever might be the force of the word "compel," unexplained by its connexion it is disarmed and rendered harmless by the precise statement of the means, by which such compulsion was to be effected. It was the agreement not to work for him, by which they compelled Wait to decline employing Horne longer.[16]

Second, Shaw rejected the view that inconveniencing nonmembers through concerted action, by itself, constituted unlawful conspiracy. As we saw earlier, he argued as follows:

Associations may be entered into, the object of which is to adopt measures that may have a tendency to impoverish another, that is, to diminish his gains and profits, and yet so far from being criminal or unlawful, the object may be highly meritorious and public spirited. The legality of such an association will therefore depend upon the means to be used for its accomplishment. If it is to be carried into effect by fair or honorable and lawful means, it is, to say the least, innocent; if by falsehood or force, it may be stamped with the character of conspiracy.[17]

In Shaw's analysis, the crucial line of demarcation between what is and what is not lawful consists in whether actions are undertaken by means of force or fraud. In the Levy decision in the *Cordwainers* case, the same line of demarcation applied to a determination of the lawfulness of individual conduct, so that regardless of whether it tended to impoverish or inconvenience others, if force or fraud were not involved, this conduct was considered lawful. But when it came to action in concert, Levy rejected this criterion, instead of distinguishing between lawful and unlawful conduct in terms of the potentially sizable impact upon for example, the tendency to impoverish or inconvenience others. For Shaw, the numerical difference was irrelevant.

It is interesting to note that Falcone attempts to discover "the reasons that influenced Judge Shaw in refusing to apply the doctrine of criminal conspiracy in this case," and proceeds to "speculate on them by examining the language appearing in his opinion and reasonably arrive at certain conclusions."[18] Falcone focuses on Shaw's mentioning that worker associations might help the poor "to afford each other assistance in time of poverty, sickness and distress; or to raise their intellectual, moral and social condition; or to make improvement in their art; or for other proper purposes."[19] Noting that Justice Shaw was probably aware of these socially desirable services initiated by the early unions, Falcone concludes: "There appear good grounds for attributing a social awareness to this courageous judge who agreed that workers might combine for the purpose of combating oppression and injustice."[20] He adds that "Shaw not only was cognizant of the distressing worker problems but was also realistic enough to concede workers the right to economic justice.... Shaw noted clearly that the trade union institution was the only means through which this justice could be obtained."[21]

On the other hand, whenever Falcone attempts to account for judgments adverse to what he regards as the just cause of workers, he invokes the idea of vested collective interests. Thus: "As in England, our early judges came principally from the propertied class, and their decisions generally favored members of their own group";[22] and: "Today it is generally accepted that the judges whose opinions then prevailed were out of sympathy with unions and their objectives and devised vague tests to narrow labor activities until impotency might result."[23] This approach to accounting for judgments—because it attempts to discern motivations, not reasons—is not consistent with the methodology being used in the present study. Nor, incidentally, is it consistent with Falcone's treatment of Shaw's reasoning.

Furthermore, Falcone's account of Justice Shaw's opinion is not borne out by a close reading of "the language appearing in his opinion,"[24] which cannot itself be distorted by Falcone's values. In this opinion Shaw clearly disavowed basing law on considerations of "socially desirable services."[25] As noted before, Shaw rested his judgment on considerations of what individuals, alone or in voluntary concert, have a right to do, regardless of whether their actions "may have a tendency to impoverish another, that is, to diminish his gains and profits."[26] Nor can we find any evidence that Shaw acknowledged what Falcone terms the workers' "right to economic justice,"[27] especially when we pay careful attention to Shaw's illustration of the principle on which he based his decision. The hypothetical case involving workers who object to intemperance has nothing to do with workers' economic matters; rather, it is a clear illustration of the principle that whatever does not involve force or fraud is to be legally permitted—that is, individuals have a right to liberty of action where no force or fraud is involved. (It does not appear that Shaws' introduction of the hypothetical case bears on "social desirability" either; only the workers' objecting to intemperance is mentioned.[28] The point of the case is that concerted action is permissible if the means and ends exclude violation of others' basic rights.)

I reflect on these matters so as to pave the way for discussion of more recent developments in national labor policy and to indicate, by example, my approach to uncovering its general philosophical (ethical, political, and social) underpinnings.

Labor Legislation: The General Welfare and Individual Rights

Subsequent to these initial, path breaking court cases, labor legislation increased throughout the United States, thus increasing the number of employment situations under state, and later federal, supervision and regulation.[29] Determination of health and safety requirements, for example, was gradually removed from the jurisdiction of the parties directly involved (employers and employees). The gradual establishment of the legal right to form workers' associations did not foreclose increased political legislative efforts to govern the relationship of employer and employee or to satisfy the desires of workers concerning their workplace, length of time spent at work, insurance against unemployment or disablement, and so on.[30] All this did not occur in isolation. In the general political climate, the more or less consistent atmosphere of laissez faire began to be repudiated. Businesses began to seek and gain the open assistance of state governments. The federal government, too, involved itself in helping various entrepreneurs whose business endeavors were deemed to be in the public interest, and often directly related to national security. Through these developments many corporations, often employing workers on whose behalf labor leaders sought political and legal measures, gained economic advantages that could not have been achieved without special governmental assistance.[31] Labor leaders, too, proceeded with efforts to obtain governmental assistance.

These political developments were largely thought to be required to secure the general welfare. This point is independent of the fact that particular measures were often initiated and advocated by spokesmen for groups who stood to reap substantial benefits from the measures. The developments were supported, in legislative debates, in court decisions, and by the spokesmen themselves, as being in the public interest—that is, as means by which to advance the general well-being of society.

From the middle of the nineteenth century onward, the general welfare was invoked as normative support for an increasing number of state and federal court decisions. At first the judgments worked to stultify what labor leaders regarded as progress for workers. For example, injunctions came to be sued widely after their first invocation in the 1877 Railway Strike, on grounds that laborers' disruption of the economy would inconvenience not only the employer, but other workers, other businesses, and the general public. Certain otherwise peaceful, albeit concerted and consequential actions of workers (for instance, boycotts),[32] could be stopped by means of a court order alone, prior to any determinations of actual legal culpability. The idea of the civil conspiracy, which does not imply criminal intent but concerns only the damaging results of action, came to be very influential. It is not possible here to uncover the full, consistent philosophical rationale of the injunction measure, nor should it be assumed that all such legal measures have arisen by way of conscious deliberation and detailed prior theoretical analysis. What is possible to ascertain, however, is that use of the injunction in labor cases was based on the view that those whose actions would produce widespread inconvenience, economic disruption, or general dismay throughout some community must demonstrate that they possess the right to carry out such action.

Here again, as in the Levy judgment, what is of primary significance is the welfare of the community, not the rights of the individual to take peaceable action (alone or in concert with others). This is not to argue that the actions stopped by the injunctions were wise, prudent, decent, benevolent, considerate, or otherwise morally praiseworthy—nor that they were not any or all of these. The point is that, in the bulk of those cases involving injunctions, the rights of individuals were considered less significant than the possible loss of advantage to those who might be inconvenienced from the perhaps unwise exercise of those rights. (A right may be exercised, if it is a right, whether this exercise is wise or unwise, desirable or undesirable, good or evil. The right to free speech may be exercised whether in defense of democracy or communism, whether in support of virtue or vice.)[33]

Nor is it clear that under no circumstances is the issuing of injunctions consistent with a full recognition of individual rights. For example, judges would sometimes need to issue restraining orders to delay actions that ultimately may be found, upon close legal scrutiny, to be rights violating. From the evidence, however, some injunctions were issued on grounds that the workers' actions did or would damage or inconvenience certain parties. And reference to such "damage" did not always conform to principles of individual rights—that is, such rights had not been violated and yet damage was declared.[34]

The issue here is not whether such development is good or bad. Many commentators on the history of the labor movement in the United States have reflected positively upon the political and legal institutions of European nations, where various measures thought to favor working people had been adopted many years prior to their mention as possible governmental measures in the United States.[35] These countries are well known to have eschewed the distinctive feature of the U.S. political system, namely, its emphasis on individual rights; yet many citizens of the United States favored their approach to working people and their employee-employer relationships over the more or less laissez-faire approach implicit in the U.S. political tradition.[36] The point here is not to take sides but to identify trends, although not every development will reflect the trend, and some will do so more than others.

These early legal developments do not reveal a clear direction or trend but only certain mixed inclinations, and some reigning ideas, and those of a negative sort. What is usually identified as the distinctively U.S. legal framework did not have uniform influence in the courts, the legislatures, and the ranks of business and labor. Instead, a concern for the overall advantage of those generally linked with various sides of controversies gave direction to the arguments, pro and con. For example, when those speaking for "labor" saw advantage to be gained for laborers by insisting on the large recognition of every individual's right to liberty, this line of argument was stressed. Opposition to the use of the injunction best exemplifies the approach. On the other hand, when the advantage of laborers appeared to consist in obtaining state support for purposes of limiting others (employers) from exercising their individual rights, advocates defending "labor" pursued just that course. For example, in *Lochner v. New York*,[37] labor leaders and spokesmen argued against the principle of freedom of contract and in support of the state forcing employers and employees to refrain from various labor practices not desired by "labor."

We must not think, however, that those who claimed to advance the interest of workers were alone in following this inconsistent course. The courts in both U.S. and English law voiced contradictory positions, sometimes with reference to the same general group of citizens such as workers or professionals, sometimes with reference to divergent groups.[38] Thus, in *Mogul Steamship Co. v. McGregor, Gow and Co.*,[39] the English courts upheld the right of businesses to combine in ways that would be severely detrimental to one who would not join them, but denied this right to combine when it was claimed in defense of the conduct of labor groups in *Allen v. Flood*.[40] In the United States these matters did not reach the federal judiciary at this time, but the influential courts of Massachusetts and New York may fairly be regarded as reflecting judicial trends.[41] Although in *Bowen v. Matheson*[42] the Massachusetts court in 1867 also granted the right of combination to members of Boston shipping masters at the expense of a John Bowen in 1870, in *Carew v. Rutherford*[43] the court did not uphold the right of a union to make a closed-shop agreement. However, historians frequently single out Justice Holmes's dissent in *Carew v. Rutherford*, in which he argued that this case should have been analyzed by analogy to *Bowen v. Matheson*. Yet in his reasoning Holmes relied, not on an affirmation of the right of individuals (in concert) to act regardless of what the larger society might expect of them or even have come to depend on them for, but on the claim that "free competition is worth more to society than it costs, and that on this ground the infliction of the damage is privileged [provided] the damage is done not for its own sake, but as an instrumentality in reaching the end of victory in the battle of trade."[44]

Conflicting judicial trends, centered around the same issues, are also found in the development of the concept of due process within U.S. law. While social developments (including the adoption of certain ethical, political, and general philosophical perspectives) often produced legislative efforts to achieve goals sought by workers and other groups,[45] courts variously granted or denied the validity of these efforts based on different conceptions of the nature of due process. Generally put, there is a long-standing dispute within legal circles as to whether the idea of due process of law, derived from the idea of the law of the land, is a substantive or a procedural doctrine.[46] Does it refer to certain absolute limits on the scope of legislation or to the requirement that certain procedures gradually established within the legal system be followed in the process of enacting legislation? This dispute is not yet resolved.[47] That is not surprising, because it has it sources outside of legal theory proper, in ethics and in metaphysics.[48]

The issue is significant because, in numerous cases involving challenges to labor legislation, courts have appealed to substantive due process.[49] An influential and still widely discussed example is *Lochner v. New York*, in which legislation was overturned by the U.S. Supreme Court on grounds that collective aims not shown to be necessary do not suffice to override such individual rights as freedom to enter into contract. As William Letwin has noted, "before the Lochner decision, the Supreme Court had upheld state legislation in the leading cases and had voided it in a number of others, and so had the state courts and lower courts—the batting record on both sides is recited fully in the Lochner pleads and opinions." [50]

Lochner is perhaps the most famous of the cases involving the issue of substantive versus procedural due process. While Justice Peckham's majority opinion is often discussed, very frequently it is Justice Holmes's dissenting opinion that receives special attention. It was Holmes who argued that the New York legislature could regulate bakers' hours of labor even though this regulation was clearly not part of the "police power" of the state (since the regulation was evidently concerned, not with the uniquely unhealthy condition of bakeries or baking, but with the hours of labor per se). His argument is well remembered for the famous quip we have already recounted, concerning how "the 14th Amendment does not enact Mr. Herbert Spencer's Social Statics."[51] Although this is one of Holmes's many famous contributions to legal history, it did not directly address the reasoning of the majority opinion, as Letwin shows.

[The quip] is gratuitous. Herbert Spencer was not cited as authority by anyone in the case, and Social Statics had no direct bearing on it. Spencer was of course recognized as exponent of the doctrine that the state ought not to protect the weak because to do so would interfere with the evolutionary process of natural selection, whereas the majority of the court insisted that to protect the weak was well within the police power. It might equally well have been said that the Fourteenth Amendment did not enact Plato's *Republic* or the platform of the Populist Party, or, as Holmes went on to say, any "particular economic theory." It missed the point to suppose, as Holmes did, that "this case is decided upon an economic theory which a large part of the country does not entertain." It was decided, no doubt, by justices who held economic views, but they decided the case on a well-established constitutional principle that a health law would be constitutional where there was a danger to health and unconstitutional where the danger to health was insubstantial. What could well be argued was the point presented by Harlan, about presumptions and burdens of proof—again a point of constitutional law and not economics. Holmes's witticism amounted nearly to ad hominem attack.[52]

In fact, when we go beyond the witticism, Holmes's argument came to something more than ad hominem, and Letwin is aware of this. Holmes did take a position on Justice Harlan's point about "presumptions and burdens of proof." Siding with Harlan, Holmes argued that the criterion by which to evaluate the validity of the legislature's action should be, not whether it did in fact secure health as intended, but whether "a rational and fair man necessarily would admit that the statute proposed would infringe fundamental principles as they have been understood by the traditions of our people and our law."[53] So state action limiting freedom of contract between employer and employee is only objectionable if Holmes's criterion is satisfied, that is, if a rational man would necessarily regard such interference as in violation of fundamental principles. And "necessarily" clearly places the burden of proof on those who would protest the state actions, not on the state. While the majority of the Supreme Court held the statute unconstitutional, on grounds that it did not fairly state its "means and ostensible purpose,"[54] Holmes appears to have argued that the legislature's act need not be justified. The legislature, according to Holmes, can do what it willed, as it were, and the burden of proof of a violation of principles of justice was on the side of those whose lives and property were directly or indirectly regulated by such acts. The legislature, not the individual citizen, was sovereign.[55]

Holmes was not alone in this view, and even the judges most suspicious of legislative power often affirmed a similar position vis-à-vis certain areas of state (police) power.[56] But it is important to notice that, for due process of law to have been observed in lawmaking, Holmes required only for the legislature to have acted (that is enacted some statute or policy) independently of whether this action accorded with (extralegal) principles of justice. Holmes's idea of what could constitute a limitation on legislative action is not very precise. When he referred to fundamental principles "as they have been understood by the tradition of our people and our law," he was skirting the fallacy of circular definition.[57] For him these principles appear to consist in previously enacted statutes and earlier court decisions and thus to be determined by the very process he believes should be limited by them.[58]

In criminal law, the individual's right to life, liberty, and property may not be infringed upon unless it has been demonstrated that he has acted in violation of fundamental principles of justice (and, in consequence, of law). However, as we saw in Chapter 1, by Holmes's reasoning, legislatures may place burdens on those not proven guilty of any wrong-doing unless "a rational and fair man necessarily would admit that the statute proposed would infringe..."[59] Majoritarian democracy appears to accept that a majority of its representatives may place burdens on the minority without demonstrating that those burdens are deserved or otherwise justified. This differs from limited (constitutional) democracy, wherein deprivation of life, liberty, and property—at least in the conduct of crime prevention—are commonly regarded as actions that may not be undertaken without due process. In Justice Holmes's dissenting opinion, which was to prove extremely influential after Lochner, substantive due process could not be invoked to strike down legislation in matters of economic interest such as contract, employment, or labor. As Holmes put it elsewhere, "the Truth seems to me to be that, subject to compensation when compensation is due, the legislature may forbid or restrict any business when it has a sufficient force of pubic opinion behind it."[60]

Although in Lochner, then, we find certain considerations involving substantive due process successfully raised in opposition to state regulation of some aspects of people's economic activities, such regulation had gained ample, firm footing in U.S. legislative and judicial history by Lochner's time and would continue on the same path thereafter.

Early Trends: Dual Influences

What is evident from the above is that no single perspective governed the early development of labor law, even in the most influential centers of judgment on relevant matters. Despite this, a certain pattern can be identified. Two basic frameworks seem to have exerted influence.

One was the uniquely U.S. framework of individualism, in terms of which a person's actions are judged legally permissible, not by reference to whether they tend to yield benefits or losses to others (society) or the individual, but by reference to whether they involve force or fraud. The underlying perspective here is that each person is an independent agent and, what he or she does cannot be proscribed by law unless it involves force or fraud against others. In this view, the purpose of law is to protect and preserve the rights of individuals to engage in noncoercive actions—that is, in conduct that intrudes in no unavoidable fashion on the lives and property of other persons—and governments, which administer and execute laws, are bound by this limitation. This is clearly the unique normative political philosophy, namely, individualism, that distinguished the United States from other nations of the time, and it is no surprise that this point of view showed its influence upon developments in labor law.

It is not unfair to characterize the second framework as collectivist, rather than individualist, in nature. Here, the primary concern is with overall social progress, the good of society, what is now often called "public interest." From this perspective, a person's actions are judged legally permissible by reference to whether they tend to yield benefits or losses for others, and the purpose of law is to protect the pursuit of societal, not individual goals—at least when those sets of goals seem to conflict.

Evidence of the influence of these two frameworks is clearly found in U.S. political developments in general in the courts' rulings on labor activities and labor legislation. Particularly in the judicial system, there has been a concern both with whether individual rights are protected and with whether the law aids the public good, and not with one to the exclusion of the other.

One might ask why only these perspectives made themselves felt in most legal situations, whether legislative or judicial. Here, we can note that the law generally abided by certain explicit restrictions against emphasizing some goals or values that were influential in other societies. For example, considerations of what is supportive of religious values, of status, or of title nobility, for example, were mainly absent from U.S. law. But two factors did permeate U.S. society from the start, in both matters of conviction and of practice. On the one hand, most citizens were self-conscious supporters of limited government, of the idea that governmental power should only be used against those engaging in (or threatening) force or fraud. On the other hand, most citizens were believers in each person's duty to further the well-being of others. In the law, these points of view might have been reconciled in two ways.

First, one might have stressed that protecting individual rights would preserve the moral responsibility of each person for his own virtuous conduct, whatever that might be. Second, one could have stressed that protecting and preserving individuals' rights would (very likely) lead to the greater general welfare, or public good.

The first alternative would leave virtuous conduct unspecified. Although the protection of individual rights would allow people to pursue their own well-being instead of different objectives, including the welfare of others, it was widely believed, following Adam Smith, that such "selfish" action would in fact maximize the general well-being of the community.[61] Thus the second alternative came more naturally; it did not unduly stress the outcome for individuals and incorporated the widespread view of what is to count in normative matters: others' welfare. And it would not be unfair to speculate here that it is difficult to advocate publicly the opposite viewpoint: ethical individualism, that is, the view that everyone should pursue personal happiness in life as a matter of moral principle.[62] This doctrine has not fared well among those most vocally concerned with ethical issues, namely, the clergy. Nor have many philosophers, excepting the ancient Greeks and a few moderns, found the idea compelling.[63]

In the nineteenth century, the idea of self-interest was understood mainly as referring to certain inclinations for self-gratification built into human nature, not to the self-development of one's unique (yet human) personality.[64] Most of those who discussed the matter agreed that people will, as a matter of innate drives or instincts, strive to benefit themselves. So the view that pursuing one's true self-interest might be morally significant—that is, constitute a responsibility everyone has in life as a human being—simply did not receive any serious consideration. Instead, ethical discourse on all levels tended to stress service to humanity, the nation, God, society, and the various other allegedly more important beings that issued claims upon individual persons' conduct. Most political systems incorporated this emphasis. Thus, although the Founding Fathers had been—sometimes only indirectly—influenced by the British philosopher John Locke and his individualist, natural rights political theory,[65] by the nineteenth century the utilitarian political ideas of Jeremy Bentham and John Stuart Mill were more widely respected. In a way Mill, with his insistence on political individualism for the sake of social progress, provided a political viewpoint more in accord with popular morality than did John Locke's natural rights views, which implied (or at least seemed to presuppose) an ethics of personal aspirations (if any ethics at all).

These are plausible suggestions, based on a general familiarity with the period. It seems, also, that the conjunction of an essentially individualist political and legal framework with an essentially altruist ethical climate will have fairly definite social and legal consequences. Therefore, when legislatures or judges were concerned with matters of social life, especially questions about social progress and economic prosperity, the natural rights or individualist framework was superseded.

Altruism in the context of politics (whether judicial reasoning or legislation) can very easily lead to collectivism, since it stresses that each is primarily responsible for advancing the welfare of others, which in political and legal terms means that the rights of individuals are less significant than the good of the community (others)—something everyone has an enforceable obligation to promote.

These suggestions are borne out by history. Contrary to widespread beliefs, there was never a steady laissez-faire policy in the United States, at either the state or the national level, especially toward economic activities. U.S. legislative and judicial history shows that so-called personal and political rights (ergo, substantive due process involving them) seems always to have been regarded as morally, politically, and legally more significant—or, at least, in need of more explicit protection—than property rights, despite occasional denials of this separation and insistence that human freedom is indivisible in the final analysis.[66]

The focus on material wealth in conjunction with the dominant ethics appears to have convinced the socially conscious in the country to use the state for purposes of reaching collective economic goals, even where so doing could lead to abandoning political individualism. The point here is only that these trends were in evidence early in U.S. legal history, specifically with respect to developments in labor law.

Federal Labor Legislation

By the beginning of the twentieth century, federal involvement in labor matters was well established, and a national labor policy began to emerge as labor legislation at the federal level was enacted. For purposes of discovering the philosophical underpinnings of the trends in that policy, the most significant piece of legislation is the National Labor Relations Act—or the Wagner Act—which in 1953 succeeded the National Recovery Act after the latter was declared unconstitutional.[67] Although the Wagner Act was and is widely regarded as a turning point for the labor movement in the United States, its legislative and judicial context, in conjunction with the working of the act itself, reveals an identifiable trend in national labor policy in the twentieth century.

Federal Involvement: The Police Power

Federal dealings with labor began with an 1884 congressional act establishing a Bureau of Labor, which was to gather information on wages, working hours, and "the means of promoting [workers'] material, social, intellectual, and moral prosperity."[68] This agency was made into a department in 1888, incorporated into the newly created Department of Commerce and Labor in 1903, then separated off into a cabinet-level Department of Labor in 1913. With the latter development, the function given it by Congress was "to foster, promote, and develop the welfare of the wage earners of the United States, to improve their working conditions, and to advance their opportunities for profitable employment," and its secretary was to attempt to mediate labor disputes.[69]

During this period, there was widespread dissatisfaction voiced (or alleged) concerning private employment agencies.[70] These private businesses and organizations existed throughout the country to enable seekers of work to obtain suitable employment, but they were said either to be ineffective (when run by philanthropic organizations) or to "lack the neutrality essential to the satisfactory organization of the labor market," as J. Commons and J. Andrews said when pronouncing unemployment "the most serious labor problem of the period, warranting extensive legislative action on the federal level."[71]

Perhaps the defense of such action is best illustrated by D. Lescohier's observations in 1919 that irregular employment

> undermines the physique; deadens the mind; weakens the ambition; destroys the capacity for continuous, sustained endeavor; induces a liking for idleness and self-indulgence; saps self-respect and the sense of responsibility; impairs technical skill; weakens nerve and will power; creates a tendency to blame others for failures; saps courage; prevents thrift and hope of family advancement; destroys a workman's feeling that he is taking good care of his family; and sends him to work worried and underfed; plunges him in debt.[72]

Sound or unsound, such considerations were coupled with the disparaging characterization of private employment agencies noted above and were offered as support for legislation aiming to abolish and restrict such agencies.[73] These ideas gave considerable support to efforts to have the federal government concern itself more and more with employment and labor matters.

Establishment of the Department of Labor marked the beginning of such involvement. This is not to say that there was no other way to alleviate the problems involved nor that attempted remedies should have involved governments in such a way that private solutions were eliminated or seriously diminished. A number of other human problems can produce the results listed by Lescohier, yet governments should not attempt to solve them.

In retrospect it is not at all clear that bringing the government's powers and resources to bear on the unemployment problem and other labor matters in fact solved more problems than it created. My concern here is only with the avowed rationale for instituting governmental involvement in the labor market. That is, we are merely noting the justification offered for introducing governmental—in other words, coercive—activity into the area of human social life that consists of productive work.

I noted earlier that, from a legal perspective, governmental concern with such matters is justified, in the main, on grounds of the traditional police power. Ernest Freund traces the concept of the police power to the "royal power of controlling the internal police of the realm... exercised by the King through his council sitting in the Star Chamber," and seen as "a normal and legitimate function of state, namely, an inherent executive police power."[74] In the United States this police power was thought to have been transferred to the legislatures—as a number of U.S. court decisions clearly implied or asserted.[75] This concept is explained by Commons and Andrews as follows:

> The police power is an indefinite authorization for the American state to abridge liberty or property without consent or compensation, in addition to its other more definite powers. An individual is sick with diphtheria. The state draws the line of quarantine beyond which his family and friends are deprived of their liberty of movement. Valuable animals have foot-and-mouth disease. The state may order them to be shot and buried without consent or compensation...The bulk of labor legislation by the states looks for authorization to the police power....
>
> The other powers of the state...are in theory definitely limited. Either they accomplish only a specific object of government, such as conquest, peace, the execution of laws, the acquisition of revenues, or the purchase of property, or they extend only to a limited class of people, such as children or public employees. But, in addition to these objects and persons, there are those large and indefinite purposes of public safety, health, morals, welfare, and prosperity, and those many but indefinite classes of producers and consumers, buyers and

sellers, employers and employees, who often are restrained by government under the police power.[76]

Justice Field, in *Barbier v. Connolly*, is more explicit about the uses to which such power may be put.[77] The police power consists of authorization "to prescribe regulations to promote the health, peace, morals, education, and good order of the people, and to legislate so as to increase the industries of the state, develop its resources, and add to its wealth and prosperity."[78] Echoing the origins of the concept, Chief Justice Taney noted that the police power amounts to "nothing more or less than the powers of government inherent in every sovereignty to the extent of its dominions."[79]

Not only state legislatures, but the federal government, too, exercises the police power; as Robert E. Cushman explains, this is constitutionally unobjectionable.[80] An investigation of the major pieces of federal labor legislation in recent times shows that the legal authority for such actions is long established.[81]

Outside of the idea of police power, with its origins in common law, the federal government's regulation of labor gained authority from the explicit constitutional ascription to Congress of the power to regulate commerce with foreign nations and among the several states. In addition, on several occasions the Supreme Court has overruled state courts in cases involving activities relating to property or businesses "affected with a public interest," an idea also derived from the common law. The innumerable decisions relating to the various antitrust cases adjudicated by the U.S. Supreme Court prior to the enactment of the Railway Labor Act (1962) and the National Labor Relations Act (1935) drew heavily from the legal authority established via the commerce clause and the common-law idea of legislative power over property affected with a public interest.[82]

It is clear from the above that the federal government did not initiate involvement in the labor-related affairs of the citizens of the country with certain legislative acts of Congress. The purpose of considering specific pieces of legislation within the present study is not to single them out as giving special or even new direction to national labor policy. It is, rather, to focus on certain official statements of the federal government in which the crucial ideas and arguments for subsequent (and prior) national labor policy are relatively clearly announced. Such laws as the Wagner Act are by necessity general in their scope, unlike many rulings on the part of the Supreme Court.

As the idea of the rule of law, or law of the land, implies, an act of Congress puts forth a broad principle, probably as broad and explicit as the content of positive law could ever be within a political tradition such as that of the United States. It is important, therefore, to examine such broad pieces of legislation in order to unearth the philosophical under-pinnings of national policy. But it would not be correct to infer that the Wagner Act itself, for example, gave the philosophical impetus to na-tional labor policy. As has been indicated in the preceding pages, that impetus had been present throughout the history of U.S. law.

The Wagner Act: A Conception of Rights

The National Labor Relations Act (Wagner Act) of 1935 contains precisely the sort of statement that is valuable and interesting for our purposes. Section 1, "Findings and Policy," is reproduced here in full.

> The denial by employers of the right of employees to organize and the refusal by employers to accept the procedure of collective bargaining lead to strikes and other forms of industrial strife or unrest, which have the intent or the necessary effect of burdening or obstructing commerce by (a) impairing the efficiency, safety, or op-eration of the instrumentalities of commerce; (b) occurring in the current of com-merce; (c) materially affecting, restraining, or controlling the flow of raw materials or manufactured or processed goods from or into the channels of commerce, or the prices of such materials or goods in commerce; or (d) causing diminution of em-ployment or wages in such volume as substantially to impair or disrupt the market for goods flowing from or into the channels of commerce.

> The inequality of bargaining power between employees who do not possess full freedom of association or actual liberty of contract, and employers who are orga-nized in the corporate or other forms of ownership association substantially bur-dens and affects the flow of commerce, and tends to aggravate recurrent business depression, by depressing wage rates and the purchasing power of wage earners in industry and by preventing the stabilization of competitive wage rates and working conditions within and between industries.

> Experience has proved that protection by law of the right of employees to organize and bargain collectively safeguards commerce from injury, impairment, or inter-ruption, and promotes the flow of commerce by removing certain recognized sources of industrial strife and unrest, by encouraging practices fundamental to the friendly adjustment of industrial disputes arising out of differences as to wages, hours, or other working conditions, and by restoring equality of bargaining power between employers and employees.

> It is hereby declared to be the policy of the United States to eliminate the causes of certain substantial obstruction to the free flow of commerce and to mitigate and eliminate those obstructions when they have occurred by encouraging the practice and procedure of collective bargaining and by protecting the exercise by workers of full freedom of association, self-organization, and designation of representa-

tives of their choosing, for the purpose of negotiating the terms and conditions of their employment or other mutual aid or protection.

The central point to be noticed here is that what is called "the right of employees to organize" is deemed to be in need of protection because failure to render such protection will harm society, or the public, by injuring, impairing, damaging, or otherwise obstructing commerce. From (a) to (d) the emphasis is on what is likely to happen to commerce if "the right of employees to organize" is denied and "the procedure of collective bargaining not accepted by employers." Based on these paragraphs, then, such denial or refusal by employers is said to cause harm to commerce; the Wagner Act is explicitly designed to "eliminate the causes of certain substantial obstructions to the free flow of commerce."

The Wagner Act follows trends previously begun. It is consistent with long-standing interpretation of the commerce clause of the U.S. Constitution, the Preamble to which states that the Constitution had been ordained and established, in part, "to promote the general Welfare." It is consistent with the numerous legal grounds for authorizing government action pertaining to the action of the citizens (including labor and business) of the United States. Whether it is consistent with the rest of U.S. legal and political principles and ideals is not the issue at this point. What is important is that government interference with people's lives has throughout U.S. legal history been justified, in large part, by reference to what legislatures have considered necessary to promote the general welfare.

This is a critical point because there are alternative approaches to justifying the rights individuals are said to possess as well as their protection and preservation by government, and different approaches to justifying individual rights yield different conceptions of these rights. For instance, to take a drastic example, there were numerous references to human rights in the former Soviet Constitution, just as there were in the constitutions of Western nations. Yet the idea within the context of the Soviet's avowedly Marxist-Leninist, centralized socialist system was not the same as the idea within the essentially Lockean, individualist-capitalist system that is the theoretical base of the U.S. political tradition.[83] An essay in *Pravda* provides a clear illustration of this.

As regards genuine human rights, historical experience has shown that such rights can be ensured only by the socialist system. The right to work, the right to education, to social security, the right to elect and to be elected to government and administrative bodies of all levels, the right to criticize and control their work, the right to participate in the discussion and adoption of decisions, including decisions on matters of national importance—such is our socialist democracy in action.[84]

The essay indicates just how clearly this conception of human rights differs from that traditionally entertained within the U.S. framework:

Legal action is taken in conformity with Soviet law in the case of individuals who engage in anti-Soviet propaganda and agitation, designed to undermine or weaken the established social and political system in our country, or who systematically spread deliberate falsifications vilifying the Soviet state and social system.[85]

To put it more plainly, the exercise of human rights in the former Soviet Union was expressly (constitutionally, by statute) limited to activities that promoted or did not impede the realization of those all-embracing sociopolitical objectives around which the Soviet state was organized.

Two differences can be seen between the U.S. (Lockean) idea of human rights and the ones that were conveyed in the pages of *Pravda*. Both help, in their drastic contrast, to make clear the point about how human rights can be conceived and thus what conception of human rights is prominent in the language of the Wagner Act.

First, the Lockean idea of rights is natural, not positive. It ascribes rights to human beings on the grounds that they are a certain kind of entity, that they have a specific nature that requires that these rights be recognized for all persons in society. Laws should be enacted, and individuals and governments should act, in compliance with natural rights because only to protect or secure these rights may government—otherwise a very dangerous institution—be established among human beings.

The Soviet or Marxist-Leninist idea—which is actually simply the most explicit version of similar ideas embodied in anti-individualist theories of the state—sees human rights as conditional, based on the goals of society as guided by the government. Not human nature, but the overall purpose or aim of society, is the basis for the rights one is supposed to have. Rights are regarded as conditions to be granted legal recognition by the government or state, acting on behalf of the society (or its purpose).

Second, Lockean natural rights are generally prohibitions, specifying what others may not do to one, establishing one's sphere of personal moral authority that ought to be protected and preserved. No positive obligation on the part of others flows from the mere possession of natural rights; the negative obligation that everyone should refrain from encroachment upon the personal moral sphere of others is the only duty

Lockean right theory identifies. (There is no concern here with whether the Lockean idea allows for positive obligations or responsibilities among friends, family members, or colleagues. There is concern only to note that Locke's idea does not actively bind anyone to anyone else qua human being.) Generally, the human rights listed in the *Pravda* essay are of quite a different character. One has the right to be provided with goods and services that can exist only if others produce them. The right to education or health care, for example, means that someone is obligated to provide education or health care to everyone who has that right—to every human being, if this is a human right.

It is not always the case that the rendition of important concepts in different political or moral theories will be in such direct opposition. The above drastic case does, however, serve to illustrate the point that it is important to look closely at the theoretical underpinnings of an idea that can have crucial normative significance. What, then, is the conception of rights underlying the Wagner Act? Reference is made to "the denial by employers of the right of employees to organize." The central concern is that employers sometimes refuse to employ those who have chosen to organize into or join labor unions. Does this refusal constitute a denial (violation would be a better word here) of the right of employees to organize?

If having a right means that one should be provided with certain conditions, then one's right has been "denied" if someone who is obligated to do so refuses to provide those conditions. A typical case is that of a contractual right—for example, a right to payment for services rendered. This right is violated if the other contracting party refuses to pay.

If it is believed that individuals owe one another certain services, values, considerations, or economic benefits by nature (versus by contract or upon specific agreement), then refusal to provide these would also be held to constitute the violation of rights. Thus, if employees have the right to certain conditions—namely, employment and the option of labor union membership—then refusal of employment when the option is exercised would be a "denial" of the right of employees to organize.

If having a right means, however, that one may not be prevented from taking actions that constitute the exercise of that right (without obligating anyone to provide certain conditions to which he has not previously agreed), then one's right has been denied if someone prevents those actions. To have a right to free speech, then, means one may not be prevented, for example, from writing down and securing publication of one's ideas (without obligating anyone to provide whatever conditions would facilitate one's doing so.) This right is violated if force is used to prevent one from taking those actions, but not if someone under no prior agreement to do so refuses to provide pen and pencil, magazine space, or the like.

On this conception of rights, employees' right to organize is violated if they are prevented from joining a union. In terms of the common sense idea of prevention (incorporated in the bulk of Western law), to prevent someone's actions means to use or threaten to use force to obstruct his or her actions. Thus, employees' right to organize is violated if they are barred by private force or by government from joining a union.

It is sometimes maintained, however, that not doing something for someone (for example, not employing him when one could) is a form of prevention.[86] This clearly relies on some idea of individuals' being owed certain services or conditions. Thus, the conception of rights has shifted to the former sense above, where some individuals have a (noncontractual) obligation to provide others with certain conditions. The Wagner Act assumes just such an obligation on the part of employers, and this obligation seems to be derived from the general goal of advancing commerce (as part of the general welfare). The rights of the relevant individuals are justified in terms of that goal, yielding the specific rights individuals are said to possess. Thus it is held that employees have the right to organize and, consequently, may not be denied employment upon doing so; and it is held that employers do not have the right to free association with employees when the exercise of that right would (very likely) disrupt the free flow of commerce.

Another crucial point in the first section of the Wagner Act is the discussion pertaining to inequality of bargaining power between employees, who supposedly do not possess full freedom of association and actual liberty of contract, and employers, who are organized in the corporate or other forms of ownership. It is maintained, again, that this inequality substantially burdens and affects the flow of commerce and therefore requires mitigation and elimination via governmental measures specified in the act.

What is equal bargaining power?[87] "Bargaining power" is an economic concept, yet political theory may offer insight into what it means. This is not surprising, since political theories aim to identify what kind of very general principles (laws) are proper or suited to a good human community, and human communities will nearly always include economic elements—that is, production, trade, consumption, and so forth. Different economic and political theories may differ on the nature of bargaining power, or even on the validity of the concept (in some systems, no bargaining is possible, since sharing, and not profiting, is the governing principle required by law).[88]

As well as the expected economic factors, noneconomic considerations have also been brought to bear on the understanding of bargaining power. Many concerned with these issues assert that most of those who work for wages are not really free to leave their work and thus to hold out for better conditions. A good discussion of this is provided by John Spargo and George Louis Arner.

> Socialists frequently speak of the condition of the proletariat under Capitalism as "Wage Slavery." This term is sometimes objected to on the ground that the worker is free to give up his job and move from place to place at will. He is thus in a very different position from that of the chattel slave of antiquity, or even that of the feudal serf.

> The Socialist replies that while the worker is theoretically free he is in fact enslaved; that while the law does not enforce wage slavery, it is enforced by conditions more effectually coercive than statutes could be. There is always an army of unemployed ready to take the jobs that the discontented may vacate, and the choice that confronts the worker is usually a choice between holding his job or falling to poverty or even pauperism. If he moves from one factory to another, he only changes master, still working under the same general conditions. The average worker cannot hope to find relief in private business enterprises. The risk is too precarious, for the majority of small businesses fail.[89]

It is interesting that while Spargo begins by denying that workers were free to move, he then goes on to entertain the possibility of their moving. But then he denies that there is any advantage in that for workers. This engenders a problem: If the disadvantage consists of not being able to move, then when they do move, the possibility cannot be foreclosed that they will have at least some improved condition. If, however, moving holds out no improvement, one wonders what would satisfy a critic. What would have to obtain for workers to be in an improved condition?

It is also noteworthy that the socialist thesis rests, in large measure, on the popular understanding of the analysis of a nonsocialist, namely, Thomas Malthus (1766–1834), of population growth under capitalism.

Malthus was generally taken to have argued—never mind the exact technical rendition of his views, which are quite complex—that workers would reproduce much faster than jobs would increase. This view relied extensively on certain beliefs about workers that are extremely doubtful and, to say the least, highly demeaning. As a class they were supposed to lack the initiative to stem their condition of subservience and dependence. This produced a constantly growing laboring class, an easy prey for exploitation by capitalists.

Not only socialists picked up on these types of beliefs. Oddly, perhaps, Herbert Spencer, a late nineteenth-century advocate of laissez-faire capitalism as the proper next stage in evolutionary development, also argued the Spargo position.

> The wage-earning factory-hand does, indeed, exemplify entirely free labor, in so far that, making contracts at will and able to break them after short notice, he is free to engage with whomsoever he pleases and where he pleases. But this liberty amounts in practice to little more than the ability to exchange one slavery for another; since, fit only for his particular occupation, he has rarely an opportunity of doing anything more than decide in what mill he will pass the greatest part of his dreary days. The coercion of circumstances often bears more hardly on him than the coercion of the master does on one in bondage.[90]

These points are disputed by those who claim that the helplessness of workers not only is exaggerated but is focused on to the point of being an insult, a kind of chauvinism. Only a view of workers that bars them from being able to embark upon careful planning, learning, saving, organizing, and other types of prudential action would characterize workers as so incapacitated. Moreover, such a thesis ignores the basic similarities between workers and other sellers of goods and services on the market and between what the two offer for sale.[91] And if workers are in bondage, what about capitalists?

Marx at least recognized this implication. In his view only the utopian (as distinct from his scientific) socialist position contends that the inherent constraints on workers must be remedied by constraining the "capitalists." For Marx the workers are where they are by historical necessity and there is a historical purpose to their clash in the marketplace. It would be futile, within Marx's perspective, to try to soften the situation by way of provisions such as the Wagner Act. Indeed, as some Marxists see it, such measures merely stave off the real solution, namely, social revolution.

The normative concepts "just price" and "just wage" also underlie the understanding of bargaining power. These concepts apparently account for the fact that "equal bargaining power" is usually not taken in an exclusively economic sense, whereby an agreement would never be reached. Rather, the point is for workers to have bargaining power equal enough to enable them to hold out for a "decent" or "just" wage. The idea of a just price or just wage—one not necessarily coinciding with whatever payment the "market" commands—can be traced back at least to Aristotle.[92] The belief that workers are owed more than they (generally) receive has been a prominent feature of national labor policy insofar as the objective has been to improve the financial and related conditions of workers (with what probable degree of success is not the issue here).

From the earliest times of federal labor legislation the intention of Congress to enhance the well-being of workers was explicitly declared. The Labor Department was at first an information-gathering agency, but as federal legislation concerning labor matters proceeded, the task of actively improving the financial and related situation of workers was also assumed. The early attempts to unionize labor throughout the country did not fare well with the Supreme Court, but in several of these the dissenting opinions made it clear that "labor's progress" had been avowed as a goal by legislatures and in various courts at the state and federal levels.[93] Further evidence of this trend comes from Senator Robert F. Wagner's testimony on behalf of the National Labor Relations Act before the Senate Committee on Education and Labor, March 11–14, 1935. During these hearings, he quoted from the report, *Recent Social Trends in the United States*, published in 1933 by a committee established by President Hoover: "In spite of the deliberate attempts to promote the wider diffusion of wealth there is little evidence that any change in the distribution of wealth has taken place in the country during the past several decades."[94] Senator Wagner added: "It is well recognized that the failure to spread adequate purchasing power among the vast masses of the consuming public disrupts the continuity of business operations and causes everyone to suffer." (Statistics were presented to substantiate both of the above claims.)[95]

A good deal of labor legislation, including that pertaining to bargaining power, is justified by the belief that the law should remedy the moral shortcoming of workers' receiving unjust wages. In the history of Western thought, there has always been the inclination toward an ethical view-point in terms of which the less well-off are owed help from the more fortunate. There has been less acceptance of the proposition that this responsibility—or even duty—should be enforced by law, which would transform a moral duty, to be done by choice, to a legal obligation.

As can be seen from Senator Wagner's remarks above, the rationale for politicizing such a moral duty—by having the government step in, for example, to ensure equal bargaining power via the imposition of collective bargaining—is to prevent commercial disruptions and thus general suffering. Likewise, the Wagner Act specifies that the inequality of bargaining power is to be remedied by federal policy because it "substantially burdens and affects the free flow of commerce."[96]

We can now advance to another crucial idea in the Wagner Act, namely, full freedom of association or actual liberty of contract. What do these concepts mean in the act, and what are their broader implications as employed there?

We can take association to be the voluntary action of at least two individuals culminating in their joint pursuit of some mutually intended (though not necessarily commercial) endeavor. That people should be free to associate means that they cannot justifiably be prevented from embarking upon such joint endeavors. It does not mean that what they do in their association is always good or the most worthy thing for them to do. The issue here is a moral and political one, concerning what human beings ought or ought not do to each other—to wit, they ought not interfere with associations among others even if the association has not the best objectives.

"Contract" means the voluntary actions that constitute association as legally defensible or protected endeavor, something that the relevant governmental bodies such as courts and police should in appropriate ways (via due process, for instance), protect. When association is legally defensible or protected, parties who might act, for instance, to breach the ensuing relationship contrary to the terms of the contract could be acted against by force of law. Liberty of contract, then, focuses on the normative point that it should be possible for individuals in a human community to establish such legally binding associations as they desire. The issue here is a political one, concerning the proper relationship between citizens and their legal system; none should be barred in his or her association from gaining legal protection for them. (This is different from the economic analysis of contract, which aims to be purely descriptive.)

The Wagner Act does not employ these phrases exactly as rendered above. However, the act implies that voluntary acts of association and formation of contractual relations should not be barred. It implies that if someone not party to those actions acts to disassociate himself from those so acting, the freedom of association or the liberty of contract is violated. Specifically, if employers choose to base employment relationships on whether or not an employee or potential employee has associated with others in a labor union, this is construed in the Wagner Act as a violation of freedom of association or liberty of contract. Section 8(3) provides: "It shall be an unfair labor practice for an employer... [b]y discrimination in regard to hire or tenure of employment or any term or condition of employment to encourage or discourage membership in any labor organization."[97]

In other words, the full freedom of association and actual liberty of contract referred to in the act involve, not only the employer's abstaining from interference with the employee's voluntary action to join or not join a union, but also his maintaining the same relationship with the worker that prevailed prior to this voluntary action. Again, this understanding of "full freedom of association and actual liberty of contract" is justified in the act in terms of the goal of maintaining the free flow of commerce.

It should be noted that earlier in the history of labor law, some judgments emphasized the individual's so-called freedom rights without employing the sense of "full freedom" incorporated in the Wagner Act. Recall Judge Shaw's opinion in *Commonwealth v. Hunt*. Another example is the decision in *Coppage v. State of Kansas*, in which the Supreme Court employed the idea differently from the Wagner Act.

Conceding the full right of the individual to join the union, he has no inherent right to do this and still remain in the employ of one who is unwilling to employ a union man, any more than the same individual has a right to join the union without the consent of that organization.[98]

So there have been more or less important decisions supporting different conceptions of the right of individuals and the freedom these individuals should have. The Wagner Act's reference to full freedom and actual liberty no doubt relies on the belief, previously noted, that workers, because of their material situation, are not actually free to withhold their work for better wages or working conditions. But we have seen, also, that such a view is most comfortable within a framework that does not regard either the worker or the employer actually free but sees both as moved, at least as a class, by impersonal forces of history.

We turn now to some additional sections of the Wagner Act. Section 8(1) forbids employers to "interfere with, restrain, or coerce employees in the exercise of the rights guaranteed in section 7." Section 7, in turn, specifies: "Employees shall have the right to self-organization, to form, join, or assist labor organizations, to bargain collectively through representatives of their own choosing, and to engage in concerted activities, for the purpose of collective bargaining or other mutual aid or protection."

The interference in which employers are forbidden to engage is explained more specifically in paragraphs 2–5 of Section 8: they are not to dominate or interfere with" or "contribute financial or other support to" labor organizations; they are not to "encourage or discourage" unionization by any policies of "hire or tenure of employment or any term or condition of employment"; they are not to "refuse to bargain collectively" with employees' (legitimate) representatives.

What philosophy underlies Section 8 of the Wagner Act? In other words (to refocus our attention on the broad task of this project), by reference to which broader social, political, and ethical principles would one be most successful in an effort to justify these provisions as laws by which members of a human community should conduct themselves, quite apart from considerations of positive law, statute, or majority will?

In the Wagner Act, the interference, coercion, or restraint being discussed is not the kind involved in, for example, ordinary assault. (Indeed, the latter, illegal under statutes predating the Wagner Act, would not require prohibition by it.) It comes close to the sort of coercion or interference commonly associated with violation of binding contracts. If one has entered into a contract with a house painter, but upon completion of the work refuses to pay the agreed amount, he has interfered with the painter despite having taken no overt aggressive actions against him. The contract requires payment, and failure constitutes a breach, thus interfering with or coercing the painter in the exercise of his rights (or in other words preventing him from enjoying his property—the money earned through his performance).

The interference contemplated in the Wagner Act, while more like contract violation than like physical assault, is also quite different from the former: the employer has not entered into any contract whereby his discrimination against workers who choose to support labor organization is precluded. (The cases in which the employer and employees have so contracted are not at issue here.) It is the Wagner Act itself that institutes legal acceptance or recognition of something like a contractual provision, namely, a natural obligation, specifying that support given to labor organizations shall not suffice as grounds for withholding employment, promotion, or other benefits from the employee. In this respect the unfair labor practices of an employer are conceived of in the Wagner Act as analogous to the practices of parents who, for various reasons, such as disapproval of their children's friends or choice of religion, withhold from their children the ordinary benefits due a child from parents or guardians—and recognized as due, clearly, not as a matter of contract, but as the function of the parent-child relationship. The Wagner Act appears, then, to regard the employer's obligation as similar to that of the parents, not requiring prior agreement—indeed, not justifiably discharged by any agreement contrary to the implicit natural obligation or duty. (In Lochner the dissent argued in similar fashion for the authority of states to void contractual agreements that would not conform to conditions thought by state officials to be proper for workers, deeming workers incapable of deciding where their welfare lies and implementing their judgments.)[99]

The Wagner Act implicitly identifies certain actions as the employer's natural duty on grounds of the nature of employment, namely, that it can contribute to the free flow of commerce in a given community. The authority to enforce fulfillment of this obligation would be derived, of course, from police power. Employers are thus taken to be duty-bound to maintain between themselves and their employees whatever relationship the legislature, upon investigation, deems required for the enhancement of the free flow of commerce. The result is that this "natural" duty is conditional upon the particulars of the goals and desires of the majority within the community (the United States), presumably expressed through the legislators. Thus the Wagner Act stipulates that, upon certain choices of the employee, the employer may not exercise certain choices of his own, such as disassociating himself from the employee. The act does not require an employer to maintain the association under whatever circumstances of the employee's making—for example, should the employee turn to crime, or should he dress unsuitably for work, even if by virtue of religious, political, or personal convictions. Yet, would not dissociation under these circumstances also contribute to the obstruction of the free flow of commerce? What emerges is that the Wagner Act, while broadly concerned with the continuity of business activities, was quite specifically concerned with the overall "progress of labor," at the time widely construed to involve unionization.

Still, the wording of the Wagner Act does not give us this view explicitly. The language simply indicates the need for invoking certain police powers so as to forbid persons to act in ways that would obstruct goals deemed worthy by the government of the United States (as directed by the Constitution or its Preamble). The collective goals referred to are thus considered of sufficiently greater significance than the freedom of choice of various citizens whose exercise of this freedom appeared not to contribute to those collective goals.

The Wagner Act's implicit view of the relationship between the welfare of the group and the rights and welfare of individuals also appears in the act's specification of majority rule or the democratic method as the proper means of expressing the collective will of the employees— This specification may be termed its underlying commitment to certain elements of the theory of industrial democracy. Section 8(a)(5) prohibits an employer from refusing "to bargain collectively with the representatives of his employees, subject to the provisions of Section 9(a)," which specifies what will constitute legitimate representation:

> Representatives designated or selected for the purpose of collective bargaining by the majority of the employees in a unit appropriate for such purposes, shall be the exclusive representatives of all the employees in such unit for the purposes of collective bargaining in respect to rates of pay, wages, hours of employment, or other conditions of employment.[100]

The importance of this provision becomes clear upon examination of the different ways in which the democratic method may be conceived. Sometimes it refers to an agreed method by which members of a voluntary association (a corporation, a club, and so on) will arrive at directives, goals, rules of procedure, and so forth, without or within certain limits as to what the method may affect. The method itself, with any specified limitations, is chosen when one chooses membership in the group. The idea of the democratic method also refers, however, to the best (proper) means to be used in identifying a given group's or community's policies, rules, goals, and so forth, whether or not each of those affected by the results concurs.

It is this last sense of the idea—democracy as the proper method of substantive decision making—that is incorporated in the Wagner Act. The act takes it as natural that where employees may have a stake in certain decisions, majority rule should apply, whether or not agreed to as a method by those so involved. Representatives chosen "by the majority of the employees in a unit...shall be the exclusive representatives of all the employees in such unit."[101] (Yet, interestingly, once elected as exclusive representative, a union need not return to the employees for any further mandate for its decisions or actions. No labor law, for example, requires a union to submit contracts it has negotiated to its members—much less to the entire bargaining unit—for approval, although some unions do so as a matter of internal rules. It can be argued that this is something in which employees have a stake, yet the Wagner Act does not provide for majority rule in these matters. In this respect the Wagner Act is philosophically inconsistent and ambivalent.)

The Wagner Act's stance is reiterated in the Supreme Court's decision in *J. I. Case v. National Labor Relations Board*. In the Court's majority opinion we find a candid discussion of the point.

> The practice and philosophy of collective bargaining looks with suspicion on . . . individual advantages....[I]ncreased compensation, if individually deserved, is often earned at the cost of breaking down some other standard thought to be for the welfare of the group, and always creates the suspicion of being paid at the long-range expense of the group as a whole.[102]

The point is made, not so much as advocacy, but as a report of the nature of employment within the framework of the Wagner Act's provisions and the NLRB's authority to determine fair labor practices. As such, it gives support to the interpretation of the Wagner Act advanced here.

It seems likely that the Wagner Act's preference for democratic determination of working conditions and other terms of employment derives from the fact that the U.S. political system includes a large measure of democracy (in both senses of the term). When the Wagner Act proposed that government become more immersed in the nation's economic life, the fact that the United States government could be characterized as democratic would, not surprisingly, influence the nature and specific content of the involvement. Moreover, the philosophical climate of opinion that had given support to the idea of absolute property rights, absolute freedom of contract, absolute freedom of association, and similar limits on the scope of majority rule had been greatly undermined.[103]

Philosophical Underpinnings: The Individual Versus the Group

Consider the main thrust of the Wagner Act: Individuals—employees and employers—have rights and obligations insofar as legal recognition and enforcement of these will contribute to the free flow of commerce in the community, as determined by the majority of employees in a given group. What emerges is a philosophical-political outlook that may be characterized as collectivist utilitarian, whereby the interests of the collective (the public good, the general welfare, employees' welfare) are politically prior to the interests of the individual members of the group. The utilitarian twist is that the preferences of the majority (the greatest number) are to determine the goals to be pursued and their method of pursuit.

The issue at hand is not whether the Wagner Act actually achieved or helped achieve the goals that figured in the justification of the provisions. Various governmental powers are justified even if their exercise fails to achieve their purpose. For example, numerous military operations in defense of a country are usually regarded as exercises of properly governmental powers, yet they might and often do fail. The same sort of thing may be true regarding other functions deemed to be proper to government. Bad verdicts might be reached. Legislators can be ill-prepared. Prisons can be badly managed. Whether or not a goal is properly achieved by way of governmental activity is independent of whether the means employed and people administering these means manage to attain the goal.

Why were the goals deemed achievable by the Wagner Act thought to be properly pursued by governmental activity? Within the history of the United States, it has not been thought to be the proper function of government to pursue various ends—for example, the propagation of some religious faith. If Congress enacted legislation for purposes of propagating the Roman Catholic faith, justifying various provisions of such legislation by reference to this ultimate goal, the act would most likely be declared unconstitutional by the Supreme Court. As noted earlier, in *West Virginia State Board of Education v. Barnette*, for example, the Supreme Court held that "The very purpose of a Bill of Rights was to withdraw certain subjects from the vicissitudes of political controversy, to place them beyond the reach of majorities.... One's...fundamental rights may not be submitted to vote; they depend on the outcome of no elections." The legal history of the Unites States reveals divergent tendencies concerning what are the fundamental rights that "may not be submitted to vote." It is clear, for example, that most of the judicial decisions concerned with the exercise of the rights of free expression, free religious participation, freedom of the press, or freedom of assembly have been modeled on the idea expressed in the Barnette decision. Even here, however, it appears that no constitutional provision has been considered so restrictive as to warrant its application absolutely.[104]

Of course, in legal discussion there has been a great deal said on the precise meaning of freedom of speech, press, and association. In *Schenck v. United States*, for example, the Supreme Court stated: "The most stringent protection of free speech would not protect a man in falsely shouting fire in a theatre and causing a panic."[105] Freedom of speech could not legitimate such conduct under any circumstances, any more than it would protect standing up to give a speech while a play or movie is in progress, although this would not result in "causing a panic." The protection of the right to freedom of speech does not mean that the police would protect someone as he or she is giving a talk during a church sermon, scientific lecture, funeral, open heart surgery, or even a dinner party, unless one is the pastor giving the sermon, etc.

Nor does it mean a host of other rather peculiar alleged implications that are often cited in arguing against the absoluteness of the freedom. The right to freedom to speak one's mind means that one may advance ideas, complaints, or outrage within one's own sphere of jurisdiction or authority, including home, business, hired hall, or others' homes or publications when voluntarily offered for this purpose. Nor does it mean selling false information while claiming it is the truth, for that would be fraud. It does not mean shouting fire anywhere unless in one's own home or where this is the function one has (or must assume under special circumstances, as during a fire). The right to freedom does mean, however, that the inconvenience, fear, or offense of others, including the government, cannot count as adequate grounds for prohibiting someone's saying, writing, or publishing what he will within his own sphere of authority.[106]

Even so understood, however, the right to free speech has not been held to be absolute.[107] In labor matters an employer is often forbidden to speak even though his speech would occur on his own property, on grounds that his doing so—given the context, timing, or audience of the speech—would constitute an unfair labor practice.[108] Such apparent First Amendment violations are held constitutional on the grounds given in Schenck: "The question in every case is whether the words used are used in such circumstances and are of such a nature as to create a clear and present danger that they will bring about the substantive evils that Congress has a right to prevent."[109] (Since matters of speech are frequently intermingled with those of commerce and Congress has the power to "prevent evils" in this realm, the courts have tended to yield to such considerations more often than First Amendment absolutists would wish even while they might sanction government economic regulation.)

In general, the distinction between cases concerning interference with speech, assembly, association, or religion and those where business or commerce is regulated, has to do with the issue of burden of proof. While the courts have allowed interference with freedom of speech, etc., in specific instances in which clear and present danger is demonstrated, they have disallowed general legislation curbing these freedoms.[110] This is not so with respect to commercial activities. Yet, commercial activities often involve speech, assembly, and even religion. So the distinction cannot be upheld consistently, as illustrated in the impact of labor legislation on the freedom of speech and association of employers.[111]

In spite of the difficulties we have noted in justifying such developments, as the U.S. legal system has evolved it has exhibited an acceptance of intrusive legislation relating to commercial (and therefore labor) activities. It has not, however, done so, at least on the federal level, vis-à-vis legislation pertaining to matters associated with activities covered by the First Amendment. William Letwin has described the judicial move toward this position and notes its culmination in *West Coast Hotel Co. v. Parrish*, in which "the court based its decision, so far as logic goes, on the distinction frequently made between 'property rights' and, 'human rights.'"[112] The same distinction lies behind Freund's comment: "We have heard much of freedom of contract. Would anyone be prepared to place this right by the side of freedom of press and religion without definition or qualification?"[113]

This trend is also obvious when we consider the emphasis usually placed on what are often treated as distinctively civil rights—the rights to free expression, assembly, equal protection of (or benefit from) the law, protection from unreasonable search and seizure, and the rest— versus the stress on "mere" property rights which are the rights to hold and exchange belongings, to set the terms of trade, to draw up contracts, to hire and fire, to enter or leave a trade or profession, and so on. (This is especially evident in Western concerns for human rights in the discussion of the topic during the Carter presidency [1977–1981] as well as in the history of talk about human rights associated with the United Nations.)

What is not so obvious as the trend toward greater and greater abridgment of private property rights itself is the philosophy underlying it. Of course, there are different kinds of pressures that have an impact on legal developments: some are purely emotional, some stem from unprincipled pursuit of profit or special interests, and some from political bargaining. But there are also ideas that support significant developments, usually at the stage where these developments must be provided with a palatable intellectual or moral rationale.

Why should a dichotomy between civil or human and property rights be so widely accepted when the Constitution conjoins life, liberty, and property when referring generally to what the law needs to protect in the case of all persons?

As related to commerce, of course, Article I, Section 8, of the Constitution invests regulatory power in Congress, albeit somewhat restricted by the Fifth and Ninth Amendments. We considered this briefly in chapter 1. Where commercial factors have been thought to dominate or the right to property come under consideration, the commerce clause—along with the "general welfare" provision of Article I, Section 8—has seemed to many to sanction the police power's extensions far enough to authorize Congress to enact legislation such as the Wagner Act.

Yet the police power doctrine fails to support the dichotomy. That power has been construed as sanctioning the exercise of governmental action not only for the public health and the public safety, but for the maintenance of "public morals, the general or common good, and for the well-being, comfort and good order of the people." This could readily imply legal support to foster religious observance, a "clean" press, moral uprightness, or artistic excellence.

Maintaining the free flow of commerce does not stand out as the sole special goal that one might see supported by the Constitution for which the violation or abridgment of negative or freedom rights could be legally justified. Furthermore, the Constitution's "general welfare" provision might be taken to permit more moral or religious or intellectual interference than has traditionally been tolerated. Welfare need not apply only to the nation's collective economic well-being; it could also include spiritual, intellectual, and aesthetic conditions. Moreover, the courts could have interpreted the commerce clause differently, as only empowering Congress to prevent state actions limiting the rights of individuals to engage in commerce.

Ultimately, government regulation of commerce for purposes of the national (aggregate) economic welfare is best explained, at least in part, if we see these as having been provided with intellectual and moral legitimacy by certain prominent philosophical ideas. Developments in modern philosophy have been favorable to several views: that there are no moral and political absolutes; that the knowable consists of what is composed of material substance (that is, capable of measurement); and that what is right and good is a matter of widespread preference on the part of members of the community. The last-named view has become evident in our time from the extensive advocacy of exposing many substantive political issues to democratic choice. One suspects that if the doctrine of the right to free speech did not have the popular press backing it so fervently—in other words, if it did not enjoy a very vocal lobby in the media—it too could easily be deemed subject to democratic rule. It appears that from a constitutional republic the culture has slowly but surely moved in the direction of social democracy. And the philosophical groundwork for this development is evident enough.

The social democratic view is well expressed in the philosophy of pragmatism.[114] This position is generally known to hold, in essence, that the truth of an idea or belief consists in its applicability; that is, if one can use an idea or belief and achieve satisfactory results, it is true or sound. It is perhaps a less well-known feature of the pragmatist tradition that the satisfaction must be widespread, ideally within the community of those concerned with the issues at stake, such as scientists in some field, or political thinkers. What is also true is that pragmatism rejects all absolutes—meaning all claims to the effect that there are certain true beliefs that are fundamental and serve as part of the foundations of our knowledge—as incapable of being defended and as impediments to the task of open-minded inquiry. It contends, among other things, that some ideas are at any given time acceptable within (that is found useful by) the (ideal or best or ultimate) community whose members concern themselves with the issues explored, for example, within the community of nuclear physicists. Ideally, the ideas are to be regarded true only if unanimous acceptance obtains, but in practice majority acceptance will suffice.

This view of knowledge and truth, in line with some of the most prominent currents of modern philosophy, is basically intersubjectivist. The pragmatist contribution was that individual subjectivity could be abandoned for a sort of democratic, social or collective intersubjectivity: if most of the relevant people agree on an idea, it should work well enough and is for practical purposes— the only ones that count—true.

In the hard sciences this view had little immediate influence, probably because among the members of the community of sciences certain methods of research and testing were adhered to anyway and agreement was usually not difficult to come by. But since ethics and politics involve everyone in a community, a kind of democratic determination of ethical and political truth is favored within the pragmatist philosophical outlook. And when the topic of determining truth is brought up by the few who are called upon to deal with the subject in an official capacity, such as members of the U.S. Supreme Court, the prevailing philosophical views have an influence even when the general culture may not accept them. For example, Justice Holmes was an explicit pragmatist who wrote critically of the doctrine of natural law, a clearly antipragmatic (foundationalist) philosophical viewpoint pertaining to the nature and standard of human law.[115]

Empiricism, in turn, has been very influential since at least the eighteenth century, when the British empiricist David Hume developed it most completely.[116] Empiricism in the theory of knowledge and materialism in metaphysics have been intellectually very respected, especially among those who considered a scientific approach to human affairs, including (and especially) politics, the most promising.[117] This view also offers anyone concerned with improving human life certain experimental techniques that would not be available if it were admitted that there can be knowledge of what is not directly sensible. (Modern behaviorist psychology is perhaps the most explicit application of the empiricist, materialist philosophy for purposes of understanding and controlling human affairs.)

Finally, utilitarianism construes the good to strive for as the greatest happiness of the greatest number.[118] Drawing, however, on the empiricist view of knowledge, utilitarianism regards happiness—what is of benefit to or the satisfaction of people—as a subjective matter: whatever people actually do or seek is ipso facto good for them. Thus in determining what will most benefit the greatest number, the democratic process has been regarded as an appropriate means of, in turn, determining what people desire (which is, by assumption, what will bring them happiness). On the other hand, since empiricism confines knowledge to that which is observable and measurable, when utilitarianism and empiricism are combined the result is an emphasis on material or economic well-being. At the aggregate level, determination of the greater happiness by the democratic method is supported by pragmatism, with its intersubjective theory of truth. So, while good is subjective or intersubjective, the utilitarian outlook is predisposed to stress material or economic goods that have been democratically selected.

Aside from the general intellectual respectability enjoyed by these positions in philosophy and related fields, other reasons have contributed to the collectivist utilitarian trends in national labor policy. For one, quite a few people in the United States deny that political or civil rights, and their corollaries (such as freedom of contract) have actually prevailed. True or not, much talk persists calling into question the claim that the United States is the freest country, one in which individuals can aspire to and reach success. Many labor organizations are led by men and women who adhere to and promulgate this skepticism. While this skepticism has not affected belief in freedom of religion and the press—what with many people regarding such freedoms as worth the risk even when thoroughly abused—it has promoted the concept of government regulation of economic affairs.

Furthermore, it is also noteworthy that while John Locke's case for natural rights has lost its intellectual respectability, the defense of almost the same rights by John Stuart Mill and many of his followers in our time on utilitarian grounds does command considerable respect. Mill defended the right to freedom of thought and speech, but on grounds that their free flow would ultimately assist in the discovery of truth. For Mill, both the free flow of ideas made possible by protection of civil or political rights and the occasional state intervention in the commercial life of the community (in a situation of natural monopoly, for instance), promote general utility—the greatest happiness of the greatest number.[119] But the position's philosophical roots are no doubt older than Mill. The dualism implicit in stressing liberty with respect to intellectual matters versus liberty with respect to material matters has been with us since the time of ancient Greek philosophy—for example, in Plato's radical metaphysical separation of the world into the ideal and the actual. The former is thought to deserve great respect while the latter is taken to be but a flawed rendition of what can be found in the ideal realm.

With respect to human nature, dualistic theories have dominated Western philosophy. Human beings have been thought of as composites of two essentially different substances, one material and one nonmaterial (that is spiritual or intellectual)—body and mind, or body and soul. Man is distinguished from other animals by his mind (soul), which has thus often been considered the link between humanity and divinity. Thus, many religions have emphasized guarding the mind or spirit of man, to keep it pure and untainted—by, for example, the passions, arising from man's bodily, animalistic side.

In the political arena, this dualistic tradition has fostered two different trends. On the one hand, many authoritarian regimes impose censorship in educational, artistic, and religious matters, without an equal emphasis on economic controls or economic management. On the other hand, some systems jealously guard intellectual liberty but insist on the "rational organization of production and distribution." For various reasons—perhaps, most importantly, the "measurability" of material aspects of human life—utilitarianism has supported the latter trend.

No doubt many other factors have contributed to the developments in America's general political climate, including its national labor policy, than it has been possible to identify in this chapter. I have tried to sketch some of the intellectual or philosophical currents that seem to explain the trends recounted here. Some argue that philosophical influences are illusory; Marxists, for example, assert that what people think is caused by their economic situation. Some neoclassical economists regard only self-interested urges as making a difference in social change.

But I leave this issue untreated. My limited methodological claim here is that prominent ideas, which are intelligently and spiritedly advanced, tend to place limits on the morally and politically possible or likely. This simply means that if some philosophical outlook reigns, the arenas of moral and political disputation—including those in judicial and legislative chambers and the related scholarly literature—will gain guidance from it. It is for this reason that I take it as appropriate to attribute significance to the philosophical viewpoints discussed above.

The Taft-Hartley Act: A Continuing Trend

The Wagner Act is widely regarded as a turning point in the history of U.S. labor law. Its crucial passages, employing terms most directly linked to more general philosophical, political, and ethical ideas, have been discussed. In 1937, two years after the act's passage by Congress, the Supreme Court supported its constitutionality in five separate decisions.[120] The act was amended by Congress, however, in 1947 with title I of the Taft-Hartley Act.[121] With the latter act, and in general following the New Deal period and the Second World War, some scholars have claimed to detect a fundamental shift in national labor policy, in that the freedom—or power—secured for organized labor in the Wagner Act was curbed.[122] Yet, at the basic level of interest to us in the present study, no such shift can be detected. Before this is discussed, something needs to be said about the difference between benefiting workers and benefiting labor organizations.

It is often held that the well-being of workers can be measured by the achievement of goals pursued by those who speak for labor organizations within either the labor union movement or the political arena. Once this view is accepted we have an apparently clear measure of the success of workers in their effort to improve their lot; but if the equation between workers and organized labor does not pass scrutiny, that appearance can be correspondingly deceptive.

It is necessary, then, to ask about the measure of the progress of organized labor. Must it be the achievement of its avowed (perhaps ulterior) goals or purposes? Not necessarily, for the standard for success will have to be identified by reference to the nature of such an organization. Consider, for illustrative purposes, a physician. Does his wealth alone determine whether he is successful? Only in terms of the shallowest of standards. His (professional) success depends mainly on his medical proficiency, which is by no means incompatible with economic prosperity. Likewise, if labor organizations have as their proper purpose the achievement of other goals besides their members' economic welfare, mere improvement of the latter will not suffice to judge the organization's activities productive or successful. Thus, suppose that workers become better off by growing as human beings, advancing in their professional competence, improving as citizens of their country, or being good parents and examples to their children; and suppose that labor organizations achieve only the economic success but fail to help, and even hinder in, these other areas of betterment. One would have to recognize that these organizations did not advance the welfare of their members, even though they advanced their members' financial or economic status.

Another issue also has bearing on this question of progress or failure. Suppose the physician did in fact succeed as we have defined success, but in doing so engaged in immoral conduct—say, stole medicine in order to save patients. We might consider such a person a good doctor, but a bad human being. Now suppose that a labor organization benefitted its membership in the proper respects, whatever that may involve, by using force to undermine the well-being of others—for example, forcing nonmembers out of jobs or bankrupting businesses by coercive measures such as assault, extortion, or violation of contract. Surely the benefits reaped for the members of the organization would not suffice to make the organization a success, since any human institution is accountable for how it achieves even its proper purpose.

The general point is that, even though the Taft-Hartley Act and later measures limited union activities in certain respects, it is not necessarily the case that they thereby "retarded labor's progress." Of more interest in the present context, however, is the rationale underlying Taft-Hartley, as compared to that behind the Wagner Act.

Subsequent to the Wagner Act's passage and its blessing by the Supreme Court, it became evident that its provisions did not succeed in averting strikes, one of its primary purposes (4,700 strikes occurred in 1946 alone). In 1947 the Taft-Hartley Act was passed by Congress over a presidential veto. This act included numerous provisions that were supported by critics of the Wagner Act and opposed by organized labor. It was intended to prevent certain labor union abuses of power left open by the Wagner Act and the Act's implications. Yet the arguments invoked in its support were essentially unchanged. By the time Taft-Hartley was put forth as a part of national labor policy, the philosophical presuppositions of that policy were well entrenched. It remained only to work out details regarding the bargaining power of employers and the opportunity of state legislatures to govern labor matters. Yet even these details were proposed (and accepted) on the very same grounds on which the Wagner Act had been found acceptable. Both proponents and opponents of what has been thought of as organized labor's strength made use of the same philosophy to accomplish their specific goals.

Put more generally, the power of the federal government to regiment labor matters throughout the United States had by this time become fully accepted as legitimate, and the union powers relinquished or limited by Taft-Hartley were relinquished or limited only because that seemed to be required for purposes of accomplishing the goal that guided government policy. Considerations of the collective welfare governed national policy, even with respect to which powers the states should be allowed to exercise and what strength employers might possess in dealing with labor organizations. No consideration pertaining to the rights of employers and employees based on other than utilitarian concerns entered the discussion and wording of the Taft-Hartley Act. In short, no fundamental philosophical change in perspective occurred between Wagner and Taft-Hartley.

The evidence for this is not difficult to detect. Title I of the Taft-Hartley Act adds to the Wagner text the following passage:

> Experience has further demonstrated that certain practices by some labor organizations, their officers, and members have the intent or the necessary effect of burdening or obstructing commerce through strikes and other forms of industrial unrest or through concerted activities which impair the interest of the public in the free flow of such commerce.[123]

Although the concrete results of the provisions that were to be adopted and implemented via Taft-Hartley to help remedy the situation described in this passage would differ from those of the Wagner Act, the reasoning invoked had not changed at all. Indeed, the addition of the phrase "the interest of the public in the free flow of...commerce" makes the collectivist utilitarian implications of the underlying argument even more explicit than they had been in the Wagner Act. In the latter, the concept of the public interest is only implicit. We can infer it without difficulty by reference to the legal power that is being exercised via the Wagner Act, namely, the police power of the federal legislature implicit in the commerce clause. This is just how the Wagner Act was justified by the Supreme Court in, for example, *NLRB v. Jones Laughlin Steel Corp.* The Court, in justifying its support of the Wagner Act's relevant provisions, referred to how "industrial strife would have a most serious effect upon interstate commerce."[124] It supported the Wagner Act's definition of "affecting commerce" and argued that the steel industry demonstrates "the close and intimate relation which a manufacturing industry may have to interstate commerce."[125] It upheld "the right of employees to self-organization and to select representatives of their own choosing for collective bargaining or other mutual protection," as well as the authority of Congress to safeguard this right, making "appropriate collective action of employees an instrument of peace rather than strife."[126] The Taft-Hartley Act makes explicit the link between "the free flow of commerce" and the public interest (or general welfare).

We could pursue this line of inquiry further, but in all subsequent legislation and in the bulk of the Supreme Court decisions we would find the same pattern of argumentation. However different the actual consequences of particular amendments or decisions (as well as further major pieces of legislation, NLRB rulings, and so forth), the central philosophical theme has been, and remains at this time, the same. Congress, via its various regulatory agencies, and the executive branch, via its various departments, should govern so as to pursue the goal of the public interest. And in labor matters, as a part of business activities, the determination of the public interest has been the representative democratic method. As indicated earlier, some decisions by the Supreme Court make reference to strict limitation on the democratic process: "One's... fundamental rights may not be submitted to vote; they depend on the outcome of no elections." However, such a view appears not to have been extended to commercial, and therefore not to labor, activities. As Justice Holmes argued in an influential dissenting opinion, "the legislature may forbid or restrict any business when it has a sufficient force of public opinion behind it."[127] So the public interest could be, and was, conceived within relatively definite limits, concerning some matters, and the observation of these limits was regarded as crucial.

Indeed, government is often urged to use its powers for purposes of observing such limits, for instance, via separation of powers. But in cases pertaining to commerce, the legislature itself is now virtually unlimited in its power to follow public opinion, whatever its content. This, in turn, means that the opinions thought—or persuasively said—to reflect most accurately the viewpoint of the majority should govern national labor policy. That is a form of collectivism—the goals, purposes, and methods (active) of the majority are politically prior to those of the individuals who constitute the membership of the community.

Although many more of the details and specifics that make up the general tendency identified above could be introduced, enough has been covered to indicate the broad trends in national labor policy.[128] There are cases indicating that different conceptions of the function of government have not been abandoned completely. Others show that additional philosophical assumptions support the tendencies we have detected. Some of these matters will emerge as the collectivist utilitarian point of view is examined and contrasted with one that is generally thought to be unique to the U.S. political tradition, namely political individualism.

In the most important federal measures that have formed national labor policy—most notably, the Wagner Act and the Taft-Hartley Act—the trends established earlier (as we have noted throughout this chapter) did not really change a great deal. Although in comparative terms one might argue that labor organizations were treated somewhat differently from business combinations, it is not possible from our study to draw this conclusion. Generally, labor organizations wanted support from government, and government gave it by becoming the manager of labor through the National Labor Relations Board. (In some respects this is paralleled by business organizations, but we have not examined this in detail.) Some decisions made by the board were not and are not fully welcomed by labor organizations, but its general intervention clearly was encouraged.

The main conclusion is that national labor policy has firmly crystallized into a collectivist framework, with a utilitarian approach. Considerations of the quasi-democratically determined welfare of the whole nation have been used as the grounds for forging a national labor policy and have dictated its shape. The specific directions or details of current national labor policy cannot, however, be gleaned from this realization, not even to a degree that the principle of the rule of law would ordinarily permit. Utilitarianism allows for virtually any turn of events, depending on the expressed wishes of those who participate, with more or less effectiveness, in the quasi-democratic process. Recent data have indicated a decline in the percentage of unionized workers, for example, while at the same time the actual power of unions appears to be increasing. For instance, firms, as well as numerous pubic professions, including teaching, police, and social work that have not been unionized before are now becoming subject to collective bargaining.[129] (Sometimes this is itself understandable in terms of the various provisions of national labor policy. e.g., that only a fraction of the employees in some firm are necessary in order to bring about unionization.)

Still, nothing can be predicted about the continuation of this or any other trend, since national labor policy can yield to different sentiments about unionization different from those that have prevailed in the past. There is no definite legal constraint on the progress or regress of labor, should popular sentiment change. The law itself is entirely ambiguous, providing mostly for the exercise of almost unlimited power, but with little guidance. In this respect, the most feared aspects of unlimited democracy now prevail.[130]

The philosophical underpinnings of the position that has served to justify these developments may be compared with those of the uniquely U.S. political tradition, identified as individualism (but in politics characterized as a form of constitutional republicanism based on natural rights). This is the subject of the next chapter.[131] Although never consistently implemented in the United States (or elsewhere), this viewpoint implies numerous related ideas about human nature, society, and values, many of which conflict with the collectivist utilitarianism that is characteristic of national labor policy, as well as of many other legislative and judicial developments in the United States.

Notes

1. National labor policy was not always what is has come to be in the last fifty or so years. See, for example, H. Farnam, *Chapters in the History of Social Legislation in the United States to 1860* (New York: Carnegie Institute, 1938). Farnam (p. 264) points out that during the early days of the labor movement in Massachusetts, various committees of the Massachusetts House refused to recommend action" on "proposal[s] of a ten-hour day." He offers the following explanation for the action:

   The opponents of reform took the ground, the general, that the effect of the ten-hour law in Massachusetts would "be to close the gate of every mill in the state." They also asserted that an inevitable effect would be a material reduction in wages. Both House and Senate fell back upon the laissez-faire doctrine. They admitted that abuse existed, but the committee felt that the remedy was not with them. They "look for it in the progressive movement in art and science, in a less love for money, and a more ardent love for social happiness and intellectual superiority." (quoting C. Persons et al., *Labor Laws and Their Enforcement* [New York: Arno, (1911), 1971], p. 49.)

Farnam (certainly a prominent recorder of social development, including the labor movement, in the United States) was fully aware of the general philosophical background that influenced certain legislative attitudes and actions with respect to the U.S. labor force during the early part of the nineteenth century. Others, therefore, have considered sets of values, general systems of ideas, as the possible source of labor policy at earlier times.

2. In this work I also accept the possibility of objective truth in ethical, political, or social philosophy, that is, the possibility of statements, judgments, or theories that correctly express what human beings should or should not do in their personal, legal, or social conduct and relations. This highly controversial position cannot be justified here, but it is important to note that the same view is evident in the various pieces of legislation concerning labor. For example, the Wagner Act, 29 U.S.C. 151 (1935), perhaps the most important national labor legislation to date, makes it plain that it is a valid function of legislation to "[safeguard] commerce from injury, impairment, or interruption, and to [promote] the flow of commerce by removing certain recognized sources of industrial strife and unrest." Moreover, in the body of literature advocating various reforms, the issue whether it is proper to pursue one or another goal is treated as capable of resolution.

3. The report of this case was taken in shorthand by Thomas Lloyd of Philadelphia and later printed by B. Graves. It is most readily accessible in J. Commons and E. Gilmore, *A Documentary History of American Industrial Society* (New York: Clark, 1910), p. 59.

4. Nicholas S. Falcone, *Labor Law* (New York: Wiley, 1962), p. 32, n. 1.

5. *Ibid.*, p. 32.

6. *Ibid.*, p. 35.

7. *Ibid.*, p. 34.

8. *People of New York v. James Melvin, et al.*, in Jacob D. Wheeler, *Reports of Criminal Law Cases* (New York: Gould and Banks, 1824), pp. 262–2828. Cited in *ibid.*, p. 38.

9. *Ibid.*, p. 38.

10. *Commonwealth v. Pullis*, reprinted in Falcone, *Labor Law*, p. 33.

11. *Ibid.*, p. 34.

12. *Ibid.*, p. 36.

13. *Ibid.*, p. 37.

14. 45 Mass. 111 (1842).

15. Reprinted in Falcone, *Labor Law*, p. 40.

16. *Ibid.*, p. 41.

17. *Ibid.*

18. *Ibid.*, p. 42.

19. *Ibid.*, p. 39.

20. *Ibid.*, p. 42.

21. *Ibid.*

22. *Ibid.*, p. 32.

23. *Ibid.*, p. 45.

24. *Ibid.*, p. 42.

25. *Ibid.*

26. *Ibid.*, p. 41.

27. *Ibid.*, p. 42.

28. *Ibid.*

29. While many believe that the era of laissez-faire lasted until the 1930s, there never has been such an era in any consistent sense of the term—see J. Hughes, *The Governmental Habit: Economic Controls from Colonial Times to the Present* (New York: Basic Books, 1977)—although at one time support for it was widespread. By 1867, Charles Astor Bristed could write, in *The Interference Theory of Government* (1987): "Many intelligent men have lately noticed—indeed scarcely any intelligent man can have failed to notice—a great recent change in the popular conception of a free government's duties and functions" (p. 7).

30. J. Commons and J. Andrews, *Principles of Labor Legislation* (New York: Harper and Brothers, 1916).

31. See Roy A. Childs, "Big Business and the Rise of American Statism", in *The Libertarian Alternative*, ed. Tibor R. Machan, (Chicago: Nelson-Hall, 1974), p. 208; Brozen, "Is the Government the Source of Monopoly?" in the same volume, p. 149.

32. C. Swayzee, *Contempt of Court in Labor Injunction Cases* (New York: Columbia University Press, 1935). It is arguable, however, that the central point of injunctions in labor law relates closely to the fact that labor unions lacked clear legal status—in contrast to, say, partnerships or corporations. Thus it was not a simple matter to cope with any legal wrongdoing that they might engage in. Injunction, while it has the smell of prior restraint, might have had to be resorted to in some cases where without it no further legal remedy would have been possible. Injunctions, of course, still ought to conform at least to the principle of responding only to a clear and present danger to innocent parties of violation of the rights. (I thank Howard Dickman for his discussion of these matters with me as I was preparing the present volume.) That injunctions had been used with such intent is also evident from the fact that few if any were ever contested. See Sylvester Petro, "Unions and the Southern Courts: Part 3—the Conspiracy and Tort Foundations of the Labor Injunction," *North Carolina Law Review* 60 (1982): 544ff.

33. See, for example, my book *Human Rights and Human Liberties* (Chicago: Nelson-Hall, 1975); John Finnis, *Natural Law and Natural Rights* (London: Oxford University Press, 1980); Richard Tuck, *Natural Rights Theories* (Cambridge: Cambridge University Press, 1979). Not each of these gives support to the same or even any doctrine of natural rights. But see, Douglas B. Rasmussen and Douglas J. Den Uyl, *Liberty and Nature, An Aristotelian Defense of Liberal Order* (LaSalle, IL: Open Court, 1991) and Machan, *Individuals and Their Rights*.

34. Swayzee, *Contempt of Court*. I have been using "individual rights" here in a sense explained earlier in this work. For now let us recall that the concept of rights is not unambiguous. Here I am using it in the respect sometimes clarified as "freedom (or negative) rights" as opposed to "welfare (or positive) rights." See also, Tibor R. Machan, "Wronging Rights," *Policy Review* no. 17 (1981), pp. 37–58. For a detailed discussion of the problems with the welfare rights thesis, see Machan, *Individuals and Their Rights*.

35. Commons and Andrews, *Principles*; G. Miller, *American Labor and the Government* (Englewood Cliffs, NJ: Prentice-Hall, 1948).

36. It is important to note here that individualism and laissez-faire are not the same. Individualism as a political position is a normative theory about what is most important in community life. Laissez-faire refers to a government policy of noninterference in people's commercial or economic endeavors. Since individual-

ism holds that governments should not interfere with any peaceable individual actions, it implies, but is broader than, the policy identified as laissez-faire. Moreover, laissez-faire can be supported on nonindividualist grounds; that is, it is held to be appropriate, not because individuals have certain rights, but because it is economically efficient, meaning that it is the social arrangement by which to maximize economic well-being. See more on this in the following chapter.

37. 198 U.S. 45 (1905).

38. Falcone, *Labor Law*, p. 21.

39. [1892] A.C. 25.

40. [1895] 2 Q.B. 21, revd, [1898] A.C. 1.

41. Both Falcone, *Labor Law*, and C. Gregory, *Labor and the Law*, 3rd ed., (New York: Norton, 1979), suggest this. Judging by the cases usually cited to illustrate early trends, there is nothing controversial about this claim.

42. 96 Mass. 499 (1867).

43. 106 Mass. 1 (1870).

44. Gregory, *Labor and the Law*, p. 61 (quoting O. W. Holmes, dissenting in *Carew v. Rutherford*). Holmes even relied on a view that may fairly be characterized as historical determinism, namely, "that the organization of the world, now going on so fast, means an ever increasing might and scope of combination. It seems to me futile to set our faces against this tendency." (Ibid. p. 62). While in common or unreflective contexts to offer this remark may not commit one to the broader outlook of which it is a fragment, in a carefully constructed legal dissent one must regard it seriously—even if, in fact, it was not carefully thought out. This is especially true of Justice Holmes's opinions, since his influence on the law extended far beyond the borders of Massachusetts.

45. Commons and Andrews, *Principles*; Farnam, *Social Legislation*; Arthur Ekirch, Jr., *Progressivism in America* (Boston: New Viewpoints, 1974); Ernest Freund, *Standards of American Legislation* (Chicago: University of Chicago Press, [1917], 1965). These works record the ideas, and the resulting social and political movements and eventual legislation, that have shaped these developments (although I do not contend that only ideas influence social and political developments).

46. R. Mott, *Due Process of Law* (New York: Da Capo, [1926], 1973).

47. See, for example, J. Pennock and J. Chapman eds., *Due Process* (New York: New York University Press, 1977); William Letwin, "Economic Due Process in the American Constitution and the Rule of Law," in *Liberty and the Rule of Law: Essays in Honor of F. A. Hayek*, ed. Robert L. Cunningham, (College Station, TX: Texas A and M University Press, 1979), pp. 22ff.

48. Shirley Robin Letwin, "Modern Philosophies of Law," in *The Great Ideas Today*, ed. R. Hutchins and M. Adler, (Chicago: Encyclopedia Britannica, 1972), p. 104. The point here is fundamental and extremely important. The concept *due process* means those procedures that are warranted in the relationship between governments and their citizens, hence "due" process. If they are conventional, then they are changeable either by legislation or by other means used in some community for purposes of establishing standards of justice. If they are derivable from the nature of man and community life, they are not subject to legislative or related alteration.

49. Shirley Letwin, "Modern Philosophies...," p. 104.

50. 198 U.S. 45 (1905)

51. William Letwin, "Economic Due Process," p. 56.

52. 198 U.S. at 75 (Holmes, J., dissenting).

53. William Letwin, "Economic Due Process," pp. 53–54.

54. 198 U.S. at 76 (Holmes, J., dissenting).

55. William Letwin, "Economic Due Process," p. 55.

56. 198 U.S. at 76 (Holmes, J., dissenting).

57. Thus, contrary to Harry N. Scheiber, "The Road to Munn," in *Perspectives in American History*, ed. D. Fleming and D. Bailyn, (Cambridge, MA: Charles Warren Center for Studies in American History, 1971), p. 329, not even Justice Field, whom Scheiber calls the "paragon of judicial activism on behalf of laissez-faire doctrine" (p. 348), and the "champion of inviolable private property rights" (p. 349), denied all regulatory powers to the government. Rather, Field held in "The Slaughterhouse Cases," 83 U.S. (16 Wall.) 36, 87 (1873) that the police power "undoubtedly extends to all regulations affecting the health, good order, morals, peace, and safety of society, and is exercised on a great variety of subjects, and in almost numberless ways."

58. *Lochner v. New York*, 198 U.S., p. 76 (Holmes, J., dissenting). Holmes was not advancing complex philosophical theses, of course, so it is not appropriate to hold him responsible for the resolution of these difficulties. Reportedly, Holmes was close to the pragmatist philosophers, including, mostly, C. S. Peirce. See Miller, "Holmes, Peirce, and Legal Pragmatism," *Yale Law Journal* 84 (1975): 1123; and G. Gilmore, *The Ages of American Law* (New Haven, CT: Yale University Press, 1977). It is interesting that in our own day it is the dominant pragmatic trend in philosophy that rejects the doctrine of natural law and natural rights. See, for example, Richard Rorty, *Objectivity, Relativism, and Truth* (Cambridge, UK: Cambridge University Press, 1991), pp. 31ff.

59. *Lochner v. New York*, 198 U.S., p. 76 (Holmes, J., dissenting).

60. Tyson and Brother V. Banton, 273 U.S., pp. 418, 446 (1927). (Holmes, J., dissenting.)

61. Adam Smith, *The Wealth of Nations* (New York: Nelson, [1776], 1854). See also A. Hirschman, *The Passions and the Interests* (Princeton, NJ: Princeton University Press, 1977). Tibor R. Machan, *Capitalism and Individualism* (New York: St. Martin's Press, 1990).

62. For development of what I have called the classical individualist or egoist ethics, see David L. Norton, *Personal Destinies: A Philosophy of Ethical Individualism* (Princeton, NJ: Princeton University Press, 1976); Ayn Rand, *The Virtue of Selfishness, A New Concept of Egoism* (New York: New American Library, 1964). For a discussion of the contrast, see Machan, *Capitalism and Individualism*.

63. See W. F. Hardie, "The Final Good in Aristotle's Ethics," *Philosophy* 40 (1965): 277–295; Jack R. Wheeler, *Ethical Egoism in Hellenic Thought* (Ph.D. diss., University of Southern California, 1976). For some modern examples, see works by Jesse Kalin, Eric Mack, and Tibor R. Machan.

64. Hirschman, *Passions*; Leo Strauss, *Natural Right and History*, 2nd ed., (Chicago: University of Chicago Press, 1970).

65. See Tibor R. Machan, "On Reclaiming America's Unique Political Tradition," in *The Libertarian Alternative*, pp. 495–502. The Lockean influence is discussed in Charles Becker, *The Declaration of Independence: A Study in the History of Political Ideas* (New York: Harcourt Brace, 1922); D. Raphael, ed., *Political Theory and the Rights of Man* (Bloomington, IN: Indiana University Press, 1967). But see Wilmore Kendall, *John Locke and the Doctrine of Majority Rule* (Chi-

cago: University of Illinois Press, 1965). Kendall argues that Locke was more of a democrat than an individualist. My own reading of Locke does not confirm Kendall's interpretation.

66. See Edwin Corwin, *Liberty against Government* (Baton Rouge, LA: Louisiana State University Press, 1948). My next chapter will further illustrate this point.

67. National Labor Relations Act, ch. 372, 49 Stat. 449 (1935) current version at 29 U.S.C. 151 et seq. (1980). See *Schecter Poultry Corp. v. United States*, 295 U.S. 495 (1935).

68. Act of June 27, 1884, ch. 127, 23 Stat. p. 60.

69. Act of Feb 14, 1903, Pub. L. pp. 62–426, 1, 8, 37 Stat. p. 736.

70. D. Lescohier, *The Labor Market* (New York: Arno, 1919).

71. Commons and Andrews, *Principles*, p. 6.

72. Lescohier, *The Labor Market*, p. 107. Let us note here that failure to marry, to attend religious service, to abstain from sexual indulgence, etc., have been said to produce a similar litany of consequences. Yet these sorts of human activities have not generally been thought to fall within the scope of proper governmental actions, despite interpretations of the police power of the state as the power "to promote the health, peace, moral, education, and good order of the people...." J. Field, in *Barbier v. Connolly*, 113 U.S. 27, 31 (1885). The numerous problems people face in their lives within a community are not always thought to be remediable by political means. Indeed, a prominent interpretation of Plato's Republic has it that Socrates and Plato both tried to teach us that genuine human happiness is not attainable by political means. (See works by Leo Strauss and his students for more on this.)

73. Commons and Andrews, *Principles*, pp. 7–12. See also H. Millis and R. Montgomery, *Labor's Progress and Some Basic Labor Problems* (New York: McGraw-Hill, 1938) for the details of the statistics cited throughout the period in support of various types of labor legislation.

74. Freund, *Standards*, p. 38.

75. For instance, "The Slaughterhouse Cases," p. 36; *Barbier v. Connolly*, 113 U.S. p. 27 (1885); *Thurlow v. Mass. License Cases*, 46 U.S. (5 How.) p. 504 (1847); *Henderson v. Mayor of New York*, 92 U.S. p. 259 (1873). See also Robert E. Cushman, "National Police Power Under the Commerce, Taxing, and Postal Clauses of the Constitution (pts. 1–4)," *Minnesota Law Review* 3/4 (1919, 1920): 289, 381, 402, and 452. See, finally, Ernst Freund, *The Police Power: Public Policy and Constitutional Rights* (New York: Arno, 1904).

76. Commons and Andrews, *Principles*, pp. 513–144.

77. 113 U.S. 27 (1885).

78. *Ibid.*, p. 31.

79. *Thurlow v. Mass. License Cases*, 46 U.S. (5 How.) pp. 504, 583 (1847).

80. Cushman, "National Police Power...", p. 81. The establishment of legal authority means only that some edict or principle has been officially accepted (that is, by those widely enough recognized) to be the government of a given community. Different legal theories will differ on whether legal authority alone legitimizes, or establishes as binding, a government or a system of law or a particular law. Among the various schools of thought relating to this issue are (the several versions of) the historicist, positivist, realist, libertarian, socialist, communist, elitist, and democratic theories of human community life—not all mutually exclusive, of course.

81. U.S. Constitution, Article I, Section 8, paragraph 3.
82. See, for more, Walter Dodd, *Cases and Materials on Constitutional Law*, 5th ed., (St. Paul, MN: West Publishing Co., 1954), pp. 389–437, 671–695 . In *Munn v. Illinois*, 94 U.S. 113 (1877), Chief Justice Waite attributed clarification of the idea to Lord Chief Justice Hale.
83. For a clear development of the Lockean view as it applies to labor matters, see Thomas Haggard, "The Right to Work—A Constitutional and Natural Law Perspective," *Journal of Social and Political Affairs* 1 (1976): 215–242.
84. Quoted in "Behind the 'Human Rights' Hullabaloo," *New Times* (Moscow), (February 1977): 7.
85. *Ibid.*, p. 5. In contrast, consider the points raised by Andrei Sinyavsky, a Russian intellectual who left the Soviet Union in 1973: "'Human rights' do not exist in the Soviet Union.... You see, our men and women ('the people') have entrusted their rights to the state, and the state decides what is useful to them and what is harmful to them. The state knows best." *Times* (London), quoted in *Wall Street Journal* (July 26, 1977): 20.
86. See John Harris, "The Marxist Conception of Violence," *Philosophy and Public Affairs* 3 (1974): 192. But see also Eric Mack, "Causing and Failing to Prevent," *Southwestern Journal of Philosophy* 7 (1976): 83; and Eric Mack, "Bad Samaritarianism and the Causation of Harm," *Philosophy and Public Affairs* 9 (Summer 1980): 230–259. If, as Marx wrote, "the human essence is the true collectivity of man," then "not helping" will cause harm. Individualist conceptions of human beings tend, in contrast, to see causing harm only where the harm is actually inflicted by some action of one person that leaves the other person injured (unless a previous compact to provide help has been violated). Yet, of course, there may be the obligation to help when help is needed, for instance, as a matter of generosity or charity—not, however, as respecting a right.

    It should be noted here that certain "antiunion" arguments employ the same interpretation of "prevention,"—as, for example, when it is maintained that workers who withhold their work thereby violate the employer's rights, that is, "prevent" him from exercising his liberty to produce and sell goods or services.
87. The economic discussion of this issue has a long history, and this discussion will not examine the merits of the numerous contributions. One early discussion of bargaining power that supporters of labor unions have generally approved is in T. Dunning, *Trade Unions and Strikes* (1859), while another, which was critical of labor unionism, can be found in S. Jevons, *The State in Relation to Labor* (1882). It may help here to note that opponents on this issue tended to approach it from drastically different perspectives. Most prounionists have argued their case within a value-laden framework—one that admits social goals a community should pursue—while their opponents have held a value-free economic position as, for example, W. Hutt, *The Theory of Collective Bargaining, 1930–1975* (New Rochelle, NY: Arlington House, 1975). A difficulty with such a treatment of the issue is that critics of the concept of bargaining power tend to assume a perfect laissez-faire model of commerce. If one accepts this model as sound (indeed, perhaps even as the most desirable), issues of bargaining power will not emerge, since in terms of "what the market will bear," talk of bargaining power makes no sense. Adherents to the idea, however, either are critical of the assumption of perfect competition or are opposed to the implications of such a model, charging it with injustice. The remedy they then envision—to compensate for market im-

perfections or its moral shortcomings—is governmental action. It should also be noted that government intervention in support of various enterprises (such as the rail industry), in support of certain social goals (such as transcontinental transportation), began almost at the same time as organized labor became active. See Hughes, *Governmental Habit*; Childs, "big Business and the Rise...."

88. For the economic explanation of why trade is impossible when bargaining power is equal (as this is understood here), see E. Mason, *Economic Concentration and the Monopoly Problem* (Cambridge, MA: Harvard University Press, 1961).

89. John Spargo and G. Arner, *Elements of Socialism: A Textbook* (New York: Macmillan, 1912), pp. 9-10. For a more recent development of this idea, approaching the issue from what is called the "analytic Marxist" perspective, see G. A. Cohen, "Are Disadvantaged Workers Who Take Hazardous Jobs Forced to Take Hazardous Jobs?" in *Moral Rights in the Workplace*, ed. Gertrude Ezorsky, (Albany, NY: State University of New York Press, 1987). Compare with Tibor R. Machan, "Human Rights, Workers' Rights, and the 'Right' to Occupational Safety," in the same volume, pp. 45-50. See also, James Chesher, "Employment Ethics," in *Commerce and Morality*, ed. Tibor R. Machan, (Totowa, NJ: Rowman and Littlefield, 1988). Cohen argues that since no one prevents workers from taking jobs (or makes them take one), they are free to do so. But since they cannot do anything else but take a job, they are forced to do so. Ergo, they are both free and forced. Of course, this again exemplifies the idea of causing harm to someone by not helping the person when he or she is in dire straights. Yet, first, nature itself places us into hardship; if it turns out that even if no moral wrong has ben done to someone, yet that person suffers from unsatisfied need, it is not necessarily the case that anyone is forcing him or her to have that experience. For more, see Mack, "Bad Samaritarianism...."

90. Herbert Spencer, *The Principles of Sociology* (Garden City, NY: Anchor Books, [1876-1896] 1969), p. 525. It should be noted that in his later years Spencer made numerous concessions to socialism, as did John Stuart Mill. Also, Spencer's support of laissez-faire did not derive from an individualism based on natural law but from the belief that evolutionary progress required such an economic arrangement for purposes of sustaining and improving the species—an improvement that involved, in part, greater and greater diversification and individuation.

91. For a discussion of various aspects of these points, see Robert Nozick, *Anarchy, State, and Utopia* (New York: Basic Books, 1974), pp. 253-265; William Hutt, *The Strike-Threat System: the Economic Consequences of Collective Bargaining* (New Rochelle, NY: Arlington House, 1973), pp. 3-32; G. Velasco, *Labor Legislation from an Economic Point of View* (Indianapolis, IN: Liberty Fund, 1973), pp. 4-11, 19-23; Howard Dickman, *Industrial Democracy in America* (LaSalle, IL: Open Court,1987). This last work is a detailed study of the topic discussed in this chapter and it substantially agrees with the analysis advanced herein.

92. H. B. Acton, *The Morals of Markets* (London: Longman, 1970), pp. 27-29, 60-63, contains an excellent discussion of these ideas. See also, Barry Gordon, *Economic Analysis before Adam Smith* (New York: Barnes and Noble Books, 1976).
    The idea of the just price was further developed by Aquinas and his followers, although what Aquinas believed may be close to the notion that the just price or just wage is most effectively approximated in a unregulated marketplace. If we factor into this analysis the Mises-Hayek thesis about the impossibility of rational allocation of resources without a free market in which prices, wages,

etc., are determined by means of individuals and firms reaching agreement on terms of trade, then the notion is that justice in the marketplace requires freedom of trade. Not that each instance of trade will necessarily be just. Morally misguided activities are evident enough in free markets; clearly, when men and women are free to act according to their own judgments, these judgments will not always be morally praiseworthy. Yet, when we compare the likelihood of morally just conduct becoming more pervasive in different settings, it seems clear that freedom can only enhance morality—without it morality is impossible. See Machan, *Individuals and Their Rights.*
93. Millis and Montgomery, *Labor's Progress*, p. 278.
94. Senate Committee on Education and Labor, *Hearings on S. 1958*, Seventy-fourth Congress, First session (1935), p. 34, quoting from the U.S. President's Research Committee on Social Trends, *Recent Social Trends in the United States* (1933).
95. Senate Committee on Education and Labor, Hearings on S. 1958, p. 34.
96. National Labor Relations Act (1980), p. 1.
97. *Ibid.*, p. 8.
98. *Coppage v. State of Kansas*, 236 U.S. 1 (1914), p. 19.
99. The majority opinion in other cases has been along similar lines. In *Holden v. Hardy*, 169 U.S. 366 (1898), the Supreme Court said that "the fact that both parties are of full age and competent to contract does not necessarily deprive the state of the power to interfere...where the public health demands that one party to the contract shall be protected against himself" (p. 397). Note, however, that the Court supports its decision with the idea that in most labor disputes "the proprietors lay down the rules and the laborers are practically constrained to obey them" (p. 397). This is another way of asserting the thesis of unequal bargaining power. (More recently a similar argument has been advanced in support of decisions that void contracts on grounds of unconscionability. See Chapter 3, especially note 54, for a more detailed discussion of the unconscionability provision for invalidating contracts.) To underline further its belief in the powerlessness of workers, the Court in Holden observed that "in such cases [where "the laborers are practically constrained to obey"] self-interest is often an unsafe guide, and the legislature may properly interpose its authority" (p. 397). For criticism, see four works by R. Hale: "The Supreme Court and the Contract Clause: III (pts. 1-3)," *Harvard Law Review* 57 (1944): 512, 621, 852; "Bargaining, Duress, and Economic Liberty," *Columbia Law Review* 43 (1943): 603; "Economic Liberty and the State," *Political Science* 66 (1951), p. 400; *Freedom Through Law* (New York: Columbia University Press, 1952).
100. National Labor Relations Act, (1980), p. 8.
101. Ibid., p. 9.
102. *J. I. Case v. National Labor Relations Board*, 321 U.S. (1944), pp. 332, 338-339.
103. The sense of "absolute freedom of association" here is that no one (neither employees nor employers, for instance) may be prevented from entering into or dissolving voluntary associations, not that some must be spared certain consequences of such actions—as in the Wagner Act. See James E. Bond, "The National Labor Relations Act and the Forgotten First Amendment", *South Carolina Law Review* 28 (1977): 421-450, for the judicial history of the right, which gradually came to be regarded as implicit in the First Amendment.
104. The establishment clause is possibly an exception to this statement. For whether the establishment clause should be balanced in a manner similar to all other First

Amendment liberties, see Wendell R. Bird, "Freedom from Establishment and Unneutrality in Public School Instruction and Religious School Regulation," *Harvard Journal of Law and Public Policy* 2 (1979): 125, 132–138.

105. 249 U.S. (1919), p. 47.
106. This apparent digression on the meaning of "the right to free speech" is important because the idea of one's sphere of authority is crucial to any determination of whether specific rights have been upheld absolutely. Furthermore, as we have already noted in chapter 9, note 23, in recent years some feminists have been advocating banning publications, films, and other forms of communication that demean women. See Catherine A. MacKinnon, *Toward a Feminist Theory of the State* (Cambridge, MA: Harvard University Press, 1990). MacKinnon was instrumental in convincing the Supreme Court of Canada to refuse free speech protection to pornography on grounds of such reasoning.
107. Some notable classes of cases are those involving obscenity and commercial advertising. A word needs to be said here about the issue of whether the First Amendment, pertaining especially to speech, could reasonably be said to be absolute. First, would slander, libel, and defamation laws have to be repealed if we were to accept it as such? In one respect, yes; in another, no. The speaking of lies, falsehoods, and abuses could not be punished per se, nor, presumably, could their being written be punished. If one wrote a personal letter and slandered someone, this could not be punished. If one were to sell a slanderous book or article, some actions could be taken, especially if, at least by implication, the claims were to be sold as truth, as reports of fact. Action could be brought against the author or seller on grounds of fraud, for example. Of course, such action may not produce liability for damages to the party slandered and this is the bitter pill of taking the First Amendment in an absolute sense. The philosophical grounds one might raise in support of swallowing this bitter pill include: (1) no one is forced to action a libelous, slanderous, or defamatory claim; (2) everybody is free to publish criticisms of such claims; (3) upon reading something, the human mind is not necessarily compelled to accept it; and (4) no one owns the opinions others have of one (that is, one's reputation).

   Should these philosophical ideas be denied and it be argued that slander, libel, and defamation can be damaging, or in other words be the objective (necessary) causes of harm to others (without the intervening factor of other people's free will to believe or dismiss a claim), then one could argue that the First Amendment is not really compromised at all by prohibiting libel, slander, and defamation, since such acts of free speech are attacks on others. This would be analogous to rejecting a charge that laws against murder compromise the right to bear and use arms or that laws against trespassing compromise the right to travel. In short, the First Amendment could be held to be absolute, depending on what it actually means; and if it means either of the above, it could be taken absolutely. Its absolute status would, however, be compromised if freedom of speech were denied when someone expressed himself, within his sphere of authority, about commerce, politics, religion, race, unionism, or any other such matter.
108. NLRB rulings and court decisions on this subject are surveyed in Falcone, *Labor Law*, pp. 133–136, 272–275.
109. 249 U.S., p. 52. The Supreme Court has since amended the standard, via *Brandenburg v. Ohio*, 395 U.S. 444 (169), but the restriction of speech is still permitted.

110. See *Schenck v. United States*, 249 U.S. 47 (1919); L. Tribe, *American Constitutional Law* (Westburg, NY: Foundation Press, 1978), pp. 608-617. *Brandenburg v. Ohio*, 395 U.S. at 447 (1969), imposes even stricter limitations on regulating speech, namely, when speech is "directed to inciting or producing imminent lawless action and is likely to incite or produce such action." It is also notable that commercial speech has itself been excluded by some courts from First Amendment protection (see Chapter 8).

111. On the latter, see Bond, "The National Labor Relations Act...."

112. The case is recorded at 300 U.S. (1937), p. 379; see William Letwin,"Economic Due Process...," p. 28. In his *The Spirit of Liberty* (New York: Knopf, 1960), p. 206, Judge Learned Hand posed the question: "Just why property itself was not a 'personal right' nobody took the time to explain." I suggest, in the following chapter (11), what very likely accounts for the puzzle to which Judge Hand alluded.

    Consider, too, Chief Justice Taft's dissenting opinion in *Adkins v. Children's Hospital*, 261 U.S. (1923), p. 525, where he declared that "it is not the function of this Court to hold congressional acts invalid simply because they are passed to carry out economic views which the Court believes to be unwise or unsound." The implicit view is that political systems and economic systems are independent of each other. Of course, Marx, who was certainly influential in the development of intellectual trends around the turn of the century, had argued that the right to property is not universal but an outgrowth of certain transient economic circumstances—indeed, that the advocacy of this right was little more than an expression of the vested interest of the capitalist class. See David MacLellan ed., *Selected Writings of Karl Marx* (London: Oxford University Press, 1977), pp. 34-69. This view seems to have had some influence, while the further idea—also endorsed by Marx but not by other socialists and supporters of labor organization—that political civil rights have a more independent (perhaps universal) status continued to impress legal authorities and intellectuals.

113. Freund, *Standards*, p. 3.

114. Richard Rorty, *Objectivity, Relativism, and Truth* (Cambridge: Cambridge University Press, 1991). Rorty is only the latest among pragmatists who find the substitution of social solidarity for the idea of objectivity philosophically and politically very appealing. Of course, whether philosophers of pragmatism would all support such a development is not at all clear. See, Tibor R. Machan, "C. S. Peirce and Absolute Truth," *Transactions of the C. S. Peirce Society* 16 (1980): 153-161. For a general criticism of the relativist trends in contemporary philosophy, including philosophy of science, see Roger Trigg, *Reality at Risk* (New York: Barnes and Noble Books, 1980).

115. Lochner v. New York, 198 U.S., p. 76.

116. As is not uncommon, debates persist about just how much of an empiricist Hume had been. Some argue that his empiricism was merely a device to discredit a certain understanding of what knowledge must be. For a discussion of this see *Reason Papers* no. 15 (1990), "Essays to Commemorate the 250th Anniversary of the Completion of David Hume's *A Treatise of Human Nature*," edited by Stuart Warner. See, especially, the essays by Donald W. Livingston and Douglas B. Rasmussen, for contrasting positions on this issue.

117. See Eugene F. Miller, "Positivism, Historicism and Political Inquiry," *The American Political Science Review* 66 (1972): 796-817.

118. See Ellen Paul, *Moral Revolution and Economic Science* (Westport, CT: Greenwood Press, 1979); Gertrude Himmelfarb, *On Liberty and Liberalism: The Case of John Stuart Mill* (New York: Knopf, 1974).
119. John Stuart Mill, *On Liberty* (Indianapolis, IN: Bobbs-Merrill, [1861], 1957), p. 66; John Stuart Mill, *Principles of Political Economy* (New York: D. Appleton, 1865), pp. 189–190.
120. See Falcone, *Labor Law*, pp. 193–197. The most significant case was *NLRB v. Jones and Laughlin Steel Corp.*, 301 U.S. (1937), p. 1.
121. Act of June 23, 1947, Eightieth Congress, First session, ch. 120, p. 61; Stat. 136, 29 U.S.C. pp. 141–144, 171–188.
122. Falcone, *Labor Law*, pp. 247–248; C. Gregory, *Labor and the Law*, pp. 413–457.
123. 29 U.S.C. (Supp. III), p. 151.
124. 301 U.S. (1937), p. 41.
125. *Ibid.*, p. 33.
126. *Ibid.*, pp. 33, 34.
127. *Tyson and Brother v. Banton*, 273 U.S. 418 (1927); (Holmes, J., dissenting).
128. Numerous labor-related pieces of legislation and executive orders were introduced in the wake of the Depression and the Second World War; some of these were promoted as temporary measures only but have since become permanent government policy. For a history of national labor policy to the mid-1940s, see H. Metz, *Labor Policy of the Federal Government* (Washington, DC: Brookings Institution, 1945). Many of these government actions established precedents for further measures. Some major pieces of legislation came to be modified or mitigated by court decisions. Today we find that labor policy is still somewhat volatile, what with courts changing their interpretations, the NLRB altering its priorities, and Congress proposing and passing new labor-related bills. As we approach the present, it would be possible to enter into greater and greater detail, but that would not be wise for our purpose. In this discussion we are talking about the broad trend of national policy—its philosophical aura, as it were—and it is not relevant to enter into the details of NLRB rulings or the follies and foibles of particular pieces of legislation. Some people will not fail to criticize policy and law on the basis of obvious blunders and paradoxes—e.g., that the NLRB ruled that a worker who became drunk at an office party and injured himself in a fall must be paid worker's compensation. But theoretical discussions about the merits of competing systems of law cannot be resolved on the basis of sporadic oddities, paradoxes, and abuses.
     Of course, if many such paradoxes emerge, worries are justified, but in theories about human institutions one can almost always resort to the view that the problems are caused by people, their lack of character, their inattention, their biases, and so on. The fact that some governmental regulatory process does not work may be due to bad regulators, and it is the analysis of the blunders, in broad theoretical terms, that will show whether this or something even more basic—such as the complete breakdown of the system, or certain unsuitable features of it—account for the troubles being experienced.
129. For example, in the NLRB, administrative law judge Joel Harmatz ruled that despite the Amalgamated Clothing and Textile Workers Union's loss (404 to 540) in a vote at the J. P. Stevens Co. plant in Wallace, NC, the company must accept the union as the bargaining agent for the workers, on the basis of a majority having earlier consented to an election on the issue of unionization. The facts in

this case concerning the company's alleged violations of fair labor practices are complicated. Since Harmatz did not order another election, however, but instead relied on the workers' earlier willingness merely to test the union's bid for representation, it is entirely unclear that any democratic procedures are evident in these proceedings. Some will argue that this is a desirable feature of current national labor policy, inasmuch as there is no fixed policy at all and ample flexibility is permitted, something suitable to the fast pace of changes within our society and the arena of labor relations. (This had been argued by Bentham against Locke's natural rights theory, when the former held that such rights were "nonsense upon stilts" because they impeded progress.) See Jeremy Bentham, "Anarchical Fallacies," Part 2 of *The Works of Jeremy Bentham* (1843) in A. I. Melden, *Human Rights* (Belmont, CA: Wadsworth, 1970) p. 28-39.

130. See F. A. Hayek, "Miscarriage of the Democratic Ideal," *Encounter* 14 (March 1978): 50.

131. This position is developed in Harry V. Jaffa, chapter 5 of *How to Think About the American Revolution* (Durham, NC: Carolina Academic Press, 1978). The idea is that a constitution, with a well-defined bill of rights that is internally consistent and suitable (based on human nature), cannot, of course, be a guarantee against eventual basic alterations of the system, because human beings can change their minds and overcome all institutional obstacles to their new intentions (even if in the end this will not result in what they wish for). But a sound constitution can serve—as law itself, when rightly conceived, must serve—in the capacity of a guideline, by way of broadly understood public principles of conduct that define (not limit) human freedom of conduct with respect to members of the community, as well as those who have been selected to uphold its laws.

11

Philosophies of Public Policy in Conflict

The human essence is the true collectivity of man.

—Karl Marx

I wish now to summarize some of my earlier points and place them in a broader intellectual context. My main theme has been that individualism is essentially right—with some serious modifications, of course, in the *homo economicus* models of it. I have tried to suggest an alternative way of characterizing individualism and I will carry that project a bit farther. And I also wish to strengthen my case for the proposition that collective utilitarianism has guided much of U.S. politics and that this has been a mistake.

Throughout this work I have been exploring the proper scope of public policy and the significant departures from that scope in our actual political system. At this point I want to spell out the two political outlooks that have competed with each other during most of our history of public policy in the United States. I want to relate these two positions to the field of labor policy and here and there, to some other ways in which the government regulates the economy, although I do not doubt that it would be possible to show that many different areas of public policy have been influenced by them.

No doubt, in reality all sorts of forces—economic, religious, philosophical, climactic, psychological, and many more—are involved in the development of a society's way of handling its various problems. Still, the philosophical—or, rather, political philosophical—ideas involved will have a significant impact. As Mancur Olson has argued, even if one admits that much in relatively democratic societies depends upon the impact of the political lobbying of special interests such as business,

337

labor, and ideological groups, there are crucial phases during the system's evolution when ideas will have the most serious consequences.[1]

Essentially my argument is that the collectivist utilitarianism I referred to in the previous chapter has reigned as the dominant influence in U.S. history in forging economic public policy decisions and laws, despite the fact that the unique or distinctive features of the U.S. political tradition conflict with such developments. I want to elaborate on that point in the following passages by drawing on examples I have examined earlier, for example, labor regulation.

Scrutiny of the major pieces of legislation and court decisions pertaining to the economy in the recent past provides a relatively clear picture. U.S. government regulation has gained its philosophical support primarily from what can most appropriately be called collectivist utilitarianism. The main thesis of this position is that the proper actions, policies, and institutions are those that achieve the greatest happiness for the overall community, as reflected by the weighted preferences of the people (often assessed by means of the democratic method).

The difference between an individualist and collectivist utilitarianism might be worth noting here. The former would treat personal autonomy as a kind of intrinsic good or condition of reaching for human happiness, while the latter would treat the unity—not, necessarily their equality—of all humankind in nearly all respects as a kind of intrinsic good or condition for its realization. The difference is mainly ontological, concerned with just what kind of being a human being is, mainly a collective being, but with the qualification (as distinct from Marx) that this is one of innumerable equally important elements of human goodness. Collective utilitarianism does not hold collectivism as inherently dominant, but only equally valuable, politically, with other high values.

Utilitarianism can lean in several directions. Observe, for instance, how some defend animal liberation from a utilitarian position. The U.S. version of it leans both ways some of the time, but the aspects of it responsible for government regulation of the economy stem mostly from its collectivist utilitarian leanings.

The description "collective utilitarianism" is deliberately technical, rather than pejorative. The terms are chosen from among those available throughout the relevant historical period. Collectivism and utilitarianism are philosophical positions with long and distinguished histories, albeit with frequently modified varieties in both cases. Concrete results—policies, legislation, court decisions, and so on—might be justified by positions formulated more recently than in the period under consideration. The purpose of this chapter is to explicate the concept and effect of collective utilitarianism and of a quite different ideology—individualism, often and properly associated with the unique U.S. political tradition. The soundness of neither position is at issue here; the two ideas are discussed primarily for purposes of comparison.

Collectivist Utilitarianism

Utilitarianism is a normative theory of the nature of the good. It focuses on the consequences (rather than the inherent merits) of actions and, specifically, on the production of pleasure, happiness, or well-being. Although glimmers of utilitarianism can be found in Greek thought, it was first comprehensively developed in the eighteenth and nineteenth centuries by Jeremy Bentham and John Stuart Mill and has since developed many variations, of course. Broadly, as the contemporary philosopher J. J. C. Smart explains, utilitarianism is the view that the rightness or wrongness of an action depends on the total goodness or badness of its consequences. A hedonistic utilitarian will hold that the goodness or badness of a consequence depends only on its pleasantness or unpleasantness. An ideal utilitarian, such as G. E. Moore, will hold that the goodness or badness of a state of consciousness can depend on things other than its pleasantness.[2]

Strictly speaking, utilitarianism permits relevant consequences to include only those for the individual taking action. Historically, however, its idea of "total goodness or badness" has led to the inclusion of all the individuals—human and even animal—on whom the action will (or might) impinge.[3] Thus, utilitarianism as an ethical theory has been taken to involve the broad prescription: individuals should act so as to further the greatest happiness of the greatest number. As such, it is a collectivist ethic in that it gives priority to the (net) good or happiness of the relevant group (or collective), even if this can be easily identified to be in conflict with the good, happiness, well-being, or liberty of one or more individuals. What matters is not the consequences of an action for particular individuals (even the agent) but whether, when the resulting gain or loss of each person is aggregated, there is a net benefit.

Versions of utilitarianism are numerous. In some, the measurement of the happiness of the greatest number involves aggregating the degree of intensity of pleasure distributed throughout the community (hedonistic utilitarianism in its original, Benthamite form). Some, such as Peter Singer's, include lower animals in the count; most confine their count to human beings. Some leave the character and measure of benefits to subjective determination, so that an individual's desires or preferences take priority in the calculations, while others confine the count to measurable, material indications of well-being, ignoring subjective, psychological, spiritual, or intellectual factors. Some, such as the ideal utilitarianism of G. E. Moore, permit the meaning of "good" or "happy" to be determined by common intuitions, that is, by the widest considered opinion on the topic.

As described thus far, utilitarianism is an ethical theory, relevant in explaining and guiding how a person ought to live his life: namely, so as to bring the greatest benefit to the greatest number. However, utilitarianism is also a political theory, pertinent to the nature of a good community and the proper goals to be pursued by political institutions.

As a political theory, utilitarianism maintains that communities ought to be organized and governments ought to act so as to secure the greatest happiness of the greatest number, with the result that utilitarian ethics are legally enforced instead of being reserved to individual decision or choice. This "greatest number" applies to the society or political unit, although certain trends of thought in recent years have expanded the relevant community not only internationally but to all sentient beings. The same varieties of aggregate happiness mentioned above are found in political utilitarianism. Again, it is collectivist in that it gives priority to the good of the totality of the community—to the perceived net social benefit of actions and policies.[4]

It is this utilitarianism that is best identified with the philosophical position that underlies much of U.S. political philosophy today, including, as we saw, national labor policy and other areas of government regulation—such as the regulation of insider trading by the Securities and Exchange Commission. On the issue of the precise nature of the good that is to be widely distributed over the collective, the vagueness that has characterized the emergence of utilitarianism in philosophy has also been a feature of its application in developing advertising or health and safety regulation and in forging labor law. Since the doctrine leaves quite unspecified a method of determining the greatest happiness of the greatest number, politically active members of the community, claiming to represent the public interest or the common good, gain authoritative influence over public policy as reflected in legislation, federal and state government regulation, and court adjudication. In short, no objective standard (that is, one measurable by a commonly identifiable rule or principle) constrains the policy maker, legislator, or judge concerning the directions in which law should guide the conduct of members of society. This result is particularly ironic, since utilitarianism was initially forged in order to overcome skeptical implications for ethics and politics stemming from a prior and rationalist philosophical systems such as Thomism, Spinozism, and Cartesianism. The hedonism of Bentham was conceived as an empirically-based ethics, tying the concepts of good, bad, right, wrong, just, and unjust to the allegedly measurable phenomenon of pleasure. However, pleasure was not found to be measurable; thus substantial subjectivism had to be accepted within the hedonistic position. Moreover, advocates of utilitarianism were not satisfied with identifying goodness with pleasantness and badness with unpleasantness.[5]

Collectivism

At this point, it will be helpful to elaborate some of the crucial features and types of collectivism. The different types are not necessarily mutually exclusive or incompatible. Normative collectivism emphasizes the rightness of pursuing the overall good (however defined) of the relevant community. Other versions conceive of the good of the whole as an inevitable historical result (whether by evolution or revolution).[6] Some specify certain methods as the best means to determine the good of the whole—for example, consulting each member of the community, or elected representatives, or an elite, or experts in various fields. Others are more organic in their collectivism; viewing the state, society, or mankind as an organism, they identify the good of the whole by reference to an understanding of that organism.

Despite differences, however, all collectivists embrace the central idea that it is the totality whose good should or will be achieved. Utilitarian collectivists distinguish themselves by conceiving of the good in terms of consequences (the state of affairs to obtain as a result of action, versus, say, the intrinsic value of the action or the process of acting).

If utilitarianism however, is already collectivist in that it places priority on the greatest happiness of the greatest number in community, why attach "collectivist" to "utilitarian" in characterizing U.S. regulatory policy? One reason is to emphasize that, within this framework, the society or community itself is conceived to have goals and interests that are independent of the divergent myriad goals and interests of each of its individual members. A second and more important reason is to distinguish the apparent redundancy of the utilitarianism discussed thus far as it developed within philosophy from a somewhat different tradition in economics.

An acknowledged assumption within the discipline of economics is that each individual acts so as to maximize what he perceives to be his own well-being or utility, with "well-being" remaining undefined (as is "goodness" in the philosophical utilitarian tradition). This is not a normative position; it says nothing about what people should do but rather postulates what people as a matter of fact will do. It is often labeled "utilitarian," however, because, like normative utilitarianism, it focuses on the consequences of action—the total consequences (although for the agent only)—and, specifically, on the production of well-being. Moreover, economists have sometimes espoused individualism (or laissez-faire) as a parallel political position. In some instances individualism is considered compatible with the above assumption about human conduct: since people act so as to maximize their own well-being, the "natural" political arrangement is to leave people alone to do just that.

In other cases, it is supported on essentially collectivist grounds: when people pursue their own well-being they in fact further the overall, maximum well-being of the community; therefore, they should be left to do so.

A laissez-faire political arrangement, even when justified on the latter collectivist grounds, is not collectivist in outcome; pursuing the community's well-being at the expense of particular individuals' well-being is never an issue (either because it is unnatural or because it is unnecessary, by the above accounts). The phrase "collectivist utilitarian" is used in this study to distinguish the economic "utilitarianism" in which this individualist position is rooted from the utilitarianism previously outlined.

To reiterate, the previously noted trend in labor and other regulatory policy may be considered collectivist utilitarian because the arguments most often advanced to justify the measures introduced focus on the well-being of the entire community. To better understand this trend it will help to look at the related philosophical substance underlying this feature of U.S. politics and culture. Neither utilitarianism nor collectivism stands in a philosophical vacuum. Both doctrines rest on more basic arguments and theories, including some concerning human nature, reality, life, society, and human relations. Of course, such bases are found underlying any general normative perspective. As an example, suppose one holds that each person's moral duty is to act in this life so as to secure a good afterlife. This position relies on the premise, among others, that the soul (or some part of the individual) can survive apart from the body, after the body dies and decomposes. Adequate support of the normative thesis requires that this supporting thesis be true.

Normative Collectivism

What does the collectivism involved here assume? What needs to be true in order for this collectivism to be a potentially correct guide to personal and political actions?

First, it must be true that human beings individually are essentially part of a larger entity—humanity, society, the nation, the race, or the like. Collectivism holds that individuals must be defined at least partly by their relationship to the group. This requires far more than mere membership in or identification with some group, however. Ordinarily, individual members of groups are considered capable of existing as whole, entire beings apart from the larger entity to which they belong. A singer who joins a choir is still a singer outside the choir and, although outside, neither more nor less a singer. In collectivism, however, being part of the larger entity is not so conceived. Rather, any individual who is part of the relevant collective is what he or she is partly or wholly by virtue of belonging to the group. Specifically, collectivism requires that (some of) the functions or ends of human beings be identified within the group context.

The group context need not be identical in the various types of collectivism. Some take humanity to be an entity to which each person stands in an organic relationship, with each contributing to the sustenance or well-being of that entity and having no independent function or end. The model here visualized is the relationship between a living organism and its components.[7] Some maintain that ideally the collective is an entity to which each person should stand in a complex relationship such that human beings at their best (when functioning properly) support the well-being of the entity. The difference between these two is significant. In the former case individuals are linked inevitably to the group, independently of choice and conduct.[8] However, this discussion concerns the second type, which considers individuals morally responsible for achieving the collectivist ideal. This is the only form of collectivism in which some sense may be made of claims as to what actions, policies, and institutions (such as laws) should be taken and supported. This raises another assumption underlying collectivism.

In order for collectivism as an action-guiding system to be sound, it must also be true that individuals can act so as to pursue the good of the whole. The philosophical idea that "ought implies can" applies to all normative theories.[9] As we have seen, the violation of that principle invalidates any action-guiding system, moral or political.

So the normative collectivism here being discussed could not be a sound system if it were impossible for individuals ever to know what the good of the whole is or to act on this knowledge.[10] It must be possible, if collectivism is to be a plausible goal, to identify and act upon a standard of the collective welfare. In the case of labor law, for example, we have seen that the standard is to be provided by this form of utilitarianism, the ultimate goal being the greatest happiness of the greatest number within the specified community. Utilitarians have proposed various measures of this happiness.

In the U.S. political arena, parameters have included material well-being, individuals' (subjective) desires, and a combination of these. Individual desires are assumed to be given expression through the democratic process and the resulting laws and regulations. "Objective" factors, such as economic well-being, are gauged by testimony from experts and professionals through agency and congressional studies.

Impartial Utilitarianism

What assumptions underlie this form of utilitarianism? What would have to be true for this aspect of the trend in "public" policy to have a sound foundation? The answers here can become extremely complicated but a few points may be made to convey the general ideas that weigh most heavily.

First, the form of utilitarianism here considered assumes that the desires (or preference hierarchy) of each member of the relevant community are of equal significance. The equality of the value of the input within the quasi-democratic[11] calculus is a necessary presupposition of the view that by (community-wide) democratic processes we can come to know the greatest happiness of the greater number, at least where subjective factors are involved.[12] (Thus, for instance, if the majority of the relevant community regard some item as undesirable—for example, obscene—it shall not be allowed; but if the majority do not so regard it, it shall be allowed. Each individual is an equal part of the whole, permitted one equally weighted vote.)

Second, utilitarianism assumes that no individual's beliefs are better or worse than those of another person. Only in relation to the outcome—in this case, the well-being of the whole—might her actions or beliefs be evaluated as right or wrong. For this evaluation to be possible, at any given point of considering the good of the whole, everyone must be given equivalent determination capability. It is irrelevant that some wishes may arise because of, for instance, personal failure. Thus, if a business owner has mismanaged affairs for twenty years and is now bankrupt, his desires for such things as subsidies, tariffs, or legal restrictions on competitors are equal in weight to those of a business owner who has been, as we might ordinarily put it, conscientious, thrifty, prudent, and so forth. These judgments, which are introduced from ordinary discourse, make no sense in the utilitarian perspective, which focuses on the total outcome of actions, not on their quality or the agents' character. What matters is only that each person has spoken, since the good of the whole, the greatest happiness of the greatest number, is determined by computing the preferences or interests of the entire relevant population.[13]

Third, by the tenets of utilitarianism, as applied to the determination of collective public affairs, there can be no firm commitment to (binding) moral or political principles (such as natural rights and political or racial equality). Outside the goal of achieving the greatest good or happiness of the greatest number via collective public policy, there is only a commitment to methods thought to be required for this end. (This approach may, of course, coexist with elements of a system left from periods under different theoretical influence, for example, natural rights theory. Some of the concerns about equal distribution of welfare may be attributed to such influences, harking back to equal rights.) For example, a utilitarian approach can lead to such official practices as discrimination. That no one should prejudge others by reference to race is often advanced as a moral or political principle, but utilitarian theory sees it differently. By this theory, racial equality could emerge by the more or less democratic process as a desired state of affairs. But it is then a (collective) goal of public policy, not a principle binding individuals, morally, or governments, politically. Thus, the process of achieving the desired state of affairs—equality—could involve (would require, it is often argued) practices whereby individuals are treated unequally until that state is reached. An example of such practices is an affirmative action policy, which must be considered discriminatory in that individuals are treated on the basis of their membership in racial, sexual, or ethnic groups.[14] Utilitarianism is committed to achieving desired ends and not to principles that might, by other theories, be embodied in those ends.

I have now spelled out a reasonably complete characterization of collective utilitarianism. I am using this term here because "collective" indicates that welfare is to be identified by reference to equally weighted, quasi-democratically determined desires or preferences of those who make up the group, thus fitting the theory of utilitarianism. It is fair to say, I believe—and we have noted this in the context of national labor policy as well as some other features of what public policy is widely understood to involve—that this outlook guides much of the affairs of government in our time. These affairs lead government to regulate the economic activities of the nation, although there are other spheres of human community life that are guided by this outlook as well.

Individualism

At this point it will be useful to outline briefly the political philosophical outlook that is traditionally associated with the U.S. polity, namely, individualism. I am not claiming, of course, that this outlook fully expresses the U.S. political philosophical tradition.[15] But it does distinguish that tradition in the minds of most of those who find it to be notable, remarkable, and distinctive among history's various political systems.

Individualism, as I have been trying to make clear throughout, is the view that the proper or right actions, policies, and institutions in the political realm are those that aim to secure the political conditions suitable to the flourishing of individuals of the kind a human being is. By this view, the individual is the most important unit or entity in a politically organized unit, and government is an agent or organization established to serve (in very specific respects) each individual. Perhaps in some other context individualism might have to be suspended—military service, for instance, or the priesthood—but politically, as I have been arguing, it is superior to all live options.

America's Individualism

To see why the unique tradition of U.S. politics is individualist, consider this important passage from the Declaration of Independence:

> We hold these Truths to be self-evident, that all Men are created equal, that they are endowed by their Creator with certain unalienable Rights, that among these are Life, Liberty and the Pursuit of Happiness. That to secure these Rights, Governments are instituted among Men, deriving their just powers from the Consent of the Governed....[16]

A brief look at the issues raised here will help us identify the unique U.S. political tradition, as distinct from its actual legal and political history. In other words, I propose to treat the reasonably distinctive political theory from which the Founders and others drew for purposes of conceiving and establishing the U.S. political system independently of the implications of subsequent U.S. legal and political history.

Stated in the philosophical and political context of the Declaration, the phrase "all men are created equal" means that each individual is equal to others in the relevant, political respect: no one may justifiably be subjugated by any other(s); beyond childhood, no one's actions may be compelled by others through the use or the threat of force or fraud. The thesis is not that people are, or ought to be made, equal in their physical or intellectual characteristics and abilities or in the results of having and applying them, or even in their material opportunities. Nor is the idea that, given political liberty, individuals will do equally well in controlling their own lives. Rather, it reflects the idea that whatever differences exist among individuals are politically irrelevant; no such differences entitle anyone to compel another. Force is justifiably used only against individuals who have violated this very principle of voluntarism in their dealings with others.

The abstract notion of political equality is made more concrete by identifying the standard by which it should be implemented in community life (and by which public policy should be evaluated), namely, the "unalienable Rights,...Life, Liberty, and the Pursuit of Happiness." One's efforts to sustain oneself by actions that accord with the principle of voluntarism may not be obstructed by others. One may not be prevented from taking peaceful actions in the course of living; nor may anyone coercively interfere with one's choice of a peaceful route toward success in life, or happiness—the latter extending the first right further, as its implication. It is by respecting these rights that the equality shared within a political context is upheld, not by trying to force everyone into a procrustean uniformity.

Individuals are equal, then, insofar as in adulthood none is involuntarily subject to another. Each has the rights to life, liberty, and the pursuit of happiness, by virtue of being a human being—that is, a moral agent with the task of living his or her life successfully.

Some have actually argued that within such an individualist outlook, nothing justifies political authority. But, as must have been apprehended by the Founders, it is these very rights that provide the basis for political authority.[17] The purpose of political organization is to ensure respect and protection for these rights. The force that politics justifies may be exercised only against those who violate these rights or threaten to.

The individualism characteristic of the U.S. political tradition is almost exclusively political. The Declaration of Independence, the most philosophical document of the U.S. founding, does not invoke basic ethical principles by which a good human life must be guided. Nevertheless, the idea seems to be implicit, in that the right to the pursuit of happiness would seem pointless unless the pursuit of happiness were itself morally proper. This was clearly perceived by such critics of individualism as Karl Marx.[18] Were this not implied, one would be hard put to explain why a system of community life should have, as its basic principles, guidelines that take the pursuit of happiness to be of great importance. It might also be noted that John Locke, from whose writings the content and even the wording of much of the Declaration derives,[19] suggested a form of ethical individualism or egoism.[20]

"Individualism," like "utilitarianism," can designate both an ethical and a political theory. As an ethical theory, individualism is the position that it is each person's moral responsibility to strive for personal success in life—which means being excellent as a human individual.[21] (This position is sometimes called "ethical egoism.") Political individualism is supposed to provide the social conditions whereby such an ethical system may (but might not) be implemented by individuals (and some theorists have argued that the soundness of the former position depends on the soundness of the latter).

In this connection, the political individualism embodied in the Declaration of Independence shares with utilitarianism a reference to happiness. A crucial difference, however, is that an individualist political system expects the pursuit of that happiness from each individual, while a utilitarian system, in the main, would make it part of the task of politics to secure the happiness that is such an admitted value. Collectivist utilitarianism, especially, makes the achievement of happiness the object of public policy and changes the focus from individual happiness as such to the greatest happiness of the greatest number—that is, to a kind of aggregation of the states of affairs that happiness amounts to. Put more broadly, political utilitarianism must be coercive with respect to those ethical principles identified by natural rights theory.[22]

In general, collectivist political theories and systems combine the ethical and the political aspects of human life into one organic scheme, while individualism does not. Individualist political theory does not deny that human beings share innumerable common aspiration and problems, but it restricts its focus to the problem that is unique to their being members of a human community—namely, how to act toward one another as fellow human members of the community.[23]

It is this problem, the theory holds, that calls for the identification of certain universal, equally applicable principles of community conduct (natural rights), justifies political organization, and provides a definite standard of proper governmental power and action ("to secure these rights"). But beyond this necessarily common problem that all face in human communities, the myriad possible problems pertaining to human beings, as particular individuals, or as members of special associations or groups, are not of political concern.

Grounding Political Individualism

What are the assumptions underlying individualism? What conditions must exist for this political perspective to be plausible?

As we have already seen, any normative theory assumes that all human beings, if not crucially incapacitated, can choose some of their own conduct and can identify standards of right action. In the case of political individualism, it is assumed that individuals can identify and act in terms of the standard by which the conduct of these individuals as community members is to be judged right or wrong. This standard is developed through a natural rights theory. Although the standard is to apply to individuals in their community life, its identification does not depend on the existence of a whole of which each person is a part. Instead, individualism can involve two approaches to such a standard.

First, certain individualist systems assume that each person's chosen or felt priorities constitute what that person should and should not do. This is a subjectivist position that comes in more or less complicated versions but leads, in essence, to a denial of the objectivity and universal applicability of any ethical standard. As related to politics, however, the position is regarded as supportive of political individualism. Starting from the belief that no one is justified in forcing another to do anything, governments are to engage in the minimal activities necessary to prevent individuals from obstructing one another's (single-handed or more often mutual) pursuit of chosen priorities; that is, governments are to protect individuals' rights to take noncoercive action. Most neoclassical economists assert this view.

Second, other individualist positions, attaching significance to the fact that the concern is with human individuals, are not subjectivist. This type of individualism assumes that what people should do and not do can be identified in terms of the nature or essence of being a human being. It is maintained that objective and universal principles thus identified are applicable to all persons. And since each person is also a unique entity, not replaceable by others as the person he is, there are many implications to be drawn from the basic ethical principles that might apply only to that person. (This is the fact partially recognized by subjectivist individualism.) Even with this objective standard of conduct, however, the fact that each person is a moral agent (capable of right and wrong conduct) implies that the standard must be adhered to by choice; human beings are properly acknowledged moral agents only if choices— the initiative to act—concerning their own lives are left to them. There is no denial here of the possibility of knowing what actions are right and wrong for an individual; but from this, it is held, it does not follow that others may compel anyone to act on that knowledge. None may interfere with an individual except to prevent or repel actions that will infringe upon another. Natural rights theory thus specifies those principles the violation of which constitutes acting in ways that impinge (avoidably) upon others' spheres of moral authority.[24]

The plausibility of political individualism depends, then, first on the philosophical underpinnings of any normative theory: metaphysically, it must be possible for at least some entities (human beings) to initiate their own conduct, or some aspect of it. Universal environmental or biological determinism could not be true along with ethical individualism.

Furthermore, the natural rights element of political individualism requires that human nature exists (that human beings are a specific kind of thing) and that this is, furthermore, knowable. With this as given, it is necessary to demonstrate, in terms of the features of human nature, that specific political conditions are right for individuals—thus the term *natural* or *human rights*. Broadly, these conditions have been taken to be the rights to life, liberty, and the pursuit of happiness or property, with others (such as the ones enumerated in the Bill of Rights) derived from these.

There are many more assumptions here that require extensive support. These include fine details of legal theory; the issue of whether government is justifiable in the first place if individuals are entitled to liberty, as individualism holds; and the justification for punishing violators of the right of individuals. These matters cannot be pursued here. It should be evident, though, that political individualism, like collectivist utilitarianism, depends on other complex and philosophical positions.[25]

Points of Contrast

Both collectivist utilitarianism and individualism have now been described. The former underlies, more or less consistently, a good deal of government intervention in the market, including, for example, both national health and safety and national labor policy in the United States. The latter underlies, more or less consistently, the unique U.S. political tradition. While critics might object that these characterizations are somewhat simple, such a sketch as provided here does enable one to get a general overview of the two contending and interacting ideologies.

Contrasting Political Ideals

What is the relationship between the two positions? They clearly share some features. For example, both make room for democracy as a means for political decision making. Individualists, however, give politics a very narrow scope, while collectivist utilitarians understand by politics virtually every facet of social life. Even more importantly, both positions employ the concept of human rights. For individualists, human rights are basic conditions that define the scope of every individual's freedom of action. For the collectivist utilitarian, such rights mean something more instrumental and can encompass both the scope of individual liberty and various positive obligations that citizens supposedly have toward society and other people. Thus while for an individualist, everyone has such rights as are spelled out in the Declaration of Independence (meaning rights that identify a person's sovereign authority or range of liberty), for the collectivist utilitarian, rights can mean whatever is useful toward securing the goals of the community.

Having the right to receive health care, vacations, a certain level of income, education, or a job fits best within a collectivist utilitarian framework, since such "rights" were meant to identify conditions suitable for achieving the greatest happiness of the greatest number. However, several nonutilitarian arguments have also been advanced in defense of such a conception of human rights.[26] Still, in the past it has been mainly in the collectivist utilitarian sense that society was understood to be owed benefits by right, with the citizenry, of course, conceived as being obligated to provide or guarantee the provision of these benefits.[27] For the individualist, rights impose on all people what are often called negative obligations. Rights are moral injunctions to abstain from certain kinds of conduct. For example, that individuals have rights to life, liberty, and property means that others are to refrain from taking their lives, from interfering with their noncoercive actions and pursuit of happiness, and from theft or extortion.

By the collectivist utilitarian point of view, rights are conceived instrumentally. They are granted recognition by the relevant group; individuals have rights only if the fulfillment of the related obligation on the part of others will bring about the greatest happiness. The task of governments is therefore to circulate what will promote happiness and to assign the corresponding rights and protect them by ensuring fulfillment of the obligations. In individualism, rights are conceived naturally. Individuals have rights by virtue of being human and living within a community, and they have these rights without regard to whether others (the majority, the government) recognize them. Such a structure is necessary or there exists no basis for criticizing governments for their disregard of human rights. Thus, it is the government's task to recognize the rights of people and to protect and preserve them by acting against any person or institution (including itself) attempting to violate them. Those not fulfilling their negative obligation to refrain from interference are seen within the individualist framework as violators of natural rights, not as obstructers of collective goals.

Yet despite fundamental differences, the concepts of rights used by these two political outlooks are deceptively and confusingly similar. In both cases the function of governments is to protect and preserve rights, but the character of these rights, as explained above, is quite different. Likewise, each political outlook conveys a fairly clear meaning of "the general welfare," an idea that is part of the U.S. constitutional tradition. Within collectivist utilitarianism, the general welfare is the greatest happiness of the greatest number. In short, "the general welfare" refers to the overall benefits of individuals' and society's actions. For political individualism the general welfare—or the public interest—is whatever good is generalizable over all members of the community. And what is most generally required (or good) for the welfare of everyone is that everyone's rights be protected and preserved. In both cases governments must secure the rights of people so that this general welfare is achieved. In the first case, government must strive for various results, such as an expanding gross domestic product, full employment, a rise in the standard of living, equal job opportunities, and, the free flow of commerce. In the latter case, governments must keep the peace; protect everyone's natural rights of life, liberty, and the pursuit of happiness; and not attempt to achieve narrow goals or to impose such goals on the entire community by requiring positive contribution to their pursuit. For the former, there are various great social goals; for the latter, each person can have an ultimate goal and the only social goal is to foster an atmosphere in which each person is free to pursue his or her own proper goal (conceived either subjectively or objectively).

In each case, finally, governments use due process. For the individualist, this provision requires governments to act in accord with the principles it is to uphold in citizens' dealings with one another. The collectivist utilitarian interprets due process conventionally—that is, as a requirement that governmental means be approved via the democratic or some other legally accepted method.

Public Affairs, Political Ideals

The similar terminology in the two positions has often obliterated the difference between the trends properly associated with national labor policy and the U.S. political tradition. For instance, consideration of both employees' and employers' rights has been prominent in the debates, court decisions, and legislation relating to labor matters, no doubt because of the centrality of rights in the individualist tradition. Yet the concept has not always been used in a way consistent with that tradition. Thus, from an implicit individualist perspective, it has been maintained that employees have the right to organize as a simple extension of their natural right not to be prevented from engaging in peaceable action, whether alone or in voluntary association. On the other hand, from an implicit collectivist utilitarian stance, employees have been said to have the right to organize because of their relative poverty or because, by so organizing, economic disruptions affecting society might be avoided.

Moreover, as should be clear from this example, the so-called prounion and antiunion groups have not divided along lines distinguished by the different interpretations of *rights*. Thus, some antiunion advocates claim that if employees withhold their work, the employer's rights have been violated. But since such action by the employees, on its own, does not constitute forcible prevention of the employer's actions, "rights" is here being used in the collectivist utilitarian sense, that is, the underlying thesis is that the employer has rights to positive contributions from others (the employees) toward the achievement of company goals. (Of course, if there were a law requiring the employer to refrain from hiring workers when the employees go on strike, or obliging the employer to permit strike-related activities on the premises, the matter would be somewhat different. Only a careful analysis of the meaning of forcible prevention would allow a conclusion about whether striking would then involve violation of [individualist] rights.)

Public Policy Mistakes

This study is concerned with fundamental philosophical issues that emerge within national economic policy. It may therefore be useful before concluding to look at some other, less comprehensive, issues related to that policy, and to consider their possible connection with the two positions outlined above.

There is the familiar idea, for example, that labor and management are classes of human beings standing in inevitable opposition to each other. This idea is derived from the works of Karl Marx, who conceived of human beings (at least for our stage of history) in necessarily opposed classes. (In the ultimate stage of human history—communism—the "new man" is to emerge; by which time classes will have disappeared.) Of course, individualism, although it accepts incidental classification, rejects the idea of classing people as such; that is, that people in different categories are thought to have different essential characteristics, interests, or modes of being. Nor, strictly speaking, can the idea of classification within a collective be accepted by collectivist utilitarianism, which as a normative theory depends on human freedom of choice.

Marx, on the other hand, held to a deterministic view of human conduct: the economic circumstances into which one is born or to which one otherwise gains access will determine one's world view, actions, treatment of members of other classes, and so on. While some governmental policies may be justified in the language and the classifications that Marxism emphasizes, they have not usually been given philosophical support in terms of exactly this classificatory system or its deterministic underpinnings. (Of course, in the complicated legal, social, economic, and related arguments put forth in a highly diversified society, it is usual to find various incompatible viewpoints combined. Thus, the essential helplessness of workers is often maintained along with the essential full responsibility of employers.)

The idea of labor versus management and owners is central to Marxist thought, but removing its underpinnings does not preclude the possibility that the same results may be based on other notions. Thus, it is popularly believed that employers would exploit their workers if they could or that employees would work less diligently if they could. Of course, there are no doubt such employers and employees, but it is open to question whether the ascription of moral traits on the basis of one's place in the commercial world has any foundation beyond the Marxism we are not going to examine here. It is fair to hold that collectivist utilitarianism does not require this division, and merely adjusts itself in the details of its provisions as it has worked itself through the legal system.

The Free Rider Problem

Another issue that arises in commercial matters is the phenomenon of "free riders," which occurs when certain arrangements make it possible for some people to benefit from others' efforts without having contributed to them. With respect to unionization, free riders are those employees who do not belong to and do not pay dues to the relevant union but nevertheless benefit from the unionization of their firm or profession or industry. This situation is a result, on the one hand, of legislation and regulatory rulings determining that, for instance in labor relations, a union comes to represent a group of employees when so elected by some percentage of that group and, on the other hand, of court rulings upholding state laws that ban the practice of requiring union membership—for example, by way of closed-shop contracts.[28] Many people concerned with union matters have taken the free rider phenomenon to be a problem, and one solution has been to in effect make union dues compulsory through agency shop fees.[29]

Whether or not the free rider presents a problem, however, depends on one's perspective. Individualism, for example, cannot view free riding as anything but occasional good fortune, nothing more. If some people find toleration of it harmful they can endeavor to eradicate it (without interfering in the life, liberty, etc., of others, including their freedom of association or contract). For example, if my neighbor finds it disturbing that I enjoy seeing his flower garden, he would be free, within an individualist political community, to build a fence—provided no prior contract constrains him—or to strike a deal with me such that I pay for the benefit and he forgets the fence. If there is some good or service from which it is difficult to limit people's benefit (an air show, for example or the preservation of an endangered species), and it would not be profitable to supply it under such circumstances, efforts could be made to secure payment by such means as persuasion, boycott, or ostracism but not, within an individualist community, by forcibly taking or legally requiring it. (This may call into question the prospect of making provisions of government, especially national defense, in such a community.

Individualists have argued, however, that this problem is avoidable because government in a free society, including national defense, is both a public and a private good and must be maintained as an integrated system of political services.)[30]

Within collectivist utilitarianism, on the other hand, the free rider problem is clear and of great political concern. If people benefit without payment, it may diminish the greatest happiness of the greatest number, happiness that might be possible to attain if it were not for the missed opportunity of extracting production from these free riders. Without the opportunity to ride freely, one might well engage in additional production so as to obtain the ride in question, thus creating wealth. Since collectivist utilitarianism (as certain other positions that focus on the quality of society and are concerned with welfare economics) implies a concern with planned distribution of benefits, it would look askance at the possibility of free riding. Such a possibility removes control of wealth distribution from "society."

It might be asked why the free rider problem focuses on wealth distribution rather than on maximizing happiness or wealth, however distributed. The reason is that securing maximum happiness still requires planned distribution, even if not equal distribution. Free rider situations could be potential losses to the community, thus threatening the goal of maximizing wealth. Therefore planning is required so that those striving to get away with something be available for control. In other words, laws and regulations need to be enacted to make getting away with some costless benefit punishable, that is, costly. Whether or not most people do or, more importantly, must act that way is one issue. Whether, in any case, it is unbearable depends on one's idea of what is most important—what is the ultimate good. If individuals should focus on their own success in life, then benefiting from the production of others (and vice versa) when this does not interfere with their rights is not morally significant. If individuals should focus, however, on some overarching collective good, some people's failure to be conscientious contributors will be of great significance.

Empowerments Galore

Another philosophically potent matter might be mentioned briefly. Much discussion surrounding "public" policy, especially in connection with labor matters, explicitly relies on a belief in personal powerlessness, ineptitude, and helplessness, reflecting a trend away from confidence in human beings' capacity to cope with the complexities of life. This is backed up by a general view in the social sciences that human beings are really not in control, and that they are driven by circumstances to act as they do, that people's problems can only be solved by alterations of environment or brains. While this outlook is not strictly tied either to collectivist utilitarianism or to individualism, it gives intellectual support to certain aspects of the former.

At the same time as personal capacities have come to be doubted, people's expectations have risen, often encouraged by political leaders and "public policy" advocates. This could well explain the widespread acceptance of the need to bring government into people's problem-solving efforts (to secure their health, financial security, and other valued ends); for government, with its capacity and promise to use force in the matter, seems more powerful initially than are individual efforts. The natural consequences of a belief in personal powerlessness, especially when combined with rising expectations, is thus quite compatible with collective utilitarianism.

Policy Trends

Having discussed the philosophical issues underlying much of U.S. "public" policy and U.S. political tradition, what remains to be said is simply that, with any awareness of U.S. culture and politics, as well as world trends, it is not surprising that such policy should be guided by a philosophy of collectivism with utilitarian elements. Many other aspects of our culture are permeated with this outlook, even while great diversity still prevails. The social sciences have for the most part accepted a framework that lends it support. Advocates of labor, business, the environment, consumers, the old, students, the sick, the physically handicapped, blacks, women, or any other special group advocate their public policy views by reference to the public interest. The government may be seen here as trying to referee or administer or, quite often, promote the efforts of all these groups to have their desires be made public policy and thus gain forcible support, backed by legal sanctions.

The point here is not to evaluate this trend but to note why government regulatory policy, as manifested most starkly in national labor policy, is part of a larger phenomenon. The purpose of this discussion has been to examine the trends in the United States respecting the disposition of government at different levels toward various segments of the society.

For example, in the context of national labor policy—but the same could be said with respect to other areas of concern such as health policy, education, or affirmative action—from the beginning, government, through the courts and legislation, judged matters by reference to the public interest or the collective. Now and then the question of individual rights (for instance, to associate freely) did emerge. With time, however, this line of argument was dropped, in view of the increasingly greater involvement of the state in market affairs. Government has simply never had a laissez-faire attitude toward the economy (or toward virtually any other part of U.S. society).

In the last analysis, the conclusion of this inquiry is not very surprising. It confirms what many have argued in more general terms, namely, the erosion of constitutionalism based on the theory of natural rights and the rise of unlimited democracy, which has begun to be undermined by the politically active majority's delegation of powers to a centralized state bureaucracy.[31]

While I have not argued for the soundness of either of the views examined in this chapter, I have noted before that I consider individualism, with its theory of natural human rights, a sound position. And I have made some effort to defend that contention both in this work and in my other books, notably in *Individuals and Their Rights*.

My aim here has been to contribute to an understanding of the U.S. legal stance toward the phenomenon of government-market relations. I have earlier explored the labor market as an instance of a government-regulated human activity and shown that regulation of that market would not be justified, or not as the term is usually understood, namely, as setting and enforcing public policy about what should essentially be voluntary actions. In this chapter I wanted to explore how the actual history of the phenomenon differs from the individualist U.S. political ideals discernible within the philosophical and legal tracts associated with the founding of the country. Only such understanding will enable those who have a hand in guiding public policy in the United States to begin a clear formulation of the directions available, and to make an intelligent, wise decision as to which of the alternatives, if either, should be supported, resisted, or elaborated in practice.

Notes

1. Mancur Olson, *The Rise and Decline of Nations* (New Haven: Yale University Press, 1982).
2. J. J. C. Smart, "Utilitarianism" in *Encyclopedia of Philosophy*, ed. Paul Edwards, volume 8 (New York: The Free Press, 1967), pp. 207ff. G. E. Moore, *Principia Ethica* (Cambridge, England: Cambridge University Press, 1956).
3. Peter Singer, *Animal Liberation* (New York: Avon Books, 1975).
4. Rolf Sartorius, *Individual Conduct and Social Norms* (Belmont, CA: Dickenson, 1975); Jeremy Bentham, *Deontology: or the Science of Morals* (London: Longman, Rees, 1834); Jeremy Bentham, *Introduction to the Principles of Morals and Legislation* (Oxford: Clarendon, [1789] 1878). The trend toward a utilitarian approach is exemplified in J. Brierly, chapters 4 and 5 of *The Law of Nations*, 6th ed. (London: Oxford University Press, 1963). A critic of the trend is John Rawls, *A Theory of Justice* (Cambridge, MA: Harvard University Press, 1971), pp. 378–379; O. Schachter, "Towards a Theory of International Obligation," *Virginia Journal of International Law* 8 (1971): 300ff. While these do not advance all or strictly utilitarian arguments, they defend the proposition that the good of the entire human community should figure in governments' actions with respect to their own citizens.

    Note also that the United Nations often judges the propriety of national and international proposals in terms of whether wealth (or what it can be used for) is properly distributed throughout the world. See, for example, its 1974 proposal, *The New International Economic Order, Report on the Sixth Special Session of the United Nations General Assembly*, Cd. 6031 (New York: United Nations, 1975). It represents a version of utilitarianism whereby the measure of well-being or happiness focuses on the material equality of either nations or the population of nations of the world.

    Contemporary developments are not all unidirectional and there are signs that utilitarianism is no longer as influential, probably because of its ties to empiricism and economic analysis. But the collectivism of utilitarianism persists, for example, in the current communitarian movements. See, Amitai Etzioni, ed., *Socioeconomics: Toward a New Synthesis* (New York: Sharpe, 1991). See also the antiindividualism in Robert Bellah, et al., *Habits of the Heart* (New York: Harper and Row, 1983); Robert Bellah et al., *The Good Society* (New York: Harper and Row, 1991).
5. John Stuart Mill is often taken to be an individualist (or at least classical liberal) and a utilitarian, but he was one of the first utilitarians to relate the doctrine to socialism. See J. Stone, *Social Dimensions of Law and Justice* (Stanford, CA: Stanford University Press, 1966), p. 119.
6. By "normative" socialism I mean what Marx referred to as utopian socialism, namely, the view that the conditions appropriate to human community life, that every person in the community fully realize his or her species-being—ought to be achieved as a matter of moral obligation. Marx saw this as a hopeless dependence on idealism. Marxist communism, in contrast, is best understood as a projected, historically inevitable social state. Marx's "scientific" prediction of this state is based, philosophically, on his acceptance of Hegel's view that history is governed by the principle of dialectic progression. For a good discussion, see Stone, *Social Dimensions*.

Marx and Hegel were not alone in projecting inevitable final stages of history. August Comte, Herbert Spencer, and John Stuart Mill all advanced views that may be considered historicist or progressivist, foreseeing the inevitable resolution of human social problems. For a criticism of Marxism from an individualist framework, see Tibor R. Machan, *Marxism: A Bourgeois Critique* (Bradford, England: MCB University Press, 1988).

7. For a popular rendition of this position, see Lewis Thomas, *The Lives of a Cell* (New York: Viking, 1974). For a philosophical defense of organicism, see J. Herder, *Outline of the Philosophy of the History of Man* (New York: Bergman, [1800], 1966).

8. This collectivism, with the group being one's socioeconomic class, was subscribed to by Marx:

> I paint the capitalist and landlord in no sense *couleur de rose*. But here individuals are dealt with only insofar as they are the personifications of economic categories, embodiment of particular class-relations and class-interests. My standpoint, from which the evolution of the economic formation of society is viewed as a process of natural history, can less than any other make the individual responsible for relations whose creature he socially remains, however much he may subjectively raise himself above them (Karl Marx, Das Kapital, [1893], p. 15).

9. While those who subscribe to the view that normative theories need only spell out values might disagree with this, if it is acknowledged, as it should be, that norms pertain to guiding conduct, the point cannot be denied. See Douglas J. Den Uyl, "Freedom and Virtue," in *The Libertarian Reader*, ed. Tibor R. Machan, (Totowa, NJ: Rowman and Littlefield, 1982), pp. 211–225.

10. Of course, even if collectivism is a genuine normative theory, it may not turn out to be a sound one if, upon comparison, we find that a different system is better. That is, we may find that collectivism is one of numerous (possible) theories that aim to answer the question, How should we live in the company of others? There will still be a difference, however, between what count as meaningful answers and the best or right or correct answer. This is the same in all fields of inquiry. Some answers are not bona fide answers: some are but are wrong or inadequate; and some are good or correct or sound.

11. The term "quasi-democratic" is used to indicate: (1) that it is representative, not "pure" democracy; (2) that expert as well as special-interest—rather than majority—opinion is often relied on; and (3) that the courts have tended to uphold an interpretation of the Constitution whereby some matters are not open to democratic decision making.

12. There is no consistent doctrine that overcomes these difficulties; but see Thomas Grey, "Property and Need: The Welfare State and Theories of Distributive Justice," *Stanford Law Review* 28 (1976): 877ff.

13. I am not maintaining that the position characterized here is ultimately coherent. See Chapter 2, where some of its problems are discussed.

14. Some who advocate such discrimination avoid the utilitarian approach, claiming that reverse discrimination is warranted, not because the majority desires (end-state equality, but because it is required for the rectification of past injustice toward members of certain groups. So reverse discrimination is defended as a means of compensating for violations of principles (here, the treatment of everyone as

equals). See, for example, Ronald Dworkin, chapter 9 of *Taking Rights Seriously* (Cambridge, MA: Harvard University Press, 1978).

15. There is, and will probably always be, controversy about what is the actual philosophical normative foundation of the political tradition in the United States. There is less controversy about what is unique in that tradition, what features of it distinguish it from previous and subsequent systems. It is this element of the U.S. political tradition, not so much what it actually is but what makes it distinctive, that we are concerned with here.

16. When the Founders said "we hold... self-evident," they did not mean, as some have suggested, that they thought it self-evident that we all have these rights. One can hold as self-evident certain facts within some context, fully acknowledging that those facts need to be established in another. Nearly all disciplines of human inquiry hold some principles self-evident, just to be able to proceed with the work at hand.

17. For an excellent but unusual analysis of equality, see Antony Flew, "The Procrustean Ideal: Libertarians v. Egalitarians,"*Encounter* (March 1978): 70ff. For the individualist anarchist view, see Murray N. Rothbard, *Power and Market* (Menlo Park, CA: Institute for Humane Studies, 1970); Morris Tannehill, Linda Tannehill, and Jarrett Wollstein, *Society Without Government* (New York: Laissez-Faire Books, 1972). I address this issue and develop the individualist case for political authority in chapter 7 of my *Individuals and Their Rights* (LaSalle, IL: Open Court, 1989).

18. Karl Marx, "On the Jewish Question," in *Selected Writings* , ed. David McLellan, (London: Oxford University Press, 1977), pp.39–62. See also C. B. MacPherson, *The Political Theory of Possessive Individualism: Hobbes and Locke* (Oxford: Clarendon Press, 1962). The type of individualism critics associate with the U.S. political tradition and with classical liberalism or libertarianism is Hobbesian. This is not by any means what the Founding Fathers had in mind, although it is an ingredient of neoclassical economic analysis, a framework often invoked to spell out the nature of capitalist economic systems. For an alternative type of individualism, much closer to what the founders had in mind, see Tibor R. Machan, *Capitalism and Individualism* (New York: St. Martin's Press, 1990).

19. For an elaboration, see Donald Devine, *Does Freedom Work? Liberty and Justice in America* (Durham, NC: Carolina House, 1978); Donald Devine, *The Political Culture of the United States* (Boston, MA: Little, Brown, 1972); For a detailed description of the intellectual climate at the time of the American Revolution, see Bernard Bailyn, *The Ideological Origins of the American Revolution* (Cambridge, MA: Harvard University Press, 1973); Bernard Bailyn, *The Origin of American Politics* (New York: Knopf, 1967).

20. Locke's views on ethics are not entirely clear, and scholars are in considerable disagreement about them. He held two views that are both related and in (partial) conflict. On the one hand, Locke thought that human beings are naturally inclined to seek happiness; he even adhered to psychological hedonism, although in an early work he rejected this position. See John Locke, *Essays on the Law of Nature,* ed. W. von Leyden, (London: Oxford University Press, 1954). He also asserted that human beings are bound by a law of nature even when they do not live under (compulsory) civil law. But this last view, first espoused in John Locke, *Second Treatise of Government,* 2nd ed. (Cambridge: Cambridge University Press, [1690], 1967), rests on a certain view of human nature that Locke makes explicit in this work, one that seems not to be fully consistent with his more philosophical

discussion. In Locke's politics, each person is essentially free to choose his or her conduct (so he or she can choose either good or evil). But Locke's epistemology and value theory, expounded in his *An Essay Concerning Human Understanding* (1690), implies a form of determinism whereby human beings are under psychological compulsion to seek pleasure or hedonistic happiness.

21. See David L. Norton, *Personal Destinies, A Philosophy of Ethical Individualism* (Princeton, NJ: Princeton University Press, 1976); Ayn Rand, *The Virtue of Selfishness* (New York: New American Library, 1962).

22. Coercion is not a descriptive but a normative concept. It means a wrongful use of force, with "wrongful" explicated in terms of natural or some other rights theory. But if one denies the significance of individual rights, then what may appear to be coercive within the above context could come to be noncoercive or morally innocent. One can appreciate this from contrasting theft with repossession: both may clearly involve the use of force, but the former is vicious, the latter quite possible virtuous.

23. It is notable, in this context, that contemporary communitarians, such as Robert Bellah and Amitai Etzioni, insist on focusing on the kind of individualism we find in economics textbooks rather than on the more robust kind found in the Lockean and Emersonian traditions.

24. Robert Nozick, *Anarchy, State, and Utopia* (New York: Basic Books, 1974), spells this point out most forcefully, although it is already made clear in Locke's political theory. See also my books, *Human Rights and Human Liberties* (Chicago: Nelson-Hall, 1975); and *Individuals and Their Rights*.

25. I attempt to develop all these stages of the case for the individualist polity in *Individuals and Their Rights*.

26. James Nickel, "Is There a Human Right to Employment?" *Philosophical Forum* 10 (Winter 1978–79): 149ff; Henry Shue, *Basic Rights* (Princeton, NJ: Princeton University Press, 1980). But see Tibor R. Machan, "Wronging Rights," *Policy Review* 17 (Summer 1981): 31ff.

    Individualists have held that the "negative" human rights of life, liberty, and property obligate others merely to refrain from certain conduct—murder, assault, and theft, for example. Shue and Nickel both defend "positive" human rights, such as to be employed, or to be provided with health care, on grounds that no sound distinction can be made between "negative" and "positive" human rights regarding the type of obligations they impose on others. Both Shue and Nickel argue that in fact the rights individualists claim impose only refrainment on others, actually call for getting protection from government, which is a "positive" contribution. Individualists have replied, however, that it is not to protection that anyone has a natural right but rather to life, liberty, and property, and that government should and may be established so as to protect and preserve these rights in the face of the obvious possibility of their being violated by some members of society, a service for which government receives compensation. No one receives compensation, however, for respecting another's rights to life, liberty, and property.

    Actually, the dispute between the individualists and the new crop of human rights theorists such as Shue and Nickel is far more fundamental than appears from a mere concern with the character of rights.

27. John Stuart Mill, who spoke about rights from a utilitarian perspective, did not always emphasize (or perhaps even approve of) welfare rights such a these. This was mainly because Mill believed for most of his life that liberty was the most useful means by which to achieve social progress, and that if people had a right to

such benefits it would (sometimes) mean that some people's liberty (for instance, to pursue their own goals instead of contributing to others' health care) must be abridged. But even for Mill the right to liberty was justified as a condition people were owed because through liberty they could enhance the greatest happiness of the greatest number. When a utilitarian changes his mind on what means best achieve this goal, he is very likely to change his mind on the question of what rights individuals possess.

There is also the other side of this coin, whereby it is society that owes certain people benefits—for example, those in dire need. In this framework individuals are conscripted to provide the labor, skill, wealth, and so on, that will enable "society" to hand out such benefits. So the same point still applies, namely, that individuals owe society certain goods and services. Recall President John F. Kennedy's famous pronouncement: "Ask not what your country can do for you, ask what you can do for your country."

28. 29 U.S.C. 151 et seo.; *Abood v. Detroit Board of Education*, 431 U.S. 209 (1977).
29. See *Burns v. So. Pac. Trans. Co.*, 11 Fair Employment Practices Cases, 1441 D. Ariz. (1976). For a competent discussion of this issue, see Merrill, "Limitations Upon the Use of Compulsory Union Dues," *Journal of Air, Land and Commerce* 42 (1976): 711ff.
30. See Tibor R. Machan, "Disolving the Problem of Public Goods: Financing Government without Coercive Measures," in *The Libertarian Reader*, pp. 201–208; Richard Tuck, "Is There a Free-rider Problem, and If So, What Is It?" in *Rational Action*, ed. R. Harrison, (Cambridge: Cambridge University Press, 1977).
31. See, for example, Robert Moss, *The Collapse of Democracy* (New Rochelle, NY: Arlington House, 1975). Moss argues that in general the usurpation of basic political (constitutional) principles in Western liberal countries threatens to usher in one of two alternatives: totalitarianism (from the left), and authoritarianism (from the right). See also, Freidrich A. von Hayek, *Law, Legislation and Liberty*, volume 3, (Chicago: University of Chicago Press, 1979).

Index